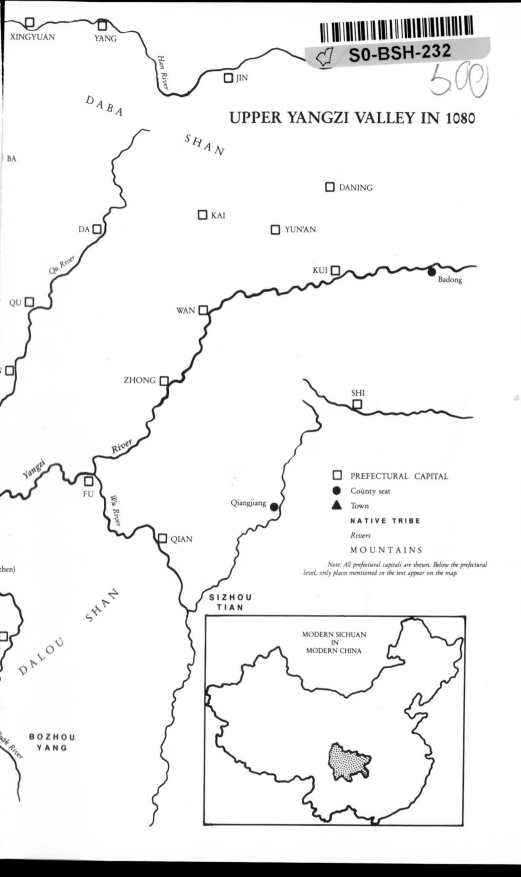

UPPER YANGZI VALLEY IN 1080

XINGYUAN
YANG
☐ JIN

Han River

DABA
SHAN

BA

☐ DANING

DA ☐

☐ KAI

☐ YUN'AN

Qu River

KUI ☐

● Badong

QU ☐

WAN ☐

ZHONG ☐

SHI ☐

River

Yangzi

FU ☐

Wu River

Qiangjiang ●

☐ QIAN

☐ PREFECTURAL CAPITAL
● County seat
▲ Town
NATIVE TRIBE
Rivers
MOUNTAINS

Note: All prefectural capitals are shown. Below the prefectural level, only places mentioned in the text appear on the map.

(hen)

SHAN

SIZHOU TIAN

DALOU

MODERN SICHUAN
IN
MODERN CHINA

BOZHOU YANG

k River

THE COUNTRY OF STREAMS AND GROTTOES

Expansion, Settlement, and the Civilizing of the Sichuan Frontier in Song Times

RICHARD VON GLAHN

Published by COUNCIL ON EAST ASIAN STUDIES, HARVARD UNIVERSITY, and distributed by HARVARD UNIVERSITY PRESS, Cambridge (Massachusetts) and London   1987

The Council on East Asian Studies at Harvard University publishes a monograph series and, through the Fairbank Center for East Asian Research and the Reischauer Institute of Japanese Studies, administers research projects designed to further scholarly understanding of China, Japan, Korea, Vietnam, Inner Asia, and adjacent areas.

Library of Congress Cataloging-in-Publication Data

Von Glahn, Richard.
    The country of streams and grottoes.

    (Harvard East Asian monographs ; 123)
    Bibliography: p.
    Includes index.
    1. Szechwan Province (China)—History.   2. China—
History—Sung dynasty, 960–1279.   I. Title.   II. Series.
DS793.S8V66   1987   951'.38024   87-13526
ISBN 0-674-17543-3

For my parents,
Richard L. and Helen T. von Glahn

Contents

Tables

Maps

A Note on Romanization

Chinese names and words in the text are romanized according to the pinyin system. In order more closely to approximate the original sound and form of words and proper names of non-Han origin these terms are rendered in Middle Chinese (M.C.) phonetic transcriptions, based on Zhou Fagao et al., *Hanzi gujin yinhui.* In cases where non-Han persons adopted Han names or titles, these names are given in pinyin.

Acknowledgments

Over the several years that went into the making of this book I have been privileged to receive the advice, guidance, and encouragement of many scholars and friends. Pride of place must go to my dissertation advisers at Yale, Professors Ying-shih Yü and Jonathan Spence, who thoroughly read and critiqued the original drafts of the thesis. Their suggestions and instruction improved the text in many places, especially in interpreting obscure texts and polishing my prose. I would also like to record my appreciation to Professors Yü and Spence for their inestimable help and many kindnesses over what became a lengthy career as a graduate student.

It is a pleasure to acknowledge the inspiration of my first teachers in East Asian studies, Professors Charles Chu, Thomas R. H. Havens, and Kent C. Smith. My former teachers at the University of California, Berkeley, Professors Edward H. Schafer and Robert M. Hartwell, deeply influenced my understanding of Chinese history and civilization. I fear that the present work does not match the high standards of scholarship which they have established, but their inspiration and insight underlie much of what is contained in these pages. Another longstanding debt going back to my Berkeley days is owed to Paul Smith. Our common interest in the social and economic history of Song Sichuan has yielded an invaluable comradeship, a profound appreciation of scholarship as a collaborative enterprise, and innumerable and substantial improvements in the final version of this study. Professors Ron Knapp, Jerry Dennerline, and Conrad Schirokauer, who sat on my prize fellowship committee, generously shared with me their expertise and advice. I am also

deeply grateful for the assistance and encouragement of Professor Shiba
Yoshinobu of Osaka University, who took much time away from his
own work to guide my research.

Over the past few years I have besieged many libraries and librarians
with countless requests. For their unstinting and gracious assistance I
would like to thank the librarians and staff at the Fu Ssu-nien Library
of the Institute of History and Philology, Academia Sinica; the Tōyō
Bunko; the National Diet Library; the Institute for Humanistic Sciences
at Kyoto University; the Genealogical Society of Utah; Sterling Memorial Library at Yale University; and the Harvard-Yenching Library at
Harvard University. I would also like to express my appreciation to Professor Ting Pang-hsin, Director of the Institute of History and Philology, Academia Sinica, and Professor Umehara Kaoru of the Institute of
Humanistic Sciences, Kyoto University, for their hospitality in extending to me the use of the facilities at their respective institutions.

Much of work that produced the dissertation upon which this book
is based was made possible by funding from the U.S. Department of
Education, which awarded me a Fulbright-Hays fellowship to pursue my
research in Taiwan and Japan, and the East Asian Prize Fellowship ad-
ministered by the Council for East Asian Studies at Yale University,
which supported my research and writing in the United States. I am
most grateful for their financial support. The final version of the manuscript was prepared during my year as a Postdoctoral Fellow at the Fairbank Center for East Asian Research at Harvard University. I would like
to thank the acting director of the Center, Professor Benjamin Schwartz,
and my colleagues at Harvard for the benefit of their support and
wisdom.

Finally, many friends—scholars all—have contributed substantially to
my thinking on many of the issues raised in the pages that follow: Pamela Crossley, Albert Dalia, Ileen DeVault, Ed Gargan, Valerie Hansen,
Kandice Hauf, Heather Peters, Pamela Price, James Silverstein, and
Roger Thompson. And I am especially indebted to my editor, Katherine
Keenum, who through her dedication to the reader's best interests has
done a great service both to them, and to me.

Preface

Since the path-breaking researches of Katō Shigeshi[1] a half century ago, scholars working in the field of Tang-Song social and economic history have principally studied the formal characteristics—such as land tenure, legal status, social stratification, and economic institutions—of the new society that replaced the crumbling aristocratic order from the mid-eighth century onwards. Japanese legal and economic historians, most prominently Niida Noboru and Sudō Yoshiyuki, shaped the direction of this research in the post-war period. The studies of Niida and Sudō described the rise of a manorial order (*shōensei*) following the collapse of the equal-field (*juntian*) system of landownership in the mid-Tang period. According to Sudō and Niida the manorial order was founded on a feudal mode of production which, they implied, was uniformly distributed throughout China from the late Tang onward. This manorial order imprisoned the rural populace, temporarily liberated from the yoke of the aristocracy, as tenant-serfs under the domination of an emerging class of large landowners.[2]

Of the many criticisms raised against this line of interpretation, two merit particular emphasis as points of departure for the present study. First, in Niida's and Sudō's model of periodization historical change was reduced to a series of transformations in the legal foundations of property. Secondly, they utilized data without regard for geographic provenance, thus reinforcing a myopic view of historical change. Consequently, the rapid advances in commercialization, urbanization, and industrial growth during the Song fit into their social paradigm only awkwardly at best. The conflict between Sudō's and Niida's model of the manorial order and the recognized economic metamorphosis of Song China resulted from their failure to take into account the varieties in human activities in different times and places.

Leading scholars of the so-called Kyoto school, represented by Miyazaki Ichisada, fashioned a wholly different paradigm of the Tang-Song transition based on the idea of a transition from a "natural" economy to a "monetary" one. In their view, the establishment of private property, circulation of money, and commercialization of agricultural production created a society based on the cash nexus and contractual relationships. Miyazaki argued that the consolidation of landownership in the Song was not a resurrection of the manorial estates of the aristocratic era but rather a profit-oriented amalgamation of fragmented and morcellated landholdings in which a purely contractual exchange between landowner and tenants or field laborers replaced personal bondage.[3]

Miyazaki's studies established the significance of the powerful role of the market in transforming rural society in the Song. Shiba Yoshinobu, in his panoramic survey of the Song economy, laid to rest any doubts about the pervasive impact of commerce throughout the whole of Song society.[4] Shiba proposed that the reciprocal dynamism generated by the commercialization of agriculture and urbanization engendered quantitative growth in production and a qualitative sophistication of the commercial system. Innovations in transport and finance, the transformation of the fiscal system, and the formation of a national market established a structure of exchange and circulation that drastically altered the social landscape, shortening the distances between far-flung parts of the empire and corroding the rigid distinction, symbolized by the city wall, between the urban and rural worlds. At the same time, Shiba drew back from Miyazaki's concept of the destructive and liberating powers of a "monetary" economy, insisting that rural change followed an internal process of historical development that was influenced, but not determined, by commercialization.

Shiba's study also detailed regional variations in the structure of commerce, which he described primarily in terms of consumer demand, market location, and facility of transport. He made no attempt to define economic regions explicitly. A few years earlier one of Sudō's students, Yanagida Setsuko, developed an hypothesis of regional patterns in Song rural society based on differences in the impact of commerce and the monetary economy. Yanagida admitted that the contractual order described by Miyazaki had indeed emerged in "advanced" (*senshin*) areas such as the Yangzi Delta and the Chengdu Plain, but maintained that the manorial order persisted in "developing" (*kōshin*) areas, particularly the central Yangzi region and eastern Sichuan. In her view, the rising value of labor in the competitive, commercialized economy of the "advanced" regions enabled tenants and field laborers to win emancipation from the conditions of serfdom that still prevailed in "developing" areas.[5] Yanagida's primary intention was to explain the conflicting evidence on land tenure in terms of regional variations. She made no attempt to define systematically her concepts of "advanced" and "developing" economies. Yet this dichotomy between "advanced" and "developing" regions continues to serve as the conceptual focus of Japanese studies on rural society during the Tang-Song transition, most notably Satake Yasuhiko's researches on Sichuan.[6]

The use of this framework of analysis implies that each region can be placed along a continuum leading from a "developing" stage to an "advanced" one. Not only does the language of modernization theory rest on a dubious presumption of an inevitable and uniform progression towards an ideal "advanced" society, it also obscures the relationship between the center and peripheral regions within the Song economy and polity. Tan Kyōji has rightly criticized Yanagida for deriving her model of "developing" regions from a system of social relationships, the bondage of the tenant-serf to the soil and to a master.[7] In a recent essay Joseph McDermott has attempted to consolidate the available documents on land tenure into more nuanced regional profiles. Elaborating on the Yanagida thesis, McDermott attributes the eclipse of coercive tenurial relations by contractual ones to the rising value of land in the core regions of the lower Yangzi valley resulting from higher levels of population density and commercialized agriculture. He also suggests that changes in tenurial arrangements may have been connected to the emergent power of the gentry and corporate kinship groups.[8] But, while acknowledging that land tenure documents alone are inadequate for describing Song society, like Yanagida, McDermott tends to define regions in terms of tenure systems.

A study of life and livelihood within a given region must instead begin with the history of local society, grounding social relationships in a mode of production that reflects both the priorities of the community and, equally importantly, the place it occupies in regional and national socio-economic structures. To employ the concept of region does not mean slicing up a given area into a set of territories and describing the differences between them; regional analysis must be based on common features that define a region as a coherent unit of space. Geographers have long insisted that the concept of region must be defined in terms of the functional integration of human activities as well as landscape features. This emphasis on the functional unity of a region in turn led to the idea of a spatial system, a network of nodes, routes, and patterns of circulation that channel the movement of people, goods, and information within a defined space.

The full significance of a regional system can be discovered only by examining how it functions as a unified system of production, consumption, migration, political administration, and social control. Such an examination requires an investigation of the spatial relationships among different regions. As Shiba and others have shown, the formation of a national market during the Song period provided a dramatic impetus to commercialization and urbanization in certain regions favored with exceptional productive resources, ease of transport, and growing demand for non-agricultural goods and services. Peripheral areas, though not directly subjected to these changes, nonetheless were part of the entire system and certainly were affected by them.

In the study of China, the concept of a region as a spatial system has been advanced by G. William Skinner, who applied the analytical methods of central place theory, originally developed to descibe marketing systems, to the study of social interaction as well as economic organization. More recently Skinner has devised a universe of "macroregions" for nineteenth-century China based on the functional differentiation of regions into core and periphery.[9] Although Skinner stresses the necessity of studying each region in terms of its own separate history, he and others who have borrowed his models have simply elaborated synchronic profiles of regional systems rather than attempting to study the history of regions.[10] In part this omission results from the theory itself, since the central place concept is much more useful for describing a region at a given point in time than for explaining its history.

The concept of core and periphery can, nonetheless, be helpful in understanding the evolution of a region over time because it emphasizes the underlying importance of the center as the ultimate determining factor of much change that may, on the surface, appear local or random. To comprehend fully the formation of spatial systems, consideration must be given to the genetic sequence of land occupance. Several layers of spatial phenomena must be mapped: the settlement and livelihood patterns which result from the initial peopling of an area, the emergence of centers of production and consumption, and the evolving relationship between metropolitan political and economic centers and peripheral areas.[11] The spatial systems that emerge from the superimposition of these networks of circulation will contribute to an understanding of the formation of a region as an extension of social, economic, and political forces originating from the center.

This book is a study of Han expansion in southern Sichuan during the Song dynasty. It seeks to discover the economic forces and political relationships that produced a characteristic regional society and landscape out of the meeting of two unlike civilizations and especially to demonstrate how pressures from the centers of Han power and culture affected life in the frontier. A chief objective of this study is to give proper weight to the structural relationship between the frontier and the center. Owen Lattimore, in an admirable essay contrasting China's northern and southern frontiers, drew attention to the implications of different forms of frontier expansion.[12] The degrees of military, political, and economic integration varied greatly, as did their form and function. The radius of military control generally ranged beyond the bounds of effective civil administration; trade routes for highly valued goods pierced national borders, while the exchange of staple commodities moved sluggishly within much more constrained geographic limits. To understand the Sichuan frontier in particular or regions in general, care must be taken to recognize the functional distinctions inherent in these different modes of regional integration. To understand the process by which a frontier developed, moreover, those features of the historical context which either facilitate or inhibit integration must be identified.

A truly full analysis of a region takes into account as many available documentary and archaeological sources from the period and region as possible, using modern analytical theories to interpret them. Most important, it must not limit such interpretation to the examination of a single factor or a single question. And it must always return again and again to the concrete particulars that gave the human experience in a given region at a given time its particular shape and texture.

The Country of Streams and Grottoes

Introduction

The "medieval economic revolution"[1] of Song China was in large part a spatial transformation, the shift of the center of gravity of Chinese civilization from the Yellow River valley to the Yangzi River basin. Beyond the great commercial towns clustered around the Yangzi delta, the surge in production, wealth, and numbers of people also propelled many Chinese to seek out and exploit the untapped resources of the more remote parts of South China. Economic opportunity created new incentives to tame a forbidding wilderness. The present study focuses on the process of settlement and economic exploitation of the southwestern frontier during the period of decisive and sustained colonization that began during the Tang-Song transition. The area chosen as the subject of this book—the southern frontier of Sichuan, especially the prefecture of Luzhou and its subordinate territories south of the Yangzi, known as Southern Lu—typified the process of frontier settlement unfolding during the Song period.[2]

Song Sichuan largely corresponded to the modern-day province, with the addition of the upper Han River valley, now part of Shaanxi province. Since antiquity Sichuan had been renowned for its starkly contrasting landscapes: the Chengdu Plain, whose agricultural wealth inspired the epithet, "Heaven's Storehouse," and the formidable mountain ranges which encircled the Sichuan Basin and sealed it off from the larger Sinitic world and from the non-Han peoples to the south and west. In the Warring States period this territory was divided between two kingdoms, Shu in the west (with its capital at Chengdu) and Ba in the east (with its capital at modern Chongqing, known during the Song as Yuzhou). The polarity, roughly following the contours of the ancient Shu and Ba kingdoms, between the rich, densely populated western part of Sichuan and the vast wilderness of the east persisted throughout much of the imperial era. The Song initially divided Sichuan into two administrative regions: the west, or Rivers, and the east, or Gorges. In 1001 these two administrative units were each further subdivided into two routes (*lu*): Chengdu and Zizhou in the west, Lizhou and Kuizhou in the east. Western Sichuan was popularly known as Shu or the Rivers region, while the east, corresponding to ancient Ba, retained the frontier character signified by its designation as the Gorges region.

The Song prefecture of Luzhou, surrounding the confluence of the Tuo and Yangzi Rivers at the southwestern edge of the basin, lay at the intersection of these two regions and shared features of both. The northern portion of the prefecture, conveniently situated along major waterways, was celebrated for its rich agricultural and mineral resources. By contrast, the area known as Southern Lu, extending southward from the Yangzi River, encompassed many indigenous non-Han tribes as well as scattered Han frontier villages. Although a formal part of the empire since the Qin unification in the third century B.C., Luzhou comprised a zone of contact between Han and native peoples down to the eighteenth century. The boundaries between Han and native continually advanced and receded; but the Song dynasty stands out as a period of vigorous Han expansion and settlement, culminating in the enduring political hegemony of the Han. This phase of frontier expansion coincided with—and, indeed, was in large part produced by—the spatial and social transformations of the Song period. The case of Luzhou, therefore, allows examination of how these changes shaped frontier settlement and regional integration, in Sichuan and in China as a whole.

The frontier, after all, is a special type of region. With its new territories and hitherto unavailable resources, it provides valuable opportunities for an expanding society. At the same time, the fragile, elongated spatial relationship between the center and the frontier limits the scope of human activities. Moreover, a frontier implies a zone of contact between two (or more) separate societies, one indigenous, the other intrusive.[3] During the Song period, the expanding empire encroached upon the territories of non-Han peoples along a vast but discontinuous frontier from the tropical jungles of Hainan Island to the cold, dry plateaus of the upper Yellow River valley. An assessment of the unique character of the frontier process in southern Sichuan and its place within this larger phase of frontier expansion requires an examination of the indigenous peoples and the environment they inhabited; the political forces, both in the capital and on the local scene, that tipped the balance in favor of warfare and conquest; and the social and economic changes that made the frontier an attractive target for colonization.

First of all, the human and physical geography of the Sichuan frontier, of course, shaped Han settlement. Landscape features such as physiography, routes, productive resources, and disease distributions presented both obstacles and opportunities to Han settlers and established a range of settlement choices. Most importantly, the native peoples of the southwest forced the Han to modify their strategies for settling and exploiting the frontier. A history of the Han occupation of the southwestern frontier must begin with a recognition of the autonomy of indigenous societies and the long and only partially successful processes of interaction, integration, and assimilation with the intrusive Han.

For the Han immigrant, the frontier appeared as a barren, desolate wilderness which impeded, or suppressed altogether, normal habits of life and work. Yet the frontier was not a pristine, empty landscape. The native peoples subtly altered the ecology of their habitat to meet their own basic livelihood needs. Although divided into myriad distinct societies, the native peoples created remarkably similar forms of livelihood under similar ecological conditions. Indeed the southwestern frontier was the meeting point of two distinct civilizations, the indigenous civilization of the forest, the product of a long history of interaction among the native peoples, and the intrusive civilization of the plain, borne by Han immigrants intent on refashioning the frontier into a typically Han world.

In this study the concept of "civilization" takes on a specific analytical meaning. Civilization, as used here, implies a focus on the settlement and domestication of a specific area, the introduction of forms of social

and economic life which create a particular pattern of ecological alteration, and the ways in which a society perceives the surrounding landscape.[4] Seen from this perspective, "civilization" is not a litany of ideas,
values, and attributes, but an active and dynamic historical force. Thus
the migration of Han to the frontier, while acting as an instrument for
the diffusion of the unified heritage of Han civilization, also ramified
into divergent forms of settlement and livelihood. The hilly terrain,
dense forest, and scarcity of land forms and soils suitable for rice cultivation demanded accommodation of social and economic organization to
an unfamiliar landscape. At the same time, the imposition of an inherited agrarian regime, the product of preconceived ideas of civilization,
proved to be a powerful tool for transforming that landscape.

This concept of civilization explains the habits of life and social
organization in terms of a creative encounter between human invention
and ecological milieu. Yet human populations are also organized as
societies and polities. Among the native peoples of the southwest the
primacy of kinship as the basis of tribal social and political organization
limited the size of the territory, the number of people, and the range of
resources that the polity could command.[5] The social and political isolation of these communities created and perpetuated ethnic boundaries.
Despite their ethnic diversity and political disunity, though, the
indigenous peoples shared well-entrenched political traditions of leadership, justice, and revenge, and alliance for trade, tribute, and war. To a
certain extent, interaction with the Han could be contained within these
venerable conventions. Yet the strain of aggressive Han settlement weakened and sometimes fractured the ethnic boundaries that divided native
societies. The incomparably greater state power at the disposal of the
Han drastically altered the political balances that equilibrated conflict
and advantage among the native peoples. New alliances to resist the Han
incursions were formed, but old habits and animosities died hard. Ultimately even the menace of subjugation to Song rule could not create a
broad and enduring unity among the native leaders.

Nor, of course, were the Han unanimous in their aims and aspirations. Peasants, landlords, merchants—and even more so, local warlords,
frontier officials, and the central government—harbored separate and
often competing interests in the frontier. But the crucial role of the Song

state in assimilating and giving a coherent direction to these conflicting aims, thus assuring a basic continuity of values, goals, and policies, decisively tipped the balance of power in favor of the Han. When the Song leadership saw its own vital interests at stake, it could undertake actions on distant frontiers with astonishing force. The active and continuing intervention of the state at the local level in frontier areas led to a radical restructuring of local power. Thus the fluctuating commitment of the Song state to frontier expansion, though only one of the many elements in the political process of the frontier, generally determined the final outcome.

Distance, as measured by the cost and reliability of transport and communication, generally fixed the limits of interaction between the frontier and the center. In most premodern societies the frontier supplied the center only with costly luxury and specialty goods from foreign lands. In Song China, however, the formation of regional and national markets based on specialization of production and the rising consumption demands of burgeoning towns and cities sharpened commercial interest in new sources of raw materials and staples. The forests, mines, rivers, and fields of the southwestern frontier contained potential reservoirs of productive resources rapidly becoming dear in the densely populated centers of consumption. The demand for non-renewable resources such as timber and minerals grew particularly acute. Furthermore, the native peoples figured not only as sources of commodities, notably horses, aromatics, medicines, and precious stones and minerals, from lands beyond the frontier but also as potential buyers for the products of Han civilization.

Initially, the question of exploiting the southwestern frontier little occupied the Song leaders, who faced a far more urgent problem in the threat of invasion by the steppe kingdoms of the Khitan (Liao) and Tanguts (Xixia). Han settlement in the southwest began largely under private auspices, spurred by the attractiveness of "virgin" lands. The growth of long-distance trade, founded on technological innovations in transport and the systematic extension of a body of commercial agents and practices throughout the empire, strengthened the links between frontier settlers and commercial centers. The distance between frontier producers and urban consumers, as measured by transport costs, diminished considerably. In Hunan, for example, newly settled frontier territories began to ship large quantities of timber, minerals, and later rice to the Yangzi River ports of Ezhou and Jiangling, where these goods were loaded onto vessels bound for the capital at Kaifeng or the cities of the lower Yangzi valley. The state's participation in the trade between the frontier and the center was principally limited to a few industries in which the state controlled the production or sale of staple goods. Thus Luzhou, with its profitable, state-run salt wells, attracted special attention from Song policymakers early on.

The need to defend Han settlers, however, drew the state into the process of frontier settlement. The state repeatedly intervened militarily to protect Han settlements, property, and trade routes. Even when Han engaged in blatantly illegal activities, such as felling timber on or cultivating the "forbidden hills" that demarcated the border between Han and native territories, the Song government invariably sided with its own subjects in the event that the natives resorted to violence to enforce treaty provisions. Although Han settlers, merchants, and state officials frequently clashed over frontier policy, they were united by a common affirmation of the sovereign proprietary rights of the Song.

From the late 1060s onward a new political creed, based on the idea of using institutional innovation and the proprietary rights invested in the state by the emperor to foster economic growth, came to the fore in Kaifeng. Inspired and patronized by Wang Anshi, prime minister from 1069 to 1077, a generation of political leadership was captivated by the belief that radical institutional innovation could not only create wealth most efficiently but also guarantee its distribution in fair proportion to all social classes. For the next half century, and sporadically afterwards, this cadre of leadership pursued these twin goals.[6]

One of the most immediate consequences of this shift in political climate was a new priority on frontier expansion. From the early 1070s to the 1120s the Song state systematically utilized its military power to secure and exploit the resources of the frontier areas of Sichuan, Hunan, Guangxi, and the northwest. Under state sponsorship, settlement in frontier areas advanced rapidly. The building of an infrastructure of towns, roads, bridges, and fortifications, combined with the enhanced military presence of the Song, paved the way for the social and economic incorporation of frontier areas into the empire. The confrontation between the civilization of the plain and that of the forest, the new role of the frontier in the productive system of Song society, and the unfolding of a political process that pitted the objectives of local Han and the Song state against those of fragmented native polities, all converged in closing the Luzhou frontier, with the loss of the native peoples' political autonomy and the implantation of Han institutions.

Yet incorporation into the larger Song sphere of social and economic circulation did not mean that the frontier areas became fully and irreversibly integrated into the Han world. The relationship between the frontier and the center remained contingent upon the frontier's functional value as an outlet for migration, a source of wealth, and an object of political aspirations. The frontier advanced and receded as these values changed. Towns carved out of the wilderness during the early vigor of a mining area, for example, were quickly abandoned when the mines gave out, leaving behind the dross of ghost towns and unemployed miners. The severing of the principal route of migration and trade connecting Sichuan with the rest of the Song world after the Jurchen conquest of the north in 1127 brought a sharp halt to frontier expansion in southern Sichuan. The fall of the prime minister Cai Jing in 1120 marked the end of frontier expansion as a political priority, yet migration to the southwestern frontier accelerated during the Southern Song as the frontier areas became increasingly integrated into the regional and national marketing systems.

Part One of this book introduces the physical and human landscapes of the Sichuan frontier, the contrasting civilizations of the forest and the plain. In addition to reconstructing an ethnic profile of the southwest and the habitats, form of livelihood, and polities of its native peoples, it investigates the distinctive features of Han frontier society. With its own traditions of defiant autonomy and communal solidarity based on personal bondage and fealty to local magnates, the "magnate society" of the Sichuan frontier posed a considerable obstacle to social and political integration.

Part Two details the political process of frontier expansion, especially during the period 1070–1120, when the Song state zealously pursued expansionary policies and sponsored an unprecedented wave of frontier settlement. Beginning with an overview of the place of salt mining and exploitation in the settlement of southern Sichuan, it traces the convergence of state and local interests in frontier expansion over the course of the Northern Song. This section concludes by considering the political institutions created by the Song court to enforce its authority in this remote territory and their impact on both Han and non-Han societies.

Part Three examines social and economic change in Luzhou during the Song. Population movements, the transformation of social institutions, the introduction of the Han agrarian regime, and the reorganization of space by trade networks all contributed to the domestication of the Sichuan frontier by Han civilization. The emergent role of the frontier as a supplier of raw materials and staple goods to metropolitan centers of consumption merits particular attention, and leads specifically to a consideration of the place of the frontier within the regional system of Sichuan in Song times.

Part One
The Setting

To the south,
The passes of Qionglai.
Heaven has arrayed formidable barriers;
Here one finds little flat ground.
Mountain ranges, extending in linked chains,
Traverse the Lu River
And sunder the valleys of the Hundred Tribes
From their neighbors.

Our backs to Hanyuan,
Facing the porous heavens above,
No day passes without rain.
Four seasons of incessant downpour.
The inhabitants, like fish, dwell underwater.
Throughout the year, constant, drenching wet.
At times the sun reemerges—
Snarling and growling, a chorus of dogs
Looks skyward and barks at the sun.
The people sleep soaked with sweat,
Half-paralyzed by lumbago.

Once more regaining the road to Yangshan;
Lethal vapors descend, condense.
The white sun sheds no light,
Its emanations shrouded in gloom.
Summer rains seep down,
"Yellow Reed" fever steams up from the ground.
Even men of the southlands dare not pass here,
Where running beasts stumble and flying birds fall.
I know not why the Fashioner of Things
Would bestow on us such a place.
The south of Shu is not fit for men;
Flee homeward, stranger from the north!

CEN SHEN, "Warning to a Stranger From the North,"
ca. 769

ONE

The Civilization of The Forest

In the spring of 906 Wang Zongruan, general and scion of the Former Shu ruling house, who was returning from a campaign in the Yangzi Gorges, decided to rest his troops and bivouac for the night at a small temple at Fang Shan, an imposing, flat-topped ridge west of the town of Luzhou. Wang ordered his aides to prepare an offering of food to the temple god and, weary from his long journey, retired to one of the temple's antechambers. The aides, likewise suffering from lack of sleep, failed to maintain a diligent watch over the offering; and a dog belonging to the temple caretaker stole off with the deity's repast. Later that night, says our informant,

a sudden thunderous roar resounded in the temple's sanctuary and several flashes of lightning darted around the temple walls. Wang and more than thirty others crouched in the corner of the chamber but found no place to hide. Then a person clothed all in white and wearing a white cap ascended to the sanctuary and sat down. Countless numbers of Lau demons [*Liaogui*] scurried about below the altar steps or waited upon the figure like rows of attendants. Soon a dozen or more demons cloaked in tiger skins emerged and carried a person dressed in a red and yellow tunic into the middle of the room. The Demon Master [*guizhu*] berated this unfortunate: "How dare you steal the food set out for me by the humans before I myself have feasted on their sacrificial offerings?" The Demon Master then ordered that the culprit receive fifteen blows with the cane, after which he was dragged out through the temple gate. After a considerable lapse of time the sounds and shadows of the demon figures dimmed, and all became pitch-dark as before. Wang immediately

commanded his officers to make sacrificial offerings, though all they could find
were some pig entrails. The following morning, upon leaving the temple, they
espied among the shrubs a red and yellow dog licking its swollen bruises.

Henceforth, we are told, those making sacrifices to the temple god became exceedingly circumspect and reverential in attending to their
tasks.[1]

The raconteur's anecdote, set down for the amusement of an urbane
audience, nonetheless conveys the fear and mystery that the tribal peoples of the southwest evoked in the thoughts of the Han inhabitants of
Sichuan. The flesh-and-blood "demon masters" haunting the dense forests of bamboo and fir beyond the edges of the rice fields were real
threats to life and livelihood. The tribesmen frequently raided isolated
and vulnerable Han settlements, "descending like swarms of bees and
ants, then departing like wheeling birds and fleeing beasts."[2] One diarist,
traveling down the Yangzi by ship, described the ominous sight of "the
natives, wearing felt even at the height of summer, peering out at our
passing boat from their storied huts on the opposite bank, almost hidden
by the verdant foliage."[3] The townfolk of Luzhou, who could see the
natives watching them from across the river, lived with the same gnaw-
ing dread.

The nearly unseen yet overwhelmingly felt presence of the native
tribes and the intimidating gloom of the forest coalesced in the imagery
of the phantom, quasi-supernatural demons of the temple at Fang Shan.
The town-dwellers of the Chengdu Plain, who since the days of the
ancient Shu kingdom had identified with the skeptical temper of Han
civilization, may have scoffed at such superstitions. But the inhabitants
of the Yangzi valley, heirs to the Ba and Chu cultures of antiquity, had
long been renowned for their vigorous shamanistic cults and abiding
awe of the spirits of the forests and rivers.[4] The capricious and intractable wilderness readily inspired notions of supernatural powers impervious to human control. As a result the Han inhabitants of the upper
and middle Yangzi valley accumulated a rich store of beliefs and rituals
focused on comprehending and controlling the frontier landscape and
its eerie denizens. Some of these practices may have originated with the
native peoples. Song officials typically blamed the obsession with the

occult and the repellent practice of human sacrifice among the Han to the malign influence of tribal customs.[5] The apostles of Han civilization sought to civilize the frontier by propagating secular cults which linked the conquest of both nature and savage to the invincible might of the great Han demiurges, from the mythical Great Yu to apotheosized historical figures such as Li Bing and Zhuge Liang.

Chief among the cults of ancient Ba was that of the primordial creator of the humanized landscape, the Great Yu. The myth of Yu existed in many permutations; but the core myth described Yu's prodigious efforts to relieve the world from the great flood, the work of serpentine rain deities, and thus achieve mastery over the elemental world. Succeeding where his father had failed, Yu delivered the world from the scourge of flood by dredging the great rivers and emptying the flood waters into the sea. In the ancient myths Yu assumed fantastic and macabre forms; his consort turned to stone at the sight of Yu transformed into a bear.[6] Yet by Song times Yu had long since been made human and dressed in the raiment of a Han sage-king. Du Fu, visiting the temple to Yu at Zhong-zhou in 765, composed a poem tinged with melancholic musings over the mortality of the once mighty creator-god:

Yu's temple lies nestled in the hills,
Exposed to the autumn wind and the sun's slanting rays.
In the desolate courtyard hang oranges and pomelos,
On the old building, traces of dragons and serpents.
The breath of clouds rises from barren cliffs,
The river's roar rushes across white sands.
Long ago I learned that he rode the Four Vehicles
To chisel the mountains, dredge the rivers, and fashion the three
  regions of Ba.[7]

For Du Fu the image of Yu existed not as the object of piety but merely as an allegory of the human condition.[8]

The related cult of the serpentine Dragon Woman (*longnü*), mistress of the rivers and the rains, lingered on much longer. In the poetry of Du Fu's contemporary Cen Shen the Dragon Woman appeared as an immanent and active deity:

The dragon woman—from whence does she come?
But when she comes—she rides the wind and the rain!
At the hall of her fane, below the blue wood,
She coils sinuously, as if about to speak to you.
Men of Shu vie there, with worshipful thoughts,
To offer her wine to the beating of drums.[9]

To the adherents of her cult in Sichuan the Dragon Woman assumed the form of a zoomorphic rain goddess who must be lured with thunderous music and sated with wine. In Luzhou a magnificent waterfall shrouded a deep, perpetually dark cavern said to be the abode of the Dragon Woman. By Song times, though, this saurian deity who once wielded the elemental forces of nature with impunity had become a tame creature routinely manipulated by men. A local historian in Luzhou recorded, in a matter-of-fact manner, that in years of drought the magistrate would send his representative to drop a golden dragon enclosed in a stone casket into the pool before the Dragon Woman's temple. She never failed to respond with her life-giving rains.[10]

Long after Yu was reduced to a mere sage of antiquity, his legendary exploits as a flood hero were invested in the person of Li Bing, the famous engineer of the third century B.C. who built the river control works, still extant today, to control flooding on the Chengdu Plain. The mythic Li, like Yu, suffered defeat before finally assuming another form (in Li's case, an ox) to defeat the malevolent kraken (*jiao*) who demanded human sacrifices from the local populace. Subsequently Li placed a stone ox at the river's edge to tame the watery spirits and quell the flood waters.[11] Yu, who received aid from a yellow ox in the course of his labors, also set up stone oxen on dikes above the rivers as simulacra representing his own power over the river-dwelling serpents.[12] Throughout the Ba-Chu cultural sphere the local populace worshipped icons of oxen to ensure the diligent protection of the flood heros. In Song times the shrine of the Yellow Ox at Xiazhou, where the Yangzi River emerges from the Gorges and enters the Hubei plain, attracted a massive cult following. Sacrifices to the Yellow Ox were accompanied by beating drums, the shrill music of flutes, and dances of the shamans.[13]

The shrine of the Yellow Ox at Xiazhou purportedly was founded by

Zhuge Liang (181–234), the heroic minister of the Shu Han dynasty who together with the general Ma Yuan of the Han dynasty became one of the most renowned paragons of Han martial vigor. According to legend, Zhuge Liang and Ma Yuan consecrated their victories over the indigenous peoples of southern China by erecting bronze pillars to demarcate the bounds of Han sovereignty; correspondingly, they placed bronze pillars, oxen, or drums in or above the rivers of the conquered domains to quell the subaqueous, reptilian deities that ruled the torrents and strategic places of passage. Ma and Zhuge symbolized the sovereignty of the Han monarch, the power to unite contrasting and hostile worlds, to subdue the gods and demons of the foreign and watery lands of the south and, by extension, the native peoples as well.[14] The widely held belief that metal objects enervated the maleficent krakens and serpents dwelling in the rivers stemmed from the putative power of metal over water expressed in Five Phases cosmology.

Zhuge Liang's spectral presence often overshadowed indigenous deities of the southwest and gained a permanent place among the native cults. The native peoples of Southern Lu (and in later times, throughout the southwest) venerated Zhuge Liang as the patron deity of horse-breeders. When those known as the Black Tribes came to sell horses to the Han, they first offered prayers at Zhuge's temple on the outskirts of Luzhou.[15] Temples to Zhuge Liang were common at horse markets in Guizhou in Ming times.[16] Of course, the Han authorities strove to supplant the "profane cults" (*yinci*) of the natives with appropriate secular exemplars from the pantheon of Han civilization. Song officials continually refurbished the temples to Zhuge Liang at Xuzhou and Luzhou, whom the emperor honored with the epithet "Numen of Loyalty" (*zhongling*).[17] Later legends among the native peoples related that their chieftains' bronze drums, the universal symbols of authority in the southwest, originally were bestowed by Zhuge Liang. In 1573, upon surrendering his bronze drums after a decisive defeat at the hands of a Ming army, the chieftain of the Tuotśiang tribe of Southern Lu lamented, "The drum emitting the most awe-inspiring sound is held in the highest esteem, worth a thousand oxen. One who obtains two or three of these drums can rightly proclaim himself king. Striking the drum at the summit of a hill will cause all of the tribes to assemble. But now, all is lost!"

Storytellers had foretold that loss of the bronze drums given by Zhuge Liang would seal the fate of the tribes.[18]

Despite the symbolic supremacy of Han civilization, natives endured in legend and story as shadowy, sinister creatures. Their profane cults attained a wide and notorious reputation among the Han. Stories were told and retold of how the Klao chose sacrificial victims with fine braids of hair, flayed their skin, and stretched it out over a bamboo frame. When dried, the effigy was venerated as a demon spirit and the Klao struck drums and danced in their propitiary rituals before it.[19] Reputedly the Klao could assume the shape of man-eating sheep, pigs, mules, and particularly tigers. A Ming author, in a play on words, equated the Luogui, one of the Black Tribes, with the Luochagui or *rakshasas,* the Ceylonese anthropophagi of Buddhist fables who haunted cemeteries and devoured unsuspecting passers-by.[20] Government officials focused their censure on the lavish ceremonies and rites of the native peoples, the costly sacrifices of oxen and horses, and the besotted celebrations that accompanied them. But in popular lore tales of headhunting, cannibalism, and selling children into slavery quickened the pulse and swelled the imagination.

AN ETHNOGRAPHIC GAZETTEER OF THE LUZHOU FRONTIER

Any modern map of the distribution of ethnic groups in southwestern China shows a confusing profusion of jumbled colors, a patchwork quilt of Tai, Tibeto-Burman, and Miao-Yao peoples, plus some as yet unclassifiable ones. Undoubtedly this situation was even more complex a millenium ago, before sustained colonization by the Han. Chinese texts from the Tang-Song era offer little help in deciphering the ethnic identities and origins of the native peoples. Rarely do they describe the native peoples in terms of ethnic categories; usually the Han identified tribes on the basis of geographical location rather than ethnicity. The simplest categorization used by the Han distinguished the "raw" tribes (*shengyi*) from the "cooked" ones (*shuyi*). This metaphor indicated the degree of hostility with which the natives reacted to Han intrusions and demands for tribute and fealty. For the most part, Song statesmen expected little in the way of cultural assimilation. Thus the terms "raw" and "cooked" do not refer to the extent of cultural change or sinicization and bear little ethnic connotation.

The history of Han expansion into the southwest down to Song times can be divided into three phases. In each phase the Han were confronted with a different configuration of indigenous peoples and cultural patterns. In the first phase, lasting from the Qin conquest of Sichuan in the late fourth century B.C. to the fall of the Shu Han dynasty in the mid-third century A.D., the Han rulers first asserted their sovereignty over the original inhabitants of southwestern Sichuan and adjacent areas in Guizhou and Yunnan, a diverse group of local cultures which I subsume under the concept of Buək civilization. The second phase spanned the Six Dynasties period (from the middle of the third century to the end of the sixth century). During this period the tide of population movement reversed; a new group of peoples, the Klao (or more broadly, Lau), began to migrate northward from their original home in the Guizhou Plateau and diffused throughout the Han-inhabited Sichuan Basin. The third phase, inaugurated by the Sui reunification of the Sinitic world, continued, with periodic interruptions, down to the modern era. Han settlement slowly spread throughout the southwest, driving out or absorbing the Klao (Lau) until their civilization reached the verge of extinction. At the same time a third major indigenous civilization, the Yi, not only encroached upon the Klao territories but succeeded in resisting the onslaught of Han expansion. In some areas the Yi remained free from direct political control by the Han until the end of the imperial era.[21]

THE BUƏK. The Buək have been acknowledged as the orginal inhabitants of the lower Jinsha River valley since the second century B.C.[22] The earliest Han word for the area around the confluence of the Jinsha and Min Rivers was Bodao, or "circuit of the Buək."[23] Textual sources shed little light on the culture of the Buək in early times except to say that of all the non-Han peoples in the southwest the Buək conformed most closely to Han standards of behavior. This bit of information suggests that Buək culture resembled that of the Han in some important ways, but beyond this the historical documents are mute. We do know that many Buək youths were brought as slaves to North China during the

Qin and Han dynasties, at the same time that Han immigrants began to outnumber the native Buək in the Min-Jinsha area and forced many Buək to migrate westward.[24]

Recent archaeological research has enabled us to go further and tentatively link the Buək with a series of cultures in the upper Jinsha valley and eastern Yunnan among peoples known variously as Buk or Buak. The sequence of neolithic and bronze-age sites in Yunnan demonstrates that an indigenous culture based on wet-rice agriculture, domesticated animals, and a fairly sophisticated metallurgical industry had emerged in eastern Yunnan by the second century B.C., culminating in the flowering of the Dian kingdom in the Lake Dian area.[25]

Excavation of tomb sites of the shaft tomb culture in the upper Jinsha valley, the pit tombs in northwestern Guizhou, and the royal cemetery at Dian attest to a widespread regional culture with distinct local variations. Most of these tomb sites are located on flat terraces above rivers, a settlement pattern that suggests a combination of agricultural and riverine subsistence resources. A spade-shaped bronze hoe associated with swidden agriculture was the basic farming tool at all of these sites, although the considerable number of ploughshares excavated at the Dian cemetery indicates that some form of irrigated agriculture was practiced around Lake Dian. Basic stylistic affinities and the recurring assemblages of bronze drums, cowrie-shell containers, bronze-handled and iron-bladed swords, reed organs, and bronze pillows all point to a consistent material culture throughout the region. The variety of burial practices—lacquered coffins in pit tombs for the royal clan at Dian, secondary burial of up to one hundred skeletons in the shaft tombs of the Anning River valley, and secondary burial in pit tombs at Hezhang in northwestern Guizhou—reveal strong local identities as well.[26]

A fourth-century text explicitly associated the shaft tombs of the Anning valley with the Buk:

Huiwu [modern Huili in the Anning valley] formerly was a town of the Buk people. At present the tumuli of the Buk still can be found there. The entrances to the tumuli are not sealed off and within the tombs there are many pieces of jade and pearl, but men dare not take them, or risk bringing misfortune on themselves.[27]

The same author also referred to the people of Dian as Buk.[28] Although ascribing archaeological sites to specific ethnic groups rightly invites skepticism, the spatial and temporal overlap of the Dian regional culture and the peoples known to contemporaries as the Buək or Buk is striking and justifies the inference of a common identity. We have sufficient evidence to postulate that the Buək/Buk/Buak comprised a regional culture of permanent village-dwellers who drew widely upon the resources of the forests, rivers, and cultivated fields for food, clothing, and shelter. The specific economy of subsistence varied from area to area. In the Lake Dian area, agriculture was far more important than at other sites. Farming tasks were performed by women, who figure as the primary actors in the numerous scenes culled from Dian artifacts depicting the rituals of supplicating the gods for good harvests, the commencement of the planting season, the harvest celebration, and storing the year's crops in the granaries.[29] Raising stock also was a basic feature of Dian livelihood. Han conquerors brought back some three hundred thousand head of horses, cattle, and sheep from Dian at the end of the second century B.C.[30] The absence of ploughshares at sites other than the Dian royal capital indicates that agricultural techniques elsewhere remained at a rudimentary level, though millet and rice were widely cultivated.

The Han conquest of Dian in 109 B.C. and the subsequent incorporation of large areas of the southwest into the Han polity brought a swift end to the development of the indigenous Buək/Buk civilization. The remarkably original culture of Dian disappeared entirely within several decades. By the end of the first century B.C. the material culture of the Dian region had shrunk to mere imitation of Han artifacts.[31] The Han introduced iron metallurgy, which spurred the transition to an agrarian society; but the Buək/Buk peoples became fragmented and dispersed, retreating into remote enclaves beyond the reach of the Han overlords. During the Six Dynasties period a confederation of White Tribes (Buak) known as the Western Cuan regained suzerainty over the Lake Dian region. The dynasty ruled by the Cuan lineage lasted for several centuries before falling victim to the Tang-Nanzhao wars of the eighth century, marking the end of Buək/Buk autonomy.[32]

By the Song period the Buək/Buk peoples had become virtually extinct in Southern Lu. They still could be found farther west in the Jinsha valley, represented by such groups as the Mahu tribes of Xuzhou. Song texts on the Mahu, like the cryptic records of a millenium before, underscored their basic affinity with Han civilization:

> The Mahu occupy lands of fertile soil suitable for ploughing and tilling. The people wear felt and tie their hair in the mallet hairstyle. Every house is tiled, just like the dwellings of the Han. In their preferences for foods and beverages and in their techniques of sowing and planting the Mahu are virtually identical to the Han.[33]

In the Yuan and Ming periods the word *Buǝk,* long unused, was resurrected and applied indiscriminately to the tribal peoples of the Xuzhou-Luzhou area, who were unrelated to the older Buǝk/Buk culture. The Buǝk/Buk survived down to modern times, though, in hybrid cultures such as the Minjia (or Boerzi, as they call themselves) in the Lake Dali region of northwestern Yunnan.

KLAO (LAU). Beginning abruptly in the mid-fourth century A.D. a new non-Han population, called Lau, appeared throughout southern and eastern Sichuan. Apparently natives of the impenetrable recesses of the Guizhou Plateau, the Lau migrated northward across the Yangzi and spread from the Jinsha River valley in the southwest to the headwaters of the Jialing River in the northeast.[34] By the Tang period the Lau extended over such a vast area that the word itself became a generic term for non-Han peoples and was affixed to any tribe between the Qinling Shan ranges in the north and Tonkin in the south.[35] From this time, too, the variety of local non-Han populations in earlier texts was dissolved and merged into a single ethnic identity. While the Lau peoples of Sichuan were known by many different ethnonyms prior to the Tang period, later texts referred to them collectively as Lau.[36] In the Song period *Lau* had roughly the same connotation as the older word *Man,* both describing a broad and indiscriminate category of southern non-Han peoples.

At the same time a number of disyllabic words for the original Lau began to appear in Han texts. These words, such as *Kiǝulau* and *Katlau,* preserve the initial consonant cluster of the Ancient Chinese word *Lau* (pronounced Klao or Tlao). Ruey Yih-fu identified the original Lau (or, more accurately, Klao), with the Gelao peoples that continued to live, in ever decreasing numbers, in Guizhou and western Hunan down to the present day.[37] Linguistic, textual, and archaeological evidence all bear out this attribution. In the Song and Yuan periods the Klao often were called *Tulaoman* or *Tulaman,* words which undoubtedly derived from the Ancient Chinese pronunciation of Tlao.

During the Tang period the Klao comprised the principal native population in Southern Lu. Tang texts depicted the Klao inhabitants of Luzhou as a warlike confederation of tribes living in the dense forests and bamboo groves on both banks of the Yangzi River.[38] Han observers of the Six Dynasties period were struck by the extremely primitive character of Lau culture, which they described as based on hunting and a rudimentary form of agriculture without any knowledge of animal husbandry or weaving. The Lau, we are told, were ignorant not only of writing and the calendar but even of the use of the bow.[39] Nonetheless textual and archaeological evidence from the Song period shows that Klao society was based on a complex forest economy centered on shifting cultivation.

In 1974 archaeologists began to investigate the "suspended-coffin" burial culture of Southern Lu. Their research focused on twenty-two sites dating from the Song-Ming era excavated at Gongxian, eighty kilometers southwest of Luzhou.[40] The deceased had been placed in wooden coffins and then either suspended on wooden frames attached to a cliff face or inserted in natural or man-made caves in the rock at heights of ten to one hundred meters above the valley floor. Although both the local populace and Qing gazetteers attribute the suspended-coffin burials to the Buək, there is little doubt that this burial practice actually was characteristic of the Klao.[41]

Recently archaeologists have studied another group of tombs in the Nanguang River valley, fifty kilometers west of Gongxian. The cliff tombs of the Nanguang valley were dug into the rock face of cliffs at heights of twenty to over one hundred meters above small tributaries of the Nanguang River. Among the distinctive features of the cliff tombs are the relief carvings of guardian figures and *ganlan*-style eaves around the mouth of the cave, evidence of stone screens used to close off the cave mouth, and relief carvings on the interior walls.[42] Unlike the suspended-coffin burials, the cliff tombs contained no evidence of coffins and only sundry human bones, suggesting secondary burial (exposing the corpse of the deceased until the flesh were rotted away, after which the bones were collected and interred in a tomb). The guardian figures and architectural motifs clearly emulated popular Song styles, indicating that the tombs probably date from the Song-Yuan era. Despite the obvious differences between the cliff burials and the more numerous suspended-coffin burials among which they are interspersed, the two share a common cultural affinity.[43] Most likely the cliff tombs represent an earlier stage of Klao culture, or perhaps a local variation on the more common suspended-coffin style.

Secondary burial had a wide and varied distribution among the peoples of southwestern China. Common themes underlying the practice of secondary burial, including exposure of the corpse, burial in stone mausoleums or caves, and the erection of a stone or stake symbolizing the ancestral deity, linked the mortuary rituals of the Klao to those of the Tibetans, the B'iu Kingdom of the Great Snowy Mountains, the cist-tomb culture of the Min Shan, the shaft-tomb culture of the Anning River valley, the forest dwellers of the Daba Shan and the Wuling Shan as well as the suspended-coffin burial culture of the Wuyi Shan in Fujian.[44] This complex of mortuary practices characterized mobile, forest-dwelling peoples who engaged in a form of ritual exchange whereby the corpses of the dead were offered to the beasts of the forest in return for the flesh of game consumed by the hunters. The sacred harmony between man and the natural world ruptured by the killing of game could be restored only through the reciprocal gift of human flesh to the animal spirits of the forest. The bones of the dead, cleansed of impurity, then could receive full recognition in the ceremonies of ancestor worship. Burial of the bones in stone tombs represented a second returning or ritual exchange, to the soil as well as the forest. Burial in permanent cemeteries of stone tombs or sacred cliffs was the inevitable consequence of sedentarization and transition to an agrarian society, just as exposure and cremation, practiced by the Tibetans and related cultures such as the Yi, typified nomadic societies.[45]

The cliff tombs and suspended-coffin burials corroborate textual evidence indicating that by Song times the Klao of the Luzhou region had adopted a mixed subsistence economy based on agriculture, fishing, and animal husbandry. Numerous Song sources attest to the practice of shifting cultivation by the Klao of Southern Lu.[46] The wall carvings in the cliff tombs were grouped into sets of productive activities such as weaving, spinning, and grinding with mortar and pestle, and ceremonial occasions, including feasting, music, and dancing. The carvings depict both domestic animals (pig, ox, and horse) and wild ones (elephant, tiger, deer, and hare). The cave paintings accompanying the suspended-coffin burials at Gongxian do not include any scenes of farming or hunting, but they give ample evidence of the importance of fishing and stock-raising, especially horse-breeding.[47]

The archaeological remains of the Klao exhibit a trend towards increasing sedentarization from the Song onward. Exposure of the corpse, cited by early authors as a Klao characteristic, was no longer practiced by the suspended-coffin burial culture. The remaining skeletons at Gongxian were discovered intact, except for the removal of teeth, undoubtedly indicative of the Klao ritual of attaining adulthood.[48] The coffins found at the suspended-coffin sites, made from hollowed-out tree trunks fitted with wooden covers, are reminiscent of the earlier "boat coffin" burials of the Jialing River valley in eastern Sichuan.[49] This burial practice suggests the idea of a boat journey in the transition to the world of the afterlife, and also betokens the central importance of the river in the life of the living culture.

The close proximity of the Klao to Han settlements in the upper Yangzi valley and western Hunan and the definitive adoption of an agrarian regime admitted the possibility that the Klao, like the Buək before them, might adopt certain traits of Han civilization. Several observers noted that Klao living within the sphere of Han influence had acquired at least the veneer of civilized habits. The assimilation of the Klao natives in Sichuan proceeded most rapidly in areas north of the Yangzi River where Klao and subgroups such as the Ñiang were completely surrounded by Han settlements and effectively subjected to Han rule. A thirteenth-century geographer remarked approvingly on the pace of assimilation in Fushun, northwest of Luzhou:

In Lainiu and Laiyi in the western quarter of the prefecture one finds the settlements of the Tulao tribes. During the Tiansheng reign (1023–1032) the chieftain Təulangtśʼiuın of Chiyai rebelled but subsequently was suppressed. He then submitted and acknowledged allegiance to the Song. The present-day tribesmen are mostly his descendants. . . . At present they have been influenced by moral teachings. Though the old customs are deeply engrained, they know something of ritual and modesty.[50]

The Klao, unlike most native peoples, did not enforce a rigid segregation of their social world into ascriptive and exclusive communities. Eighteenth-century observers noted that many Klao tribes allowed persons not belonging to their own kin groups to dwell in their villages. While some Klao groups rarely ventured beyond the vicinity of their own hamlet, more commonly the Klao interacted with Han settlers on many levels.[51]

Throughout the Song period the Klao, who typically inhabited lowland areas, bore the brunt of Han expansion into the southwest and, unlike the mountain-dwelling peoples, often became directly subordinated to Han rule. Consequently the Klao were absorbed into the Han agrarian economy to an extent unknown among other native peoples of the southwest. Many Klao, displaced from their lands, became hired laborers picking tea and litchi in the orchards of the Han.[52] Han inhabitants of western Hunan hired Klao as laborers despite their "prodigal idleness and lack of discipline," which earned Klao hired hands the derisive appellation of "slave dogs."[53] More importantly, from the point of view of the Song state, the Klao could be domesticated and converted into tax-paying subjects. As early as the 980s, well before the decisive Han colonization of Southern Lu, the household registers of Luzhou included the names of 2,415 Klao households.[54]

YI (BLACK TRIBES). Aside from the Klao and the Buək, the third indigenous non-Han population of Southern Lu in Song times was the Yi. Yi language and culture point unambiguously to an origin among the Tibeto-Burman peoples. After arriving in the valley of the Jinsha River prior to the Han Dynasty, the Yi became known as the Black Tribes (Wuman) as opposed to the indigenous Buək/Buk, or White Tribes.[55] From the Han period onward the Black Tribes steadily migrated southeastward along the western frontier of Sichuan, following the trend of the ranges of the Liang Shan and the Wumeng Shan, the easternmost extension of the Tibetan massif. By late Han times the Black Tribes had crossed the Jinsha River into Yunnan and Guizhou. Much of the area occupied by the Black Tribes lay above two thousand meters, with peaks soaring to heights of thirty-five hundred meters or more. The pastoral Black Tribes, breeders of sheep, horses, and cattle, initially preferred the high mountains to the thick forests of the lowland valleys. Ultimately, though, the filling up of the high mountains pushed the Black Tribes into the lower elevations, where the climate, generally inhospitable for stock-raising, forced them to adopt an agrarian livelihood.

Early ethnological accounts of the Black Tribes, whose habitat was far removed from the Han towns and villages, were even more cursory than descriptions of other native peoples in the southwest. Fan Chuo, a Tang official stationed in the southwest during the Tang-Nanzhao wars of the 860s, described them in extremely laconic terms:

> The men braid their hair, while the women allow their hair to fall loose and unbound. Upon meeting others they exhibit no ritual decorum, neither bowing or kneeling. Three or four translations are required before their speech is intelligible to Han. Cattle and horses are plentiful in this region, but hemp and silk are unknown. Both men and women wear the hides of cattle and sheep. . . . The women of the Black Tribes wear a black woven cloth that drags on the ground when they walk, whereas the White Tribes women wear white garments that only reach to their knees.[56]

From the Tang to the Ming, sheep-raising provided the basic means of subsistence among the Black Tribes inhabiting the higher elevations of the Liang Shan and the Wumeng Shan, supplemented by barley, buckwheat, and oats.[57] As the Black Tribes supplanted the native peoples of the lowland areas, they gradually shifted to an agrarian base; and seasonal transhumance gave way to permanent settlements. By the seventeenth century oats and buckwheat, particularly the "bitter buckwheat" (*kuqiao*), which had to be ground and steamed to remove its astringency before making flour, were the staple foods of the Yi.[58] Yet the Yi considered farming an inferior task fit only for women or slaves, while the male Yi occupied themselves with hunting and tending the herds, especially the horses raised for sale to the Han.

A noteworthy characteristic of the Black Tribes was the fusion of temporal and spiritual power in the person of a figure we have already met, the Demon Master:

> The tribesmen have great reverence for demons. The officiant at sacrifices is called the Demon Master. Each year every household must contribute an ox or sheep, which is brought to the home of the Demon Master and sacrificed. In sending off or welcoming the demons there always is a great flourish of weapons, inevitably resulting in conflict and blood feuds.[59]

> Large tribes have a Great Demon Master [*da guizhu*], while smaller tribes, numbering two or three hundred families, merely have lesser Demon Masters.[60]

The great esteem accorded to shamans by the Yi and their deep-seated fear of baleful mountain spirits translated into awe and deference before the Demon Masters, who presided over secular affairs as well as religious ceremonies. During the Tang period the Grand Demon Masters (*duda guizhu*) of the Miuətdɛng tribe achieved a certain degree of political unity among the Black Tribes of the Liang Shan and the Anning River valley. The ruling lineage of the Miuətdɛng, known as Tsio (the Chinese rendering of the Yi word for Demon Master, *zimo*), was recognized as the paramount leader of the Three Kings, the chiefs of the Miuətdɛng, Liangliɨm, and the P'iungbua tribes.[61] The Miuətdɛng maintained their control over this region and the peoples within it, including many White Tribes, until the beginning of the thirteenth century. During the eleventh century another powerful group of Black Tribes, the Demon Masters of the Luo Clan, formed a powerful confederation of tribes farther south in the Wumeng Shan.

ECOLOGY, HABITAT, AND CIVILIZATION

Apart from the histories of specific ethnic groups, the landscape of the southwestern frontier was molded by techniques of ecological adaptation shared by virtually all of the indigenous peoples. As noted above, the mortuary practices found in the southwest included certain motifs characteristic of forest-dwelling peoples in general. Similarly, economic livelihood and settlement of the landscape followed historical patterns which reveal that the native peoples of the southwest employed a common fund of techniques to alter the natural environment for human occupation and use.

The constraints of climate and topography and the biotic resources of the southwest's distinctive habitat gave rise to techniques of production which in turn ramified into specific patterns of settlement and social organization. These forms of livelihood and the artifacts and cultural behavior they engendered imparted a geographic unity to the region and its peoples. This unity of milieu and human populations was not a rigid, static phenomenon but rather a historically evolving product of assimilation and reaction to epochal changes in the ecological setting, to the human alteration of the landscape, and to pressures exerted by neighboring and competing societies. The way of life shared by the non-Han peoples of the southwest constituted a mode of civilization that contrasted and conflicted with the techniques of civilization employed by the Han to domesticate the "wilderness" landscape.

Most of southwestern China lies within the broadleaf evergreen forest belt stretching from Assam and Burma to eastern China and the southern islands of Japan.[62] Evergreen oaks with clear, straight trunks rising thirty meters in height dominated the pristine forest; even today the broad, glossy leaves of the evergreen oak crowns cover the hills for hundreds of kilometers in the undisturbed forests of southern Yunnan. The humid, subtropical climate fostered the growth of a wealth of flora, including many tropical species, under the forest canopy; but the dominance of the great oaks, with trunks often one meter in diameter, posed a formidable obstacle to habitation by primitive societies. The earliest lithic cultures of the broadleaf evergreen belt, largely restricted to clearings on river terraces, depended primarily on fish and other river produce rather than the resources of the forest.

Phytogeographic research has clearly demonstrated that rice originated in the western part of the broadleaf evergreen belt, in a zone extending from Assam to Yunnan.[63] Nonetheless the origins and antiquity of rice cultivation in this area remain uncertain. While rice cultivation in the wetlands of the East China littoral has been dated conclusively to the end of the fifth millenium B.C., we have no evidence of rice cultivation in Yunnan before ca. 1300 B.C.[64] Ecological conditions hindered the development of rice cultivation in southwestern China. Before the introduction of iron tools, the local cultures of the broadleaf evergreen belt were unable to clear the forest, a precondition for extensive cultivation. Even after rice was added to the inventory of cultivated plants in Yunnan at the end of the second millenium B.C., no significant changes in agricultural exploitation resulted.[65] The flimsy "red copper" bronze tools indigenous to Yunnan, also dated to before 1000 B.C., did not replace stone axes and hoes as agricultural implements. The use of the plough, an important instrument of wet-rice cultivation, apparently did not antedate the emergence of the Dian civilization in eastern Yunnan at the end of the first millenium B.C.[66] Throughout the Bronze Age in Yunnan, rice continued to be cultivated in dry fields using hoes and dibble sticks.

The Han conquests of the kingdoms of the southwest, such as Dian in Yunnan and Yelang in western Guizhou, radically altered the indigenous pattern of economic subsistence and spurred the transition to an agrarian economy based on wet-rice cultivation. Iron tools enabled the inhabitants of the broadleaf evergreen forest to move beyond the lake shores and river banks. By the Later Han period, rice cultivation had spread widely throughout the tablelands of eastern Yunnan and southwestern Guizhou.[67] In the Tang period the sophistication of the agrarian regime prevailing in eastern Yunnan compared favorably with contemporary Han agriculture:

South of Qujing and extending west of Lake Dian the native custom is to devote themselves solely to irrigated agriculture—the cultivation of hemp, legumes, and millet is confined to vacant areas between dwellings. The irrigated fields yield a single crop each year. Beginning in the eighth month the rice harvest is gathered. Around the eleventh or twelfth month the natives plant barley in the rice fields which will ripen in the third or fourth month of the following year. After gathering in the barley crop they again plant nonglutinous rice. The cultivation of wheat is confined to hills and knolls. By the last third of the twelfth month the wheat shoots already have begun to sprout, and the grain is reaped during the third month, at the same time as the barley. The flour made from wheat is soft and sticky, with little flavor. Barley is used solely to make flour—the natives make yeast for wine from rice, but this wine is acidic in taste and unpalatable. When ploughing the fields the natives use a meter-long share with a hafting extending over three meters in length. A team of two oxen, one walking two meters or more in front of the other, pull the plough. One fieldworker leads the front ox, another holds steady the hafting of the plough, while the third grasps the plough handle. The tribesmen are especially adept and practiced at cultivating hill fields.[68]

When Han settlers first began to colonize southwestern Guizhou in the early seventeenth century, they found that the rice fields of the natives were equally as productive, if not more so, as their own.[69]

The plough made few inroads into the Guizhou Plateau, except for the southwestern corner. Unlike Yunnan, Guizhou has no large lakes or basins. Rapid streams and rivers flowing outward to the lowland valleys of the Yangzi and West River drainage basins created a highly dissected terrain of narrow gorges, steep slopes, and subterranean rivers. The humid climate of Guizhou, the wettest part of China, was conducive to the growth of the evergreen oaks that populated the plateau up to elevations of twenty-five hundred meters, but also reduced the underlying soils to infertile podzols virtually useless for intensive agriculture. Throughout the Guizhou Plateau and in the foothills leading down to the Sichuan Basin, the inhabitants practiced shifting cultivation utilizing hardy cereals, such as spiked millet and barley, substantially supplemented by a wide variety of tuber and aquatic plants. Taro, which flourished in the warm and wet climate of Sichuan and Guizhou, achieved special importance as a staple food. Introduced from the Southeast Asian highlands at an early date, taro was widely cultivated by both natives and Han throughout the southwest and particularly in the Sichuan Basin, whence it spread to other parts of China.[70]

Rice cultivation was practicable only in a few places in the frontier areas of southwestern Sichuan, such as in the dolines (*panwa*, to use the word coined by the sixteenth-century geographer Xu Xiake; *bazi* in the parlance of the southwest)[71] that punctuated the landscape of the Guizhou Plateau. Dolines, roughly circular depressions formed by the subsidence of saturated limestone, contain rich, calcareous soils well suited for wet-rice cultivation. Han travelers in the native territories of Southern Lu marveled at the sight of lush rice fields when they chanced upon one of these closed hollows hidden in the wilderness. Outside of the occasional dolines, though, the gradients of the river valleys were too steep, and the mountain streams too swift, to permit intensive cultivation without advanced farming techniques which the natives did not possess.

The intrusion of the Yi into the limestone mountains of the Liang Shan and the Wumeng Shan brought on the first significant human alteration of the region's ecology. The pastoral Black Tribes repeatedly burned the original forest cover to create grasslands for pasturing their livestock.[72] At lower altitudes, shifting cultivators took advantage of the regenerative processes of natural forest growth cycles. In the absence of severe population pressures, shifting cultivators engaged in an ecologically balanced rotation of field and forest based on a long-range cycle of cultivation whose rhythms were invisible to Han observers accustomed to fixed fields and repeated cropping on the same plot of land. The field-clearing activities of shifting cultivators did result in the supplanting of the original evergreen oak forest by needle pines, but the natives preferred to clear and cultivate areas of secondary forest growth rather than the formidable primeval forest. Compared to the pastoralism of the Yi and the intensive cultivation and timbering undertaken by Han settlers, the shifting cultivators' activities contributed only marginally to the deterioration of the region's natural vegetation.

Animal hubandry among the Klao was restricted chiefly to pigs, with some oxen and horses. The Yi, however, practiced a much more diverse economy of stock-raising. Only hardy cereals such as buckwheat, barley, and oats could tolerate the high elevation and strong winds of their mountain habitat. The Yi raised sheep for wool, oxen for meat, and horses for warfare and trade. Oxen gradually grew in importance within the Yi livelihood as a source of protein and a trading commodity. In late imperial times Yi at lower elevations within proximity of Han settlements raised oxen and horses to trade to the Han in return for slaves.[73] In Yi legends oxen appear frequently in sacrificial feasts and ritual exchanges, while sheep are mentioned only rarely.

During the Song period the Han constantly invoked the metaphor of "streams and grottoes" (*xidong*) to denote the tribal country of the southwest. Despite its common currency, the origins of the phrase are obscure. Li Rongcun concluded from an etymological study that the phrase described specific land forms and habitats: *xi* designated the valley surrounding the source of a stream, while *dong* referred to an open space in the midst of the mountains.[74] Pulleyblank glosses *dong* as a non-Han (presumably Tai) word for "mountain valley" or "level ground between cliffs and beside a stream" and asserts that the association of this native word with the Han word "grotto" was purely adventitious.[75] The massive, vaulted caverns of the limestone regions, particularly in southern Hunan and northern Guangxi, captured the imagination of the Han, who confused the salient topographic feature of these areas with a native word for a type of settlement. Yet *dong* in the narrow sense of "grotto" or "cave" still had some validity as a description of native settlement patterns. Some groups, notably the Klao, availed themselves of the natural caverns that pierced the bluffs above mountain streams to construct fortified domiciles which could shelter a hundred or more persons.[76] Among the Yao of Hunan and the Tai-speaking Zhuang of Guangxi, though, *dong* simply meant "village," and by extension came to mean "tribe."

The placenames of native villages recorded in Song documents also bear witness to the settlement patterns of the native peoples of Southern Lu (see Table 1). The linguistic origins of these words are uncertain, but the native peoples of the southwest freely borrowed toponymic nomenclature from each other. A number of the toponyms of the Klao of Southern Lu are identical to Zhuang placewords in Guangxi.[77] The word *luo* (M.C. *la* or *lak*), signifying a fortified hilltop village (translated by the Han as *zhai*), was used by Tai, Tibeto-Burman, and Miao-Yao speakers throughout the southwest and was by far the most common toponym in Southern Lu. Other common placenames in the frontier areas of southwestern Sichuan included "mountain valley (grotto)" (*təu, tuo, ta*), "hill" (*bua, pua*), and "valley" (*lang*). Significantly, the word *si* (stream) appears only rarely. Other common toponyms, all of uncertain meaning, were *muəi, ka, tiɛi,* and *lai*. A tenth-century text on the geography of Changzhou, directly north of Luzhou, stated that "the Klao natives take their surnames from the places they inhabit, such as the mountains or the rivers."[78] In fact the most common surnames among the Klao of Southern Lu were La, Lak, Təu, Muəi, or Lai.

Prerequisites of defense, access to a supply of potable water, and

TABLE 1 Native Placewords in Southern Lu

	Ca. 1014–1115	Ca. 1220
la, lak	24	37
muəi	10	9
təu, ta, tuo	9	5
liuın	5	–
pua, bua	3	–
lang	–	4
lai	2	2
tiɛi	2	2
si	1	–
OTHER	22	14
TOTAL	78	73

Sources: Author's compilation of names of villages mentioned in annals of the Northern Song period. Names of native villages in Jiang'an county are recorded in the local gazetteer *Jiangyang pu* cited in *YLDD* 2217/18a–23b.

proximity to the cropping range determined the siting of villages. Most tribes lived in fortified villages consisting of a dense cluster of houses, often raised on piles, surrounded by a palisade of trees or log walls. Villages frequently were located on hill slopes suitable for swidden cultivation. In other cases the native peoples built their villages above steep cliffs accessible only by a single sinuous trail leading to the summit, using the natural terrain to provide a bulwark against the depredations of hostile neighbors. Such fortified settlements were virtually impregnable, as can be seen in the following description, written in 1115, of the village of Liuınpiuo:

> Liuınpiuo was built on a great hill and sits on a bluff several hundred fathoms above the valley floor, yet still encompasses an area of more than forty *li*. . . . The village is surrounded by great stones which serve as a wall-like barrier. Beyond the boulders the tribesmen had erected a palisade of trees to thwart entrance. In addition, the narrow paths, hemmed in from both sides, were obstructed by an array of great tree stumps, pits, and gullies. Not a single aspect of defense had been neglected.[79]

Kiəutsiı, the fortress of the Tuotśiang tribe recognized by the Song as an "inner dependency" in 1108, was described in almost identical terms:

Kiəutsiɪ is built on a sheer precipice, seemingly myriad fathoms above the valley. In all it is some thirty *li* in circumference. At the top there are nine hills and four rivulets. The land is broad and suitable for cultivation, but can be reached only by a single "bird track." Truly this is a natural defensive barrier![80]

These fortified hill villages enabled the inhabitants to secure not only their families and livestock but also freshwater springs and cultivated fields within a stout defensive perimeter.

The native peoples' overarching concern with defense entailed a pattern of settlement that contrasted sharply with the landscape of Han villages and towns. For the Han, a relatively flat, well watered terrain conducive to wet-rice cultivation and facility of water transport were the primary considerations in making settlement choices. The native villages, on the other hand, avoided major land and water routes and often were inaccessible by boat, cart, or even horse. Han observers in the southwest repeatedly described the native settlements as situated "deep in the mountain vales, hidden amidst the massed bamboo thickets." Thus the settlement patterns of the Han and the natives of Southern Lu were to a certain degree complementary rather than mutually exclusive, and the political dominance of the Han did not lead to the wholesale displacement of the natives. Even as Han settlers pushed into the more remote river valleys, the "nests and lairs" of the natives dotted the hills and forests all around them.

SOCIETY AND POLITY AMONG THE NATIVE PEOPLES

The social organization of the Klao, today a marginal and little-studied minority group, has never been adequately analyzed. The earliest texts described them as peoples possessing only the barest rudiments of social organization; the power of their chosen leaders was highly circumscribed and principally limited to conducting warfare and mediating endemic internecine feuding.[81] Tang accounts of the Klao in Southern Lu underscored their ferocious bellicosity, adding that the Klao "kings," called *buanəi* in their own language, were proud and arrogant—everywhere they went they were proceeded and followed by rows of attendants holding aloft banners.[82] Nonetheless the Klao chiefs apparently exercised broad authority over tribal groups only during periods of warfare. Ordinarly each village tended to its own affairs with little out-side interference.

Several sources supply us with information about the size of Klao villages in Southern Lu. An inventory of Han military conquests in 1079 stated that fifty-six villages, numbering over one thousand households, had been captured in that year. These figures suggest an average of twenty households per village.[83] Census figures from a gazetteer of Luzhou compiled about 1220 provide more detailed data. In the fifty-two primarily non-Han villages north of the Yangzi River in Jiang'an county there were 2,285 families, or an average of 44 families per village. In the remote and rugged hill country of Shengnan (a contraction of Shengjienan, "South of the Wild Frontier"), 157 families lived in sixteen tribal villages, for an average of 10 families per village. These figures contrast sharply with the population figures for the overwhelmingly Han-populated counties of Luzhou and Hejiang, which averaged two hundred households per settlement (excluding the prefectural seat).[84] The native villages of Southern Lu thus closely approximated the size of settlements in the tribal regions of Guizhou province visited by Xu Xiake at the turn of the seventeenth century. Xu recorded that larger settlements of several dozen households usually occupied slopes or foothills above streams, while settlements in lowland depressions or on ridge tops numbered fewer than ten families.[85]

Despite the absence of a unifying political authority, Klao villages existed as self-contained societies only in the most isolated settings. Beyond the small and intimate circle of the individual village, the Klao were part of a larger community, a confederation of different lineage groups spread over a large number of villages. In the annals of the Song period these confederations were typically referred to by such names as the "Eight Surnames of Shengnan" or the "Six Surnames Beyond the Mountains in Yanzhou." The segmentation of Klao society into surname or lineage groups suggests that Klao villages were exogamous and forged marriage alliances with a specific set of adjacent descent groups. For example, the Eight Surnames of Shengnan encompassed fifty-six villages distributed over the rugged hills south of the Song garrison at Naqi. These extended kinship networks maintained only a loose political structure and lacked a paramount chief. Production was organized on a domestic level and redistribution of surpluses probably was confined to the village. Village headmen and clan elders served as the principal mediators and adjudicants of conflict within and without the village and often acted independently of the larger kin group. Rarely is there any mention of specific chieftains in the annals of relations between the Song and these multi-lineage Klao confederations.[86]

Among the Yi, however, we find rigid social hierarchies and a stratified social and political leadership. Two features of Yi social organization fostered the formation of a centralized and ranked social structure: (1) the concentration of magico-religious as well as political authority in the person of the Demon Master; (2) the growing dependency of a pastoral warrior-elite on the extraction of food surpluses and agricultural labor from a subject agrarian population. Although the Black Tribes raised oxen, pigs, and chickens in addition to the major flocks of sheep, goats, and horses, grain had become their staple food source. The Black Tribes did not consume milk products and raised sheep primarily for wool. Since the Yi warriors disdained agricultural work, they relied on lower orders of subject populations and slaves to provide for their subsistence needs.

The oral traditions of the Yi of northwestern Guizhou, written down about 1700, relate that their ancestors had been driven out of eastern Yunnan by a rival Yi clan. While most of their clan was subjugated by the victors, one branch fled eastward into Klao-inhabited territories. Although the Yi and Klao chieftains agreed to a division of territory and pledged to live in peace with one another, the Yi possessed much greater military capabilities and eventually conquered the Klao and reduced them to the condition of tributary subjects.[87]

The subject peoples, primarily Klao but also including other Yi tribes conquered in war, preserved their own social organization and lived in their own villages apart from their rulers. Called *sugie*, or, in the Liang Shan, "White Bones" (even if they were ethnically descended from the Black Tribes), the subject population owed annual tribute of grain and livestock to their overlords in addition to a panoply of periodic dues and service obligations. Slaves (*dzesu*), originally from diverse ethnic origins but during the Ming and Qing periods almost exclusively of Han extraction, were attached directly to the master's household and worked both as domestic servants and field laborers. The Yi acquired slaves mostly as booty seized during raiding expeditions, but also purchased them from slave-dealers or demanded that the dependent *sugie* households submit their sons and daughters to serve as slaves in the master's household. The status of the *sugie* differed little from that of slaves with regard to their subservience to the master's will. Slave-owning Yi ("Black Bones") possessed the rights to sell, give as gifts, or execute their dependent *sugie* at will.[88]

The dominant Black Bones maintained strict endogamy within their own class and rigid racial segregation vis-à-vis the subject populations. Members of the Black Tribes defeated in battle and degraded to subservient status were forbidden to intermarry with the Black Bones and merged into the heterogeneous ethnic mixture of the subject peoples. Within their own ranks the Black Bone Yi were organized into a hierarchy of patrilineal clans headed by the *zimo*, rendered by the Han both as "demon master" and "king." The junior branches of the Yi clans did not enjoy the political and economic autonomy of the acephalous Klao tribes but rather were subordinated to the rule of the chiefdom, personified by the Grand Demon Master, the archetypal "big man" who collected tribute in the forms of grain, livestock, and slaves and distributed accumulated wealth to the various clans. Yi society thus differed markedly from the Klao of Southern Lu in the importance of political coercion, human booty, and the exploitation of a disenfranchised underclass in the productive system of the ruling class.[89]

The centralized chiefdoms of the Black Tribes steadily grew in power and influence over the decentralized and militarily weak Klao. During the eleventh century the Demon Masters of the Luo Clan (Luoshi guizhu) began to expand beyond their homeland in the Wumeng Shan and pressed northward into the Klao territories of Southern Lu. In 1042 the "King of the Black Tribes," Təkkai, won diplomatic recognition from the Song, a radical departure from the prevailing policy of denying any formal protocol rank to leaders of the "raw" tribes. Təkkai's son laid claim to the title of Demon Master, which he passed on to Təkkai's grandson Bukia. Bukia reigned as the nominal overlord of all the Black Tribes in Southern Lu but proved to be an ineffective leader. Two other chieftains, Antsi, who numbered among his subjects the "Six Surnames Beyond the Mountains," and Piuomiuang Kaśio, ruler of the "Twenty-four Surnames of Naqi," emerged as the most powerful claimants to suzerainty over the Black Tribes. After the deaths of Bukia and Antsi, Antsi's son Ṣats'iuo Lukluo inherited the title of Demon Master, but Piuomiuang Kásio and his sons continued to wield the greatest political authority throughout the region.[90] In the Yuan and Ming periods the traditions of hierarchical descent and centralized leadership under the paramount chief gradually acquired the form of permanent institutions. A rudimentary state structure was established, parallel to but independent of the segmentary clan organization, based on territorial administration of twelve *zexi* ("granaries") by appointed functionaries.[91]

The Song government, of course, was largely ignorant of the internal political organization of the southwestern tribes and established its own hierarchy of prestige based on tributary relationships. In Fan Chengda's words, "since the Tang dynasty we have distinguished among the tribal peoples seeking to become 'inner vassals' [*neishu*]. The largest ones are accorded the administrative level of 'prefecture' [*zhou*], the smaller ones are recognized as 'counties' [*xian*], while the smallest ones are known simply as 'grottoes' [*dong*]."[92] The Song state regarded the Black Tribes of the Wumeng Shan as "raw" tribes beyond the pale of civilization and steadfastly refused to grant them any diplomatic recognition until 1042. The status of the Black Tribes in the constellation of Song tributary states remained uncertain even after that date.

According to the historian Yue Shi, fifteen native "haltered-and-bridled prefectures" (*jimizhou*)—that is, tribes which accepted the yoke of Han rule and owed taxes as well as homage to the emperor—were subordinated to the military command at Luzhou in the early years of the Song. Aside from the tribes assigned this elevated rank, the Song acknowledged forty-eight other groups as "counties" subordinated to the haltered-and-bridled "prefectures"; but no records were kept of the innumerable small "grottoes."[93] The *Comprehensive Digest of Military Canons*, presented to the emperor in 1047, claimed that the registered population of the tribal regions of Southern Lu exceeded one hundred thousand households. The same source recorded a population of six

hundred for the small haltered-and-bridled district of Yuzhou, while
Yanzhou, the largest native "prefecture," purportedly encompassed a
population of thirty thousand taxable individuals (*dingkou*).[94]

These population figures appear to be the fanciful projections of an
unknown, boastful bureaucrat and are clearly inadmissible as evidence
of the scale of political organization in Southern Lu. Moreover, it is
exceedingly difficult to ascribe a single social and political identity to the
haltered-and-bridled territories. For example, at least four separate multi-
lineage groups inhabited the territory of Yanzhou. Although all of the
groups presumably were Klao, they were divided along kinship lines and
often proved to be bitter enemies. Even from the beginning of the Song
period Yanzhou, an administrative entity created by imperial fiat in 677,
ceased to have any political significance. The Song continued to employ
a hierarchy of authority and allegiance modeled after the organizational
structure of their own local administration (the *junxian* system), but this
hierarchy made little sense in the context of the dispersal of political
authority and the shifting sands of tribal enmities and alliances. The village and the multi-village kinship network were far more significant
institutions of political organization and social control among the Klao
than the nominal "protectors" (*taishou*) upon whom the Song monarchs
showered titles, gifts, and other emblems of imperial grace.

The weak authority of the central government over the southwestern
tribes left Han settlements in the Sichuan frontier vulnerable to the
depredations of hostile neighbors. The final collapse of the Tang and the
loss of central control over Sichuan beginning in the 880s ushered in an
era of increased political uncertainty and social disorder. Consequently,
a class of "local magnates" (*tuhao*), whose power and influence rested on
patron-client ties and personal bondage, rose to fill the vacuum of
political and social leadership. The social institutions formed during the
heyday of "magnate society," exemplified by the private militias of the
local magnates, established a pattern of settlement, social organization,
and land tenure that endured well into the Song. The next chapter will
trace the social forces that led to the formation of this magnate society
in the frontier areas of Sichuan and prolonged the weakness of central
political control even after the restoration of the unified Subcelestial
Realm by the Song in the 970s.

TWO

Han Society in Sichuan's Turbulent Frontier

The frontier was a dangerous place. Survival depended on providential rains, as was true anywhere in China; but even more importantly it required corporate institutions to protect the isolated pioneer family from predatory neighbors and callous gods. Some immigrant families relied solely on their kinfolk to secure a footing in the wilderness, such as the five Ren brothers who moved their families en masse from Chengdu to the valley of the Buək River, where they carved a niche out of the forest and built their own village.[1] More commonly, though, frontier settlers were forced to devise new social institutions to ensure their survival even at the risk of compromising their independence. The responsibility for defending the community came to rest upon those who could command sufficient resources to guarantee the survival of all. In the frontier regions of Sichuan an elite of diverse social origins—powerful landowners, charismatic and ambitious adventurers, anxious merchants, even native chiefs—arose who assumed the mantle of leadersip by providing for the defense of their neighbors. This stratum of leadership, known to their contemporaries as "local magnates," translated their hold over the lives and labor of their clients into a monopoly of land, wealth, and autonomous social control unimpeded by the local appendages of the emperor's flimsy latticework of statutes and administrators. Within their own domains, local magnates preserved a system of personal bondage and coercive tenurial relations which by the eleventh century was rapidly disappearing from the heartlands of the Song empire.

CRYSTALLIZATION OF MAGNATE SOCIETY

Far-off Sichuan, to the emperors ruling from the other side of the massive limestone curtain of the Qinling Shan, had always seemed ungovernable. Descriptions of Sichuan's regional character usually emphasized the arrogance and extravagance of the upper classes, who fattened themselves on the riches of "Heaven's Storehouse." The compilers of the *Sui History* recorded that the social and economic domination of the magnates of the Sichuan frontier extended over the indigenous tribal peoples as well as the Han.

> In the frontier wilderness the wealthy have secured control of "the mountains and the marshes" [that is, non-agricultural sources of wealth, properly the estate of the Son of Heaven]. By means of their wealth and power they have made themselves masters over the native peoples and exact labor service from them. Thus they act with complete impunity in illegally harboring natives within their households. Their influence subverts the authority of the magistrates and that of the state itself. Yet is this not the age-old custom of the region?[2]

Many magnates achieved their local eminence by reaping fortunes from tea plantations and salt wells, most of which were located in the western and southwestern parts of the Sichuan Basin, adjacent to native territories. Since antiquity many of the native peoples of the Sichuan frontier had become slaves or indentured servants in the households of powerful Han families, and this tradition remained very much alive in the Tang-Song era.[3] Han magnates also succeeded in imposing labor obligations on other native peoples and gradually absorbed them into their own households. In some cases the demands for labor service issued from the state, as in 648 when the Tang government attempted to muster the native peoples of the Dadu River valley to work in the shipyards at Jiazhou, an action that precipitated a revolt.[4]

Perhaps such demands and the frictions they generated underlay the rebellion of native tribes in Luzhou in 676. The Tang easily quelled the uprising and sought to mitigate further conflict by according the native chieftains the status of "inner vassals" (*neichen*) and recognizing their territories as haltered-and-bridled districts. Some years later, in 698, another official reported that border tensions could be eased only by halting all private intercourse between the Han and non-Han populations and renouncing the tribal regions as part of the imperial realm.[5] Despite these exhortations to discourage contact between Han settlers and the indigenous peoples, the Tang court opted for a policy of allowing Han settlers to "open up the country of the 'grottoes' for settlement, win the submission of the Lau, and found new cities and towns."[6] The intrusion of Han settlers into the tribal territories ignited frequent and bitter conflicts. In order to protect themselves and their property in a region where government troops appeared only as the butt of jokes, the magnates organized their own private militias, known as "Righteous Armies" (*yijun*), by drafting able-bodied men from among their own retainers and dependent households.

In the late Tang the disintegration of the central government's authority and the fierce struggles between the Tang and the Tibeto-Burman kingdoms of Tufan and Nanzhao checked the advance of Han settlers into the southwestern frontier. Sichuan was spared the ravages of civil war that swept across North China in the wake of the An Lushan rebellion in 755, but suffered repeated invasions by the Nanzhao and Tufan between 829 and 880. In response to the Nanzhao threat, Li Deyu, the paragon of Confucian statesmanship in the ninth century, recruited a crack militia corps that became known as the "Sons and Brothers in Heroic Defense of the Frontier" (*xiongbian zidi*). Li chose to model the "Sons and Brothers" after the private *yijun* militias of Sichuan's local magnates in an effort to instill, through the forms of fictive kinship, a sense of personal loyalty to their commanders.[7]

The ambivalent loyalties of the local magnates and their private armies provoked considerable consternation on the part of Tang officials like Li Deyu. When the need arose, the magnates used the *yijun* for their own local and personal ends and against the state itself. In 843, a famine year in southwestern Sichuan, many local magnates, unable to meet their clients' needs themselves, led uprisings to seize the government's food stores:

> Bandits united and joined forces; chieftains and powerful families declared themselves "kings" and assigned spurious titles and offices to their subordinates. They opened the stores and granaries, summoning the destitute and the desperate, over an area extending from Pengzhou in the east to Lu, Jia, and Xu

in the west. The rebels encouraged the native tribes to rise up in rebellion as well. The bandit gangs had succeeded in firmly entrenching themselves in this region; but the regional military governor, Lu Hongxuan, gave orders to force or persuade the bandits to surrender, which they eventually did. The cunning and powerful were given commands in the army, while the weak and doltish were returned to their homes to become peasants again.[8]

A similar rebellion, but one with more enduring consequences, broke out in western Sichuan in 882 under the leadership of a non-Han local magnate and erstwhile Tang officer named Qian Neng. Qian quickly won the allegiance of several other powerful non-Han leaders and held off the armies of the regional governor for nearly a year.[9] In the aftermath of the Qian Neng rebellion and the coincident collapse of the Tang government in Chang'an, central authority over Sichuan melted away. Henceforth the magnates exercised greater confidence and audacity in wielding power over the population within their sphere of influence. The most notable case of this devolution of authority was that of Wei Junjing of Changzhou, just northeast of Luzhou.[10]

While Qian Neng bedeviled the regional governor's army in the west, a low-ranking official named Han Xiusheng seized the opportunity to stage an uprising in the east. Wei Junjing, an untitled but influential landowner in the sparsely settled hills between the Tuo and Fu river valleys, organized local notables in opposition to Han. Together with his kinsmen and other local magnates he formed a far-flung network of self-defense militias (*yijun*). After Han's defeat in the spring of 883 the military governor appointed Wei as prefect of Puzhou. Han's rebellion was followed only a few months later by the revolt of the military governor of eastern Sichuan, Yang Shili, against the military governor in the west, Chen Jingxuan. Wei's league of militias again contributed decisively to the defeat of the rebels, leading to Wei's appointment as prefect of Hezhou. Later Wei became prefect of his home prefecture of Chang as well. All three prefectures where Wei served as prefect were in contiguous areas which essentially circumscribed the territorial range of his militia network. Imperial investiture merely acknowledged the importance of Wei's prestige and power to the preservation of the status quo throughout the region.

According to a stele inscription composed in 897, Wei's militia network linked together twenty-six separate *yijun* units, four of which were headed by members of Wei's own lineage. The military strength of the Weis was concentrated in the two garrisons of Yongchang and Jinyun, the linchpins of the entire network. Each self-defense unit guarded a distinct territorial range centered on a garrison town (*zhen*) located at key settlements, passes, and river crossings, sites chosen primarily for their military rather than their commercial significance.[11] The garrison commanders (*zhenjiang*) recruited, or conscripted, their soldiers from among their clients, who acquired the epithet of "sons and brothers" of their leaders.

Beyond Wei Junjing's immediate family, the militia system was unified into a regional hierarchy by patron-client ties. Local militia leaders over parts of five prefectures submitted to Wei's leadership in order to coordinate their defense against common enemies. Some of the local leaders acknowledged personal fealty to Wei and received titles followed by the epithet *suishen,* or "personal follower." *Suishen* was tantamount to fictive kinship and accorded the patron broad paternalistic powers over the client. As Kurihara notes, during the late Tang disorders wealthy merchants and landowners commonly adopted as their sons ambitious and capable military officers who would protect, and ultimately inherit, their property.[12] We lack specific information concerning the bonds of clientage between Wei and the garrison commanders not under his direct control, yet it is evident that Wei's personal leadership was crucial to the organizational unity of the system and his success in creating a coherent regional structure of authority.[13]

The regional scope of Wei's militia organization was exceptional, perhaps, but more localized self-defense militias had sprouted up throughout Sichuan. The local magnates' newly expanded control over their fellow countrymen can be seen in an incident concerning Zhao Shiru, a militia leader in Yuzhou, whose militia band may, interestingly enough, have been affiliated with Wei's network.[14] In 893, when Liu Pi passed through the town of Maxiaozhen to take up the post of prefect of Luzhou, he was met by Zhao Shiru, who held an honorary military appointment from the military governor and had taken upon himself the authority of a tribune. Zhao sent Liu a card with the legend *buyi,* or "homespun-clothed" commoner; but the puzzled Liu declined to

stop with him until Zhao addressed him saying, "Ba and Shu have fallen
into chaos and disorder. I, concerned for the well-being of my fellow
countrymen, summoned them together to defend ourselves and our
homes from outside bandits. I dare not usurp our emperor's rightful
authority or transgress the limits of my brevet office." Zhao provided for
Liu and his party with all propriety; and Liu, scion of one of the most
powerful families in Sichuan, concluded his tale by praising Zhao for his
"discriminating judgment and proper execution of authority."[15] With
civil rule completely discredited, the military governors willingly
countenanced the formation of private, self-defense militias. In some
cases the governors themselves initiated or encouraged the creation of
local militias. In the years after the Qian Neng rebellion the military
governors "appointed Intendants for Martial Order [*zheneshi*] in every
county and garrison town" to restore order and resettle the population.[16]
Significantly, Wei Junjing gave the title of Intendant of Martial Order to
the militia leaders under his command.

Responsibility for local defense, and the consequent extension of their
authority to include control over justice and economic resources, greatly
augmented the local magnates' domination of the countryside. Their
indispensable role as the guardians of the rural populace led to the imposition of patron-client relationships that placed the peasantry in a decidedly subservient position. After the Song reunification of the empire the
need for local militias, except in frontier areas, diminished considerably.
Yet in Sichuan, as the following document from 996 indicates, the local
magnates built an imposing structure of social control on the foundation
of social security:

> In the country of the Rivers and Gorges [Sichuan] the great households have
> many 'villein households' [*panghu*], small people [*xiaomin*], and bonded de-
> pendents [*yishu*] who serve as their tenant guests [*dianke*] and are treated as
> if they were bondservants [*nuli*]. In some families these groups number as
> many as several tens of households. All exactions of labor service and the grain
> and cloth taxes are borne by the tenant guests.[17]

This text was the preamble to a petition to restrict the social and military power of Sichuan's local magnates. During the early 990s, Sichuan
had been rocked by a rebellion led by Wang Xiaobo and Li Shun, which

was widely viewed as an attempt by the Sichuanese to throw off the reins of Song rule. In 996, after the suppression of the Wang-Li rebellion, sentiment for breaking the Sichuan local magnates' control of their militias ran high at the court. The Song ministers proposed to bureaucratize the militias by selecting promising individuals from among the villein households to serve as "community elders" (*qizhang*) in charge of local defense. But reports from censorial officials sent to Sichuan to study the viability of this plan discouraged tinkering with the delicate balance of local society:

> The villein households in the past have pledged themselves to be the bonded dependents of the magnate lineages for generation after generation. To alter this arrangement and, in the space of a single morning, place [the militias] under the authority of the military intendants will cause confusion in men's hearts and give rise to uncertainty and uproar.[18]

The matter was, in the language of the Song civil service, "put to sleep." The local magnates continued to serve as the heads of their own militias, usually with a nominal appointment as garrison commander (*zhaijiang*) or custodian of the peace (*bajie*). In 1005, forty years after the Later Shu surrendered to the Song dynastic founder, the Song court felt compelled to issue a ban prohibiting the garrison commanders of Sichuan from presiding over and adjudicating legal cases.[19]

The Song ultimately succeeded in restoring the functions of civil government to the regular administrative hierarchy, which included a military intendancy for each route. Nevertheless, local self-defense was still entrusted to the garrison commanders in the frontier and the sparsely populated, bandit-plagued Gorges region. In 1076, when Wang An-shi's controversial *baojia* ("mutual surveillance") militia system was extended to Sichuan, the court asked the military intendant of Kuizhou Route, Cheng Zhiyuan, to evaluate the feasibility of implementing the *baojia* system in his jurisdiction. Cheng informed the court that in Kuizhou Route many "aggrandizing families" (*jianbing zhi jia*) controlled as many as several hundred "guest households" (*kehu*) and proposed that the court allow each master household to compile *baojia* registers for their own client "guest households" and to serve as the commanding officers of the militia units.[20] Cheng's proposal, though tailored to match the administrative categories laid out by the designers of the New Laws, was cut from the familiar cloth of magnate society.

In many areas the role of the local magnates in frontier defense remained unchanged throughout the Song period. In 1164 officials investigating native uprisings in Jiazhou determined that consequent to the recent abandonment of the time-honored practice of employing local magnates in military posts along the frontier, the undiplomatic bungling of bureaucratic appointees often offended and provoked native leaders. The investigative team recommended that the local magnates, who knew the native leaders, understood the strategic significance of the local terrain, and enjoyed the confidence of the militia recruits, ought to be restored as garrison commanders and accorded the necessary autonomy to perform their duties efficiently.[21] In Luzhou, although most of the garrison posts were filled by bureaucratic appointees after 1082, the prefects themselves complained that regular officials who were not natives of Luzhou usually proved incompetent in dealing with the tribal leaders and urged that local people be appointed to these offices.[22]

The Song did make efforts to replace private armies with militia recruits loyal to the Song state. In the language of the Song administrators this meant replacing "stalwart conscripts" (*zhuangding*) recruited by powerful magnates—perhaps "thugs" would be a better translation—with "local conscripts" (*tuding*) drafted by civil officials from the pool of able-bodied males (*ding*) liable for labor service. In some instances the state intervened in local society to the extent of expropriating privately held resources to create a militia nominally run by the state. The Song used this tactic in the turbulent frontier area of Longpeng Garrison in Jiazhou, where the Black Tribes of the Liang Shan staunchly resisted Han expansion. At the turn of the thirteenth century the garrison commander at Longpeng was a local magnate named Ma You:

> Earlier generations of Ma You's family owned land on the northern and southern banks of the river, collecting an annual rent of four thousand *dan*. Later an imperial directive was issued ordering that their lands be used to meet the expenses of border defense. In each generation one person from the Ma lineage was selected as commandant of the garrison. The tenant householders served as local militia [*tuding*] charged with defending and securing the frontier.

Although the term *tuding* denoted local militias organized at the initiative of the state, the same document also refers to Ma You's troops as "men of his household" (*jiaren*) and "household conscripts" (*jiading*). Clearly the Song merely countenanced the existence of this private army and tried to coopt Ma by investing him with official status and specific duties. In addition to maintaining the garrison, Ma You was responsible for providing an annual indemnity—given in various commodities, but valued at three hundred *dan* of rice—to the Xioyan tribe. Ma, however, used his enhanced power mostly for his own purposes. During the period from 1202 to 1212, he carried on a private war with the Xioyan and withheld the indemnity. Finally, reports of Ma's crimes reached Chengdu and he was imprisoned and put on trial. Over a hundred members of Ma's household appeared before the judicial intendant to plead for his release. Despite their importunances Ma was convicted, though the authorities commuted his death sentence to a prison term.[23]

The example of Ma You suggests the severe limitations on the Song state's capacity for supervising and controlling the frontier militias. Local magnates used the militias as private armies to enforce their rule over their neighbors and to expand or defend their control over wealth and labor. In the early 1180s, for instance, Tan Ruyi, a Han local magnate, feuded with Tian Rubi, chief of the haltered-and-bridled district of Sizhou. When Tian died, Tan led a large army to attack the funeral. In reprisal, Tian's son Tian Zuzhou fought Tan in battles ranging over three prefectures. Lin Su, prefect of Kuizhou, considered Tan Ruyi the principal instigator and issued secret instructions to the military intendant to ignore Tan's request for aid and instead to assume personal authority over the chaotic situation in Sizhou. When the court was apprised of these events, Emperor Xiaozong personally drafted a letter to Lin, advising him to take all necessary measures to put an end to the border war.

The Song army easily routed Tan's soldiers, but Tan eluded capture. The prefect of Sizhou was banished from the civil service for having permitted Tan to mobilize the "Righteous Armies" to fight his personal feud and for opening the border passes to allow Tan to enter the tribal domain. Tan succeeded in making his way to the capital where he filed a legal petition claiming that Lin Su had been bribed with Tian Zu-zhou's gold. Lin's enemies at court added charges that Lin had over-stepped his authority in deploying the troops of the military intendant without an imperial warrant, and Lin too was dismissed. Six months later the court cashiered the assistant fiscal intendant of Kuizhou Route, Zhang Yan, for having supported Tan Ruyi's aggression against the Tian over a period of several years and for providing Tan with the necessary documents to requisition troops from the garrison commanders.[24]

In the midst of this tangle of accusations and censorial proceedings, State Councilor Zhou Bida submitted an analysis of the entire affair that clarifies the motives of the antagonists.[25] The Tian lineage had been well favored by the Song court because of their stabilizing influence over other native tribes and the service they rendered to the Song in sending troops to fight against the Jurchen. Over the previous four or five years, though, the Tian had violated Song laws by purchasing large tracts of land in Qianjiang county, Qianzhou, which adjoined Tan Ruyi's domin-ion in Shizhou. Zhou noted that the inhabitants of one area commonly migrated to and purchased property in the other.[26] The Tian, however, threatened to upset the balance of social control by amassing a huge estate valued at the extraordinary sum of 900,000 *guan*. Zhang Yan had urged the court to compel the Tian to relinquish these properties, but at first the court merely told the Tian not to make any new purchases. Zhang, rebuffed, then gave covert assistance to Tan Ruyi in his campaign to evict the Tian from the Han territories by force. In 1183, after Tan's defeat and imprisonment, Tian Zuzhou agreed to offer his holdings in Qianjiang to the Song emperor in order to purchase forgiveness of his crimes; and the frontier quieted down. Although the Song eventually reestablished its authority in this remote corner of the empire, the epi-sode underscored the fundamental weakness of the state in the frontier areas. Far from dictating policy and enforcing the laws, officials on the scene proved unwilling or unable to control the course of events.[27]

PERSONAL BONDAGE IN THE SICHUAN FRONTIER

While a few men in the frontier made themselves local potentates, most were peasants, and many were less than free. Personal bondage to powerful magnates had been a prominent feature of Chinese society throughout the early imperial age. From Han to Tang times social and political power rested in the hands of an aristocracy of great families who held sway over hundreds and in some cases thousands of persons belonging to a variety of servile statuses (*jianmin*). Aristocratic households included indentured fieldworkers who worked their agricultural estates; personal retainers (*buqu*) who manned their private armies; and domestic servants and slaves. The erosion of the aristocracy's customary privileges during the Tang dynasty, and the collapse of its political and economic power following the shocks of rebellion and invasion in the eighth and ninth centuries, brought about a significant diminution of the servile population. By Song times most of the agrarian population was legally free. Even on large landed estates tenancy usually eclipsed indentured service. Yet the decline of personal bondage was by no means universal. Conditions of life in the Sichuan frontier fostered ties of dependency that subjected the agrarian population to the will of local magnates.

Analysis of the nature and prevalence of personal bondage in Song times centers on the interpretation of a key term, *kehu* or "guest household." Once freely translated as "tenant household," the ambiguity of this term has become more apparent as historians have scrutinized the particular contexts in which it appeared. Nakagawa Manabu has helped to clarify this confusion by insisting on distinguishing between *kehu* as a fiscal category and as a social phenomenon. Nakagawa traced the origin of *kehu* as an institutional category to Yuwen Rong's tax reforms of 723, which attempted to alleviate the fiscal chaos caused by the displacement and emigration of the rural populace. Yuwen modified the tax assessment procedures to allow the re-registration of households in their place of actual abode (*xianju*) rather than their legal residence (*jiguan*).[28] Those registered in their place of abode became known as "newly appended non-registered households" (*xinfu kehu*) or simply as *kehu*. The distinction between registered or "native" households (*tuhu*) and non-registered households (*kehu*) was rendered obsolete by Yang Yan's twice-a-year tax system, instituted in 780. By shifting the basis of taxation from the individual to property (regardless of the residence of the owner), the fiscal distinction between residence and abode became moot.[29]

The concept of *kehu* was retained, albeit in altered form, under the household-ranking system that became the basis of taxation during the Song dynasty. In Song practice *kehu* signified a household that (1) originated in a jurisdiction other than its present abode; (2) was not ranked on the household registers for assessment of twice-a-year taxes and labor service obligations; and (3) did not own real property (*changchan*) in its place of residence. Thus, in the Song, *kehu* as a fiscal and administrative category embraced a heterogeneous collection of groups: landless tenant farmers, hired laborers, merchants, specially exempt landowners (*youtian wushui hu*), and immigrants from other jurisdictions, who may or may not have owned property.[30]

The customary usage of the term *kehu*, and the social status of the persons it encompassed, often diverged significantly from the institutional concept. For example, Tang authors revived the older term *fouke* (or *foulangke*) to describe the large class of itinerant, landless persons created by the demise of the equal-field system of equal distribution of landholdings and the expropriation of lands by "aggrandizers" (*jianbing zhi jia*).[31] The dispossessed became rootless laborers (*liuyong*) who sought work in transport, public works, and on large estates, or who migrated in hopes of establishing a new foothold elsewhere. Nakagawa divided the rootless laborers into two groups: (1) economically independent individuals who worked as hired laborers and tenants, or gained tenurial rights over smallholdings, and (2) bonded dependents who pledged themselves to a master and served on the great estates (*zhuangyuan*). Official documents referred to both categories as *kehu* or *fouke*.[32] The growth of the great estates was accelerated by the common practice of evading labor service by entrusting one's lands to a powerful landowner and assuming a subordinate position in the latter's household.[33]

The ambiguity of the social reality behind the term *kehu* persisted in the Song. Ouyang Xiu, in his famous polemic of 1040 on the evils of the concentration of landownership in the hands of the aggrandizers, included under the concept of *kehu* both servile dependents working on the great estates and immigrant tenants who contracted to farm lands belonging to the same landowners. He distinguished the latter by calling them *fouke*.[34] The inconsistent use of the term *kehu* betrayed the growing complexity of tenurial relationships and regional variations of social structure in the Song. Although essayists such as Ouyang Xiu, Su Xun, Chen Shunyu, and Li Gou unleashed torrents of criticism at the widespread problem of aggrandizement, the evidence indicates that personal bondage atrophied rapidly during the Song. Even on the great estates, tenancy predicated on contract prevailed. Song law accorded landlords certain legal privileges explicitly denied to tenants (encapsulated in the concept of *zhudian zhi fen*, "discriminating between landlord and tenant"), but relations between the two were subject to the emperor's laws rather than the arbitrary authority of the landlord. On the other hand, custom and legal precedent gave landowners discretionary juridical powers over permanent hired laborers and indentured servants (expressed as *zhupu zhi fen*, or "discriminating between master and servant").[35]

The persistence of bondage relationships in southern and eastern Sichuan can be discerned in a series of edicts promulgated in Kuizhou Route over the course of the Song dynasty. The Song issued the following proclamation in 1052 in response to desertions among state tenants and garrison troops:

> Guest households [*kehu*] on state lands in the prefectures of Kuizhou Route who abscond or change their residence are, in either case, to be compelled to return to their former abode and are prohibited from lingering or residing elsewhere.
>
> In the prefectures of Shizhou and Qianzhou, if anyone in the categories of (1) a master household's stalwart conscripts [*zhuhu zhuangding*], (2) the "sons and brothers" of a garrison commander [*zhaijiang zidi*], or (3) guest households subordinated to a master [*pangxia kehu*] absconds or moves beyond the frontier the authorities will send someone, within a specified time limit, to determine to which jurisdiction these persons were attached and to return them thence, where they will be compelled to take up their former station and assist in border defense.[36]

From the state's point of view, this law embodied two strategic goals. First, the state wanted to prevent tenants on state lands, who paid rent as well as taxes into the government's coffers, from abandoning their tenures and becoming the tenants of private landowners. This provision applied to all state tenants in Kuizhou Route.[37] Secondly, in the two prefectures located deep within the tribal realm, the state sought to bond certain groups to their masters in the interest of maintaining a supply of soldiers sufficient to meet the defense needs of the exceedingly vulnerable Han settlers of this region. The groups covered under this portion of the proclamation included (1) private armies of local magnates not formally incorporated into the frontier militia system, (2) quasi-official militiamen organized by magnates who were later given specific assignments under appointment as garrison commanders, and (3) heads of households who owed labor service to a master household but had no explicit militia responsibilities. All three categories implied a certain degree of bondage and labor obligations between a client household and a patron. The legal restraints on the mobility of able-bodied males were designed to prevent powerful landowners from enticing a tenant whose labor power contributed materially to the state's economic and military interests to forsake his current station in favor of a more attractive proposal. In particular, the state sought to prevent magnates from coercing state tenants to leave their tenure and enter the magnate's fold.

In 1184, immediately following the war between Tan Ruyi and Tian Zuzhou, the 1052 law was extended to a wider area, covering parts of Hubei as well as Kuizhou Route:

> The Fiscal Office of Kuizhou Route requests that the 1052 law be extended to the prefectures of Kui, Zhong, Wan, Gui, Xia, and Li in addition to Shi and Qian. Henceforth any legal suits concerning the theft or removal of "guests bonded to the soil" [*dike*] will be adjudicated on the basis of this law. If a guest household has absconded or moved to another canton [*xiang*] within the past three years, then that person and his immediate kin will be returned to their former master. A notice will be sent to all of the above prefectures stating that if transported families [*banyi zhi jia*] are returned to their former station within two months, the current master will not be tried under the statutes for criminal delinquency in repayment of debts.[38]

From this text we can infer that the intense competition for labor in the Gorges region impelled magnates to resort to illegal methods, either suasive or coercive, to acquire tenants to farm their extensive landholdings. Since the state's primary concerns—tax revenues and security—depended on maintaining the status quo, Song officials willingly condoned the system of labor bondage that had long prevailed in this frontier area. This document takes on particular relevance in the context of the Tan Ruyi incident. It seems likely that the members of the Tian lineage who began to buy up lands in the vicinity of Tan's bailiwick were also attempting to steal bonded tenants from Tan and perhaps other Han landowners. Just as the Han magnates often compelled the native peoples to abide by the customary rules of labor bondage, native leaders could force Han settlers to submit to a similar system of bondage.[39] The war between Tan and the Tian symbolized far more than inter-ethnic friction; competition for land escalated into a competition for bonded tenants and consequently a struggle for political and economic hegemony.

Another revision of Kuizhou's bondage law, issued in 1205, specified the limitations of the labor bondage system while guaranteeing the right of master households to obtain redress for the loss of their bonded guest households:

> The assistant fiscal intendant of Kuizhou Route, Fan Sun, requests that the following emendations be attached to the 1052 statute:
>
> (1) Whoever serves as a guest household may bond his own person [*yi qi shen*], but his bondage for labor service may not extend to his family's dependents, wife, or daughters.
>
> (2) Whoever mortages [*dianmai*] his lands and buildings is permitted, if otherwise in accordance with the legal code, to leave his property. He may not be compelled to submit rent and assume the station of a guest household. Even if he does pay rent as a tenant, the owner of the [mortgaged] property does not thereby assume the status of a guest household.
>
> (3) Whoever borrows cash or goods may requite the debt only according to the terms of the contractual agreement. A debtor cannot be compelled to serve as a guest household.
>
> (4) In the event of the death of the head of a guest household, if the wife of the deceased wishes to remarry, she will be permitted to do so.
>
> (5) A daughter of a guest household is permitted to make her own arrangements for betrothal and marriage.
>
> The intention of these changes is to ensure that the people dwelling deep in the hills and in the remote valleys can obtain a stable livelihood, and to protect them from suffering the depredations and misdealings of the powerful and influential, and to realize the happiness and prosperity of the entire route.[40]

These regulations, manifestly an attempt to reform current practice, limited the liabilities and obligations of a guest household to the head of the household and, it seems reasonable to infer, his male heir. Implicit in the stipulations conferring specific freedoms on wives and daughters of guest households is the acknowledgment that magnates coveted control over the reproduction of labor through marriage and procreation.[41] Three forms of bondage—only one of which was sanctioned by the authorities—are mentioned: (1) voluntary indentureship, (2) peonage, and (3) involuntary bondage of a landowner through mortgage and indenture as a "guest household." Since the first procedure was legal, it probably was the most prevalent. Peonage, or labor service to requite a debt, was a common affliction among frontier peasants. Although the infertile soils of the frontier yielded poor harvests, harvest failures probably were no more common than in the lowlands. But lacking the kin-based subsistence insurance, state-operated relief institutions, competitive markets, and ease of transport found in the metropolitan areas, the frontier inhabitants usually had only one recourse in times of dearth: borrowing from the local magnate. Thus the conditions of existence on the frontier tended to create a society structured by hierarchical bonds of clientage whereby the client pledged his labor, and less commonly his lands, to the master. From the master's point of view, the bondage system was necessitated by the scarcity of labor and the need to establish an institutional framework, beyond providing for the security and well-being of his "guests," to obtain sufficient labor resources.[42]

The state restricted legal protection of the master's right to exploit the labor of his clients to a handful of prefectures in the Gorges region. Yet customary forms of bondage, both voluntary and involuntary, persisted throughout the Song in many parts of the Sichuan frontier. Where state power was weak and the local magnates' demand for a reliable supply of labor strong, customary bondage represented a crucial adaptation to the exigencies of pioneer settlement.

Song texts on bondage in Sichuan frequently link personal servitude to a master with a social category called *pangxia kehu*, or simply *panghu*. This term lends itself at best to unwieldy translations, such as "guest households subordinated to a master," and perhaps can be best expressed by the legal category of villeinage found in medieval Europe. The two chief characteristics of villeinage in medieval England were subjugation to the legal jurisdiction of a lord (though in respect to all others the villein was a freedman, that is, under protection of the king's laws) and the obligation to perform arduous labor (such as agricultural tasks) on behalf of the lord.[43] These two features, in addition to the obligation to serve in the master's personal militia, cogently summarize the primary characteristics of bonded dependents in the frontier areas of Sichuan. Although we have no legal definition of the status of *panghu*, it seems that in the eyes of the state *panghu* were persons who were not accorded status as natives of the locality they lived in and therefore not liable to render labor service to the state, but who were accounted for under a patron household and owed the latter certain customary labor services. The *panghu* performed a wide range of tasks for the master, tilling his fields, fulfilling the master's labor obligations to the state,[44] and bearing arms to defend the master's property and interests.

Although the position of *panghu* was a decidedly servile one, bondage to the master was mediated through a personalized patron-client relationship. The word *pang* connotes an inferior kinship status, as in the words *pangfu* (concubine) and *pangshu* (subordinate segmentary lineage). The local magnate who addressed his clients as "sons and brothers" was not merely indulging in a literary trope but rather articulated a bond of fictive kinship. The master assumed responsibility for the welfare of his guest households and created a patriarchal community which resembled an extensive kin group and drew its cohesion from the customary precepts of affinal relations.

The term *panghu* seems to have been a local coinage peculiar to Sichuan. More generally this dependent relationship was subsumed under the broad and heterogeneous category of *kehu*. While the term *kehu* in itself did not denote the forms of bondage detailed above or even a general set of tenurial relations, its use along the Sichuan frontier does suggest a definite correlation between a high ratio of guest households and a social system based on bondage and labor service obligations and grounded in a tenurial system in which the master, through mortgage, indenture, or expropriation, gradually acquired the right to dispose of the guest household's labor power, and in some instances the client's lands as well. The high percentage of *kehu* in the population figures for this frontier area reflects the prevalence of subordinate households (*pangxia kehu, huxia kehu*) who owed labor service not to the state but to their patrons.

The regional pattern of bondage comes into sharper focus when one maps population density (Map 3A) and the geographic distribution of guest households (Map 3B). A line drawn on an axis running from southwest to northeast demarcates a region of high ratios of guest households from a region of low ratios. It also delineates two economic regions and conveniently approximates the ancient division between the kingdoms of Shu and Ba. In western and northern Sichuan, or Shu, a region favored with considerable productive wealth, a dense population, and a high degree of economic diversity, guest households in 1080 accounted for only 27.7 percent of the total number of households (Table 2). The countryside was more crowded than in the south and east and the demand for land was correspondingly high. Thus the low percentage of guest households in this region can be interpreted as an expression of a relatively low demand for labor and consequently a lower incidence of personal bondage. In the southern and eastern parts of Sichuan, or Ba, the percentage of guest households stood at 68.3 percent in 1080, indicating a high incidence of bondage. Furthermore, these diametrically opposed ratios were not a mere vestige of an earlier but decaying social order. During the period 980–1080 the growth in the number of households in the west and north primarily reflected the creation of new master households. Three out of four households established in that period were master households. In the south and east, on the other hand, guest households constituted 62.1 percent of the increase in registered households (Table 3). In Luzhou the preponderance of guest households was overwhelming. During the century ending in 1080 the number of master households in Luzhou grew by less than three per year, from 2,417 to 2,647. In 1080 guest households accounted for 92.5 percent of Luzhou's total population, the highest percentage in the entire empire.

Thus we can conclude that throughout the eleventh century the two regions of Sichuan reproduced essentially different societies. The contrasting geographies, societies, and economies of the country known to the Song as "the Rivers and the Gorges" warrant recognition as two distinct zones—core and frontier—within the regional system of the Sichuan Basin.

MAP 3 Distribution of Population in Sichuan in the Southern Sung

A. Population Density by Prefecture, 1080

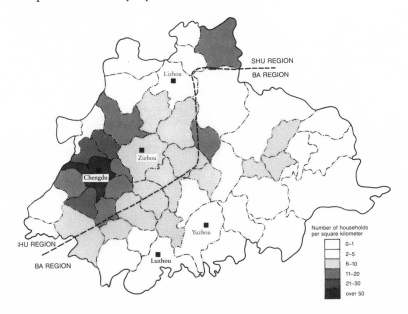

B. Distribution of Guest Households by Prefecture, 1080

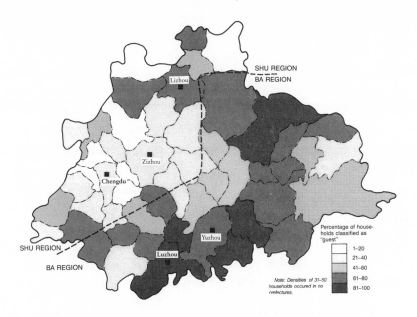

Sources for 3A and 3B: Yuanfeng jiuyuzhi 7/1a–19b, 8/1a–15b.

TABLE 2 Classification of Population in Sichuan in 1080

	Shu Region	Ba Region
Master households	920,951	212,639
Percentage of total	72.3	31.7
Guest households	353,581	459,012
Percentage of total	27.7	68.3
Total households	1,274,532	671,651

Source: YFJYZ 7 & 8

TABLE 3 Population Increase in Sichuan, ca. 980–1080

	Shu Region		Ba Region	
	Master households	Guest households	Master households	Guest households
Number of households, ca. 980	458,336	206,206	69,340	223,119
Number of households, 1080	856,298	335,878	168,656	385,713
Increase in households, 980–1080	397,962	129,672	99,316	162,514
Percentage of Total Increase, 980–1080	75.4	24.6	37.9	62.1

Sources: TPHYJ 72–88, 119, 113–140, 147–149; YFJYZ 7 & 8

Note: Prefectures which lack population data for 980 have been excluded from this calculation. These include, in the Shu region, Qiong, Mao, and Wei (6.5% of the 1080 population for the region) and in the Ba Region, Zi, Xu, Lu, Shi, and Daning (17.5% of the 1080 population).

SETTLEMENT AND SOCIAL CONTROL

The striking regional dichotomy in the ratios of guest households, and by extension the incidence of bondage, in Sichuan paralleled the geographic distribution of fortified towns and villages. The fortified town, like the self-defense militia, was necessary to frontier life. The ever-present threat of raids by hostile groups meant that problems of security figured significantly in settlement decisions among the Han as well as the native peoples.

The Han built their towns and villages at strategic and easily defended places where possible, often on the same site as an earlier village of a vanquished tribe. Yet the logistics of community defense, which favored concentrated settlement in fortified towns, conflicted with an agrarian regime based on extensive cultivation. Dispersed settlement was the logical choice for a farming population working widely scattered fields over a broken terrain and seems to have prevailed throughout much of the frontier. One compromise between the priorities of defense and production was a settlement pattern known as "ringed settlement" (*huanju*). In 1214 an official stationed in the devastated area of northern Hubei, along the Jurchen frontier, recommended surrounding the main house of an estate with the houses of the "estate guests" (*zhuangke*) as a defense against marauding bandits, who would be unable to penetrate to the master's dwelling.[45] "Ringed settlement" required a fairly compact form of land exploitation, common on the Hubei Plain but largely impractical in the Sichuan frontier.[46] Writing about an area closer to Southern Lu, one author, in an allusion to the notion that stars were strung like pearls on a latticework of invisible threads, described the houses of the Han in Qianzhou as "scattered star-like [*xingju*] along the roads."[47] The markedly lower number of households per village in the frontier areas of Southern Lu also indicates a tendency towards dispersed settlement (see below, Chapter Seven).

In the Ba region the contradiction between the priorities of production and defense was resolved by building a dense network of fortified towns that served as refuges for scattered farming households. In 1204 the officials discussing proposed sites for rebuilding Longpeng Garrison emphasized the importance of reconciling the needs of defense with the reality of dispersed settlement:

> The primary advantage [of rebuilding Longpeng at the old site south of the river rather than a more protected spot on the northern bank] is that we thereby protect the farmers south of the river, giving them no cause to fear that they have been left defenseless. During the daylight hours they can toil industriously in the fields. When twilight falls, they will be able to take shelter in the garrison.[48]

In areas where government troops were absent altogether, the frontier populace sought refuge within fortifications built by local magnates.

From the late Tang onwards the fortified town (*zhen*) emerged as the primary settlement form in the Ba region.[49] In the Tang the term *zhen* signified the seat of a garrison commander, either a military officer assigned to a locality by the military governors or a local magnate who had formed his own self-defense militia and fortified the place where he resided, such as Zhao Shiru. Since the garrison commanders usually assumed responsibility for police, judicial, and tax collection functions for the surrounding area, the *zhen* acquired an administrative status roughly equivalent to the civil administration of the counties, which they largely superseded. The Song abolished the *zhen* as a territorial and administrative unit and relegated the garrison commanders to custodial duties, such as fire protection, within the town.[50] Throughout most of the Song empire, the fortified towns passed into oblivion except for those which, owing to their favorable geographic location, prospered as commercial centers. By the Southern Song the term *zhen* had acquired its modern meaning of "market town." Yet in Sichuan, and notably in the Ba region, the fortified town and its garrison commander continued to fulfill many administrative functions. Even in places where the county administration successfully reasserted its authority over civil government, the fortified town served as the bailiwick of local magnates exercising informal rule over the town-dwellers and the inhabitants of the surrounding countryside.

A detailed examination of the lists of *zhen* recorded for 1080 shows the close affinity between the fortified towns and the privately organized militias.[51] In the Shu region there were 370 *zhen* in 1080, or an average of one per 3,500 households. The Ba region encompassed 444 *zhen,* or roughly one per 1,500 households. Whereas 38 of the *zhen* in the Shu region conducted sufficient trade to merit commercial tax stations circa 1080, only 17 in the Ba region had tax stations. The correlation becomes even stronger when the focus is trained on the areas where Wei Junjing's militia network took root. In the six prefectures of Pu, Chang, He, Yu, Fushun, and Lu there were 171 *zhen,* one for every 1,100 households. Of the twenty-one fortified towns incorporated into Wei's militia network that are still legible on the 897 stele, eleven are included in the 1080 list (Table 4). The absence of half these garrison towns from the 1080 list indicates that the latter was not a meaningless vestige of an earlier period but an actual accounting of the garrison towns still recognized by the central government.

TABLE 4 Fortified Towns in Wei Junjing's Militia Network

Name	Still Existing in 1080	Prefecture
1. Anqi	x	Lu
2. Laigan		
3. Xieyai		
4. Ganquan		
5. Longgui	x	Chang
6. Gexianzhai		
7. Lishan		
8. Laifeng		
9. Longshui	x	Chang
10. Liuqi	x	He
11. Nanfeng		
12. Dongliu	x	He
13. Dongshi	x	He
14. Yongchuan		
15. Lingyunzhai		
16. Yunmenzhai	x	He
17. Jinyunzhai		
18. Hegu		
19. Xiaojing	x	Chang
20. Jingnan	x	Chang
21. Laisu	x	Chang

Sources: "Tang Wei Junjing bei", in *Jinshiyuan,* pp. 189–193; *YFJYZ* 7 & 8.

Note: Seven other names have been effaced.

The placenames of the fortified towns of the Ba region reveal a great deal about their functional significance, but also offer a rich store of information about Han perceptions of the landscape around them (Table 5). Unsurprisingly, many *zhen* bore names that reflected the basic concern for the security of the inhabitants. The authors of names such as "Return to Grace" (Guiren), "Return to the Mean" (Guizheng), "Everlasting Tranquility" (Yongning), "Dwelling in Peace" (Anju), and "Pacified Tribefolk" (Anyi) no doubt hoped that their epithets would become self-fulfilling prophecies. The Han preference for living near rivers,

TABLE 5 Zhen Placenames in the Western Ba Region in 1080

Placename Element	Number	Placename Element	Number
Physical features		*Human values*	
Rivers	30	Social stability	26
Mountains, Vistas	14	Fortune, Wealth	5
Rapids	9	Confucian virtues	4
Rocks	8	Happiness	2
Riverbanks	4	*Human landscape*	
Ponds	3	Non-Han names	30
Trees	3	Markets	12
Cliffs	2	Wells	12
Ford	1	Soil, Grain	5
Grotto	1	Bell, Drum	3
Spiritual world		Mills	2
Dragons	12	Inns	2
Spirits	3	Palisades	2
Birds, Animals	3	Surnames	2
Buddhism	1	Building	1
		Estate	1
		Unclassified	12
		Total	215

Source: *YFJYZ* 7 & 8

Note: The Western Ba Region is here defined as comprising Pu, Chang, He, Yu, Zi, Lu, and Fushun.

virtually their only means of communication with the outside world (and under the protection of subaqueous dragons), is fully evident. Aside from providing defense and communications, the fortified towns also served as centers of commerce. Markets and salt wells figure prominently among their placenames; but notable by their nearly total absence are names derived from man-made structures such as buildings, bridges, and temples, which dominated the placenames of villages and small towns in Sichuan in the early twentieth century. Finally, the presence of non-Han peoples was manifested by the high frequency of placenames of native provenance.[52] Although the indigenous peoples were rapidly diminishing north of the Yangzi River, they left a legacy of placenames which in some cases have persisted down to the present, fossils of an unremembered past.

A major reason for the persistence of the fortified town and the garrison commander in the field administration was the high percentage of vacancies in the civil administration. Few officials from elsewhere were willing to take up a post in Sichuan, especially in the malarial areas of the Yangzi valley. Nor were officials-awaiting-appointment in the capital attracted by the thought of dealing with hostile tribes in the frontiers, especially since the poor border prefectures of Ba offered, in return for their ministrations, only one-fifth or one-tenth of the remuneration commonly provided prefects in the Shu region. Moreover, officials serving in Sichuan were paid in depreciated iron currency, for which they received a highly unfavorable rate of exchange upon leaving Sichuan.[53] Consequently native Sichuanese filled most offices in Sichuan, even at the highest levels.

The practice of appointing native Sichuanese to local administrative posts in Sichuan antedated the collapse of central authority in the late Tang. Even at the height of dynastic vigor the Tang entrusted the governors-general to select local notables for appointment to local administrative offices.[54] After the devastating rebellions that rocked Sichuan in 993–995 and 1000–1001, the Song court prohibited Sichuan natives from serving as prefect or vice-prefect in their home province, and went so far as to bar Sichuanese who served as officials elsewhere in the empire from returning to Sichuan upon their retirement. By the middle of the eleventh century, these restrictive measures had reduced the pool of qualified officials willing to serve in Sichuan to the point where the rules were routinely ignored in order to maintain an adequate field administration.[55] Once again Sichuanese occupied nearly all the local administrative posts in their native province. The predominance of Sichuanese in these offices prompted the court in 1077 to issue an imperial directive, barring the appointment of Sichuanese to the offices of both prefect and vice-prefect in a Sichuan prefecture at the same time. In 1080, the court enjoined Sichuan natives from serving more than three consecutive terms as a prefect within the four routes of Sichuan.[56] While these measures may have allayed fears of undue partiality on the part of Sichuan's local officials, they exacerbated the problem of finding qualified personnel to serve in those posts.

More often than not local administrative posts in the Ba region remained vacant, especially in the Southern Song. A report sent to the court in 1185 lamented that twenty of Kuizhou Route's thirty-one counties lacked magistrates; in some counties no regular officials had been appointed in the previous six or seven years.[57] The poet Lu You, touring the Yangzi Gorges in 1170 while en route to taking up an appointment as prefect of Kuizhou, expressed rhetorical astonishment that Song officialdom had spurned the opportunity to enjoy the untroubled life of a magistrate in a small, remote town:

> Tenth month, 21st day. Anchored at Badong. . . . Since leaving Wu and entering Chu, I have traveled five thousand *li* and passed through fifteen prefectures; yet nowhere have I found a temple or pavilion whose beauty can match that of the White Cloud Pavilion, which stands just behind the official hall of the county. There are few affairs to trouble the magistrate in Badong, who could sup and rest here in the pavilion. His joy would be boundless! Yet they lack a magistrate. Frequently two or three years go by and no one is willing to accept this appointment. How can this be?

Lu's own diary supplies a likely answer:

> The settlement at Badong is extremely desolate and dreary. Within the town there are barely more than a hundred households. From the magistrate's hall on down, all of the buildings are made of thatch; nowhere can one find a piece of tile.[58]

Predictably, the aesthete's rustic ideal of planting oneself in the nurturing spiritual soil of an unspoiled wilderness quickly dissipated upon exposure to the squalid towns of the frontier.

When Du Zheng arrived at Yuzhou in 1220, he discovered that the county of Ba, the seat of the prefecture, had not had a regular civil official serving in any capacity for seven years. The bailiff's (*wei*) post in Ba county had been vacant for over ten years, while Jiangjin county had lacked a bailiff for fourteen years. Du noted that according to the rolls of the Board of Civil Office, the "advanced scholars" available to fill openings at the level of bailiff or master of records (*zhupu*) numbered no fewer than one hundred, yet every one of them had refused these two positions. Many vacancies at the county level in this area, therefore, were filled by irregular officials, holders of honorary or purchased titles otherwise ineligible for substantive appointments. Du contemptuously dismissed this group of local magnates as venal and corrupt tyrants who regarded the territory under their jurisdiction as nothing but a personal benefice. Yet even Du Zheng approved of the policy of selecting garrison commanders from among local "property-owners of comfortable and substantial means" (jiaye wenhou).[59]

The Song ceded further control over local affairs to the magnates in the realm of tax collection. In 1026 the Finance Commission decided to close commercial tax bureaus in Lizhou and Kuizhou Routes which collected less than one thousand guan annually and sell the tax collection rights to private individuals, a system known as maipu.[60] Those with sufficient reserves of disposable capital could, in effect, purchase the right to exploit the local populace, since no officials were present to prevent them from collecting tax revenues exceeding the quotas stipulated by the government. The state's continuing effort to streamline the bureaucracy inevitably strengthened the hand of local despots, as the following case of a frontier town in the Gorges region demonstrates:

> Kaizhou formerly included three counties within its jurisdiction. The county of Xinpu has been reduced to the status of a market town [zhen] since the 1040s. Now this town is far from the prefectural seat, deep within the hills and canyons. Duplicitous, ruthlessly parasitic magnates squat among and feed upon the local town-dwellers. Formerly an official from the wine bureau was stationed at the town to oversee fire protection and other public services. In 1156 even this official was eliminated, leaving no one to curb their excesses. The inhabitants cannot live in peace and security. We recommend that a marshal be transferred to Xinpuzhen specifically to curtail these abuses.[61]

After the Song established a state monopoly on wine production in Sichuan in 1129, the wine industry quickly fell under the domination of the local magnates. In 1156 the government abolished over 230 wine bureau posts and farmed out tax collection responsibilities to magnates under the maipu arrangement.[62] Lacking funds to support an official presence in most of the market towns, the Song state was forced to rely on local magnates to collect tax revenues, especially the transit and commodity tax levies, further enlarging the local magnates' sphere of social control.

The isolation of the frontier thus protected the local magnates from the social forces that fragmented the power of the upper classes in the metropolitan areas of China and induced the dissolution of their great landed estates. The thin soils of the upland areas of the Sichuan Basin supported only small settlements of peasants but provided a fertile bed for the flowering of a dominant class of powerful magnates. Champions of the well-being of the local community by virtue of their role in organizing and supplying self-defense militias, the magnates gained a leasehold over the members of the community, a debt requited by bonds of fealty and obligation entailing not only military service but also labor service and tribute. The strong personal quality of the bonds between a magnate and his clients, whether tenants or free farmers, extended as far as taking up arms against the state and its representatives on behalf of the patron.

The magnate's power to demand labor service from the populace within his range of control gradually was extended to include the right to dispose of the clients' lands. Not a few magnates coerced their clients into relinquishing the usufruct rights of their lands, or expropriated the lands outright. Many magnates sought to perpetuate their control over local productive resources by claiming the right to sell the labor power of their "tenant guests" along with the lands they worked and the right to forbid marriages that jeopardized their control over the local labor supply. Thus the magnates manipulated a tenurial system founded on the need to control scarce labor resources to create vast personal domains. Frequently they built their own forts as havens for their clients when bandits or insurgent native tribes threatened. Where markets sprouted up in the fortified towns, they usually became the personal preserves of the magnates, who would purchase the privilege of supervising the market and collecting various taxes on trade. The combination of control over productive resources with an infrastructure of militia networks enabled the local magnates to raise substantial personal armies that could be used to extend their power and influence further.

Frequently, too, the local magnates harbored designs on the lands of the native peoples, who rarely received the protection accorded them under Song laws. The central government, handicapped by an attenuated apparatus of social and political control, lacked both the capability and the will to assume direct authority over the area. During the eleventh century, as a rapidly expanding population pushed the boundaries of Han settlement farther into frontier zones, the competition for productive resources intensified. All along the Sichuan frontier, but particularly in Southern Lu, Han settlers under the leadership of local magnates encroached upon the territories of the native tribes. One Han objective in particular stood out: to gain control of the salt-producing areas, which held out the promise of immense wealth.

Part Two
Opening the Frontier

The Great Sovereign has his laws;
  His injunctions admonish you.

Heaven has spared you,
  You dare not give offense.

Alone among you, the Nineteen Surnames
  Remained peaceful in their homes.

The civil officers will ordain your dues,
  Your labor service, your tribute of cloth.

They will instruct you when to sow your rice and millet,
  And when to reap.

Recompense begins today;
  Mend your former ways!

FAN BAILU, "Record of Vanquishing the Barbarians,"
Stele inscription erected at Wuning Garrison, 1075

THREE

Salt and the Settling of the Sichuan Frontier

The aggressive, imperialistic posture of the Tang dynastic house was shattered in the eighth century by civil war and invasions. In the southwest, as elsewhere, the domain of the Tang steadily contracted. In marked contrast to the leading statesmen of the early Tang, Song policymakers initially manifested considerable ambivalence about the role of state power in frontier expansion. Preoccupied with the menace of the nomad kingdoms of the steppe, the early Song emperors adopted a defensive stance and relinquished sovereignty over many territories in which the Tang had established a foothold. In southwestern Sichuan, for example, the Song completely abandoned the Anning River valley and the Liang Shan to the native tribes and withdrew to the northern bank of the Dadu River. Yunnan lay entirely outside the orbit of Song influence, as did nearly all of the Guizhou Plateau.

In Southern Lu, on the other hand, the Song had both the opportunity and the motive to pursue expansionary initiatives. Whereas most of Sichuan's western and southern frontiers were sharply demarcated by formidable mountain ranges, the Southern Lu area, though heavily forested, lay at relatively low elevation and was crossed by several navigable rivers.[1] Thus Southern Lu had considerable potential as an area into which the Han agrarian world could spread. Moreover, the valuable salt deposits of Southern Lu provided ample economic incentive to annex the territories of the native peoples. Initially, the Song was content to exploit the salt wells, with the consent of the local chieftains, without seeking direct political control. Over the course of the eleventh century, as frictions between Han and the indigenous tribes intensified, this position became, in the eyes of Song officialdom, increasingly untenable. In the early 1070s the court discarded the concept of shared sovereignty implicit in the haltered-and-bridled principle and began to expropriate native lands and sponsor the colonization of Southern Lu by Han immigrants.

Part Two traces the evolution of frontier policy in Southern Lu during the Song period. Since the lure of profits from the production of salt was a central feature of Song expansion into Southern Lu, the present chapter recounts the history of the salt industry in Song Sichuan and its place in frontier expansion. Chapters Four and Five expand beyond the contest for resources and territory to explore the broad political dimensions of the frontier process.

EVOLUTION OF SICHUAN'S SALT INDUSTRY

Salt, a form of wealth more widely respected than the emperor's coin, could not fail to play a leading role in the history of Han expansion into Southern Lu. The precious mineral dominated the thoughts of local magnates and native chieftains, as well as merchants, well-owners, and officials hard pressed to expand the state's sources of revenue. On the most basic level the anticipated profits from salt mining, refining, and trade provided the wedge that split asunder the screen dividing Han from non-Han, the "barren wilderness" from the imperial domain. Close upon the heels of Song officials sent to manage salt production in Southern Lu came immigrant laborers, private entrepreneurs, and farmers, who drew comfort from the presence of several thousand Song soldiers stationed in the area. Originally sent to protect the salt wells, the soldiers increasingly found themselves defending a large agrarian population.

The Red Basin of Sichuan derives its name from the mantle of reddish-purple sandstone soils that overlies the deeper layers of limestone rock. Fast-flowing streams and rivers carved the easily eroded sandstone into a landscape of sharply inclined valleys, enormous limestone caverns, and countless underground rivers. Salt deposited in the limestone, probably as a consequence of the evaporation of a huge inland sea, was dissolved by rain water and underground streams passing through the rock strata. By historical times the highly saline brine had descended to great depths. In some areas tectonic bending and breaking folded the limestone beds and brought the salt veins to the surface, as at Daning in the Yangzi Gorges; but most commonly the brine could be tapped only by digging deep wells. Shallower wells were practicable in the Fu River valley and along the Yangzi River in the Gorges region, where water flow and erosion reduced the actual depth of the salt deposits; but by the same token the salt brine in these areas, diluted by ground water, was low in salinity. The deposits of highly saline brine lay deeply buried beneath the rugged hills between the Min and Tuo Rivers in the southwestern part of the basin.[2]

The Luzhou region gained fame for its salt wealth as early as the fourth century A.D. The rich deposits northwest of the city of Luzhou, in the midst of tribal territories, had been mined by the Han since that time, but the Han population in this part of Luzhou remained small down to the Tang. The local soils, denatured by the salt, offered little attraction to Han peasants. Nonetheless the enormous revenues from salt production garnered by the state warranted a strong official presence. The Song court early on detached the northwestern corner of Lu prefecture and established the prefectural-level industrial agency (*jian*) of Fushun to supervise both salt production and civil administration.

Salt production south of the Yangzi River probably did not long antedate the Song period. The earliest reference to salt works at Yujingzhen, the only salt-producing area south of the Yangzi, dates from 883.[3] Yujingzhen, at the headwaters of the Yu River some 130 kilometers southwest of Luzhou, was located deep within the dominions of the native peoples. In 910 the Former Shu kingdom recognized the local chieftains of the La lineage as rulers of a confederation known as the "ten haltered-and-bridled prefectures and the five fortified villages" (*shizhou wutun*) in return for the right to mine salt.[4] According to one legend current in the late Song, a man named Huang had won the rights to exploit the salt deposits at Yujing in a contest with one of the La. Another version relates that two shepherds discovered pools of salt brine while seeking fresh water for their flock.[5] In any case, the Song government established a state industrial agency at Yujing (Yujingjian) shortly after subduing the Later Shu in 965. Yet the town remained an isolated enclave, populated by a few officials and the convict laborers sentenced to a life of turning the great winches that raised buckets of brine from the well bottom hundreds of meters below the surface.[6]

In Sichuan the organization of the salt industry, like its production methods, proceeded along completely different lines from the rest of the Song empire. In the eyes of the framers of Song fiscal policy, the physical isolation of the Sichuan Basin and its separate political history since the demise of the Tang required that Sichuan be treated as an autonomous economic region with its own currency system (iron coinage and, from the 1020s onward, a variety of paper instruments) and, they envisioned, a self-enclosed system of production and trade. In contrast to the state monopoly of salt production found elsewhere, in Sichuan independent well-owners (*jinghu*) extracted, refined, and marketed the salt themselves, paying an excise tax pegged to production quotas set by the state for each well. The architects of this policy originally intended that each of the four routes that comprised Sichuan would meet its own consumption needs, but almost from the beginning salt surpluses from Zizhou and Kuizhou Routes were shipped and sold to the salt-deficient cities and villages of Chengdu Route.[7]

In Yujing and five other places in Sichuan the state assumed direct management of wells that tapped especially rich salt deposits. The actual producers, or "furnace households" (*zaohu*), contracted to refine a given amount of salt per year for the state, which in turn sold the salt to private merchants. The five state-operated wells in Luzhou, including the Nanjing and Tuolu wells north of the Yangzi, produced an average of 150,000 *jin* (169,000 kilos) per well annually, a rate exceeded only by the great saltworks at Daning and Yun'an in the Yangzi Gorges.[8] Zizhou prefecture was by far the largest producer of salt in Sichuan in the early Song (3.66 million *jin* annually), but its production was scattered among 148 wells in six counties. The higher costs and logistical problems posed by the smaller wells discouraged the state from operating them directly. The state's primary interest in the salt industry of course centered on increasing its revenues, and the excise tax on small wells could generate as much income for the state as returns on actual ownership. Grounded in

Confucian principles of economic management, Song officials generally favored private development of salt resources; but a technological breakthrough in drilling techniques threatened to undermine the state's salt revenues and led to several attempts at a state takeover of Sichuan's salt industry.

The "lofty pipe well" (*zhuotongjing*, so called because of the raised derrick that supported the well pipe) was first introduced by an inventor named Wang Luan in the second decade of the eleventh century. Wang used his device to tap otherwise inaccessible salt reservoirs at Pujiang in Qiongzhou, which the government immediately appropriated. Su Shi's description of the lofty pipe well indicates that it operated on a suction-lift pump principle rather than the traditional chain-and-bucket method.[9] The bamboo pipes were fitted with an iron drill bit, touted as one of the finest products of Sichuan metallurgy, that made it feasible to drill extremely deep wells. The Yujing wells descended over one hundred fifty meters, while elsewhere wells were dug even deeper. Since the operation of the lofty pipe well did not require the elaborate equipment and dozens of workers previously needed to hoist the buckets of brine, the owner's capital and labor costs were vastly reduced. Many enterprising individuals began to try their hand at salt manufacture. The number of Sichuan's officially licensed salt wells increased from 720 at the end of the tenth century to 759 in the 1040s, about the time that the lofty pipe well technology became general knowledge, and then soared to over 4,900 by the 1130s.[10]

As the number of wells grew, so did evasion from the state excise tax. The aperture of the lofty pipe well at the surface measured less than thirty centimeters in diameter, a feature that enabled the producer to conceal the well, and the profits it earned, from the authorities. Illicit salt, by all accounts, soon became a severe problem. Legitimate producers reaped great rewards, too, as Wen Tong reported in a famous essay on the salt industry at the town of Jingyan in Lingzhou, northwest of Luzhou:

> Jingyan, located on high, uneven terrain a hundred *li* distant from the prefectural seat, is most deserving of designation as a remote, backwards area. In former times Jingyan was regarded at most as a small hamlet in the hills, but today people already describe it as a significant commercial center sorely in

need of proper government. Since the 1040s the local populace has been digging wells and drilling pipes into the earth. These lofty pipe wells are used to
extract saline brine, which is then refined into salt and marketed. Within a
short time all of the local inhabitants had become skilled in this technique of
salt manufacture. Subsequently the tax receipts based on monthly production
quotas of salt decreased, since the people relied on this device to engage in
heinous and illegal activities, applying their masonry skills to exploit the
"wealth of the mountains and marshes" to meet the expenses of their self-
indulgent extravagances. In the course of my inspection I have learned that
among the prominent families a single household owns as many as ten or
twenty wells, while those of the second rank own no fewer than seven or eight.
The court was apprised of this situation and directed the Fiscal Office of this
route to prohibit the construction of these wells. Yet at present there are nearly
one hundred households within the precincts of this prefecture operating lofty
pipe wells, which can be concealed temporarily so that the authorities remain
ignorant of the actual number of wells in operation.[11]

Wen Tong voiced concern about the threat to public order posed by
hordes of itinerant workers who descended upon frontier towns like
Jingyan in search of employment at the salt wells. He also noted the
strain on timber reserves and the rapidly rising cost of firewood that
resulted from the proliferation of salt wells in this area.

Ultimately, though, the issue that prompted the greatest alarm was
that of declining tax revenues, a prospect that vexed fiscal planners in the
capital as much as local magistrates. The Fiscal Office of Chengdu Route
had prompted the central government to issue proscriptions against the
lofty pipe well as early as the 1050s; but the ban was routinely ignored,
as Wen Tong indicated. In 1074 the newly created Bureau of Markets and
Exchange (*shiyisi*) proposed that the state shut down privately owned
wells in Sichuan and ship surplus salt from Shaanxi to markets in
Chengdu. Before this the state had been extremely reluctant to interfere
in Sichuan's internal markets. Li Qi, one of the fiscal commissioners
investigating the feasibility of bringing Sichuan within the orbit of the
Bureau of Markets and Exchange, struck a cautious note in his report.
Pointing out that court historians attributed the devastating Wang
Xiaobo–Li Shun rebellion of 993–995 to the central government's rapa-
cious seizure of the wealth of Sichuan after the conquest of the Later Shu,
Li echoed the accepted wisdom that central government interference in

Sichuan's economy risked setting off a new wave of disorders. Indeed, at the time, court officials believed that the excise tax on salt wells was a principal cause of the rebellions. In 1053 the court sent investigators to Ling, Rong, and other salt-producing areas to determine whether abuses in the collection of salt taxes might provoke a rebellion in the following year. The year 1054 would be a *jiawu* year in the Chinese sexagesimal calendar, and thus—according to prevailing concepts of cosmic regene-sis—posed the imminent threat of renewed disorders on a par with the previous *jiawu* years of 994 (the Wang–Li rebellion), 934 (the fall of the Former Shu dynasty), and 874 (the Huang Chao rebellion).[12]

Wang Anshi, the prime minister, disavowed any blame on the part of the state for the insurrections of the 990s, brusquely retorting that "he was unaware that the appropriation of the stores and treasuries of the Meng clan [the royal house of the Later Shu] made any difference to the starving masses."[13] Several months later the tea-producing routes of Chengdu and Lizhou were incorporated into the Bureau of Markets and Exchange, which immediately sought a state monopoly of salt pro-duction in the area under its jurisdiction. However, Shen Gua, the celebrated polymath whose penetrating insights into fiscal policy made him a favorite of Emperor Shenzong, convinced the emperor that de-spite its intrinsic merits the proposal was impractical and should be abandoned.[14]

The idea of state control of the salt industry in Sichuan was far from dead. In 1076 a tea agency official in Chengdu by the name of Liu Zuo, impressed by the immense profits of the merchants engaged in the ex-change of Sichuan tea for Shaanxi salt, urged the court to take over this trade. The court quickly adopted Liu's suggestion, at the same time pro-hibiting private production and trade of salt in Chengdu and Lizhou Routes and closing their markets to salt produced in Zizhou and Kui-zhou Routes.[15] The staff officer of the Chengdu Route Fiscal Office, Duan Jie, applauded Liu's plan and issued a proscription against lofty pipe wells within his jurisdiction. Duan also made an effort to close the lofty pipe wells in Zizhou Route; but the Zizhou fiscal officials, fearing the loss of revenues and employment that such an action would incur, resolutely opposed this measure.[16]

A chorus of opposition arose from leading Sichuanese officials. Wen

Tong, then serving as the prefect of the tea-producing center of Yang-zhou in Lizhou Route, complained that the state-operated salt market located in the prefectural capital failed to service the tea cultivators deep in the hills, who formerly bought salt from itinerant merchants at rural markets. The censor Zhou Yin delivered a stinging critique of the Chengdu salt monopoly, protesting that thousands of workers had been left unemployed by the closing of the lofty pipe wells so that the state could extort monopolistic prices from Chengdu's consumers.[17]

The court passed on Zhou Yin's appeal on behalf of both producers and consumers in Chengdu to the Finance Commission, headed by Wang Anshi's protégé Zhang Dun, for review. From the viewpoint of fiscal planners, the salt monopoly in Chengdu and Lizhou Routes initially was a great success. The monopoly on salt sold in Chengdu Route enabled the state to empty warehouses in Shaanxi swamped with salt, which now fetched 250–260 cash per *jin* in Chengdu, while prices in eastern Sichuan stagnated at roughly 70 cash per *jin*.[18] In addition, the state protected its profits from the state-operated wells in Pujiang from the cheaper salt produced by the privately owned lofty pipe wells.[19]

The institution of a salt monopoly in western Sichuan coincided with efforts to establish a state monopsony on the sale of all Shaanxi salt sold in northern and central China. The state's interference in the Shaanxi salt trade threatened the rate of private profit and diminished merchant interest in undertaking the shipment of salt from Shaanxi to purchasing stations in North China and Sichuan.[20] Consequently the value of state-issued Shaanxi salt vouchers, the primary instrument for financing the transport of provisions to troops on the steppe frontiers, plummeted, forcing the court to reconsider the wisdom of the salt monopoly system. In the spring of 1077, after the salt vouchers fell to one-third of their former value, the court abruptly discontinued Liu Zuo's monopoly system. A year later, on the advice of fiscal officials in Chengdu, the court reinstated the marketing of Shaanxi salt in Sichuan through the Tea Market Agency, but also limited the maximum volume of this operation to one-tenth of that proposed under the monopoly system.[21]

In 1084 the court experimented with another monopoly system drawn up by the fiscal intendant of Kuizhou Route, Wang Zongwang. Wang's plan required private producers in Chengdu and Lizhou Routes to sell their salt to state purchasing offices (*chang*) at a fixed rate of 40 cash per *jin*.[22] From the start the new monopoly system was plagued with abuses. Officials continued to demand the full quota of taxes from wells that had run dry and tacked additional levies onto the base rate of 15 percent of the producer's price. In 1087 salt of poor quality from the state-owned Pujiang saltworks sold for 120 cash per *jin*, while the market price of salt in Zizhou and Kuizhou Routes remained steady at roughly 70–80 cash. Su Che indicted the judicial intendant of Chengdu for failing to root out blatantly illegal practices. The court sustained his writ of censure and appointed a local notable in Jingyan to investigate the salt administration in Sichuan.[23] The investigator compiled a catalogue of abuses which was used by the so-called "Sichuan Party," led by Lü Tao and Su Che, to wage an offensive against the state's intrusion into the Sichuan salt industry. In 1089 Lü Tao finally triumphed in his crusade to restore private management in the salt industry and the proscription against the lofty pipe wells was rescinded.[24] The private sector of the salt industry flourished once again, until the Jurchen conquest of the north precipitated a new and much more drastic fiscal crisis.

CONSOLIDATION AND CONCENTRATION OF PRIVATE PRODUCTION

The decision to restore private production of and trade in salt in Sichuan represented a return to traditional precepts of public finance. While salt had been recognized since antiquity as a public good from which the state derived revenues for the provision of essential services, the prevailing opinion among policy makers in Sichuan held that the state would reap greater benefits from expansion of the private sector than from increased state control over the market. The enormous overhead costs inherent in state regulation of the market would consume any additional revenues caught by a more tightly woven net of regulation. Shen Gua pursued this line of reasoning in an audience before the emperor when the first monopoly system was proposed in 1074:

> As for the privately owned wells, since the state not only allows but even encourages the sale of salt excise collection rights to private individuals [*maipu*], private trade in salt is unavoidable. To stop private trade in salt entirely and replace it with a system whereby all salt is obtained from state markets would

be the ideal way of reducing penal sanctions and capturing lost revenues. Yet in the areas of Zhong, Wan, Xu, and Lu prefectures bordering on the tribal regions, the small wells [the lofty pipe wells] are especially numerous. I am at a loss to say how the trade in contraband salt from these areas can be eliminated. This being the case, if we must set out an array of watch stations and augment border patrols along the frontier, then I fear that the gains in revenues will not offset the additional expenditures.[25]

Rather than engage in a long and costly battle to close the lofty pipe wells, the Song often entrusted the collection of the excise tax to local merchants or notables in exchange for fees that provided the state a reliable source of revenues. This form of tax farming turned a levy on productive enterprise into a contractual obligation owed by the producer to a third party. When the salinity of brine diminished as a result of the intrusion of fresh water, an inevitable consequence of the mining process, the producer still bore the burden of paying his quota of excise taxes. The *maipu* system of private tax collection was unequipped to deal with this eventuality. The tax farmer demanded his due as fulfillment of a contract, while local officials were loath to forgive taxes that they had already collected in the form of fees paid by the tax farmers. Many producers were ruined while waiting for their wells to be officially certified as exhausted and taken off the tax rolls.

Faced with the increased competition of the lofty pipe wells, the Song government adopted the strategy of divesting itself of all but its most productive assets in the salt industry. In 1074 the Finance Commission agreed to a proposal, initiated by a local notable in Yujing, to sell all but two of its salt-extraction furnaces at Yujing to private producers.[26] The state also sold off its less productive wells in Yujing. The production quotas for the state-operated wells at Yujing dropped steadily, from 783,000 *jin* at the end of the tenth century to around 520,000 in 1010, then 490,000, finally falling to 419,000 in the 1130s. Yet despite the reduction of the state's direct investment in production, the profits it earned from salt remained high. In 1153, production costs at Yujing consumed a mere 43 percent of the salt bureau's revenues.[27]

The moneyed classes of Sichuan, and even those of decidedly more modest means, welcomed the government's shift towards private enterprise in the salt industry. Financially advantaged producers, as Wen

Tong insinuated, constantly strove to expand their holdings, by fair means or foul. In the 1020s, Wang Mengzheng, a notorious relative of the regent empress dowager and a member of one of the great families of Sichuan, attempted to wield influence at the court to compel the salt bureau officials in Yujing to double the production quotas of private wells, expecting that marginal producers would go bankrupt and be forced to sell their wells to him.[28] Wang's scheme was frustrated by the intransigence of the local magistrate; but in the Southern Song, the state itself undertook a series of policies in the salt industry that encouraged the concentration of ownership and capital resource.

Staggered by the debilitating costs of the Jurchen wars, in the early years of the Southern Song fiscal officials desperately tried to raise cash, which in effect meant that they were compelled to siphon off additional revenues from commerce. In 1132 the Song implemented a wide range of controls over commerce in Sichuan designed by Zhao Kai, regarded by his contemporaries as a financial wizard.[29] In the salt industry Zhao transferred the bulk of state regulation from production to marketing through the introduction of a licensing system (*qianyin*) for wholesale transactions in salt and a policy of confiscating wells from bankrupt producers and reselling them to other entrepreneurs. Whenever the government put a confiscated well up for sale, a procedure known as *toumai*, it invariably raised the excise tax quota. The lure of immense profits from salt assured a steady supply of buyers, even though many new owners borrowed heavily and soon found themselves unable to meet the costs of operating expenses and capital investments in addition to paying off their loans, not to mention the various taxes exacted by the state.[30] Bankruptcy and subsequent confiscation of the unfortunate's assets, regardless of the social repercussions, was a boon to state finances. In 1210 only one-half of Sichuan's salt revenues derived from tax receipts; the other half, amounting to one million *guan*, was generated through the resale of confiscated wells.[31] Although government officials frequently expressed remorse over their role as profiteers preying on luckless well-owners, they were much too dependent on these revenues to attempt substantial reform. To quote Yu Ruli's famous utterance in 1141, "Today, the profit from levies on commerce in salt and liquor is the Lord of Destiny [*siming*] in Sichuan."[32]

As Yoshida Tora has pointed out, the *toumai* system's transferral of ownership, at high risk, to the private sector was tantamount to granting exclusive mining rights to the highest bidders.[33] In many places only persons with considerable capital reserves could weather the vagaries of both the market and geology as well as punishing taxation. Wen Tong, writing in 1071, may have found ownership of twenty salt wells a morally ambivalent concentration of wealth; but Hu Yuanzhi, in a petition to reform the Sichuan salt industry presented in 1177, insisted that tax relief be directed towards "the lowest category [of three] of proprietors, those who own no more than ten to twenty wells and fail to meet their tax quotas because [their costs, and consequently their prices, are so high that] they cannot find anyone to contract orders for their goods." Hu reported that the previous attempt at tax reform undertaken in Jianzhou resulted in the wealthiest producers receiving reductions in their tax liabilities amounting to as much as 7,000 *guan*. To counter this excessive generosity to the rich, Hu proposed that under the new tax schedule no individual should receive a reduction of more than 2,000 *guan*.[34]

Reforms intended to protect small producers and close loopholes afforded to the rich had little impact. As the wealth of a few producers waxed, the fiscal health of the salt administration waned. Powerful producers, through collusion with officials, avoided reporting the actual amount of salt they refined. On the other end of the scale, small producers and consumers beset by sharply higher prices turned to illegal production and trade of salt. By the first decade of the thirteenth century, contraband trade had sharply curtailed the salt administration's income and jeopardized the viability of Sichuan's ailing fiscal system.

SALT MINING AND FRONTIER SETTLEMENT

The Song founders, upon recovering Sichuan from the Later Shu dynasty in 965, found themselves facing a crisis in salt consumption.[35] During the Tang period, salt produced under state monopoly in Sichuan was supplemented with imports from the Shaanxi salt ponds. In the late tenth century, after major salt-producing areas in Gansu and Hebei fell under the dominion of the Tanguts and Khitan, the Song prohibited the export of Shaanxi salt to Sichuan, reserving Shaanxi's output for North

China consumers. Despite the rapid expansion of Sichuan's salt industry in the closing decades of the tenth century, production failed to keep pace with demand. The state steadily reduced the price for salt refined at state-owned wells in Sichuan, from the 160 cash per *jin* charged by the Later Shu in 965 to a low of 70 cash in 978. However, attempts to curb the inflationary pressures of salt shortages by artificially depressing wholesale prices proved futile. The officials exercised little control over retail prices; by the time the salt reached consumers, its price had soared to over 200 cash per *jin*. In 988 the court permitted Sichuan to purchase salt from the Tanguts in a fruitless effort to reduce the perennial shortfall in local production.[36] Beginning in 1042, the Song licensed merchants to purchase Shaanxi salt and exchange it in Sichuan for Sichuan goods, principally silks and tea.[37] But few merchants took advantage of this offer. Sichuan's salt consumption crisis began to abate only after the proliferation of lofty pipe wells from the 1040s onward.[38]

Over the course of the eleventh century, Sichuan's population doubled, and the region's demand for a staple like salt undoubtedly doubled as well. At the end of the tenth century, Sichuan's salt wells produced about 16 million *jin* annually, which was consumed by a population of roughly five million people.[39] Thus we can estimate that in the early Song per capita consumption of salt in Sichuan averaged 3 to 3.5 *jin* per year. By contrast, Wen Tong reported in 1076 that consumption of salt was two *qian* (about 15 grams) per person per day, or an annual average of 4.5 *jin* per capita.[40] Official tax quotas for the eleventh and twelfth centuries remained fixed at approximately the same magnitude, or slightly less, as the figures set down at the beginning of the dynasty. Actual production presumably increased to match the growth in population, which reached ten to twelve million by the 1080s. Using Wen Tong's estimate for salt consumption, Sichuan's annual output probably lay within a range of 45 to 60 million *jin* at the end of the eleventh century. This estimate makes it plausible to accept the annual salt production figure of 60 million *jin* reported for the mid-twelfth century.[41]

Rising demand for salt provided the primary incentive to settle and explore for salt in areas where poor soils and difficult terrain inhibited agricultural expansion. The invention of the lofty pipe well spurred the exploitation of the salt resources of the upland area between the Min and

Tuo Rivers by enabling miners to recover brine from deeply recessed pools. The search for fortunes in salt brought an uprecedented influx of settlers into the prefectures of Jian, Ling, Rong, Fushun, and Lu.

In Rong, the number of wells increased from fifty-seven in 980 to one hundred seventy in 1079.[42] Neighboring Jingyan county, which contained only five state-operated wells as late as 1048, experienced the most dramatic growth, with several hundred private wells in operation by 1071.[43] Wen Tong viewed this sudden influx of fortune-seekers with dismay and apprehension:

> Each [well-owning] family must hire as many as forty or fifty laborers and craftsmen, but at least twenty to thirty. Men of this ilk are rootless drifters from other districts who, fleeing capture and changing their name after the commission of some crime, come here to find work and hire themselves out as wage-laborers. When left by themselves to dwell in peace, they remain respectful and tame. But as soon as their will is thwarted, the laborers fan agitation and incite their fellows to gang together and, in loud and boisterous voices, demand settlement of their wages. Feigning illness, they request permission to depart. Then, gathering in the rural markets and villages or entering the towns, they drink, gamble, and engage in every imaginable debauchery. Afterwards they throw themselves upon yet another place, to the point where this behavior has become an habitual part of their livelihood. . . . [Lingzhou] shares common borders with Jia and Rong prefectures; in both of the latter two places the situation is exactly the same.[44]

Employment at the salt wells remained seasonal and discontinuous, subject to the caprice of geology. Even at the biggest operations, production never continued year-round. A comparison of daily and annual production figures for the late tenth century shows that Lingzhou's salt wells operated at the equivalent of 265 days of peak production per year; in the summer and autumn production dropped to only 38 percent of the output obtained during the dry season.[45]

Han inhabitants attempted to scratch out a meager subsistence from farming; but as Han Jiang's (1012–1088) poem on Fushun reveals, the harvest of salt rather than that of rice provided the measure of survival:

> *Working the sterile earth with hoe not plough,*
> *A family has no stores at year's end.*
> *They survive on wealth from the salt wells*
> *Exchanged at market for grain from elsewhere.*[46]

Lu You, in a poem written while visiting Rongzhou, also alluded to the primacy of salt in the local economy:

Sold vegetables at the market nearby, returning home early,
Boiling well-salt preoccupies the men—wheat planting will be late.[47]

The dependence of a significant portion of this area's population on salt as the basis of their livelihood can be measured by the somber devotion accorded to the cults that grew up around the salt wells. The official cult of the deity of the Fushun salt wells centered on the figure of Muəitsək, Master of the Divine Well. According to legend, Muəitsək was a Klao tribesman who first discovered salt at Fushun in 280. As Fushun's prominence as a salt-producing area grew, the cult of Muəitsək, first officially recognized in the tenth century, prospered and gained a secure place in the pantheon of local official cults.[48]

Far more invidious, in the view of Song officials, and acutely revealing of the stake the local populace invested in the fortunes of the salt industry, was the common practice of offering human sacrifices to the salt well deities. Tradition related that Lingzhou's salt reservoirs were discovered when twelve Jade Maidens (*yunü*) showed the Taoist Celestial Master Zhang Ling (after whom Lingzhou was named) where to dig. During the Six Dynasties period, the Jade Maiden, transmogrified into a serpent, became the object of a cult of human sacrifice. Each year the inhabitants threw a male youth into a salt well to serve as a consort to the unwed goddess. Purportedly the annual sacrifices halted at the end of the sixth century when a magistrate arranged a "marriage" between the Jade Maiden and the subterranean deity or *naga* of West Mountain, who previously had been paid homage with sacrifices of human maidens.[49] But human sacrifices to the denizens of the salt wells remained common in the Southern Song.[50] The Sichuanese carefully watched for propitious omens indicating that the *nagas* dwelling at the bottom of the salt wells would favor them with a steady flow of brine.[51]

In some places the salt industry inaugurated an era of enviable prosperity. Great fortunes were plumbed from the wells sunk in the wilderness of western Jianzhou's gorges, only a few days' journey from the teeming markets of the Chengdu Plain.[52] The salt wells of Fushun and Rong achieved renown as "the springs of avarice" (*tanquan*), an allusion to the bounteous and corrupting treasures of the Southern Seas.[53]

But the rush for salt more often ended in penury than in riches. Guan Qisun, prefect of Jianzhou in 1167–1168, wrote that only a few dozen households had become wealthy from their salt ventures, while the rest of the salt well owners were impoverished.[54] In Rong, "walled in on all sides by mountains," the shallow shoals of the mountain streams on the Tuo side of the watershed barred boats from reaching the prefecture's hundreds of salt wells. Gongjingzhen (site of Ziliujing, the capital of Sichuan's modern salt industry) achieved brief prominence as the seat of Rong prefecture during the first decade of the Tang dynasty; but the town's inaccessibility convinced the central government to reduce Gongjing's status to a county seat in 627, followed by a further demotion to "market town" in 1071. The gentler slope of the Min River valley allowed boats to penetrate as far as the minor county seat of Yingling, which mushroomed into a boom town. From Yingling the merchant ships sailed down to Sanjiangzhen, where salt-laden boats from Jingyan also stopped on their descent to the Min River.[55] The merchant colonies of Yingling and Sanjiang prospered; but the producers in Rong were handicapped by salt of poor quality (described as red or black in color), nonexistent transport facilities, and wells that quickly decreased in salinity. In the 1060s, the state confiscated the property of 315 households in Rong for failure to pay the excise taxes on their salt wells before local notables and court officials allied to win a reprieve for the bankrupt producers and a reduction in their tax quotas.[56]

Rich or poor, the salt miners spearheaded Han settlement in the upland areas of southwestern Sichuan, formerly the preserve of the native tribes. In Fushun and Rong the native peoples, encircled by expanding Han populations for centuries, had been reduced to small, scattered enclaves. They meekly submitted to this final push of Han settlement and were assimilated into the dominant Han society without a struggle. Along the untamed frontier beyond the protective embrace of the Yangzi and Min Rivers, the Han did not establish their claim over productive resources so easily. In Southern Lu, after the first border conflict broke out in 1013, the Song state had to assert its sovereignty over the region's salt wealth by force of arms. The introduction of the lofty pipe well in the 1040s made the native territories around Yujing even more attractive for exploration, mining, and settlement. Unsurprisingly, the policy of frontier expansion that the court adopted in the 1070s culminated in the conquest of the haltered-and-bridled districts around Yujing within the span of a few short years.

No documents in our possession describe the annexation of the salt-producing areas of Southern Lu as an explicit goal of the state's frontier policy; nor is it possible to determine whether private salt producers and merchants influenced government actions; but military conquest indubitably served the economic interests of the salt industry. In this instance the economic interests of the state and the salt producers converged. Not only did the state continue to profit from the great quantities of salt produced under both public and private auspices at Yujing, but in addition local governments depended on the salt wells for the bulk of their revenues. After Yujing was elevated to a prefecture in 1111, all of its administrative costs were defrayed by salt revenues.[57] The vested interests of both the state and private producers in acquiring valuable new sources of salt prompted repeated Han incursions into the tribal territories of Southern Lu, and ultimately launched the Song on a course of frontier expansion.

FOUR

"A Stolen Peace": Frontier Expansion under the New Laws

Yujing's location deep within the tribal territories of Southern Lu compelled the Song to seek a rapprochement with tribal leaders that would allow for some degree of joint sovereignty over the salt wells. Through the pact of condominium enunciated in the haltered-and-bridled system, the Song hoped to stabilize the boundary between Han and non-Han by acknowledging the autonomy of the native leaders in return for pledges of peaceful coexistence. The covenants between the Song and the native leaders in Southern Lu in addition recognized the Song state's claim to exploit the salt resources of the Yujing area. After the conquest of Sichuan, the Song dispatched officials to Yujing to monitor the salt operations but laid no claim to direct political control of Yujing and its environs. The Song sought to incorporate the native peoples into its political economy through economic and military alliances rather than direct sovereignty and cultural absorption.

Yet this arrangement was subject to pressures from all quarters. Han local magnates, salt miners, and homesteaders trampled on the territorial rights of the native peoples, who resorted to violence to protect their dominions. Deng Wan, magistrate of Luzhou's Hejiang county in 1066, complained that the Song had purchased only "a stolen peace" (*touan*) by forgoing direct and centralized military domination in favor of loose and unpredictable alliances with native chieftains and local magnates.[1] Deng's plea for a more vigorous state role in frontier affairs coincided with the political ascendancy of Wang Anshi's expansionist fiscal and frontier policies. A few years later the haltered-and-bridled system and its fragile balance of competing interests collapsed, ushering in a new phase of conquest and expropriation.

BORDER CONFLICT IN SOUTHERN LU

The ten haltered-and-bridled districts in Southern Lu initially submitted only nominal tribute, in the form of the prized ornamental, purple-speckled bamboo, to the Song emperor.[2] Relations between Han and the native peoples were governed principally by tribal codes, such as the right to exact compensation for wrongful death according to the tradition of "blood money" (*gujia*). Despite Yujing's reputation as a rough and disorderly town populated by itinerant salt workers and convicts, the Song did not station soldiers there until tensions between the Han and the natives began to escalate in the early decades of the eleventh century. Attacks on Yujing by native tribes in 1008 and 1013 prompted the Song to mount a full-scale pacification campaign in 1013–1014, an intervention that led to an enduring Song military presence in Southern Lu. Although a truce was agreed upon in 1014, a pattern of aggrandizement had been initiated that culminated in the 1070s with the outright conquest of the haltered-and-bridled territories.

In 1008 the Song court unexpectedly found itself drawn into a local war between the Black Tribes of the Liang Shan to the west and the natives of the haltered-and-bridled districts of Southern Lu. The marshal (*xunjian*) of Luzhou was killed when he attempted to intercede between the warring tribes. The Song general Shiqi Wei, heedless of the court's instructions to pursue a peaceful reconciliation, rounded up and executed several dozen Luzhou tribesmen. A group of natives known as the Takang, led by the chieftains Təumiuang and Təuiin, escaped Shiqi Wei's manhunt and went into hiding. Təumiuang and his followers turned to banditry, preying on the ships of salt merchants making the laborious nine days' passage between Luzhou and Yujing.[3] In 1013 they attacked and razed Yujing, provoking the fiscal intendant, Kou Xian, to initiate a massive military buildup. Kou had considerable experience dealing with the southwestern tribes as a member of Ding Wei's staff during the latter's long tenure as fiscal intendant of Kuizhou Route. Upon arriving at Jiang'an, south of Luzhou at the mouth of the Yu River, Kou first turned to diplomacy to win the support of other native leaders. He summoned the chieftains of thirteen haltered-and-bridled districts and lineage groups and, with martial fanfare of drums and pipes in the background, displayed a hundred ships in the harbor laden with weapons and provisions for troops who stood smartly at attention beneath unfurled war banners. Kou then performed the blood oath ritual with the "awed" chieftains, who readily agreed to a pact pledging cooperation in the suppression of Təumiuang's bandit gang.[4]

Kou Xian and Wang Huaixin, the military adviser dispatched by the emperor, concluded that a campaign of extermination against Təumiuang was required. Combining over three thousand regular troops with an equal number from the "Sons and Brothers of Boji" (*Boji zidi*) militias,[5] Wang began the ascent into the upper valley of the Yu River, an area known to the Han as "south of the wild frontier" (Shengjienan). Many of the villages of the Yu and Sian Rivers supported Təumiuang but were quickly overwhelmed by the superior Song army. Emboldened by his victories, Wang pursued Təumiuang deep into the tribal territory, cutting a horrifying swath of destruction through the green hills. In one day his troops burned thirty villages. To consolidate their control of the entire Yu valley, Wang and Kou built Ningyuan Garrison at the confluence of the Sian and the Singa Rivers. After three months, his army shrunken to a terrified and undisciplined rabble, Təumiuang surrendered. Wang claimed, with the braggadacio typical of Han generals, to have killed thousands of rebels and burned thousands of their huts during the course of the campaign. While the Song soldiers set about building a wall and a series of moats around Yujing, the native peoples lapsed into sullen respect for the military might of the Song. More than thirty years passed before another incident escalated into a serious uprising.[6]

Təumiuang's uprising prompted the Song government to supplement the local militias in Southern Lu with regular army troops. The central government stationed a full battalion of one thousand soldiers at Jiang'an under the newly created command of the marshal for Xu, Lu, Zi, and Rong Prefectures. The battalion was divided into five companies which alternately served stints of several months at Yujing.[7] Despite the presence of Song army regulars, the Song still regarded local militias like the "Sons and Brothers of Boji" as the primary peace-keeping forces along the Luzhou frontier. More important than soldiers, though, was the ability of local magnates to maintain order in the interests of all. In 1019 the emperor's personal envoy in eastern Sichuan, Zang Hu, reported that crimes committed by the tribal folk usually were retaliatory actions intended to avenge some wrongdoing by Han subjects. Zang recommended that instead of sending soldiers the Song ought to entrust "householders of substantial property familiar with the moods and dispositions of the tribesmen" to mollify the latter.[8]

In the late 1040s, after a series of destructive uprisings and expensive campaigns in Southern Lu, the Song decided to rely entirely on an enlarged network of local militias to defend the Luzhou frontier.[9] In 1047 the Court of Military Affairs protested against the policy of sending imperial guards from the northwestern frontier, a month's journey away, to deal with border troubles in the southwest. Wen Yanbo, then Assistant Commissioner of Military Affairs, argued that units like the "Sons and Brothers of Boji" were far more efficient and economical than regular army troops and persuaded the court to base its defensive strategy on the Boji militias.[10] Two years later, in 1049, the court drew up laws to conscript able-bodied males of Luzhou into the "Sons and Brothers of Boji." The magnates' militias, though nominally integrated into a regional militia network, continued to operate under the direct control of the magnates themselves:

> The officials ordered that the master households select and dispatch persons registered under their households [*zhuhu mingxia*] to serve in the militias. Those with the largest numbers of persons registered under their household were empowered to establish their own militia units and take personal charge of them under appointment as battalion commanders [*zhihuishi*] or other titles. At that time the registers of the "Sons and Brothers" of Xuzhou and Luzhou altogether listed 3,363 names.[11]

Despite the state's initiative in restructuring this militia network, the militias themselves essentially were a continuation of the pre-existing pattern of privately organized militias.

At the same time the court also began to conscript the warriors of the "cooked tribes" to defend their own territories against aggressive neighbors. In the early 1050s, nine tribal lineages inhabiting the valley of the Nanguang River, squeezed by rival groups to the south, asked permission to submit their territories to the emperor and be adopted as Song subjects. The court granted their wish and bestowed Han surnames on the leaders of the lineages, henceforth known as the "Nine Surnames." Local officials in Luzhou enrolled twenty-three hundred warriors of the Nine Surnames into "Righteous Armies" under the leadership of their own chieftains.[12]

Thus in order to avoid costly military campaigns in the southwest—at a time, not coincidentally, when the treasury was straining under the crushing burden of wars in the northwest—the Song opted for a decentralized militia system supported and controlled by local leaders, both Han and non-Han. In so doing the central government relinquished direct control over the potent military forces in the frontier region. The local magnates of Southern Lu continued to exercise their traditional prerogative of organizing their personal clients into militias, although each unit was required to serve tours of duty at the state-run garrisons.[13] Similarly, the native peoples of the Nine Surnames viewed the "Righteous Armies" primarily as a means of defending the interests of the allied lineages and only secondarily as a tool of Song policy. Neither the Song court nor local officials could exert effective restraint over the actions of garrison commanders and native chieftains.

The difficulty of formulating a coherent policy towards the native peoples was underscored by a series of incidents in 1051. A Han resident of Yujing had cheated a tribesman named Təulakmuəi from the haltered-and-bridled district of Changning and, when confronted by the victim, murdered him. Təulakmuəi's fellow tribesmen threatened reprisals, but the prefect of Luzhou stepped in and succeeded in negotiating a truce. No sooner had the prefect performed the blood oath to seal the truce, though, than the saltworks officials at Yujing imprisoned a group of natives from the village of Buañiəun on uncertain charges and executed eleven natives from Changning. The arrests and executions provoked a general revolt. A large force sent by the Zizhou military intendant quelled the uprising without much bloodshed, but the incident severely compromised the credibility of Song officials.[14]

Han diplomacy proved more effective several years later in 1057 when one-hundred fifty tribesmen, under the leadership of Təuγuan of Sanli village, raided Han settlements in Jiang'an. A tribesman from the rival village of Huangtukan, Təukai, informed the Han authorities of the activities of the bandits and led the Song soldiers to their lair. More than seventy men from Sanli were captured and summarily executed. The Song amply rewarded Təukai for his loyalty and in the following year appointed him as the "magistrate" of the district of Changning. Təukai traveled to Jiang'an for an audience with the visiting fiscal intendant and invited a Han "peace-keeping" force to enter his territory and flush out any remaining bandits. The Boji commander, Bo Jinfeng, subsequently embarked on such an expedition with the aid of guides supplied by Təukai.[15]

Although the Song tried to buy peace in the Yujing area by investing Təukai as a native ruler acceptable to both Han and non-Han, the tribesmen of Sanli chafed under the bonds of even indirect Song rule. In the summer of 1073, several hundred tribesmen from Sanli and eleven other villages seized several merchant ships bound for Yujing with cargoes of currency and silver. After an indecisive battle with the local militia, some two thousand tribesmen assembled at Sian and deputed a spokesman, Təuśiaet of Lakamuo village, to deliver the following petition before the Song authorities:

> The "ten prefectures and five fortified villages" of Yanzhou formerly submitted requisitions of firewood to the state saltworks at Yujing, which were used to boil the salt brine. Since the government has sold off the salt wells, we have lost our livelihood of selling firewood. In addition the government has ordered us to submit tax payments of rice in lieu of firewood. For these reasons our host assembled and seized the ships.[16]

This statement illuminates the potential impact of integration into the political economy of the Song state on the indigenous peoples. The livelihood of the natives of Southern Lu was based on the subsistence resources of the forested uplands, which favored the cultivation of taro and dryland grains as food staples. Not only was rice impractical in the upland areas, but wet-rice cultivation would have required substantial changes in the social organization of the native peoples. In recognition of these limitations the Song initially required that the tribesmen merely sell firewood and charcoal to the Yujing saltworks. Since, however, the state had embarked on a policy of divesting from the salt industry at Yujing, its need for firewood had diminished considerably. As the subsequent investigation made clear, the prefect of Luzhou, Li Man, had begun to demand unauthorized tax payments of rice instead, provoking the natives into acts of banditry.[17]

One official on the scene, Zhang Zijin, recalling the bloody conflicts of the 1040s and 1050s, urged Li Man to adopt a policy of appeasement towards the aroused tribesmen. Instead Li enlisted the aid of the chief of the Black Tribes, Piuomiuang Kaśio, to retaliate against Təuśiaet and his allies. The first Song force sent to fight the rebels, a detachment of three hundred soldiers, was completely annihilated in an ambush. The severity of this defeat led to another campaign of extermination in Southern Lu, while Li Man's controversial handling of tribal affairs sparked a heated debate at the court.[18]

Wang Anshi was appalled by Li Man's unauthorized alliance with Piuomiuang Kásio and in an audience with the emperor vigorously opposed Li's request to bestow the title of prince on Piuomiuang and another Black Tribes chief, Bukia. Wang feared that the powerful Black Tribes confederation would swallow up the "inner vassal" tribes, erasing the buffer zone of docile "cooked tribes" and perhaps posing a direct threat to Song rule in the area. Wang remained skeptical about charges accusing Li of malicious conduct, but the emperor was sufficiently concerned to order the judicial intendant of Kuizhou Route, Fan Bailu, to investigate the situation in Luzhou. At the same time the emperor appointed, at Wang's urging, the general Xiong Ben, who had considerable experience in dealing with the southwestern tribes, as imperial inspector (*chafangshi*) in charge of tribal affairs in Luzhou.[19]

The investigation of Li Man centered not on Li's involvement with the Black Tribes leaders but rather on the charge, delivered to the court in the form of a personal letter from Zhang Zijin to State Councilor Cai Ting, that Li had taken bribes from Han homesteaders in exchange for a memorial to the court requesting that Han subjects be allowed to acquire tribal lands through mortgage (*dianmai*). Deng Wan, now executive censor, found no evidence against Li, and his verdict was accepted by Wang and the majority of the other councilors. Wang clearly favored the idea of overturning the existing statutes prohibiting Han from purchasing lands belonging to the native peoples.[20] When asked by the emperor why the laws forbade such purchases, Wang replied:

> Originally it was thought that purchase of lands through mortgage would blur the boundary between Han and non-Han and that the competition for lands would inevitably lead to border disputes. Therefore these regulations were enacted. If one can convert tribesmen into Han subjects, however, then there is no cause for anxiety. If we are willing to spend several ten thousand *guan* of state funds to buy lands along the frontier at Yujing and bring Han households to live there as state tenants, there will not be any further problems with the tribal peoples of Yujing.

The emperor agreed and abolished the proscriptions against mortgage of tribal lands. This sudden departure from the longstanding policy of strict territorial segregation received support from Xiong Ben, who reported that the tribesmen had not been coerced into selling their lands but simply wished to avoid the complicated procedures of registering deeds and transactions with the local authorities. The emperor approved Xiong's recommendation to acknowledge as legally binding land purchases made prior to the emperor's nullification of the existing statutes as long as deeds were drawn up and submitted to the local authorities and the lands were assessed for taxation.[21]

The emperor's approval of Li Man's request to permit Han to acquire tribal lands did not blunt his concern about possible improprieties on Li's part. Indeed, when Fan Bailu presented his findings to the court several months later, the emperor was impressed by the incontrovertible evidence of bribery despite attempts by officials at various levels of the censorate administration to protect Li. Li was cashiered, but not before the emperor lectured the court on the deceit and chicanery of officials trying to cover up Li's malfeasance. Wang Anshi, no friend of the Sichuanese, likewise railed angrily against the perversion of the institution of the censorate.[22]

Ironically, not only did the Song court adopt Li's proposal on mortgaging tribal lands, but Wang Anshi, upon Xiong Ben's recommendation, reversed his opinion on the question of bringing the Black Tribes within the sphere of "inner vassals." Xiong argued that if the Song strictly delimited the territories of the Black Tribes in a treaty acknowledging them as haltered-and-bridled peoples, their chieftains would be less likely to annex neighboring areas and build a strong challenge to Song authority. In the summer of 1074 the Song bestowed the title of prince on Piuomiuang Kaśio and Bukia. Another Black Tribes chief, Antsi, had arrogated to himself the title of demon master formerly held by Bukia, who apparently was unsuccessful in reasserting his patrimonial claim. The Song court intended to acknowledge Antsi as Demon Master of the Luo Clan, but Antsi died before his formal investiture and the title passed to his son Ṣats'iuo Lukluo. Xiong Ben envisioned that upon the twin pillars of Piuomiuang Kaśio and Ṣats'iuo Lukluo the Song would erect an enduring structure of diplomatic communication and accommodation.[23]

The immediate problem, though, was to suppress the uprising of the Sanli tribesmen. Xiong secretly laid a trap, despite the emperor's explicit disapproval, to ensnare the leaders of the insurgents. Under the pretext of preliminary negotiations to purchase lands from the tribal peoples, Xiong's lieutenant, Cheng Zhiyuan, summoned together the chieftains who had petitioned against Li's unilateral revision of their tribute obligations. According to Cheng's account, which the emperor regarded with some suspicion, when he interrogated Təuśiaet and the rest about the disappearance of a Han officer, the tribesmen seized their weapons—"fearing the punishment justified by the enormity of their crime," Cheng related—and attacked the Han officials. Cheng evidently expected this outcome and had positioned his troops to descend instantly on the assembled chieftains. Over ninety tribesmen were killed in the ambush. Cheng sent Təuśiaet in shackles to Luzhou to await a "lingering death" at the hands of the Song executioners, while the heads of the dead tribesmen were impaled on spears above the walls of the city.[24]

In the meantime Xiong had mobilized five thousand army regulars and militiamen. Capitalizing on the disorder among the suddenly leaderless tribes, his army swiftly marched up the Yu River valley, seizing forty-six villages with barely a struggle. The villagers "greeted him on their knees, offering their bronze drums"—the universal symbol of authority among the native peoples of the southwest. The Song soldiers began construction of forts at Xiaoqikou and West Ningyuan, erected watchtowers throughout the valley, and built roads and bridges. Only one village, Kaiem, persisted in its resistance to Xiong's army. With the aid of the "Nineteen Surnames," a rival tribal confederation, and

Piuomiuang Kaśio, Xiong pursued the Kaiem deep into the forest and ultimately subdued them. In Kaiem as well as the rest of the conquered villages, the inhabitants were registered as taxable subjects of the Song state and their lands, valuable possessions, and fine horses duly entered into the account books of Luzhou's master registrar.[25]

Xiong Ben's dramatic sweep through the Yu and Sian River valleys pushed the frontier back, according to Xiong's reckoning, "two hundred forty *li*," bringing a sizable area under direct Song control. The enhanced military and political domination of the Song soon led to further, albeit "negotiated," aggrandizement. A brief passage in the *Veritable Records* states simply that in the winter of 1075–1076 the tribal peoples of Changning and nine other haltered-and-bridled districts submitted their lands and salt wells as tribute to the Song emperor and were placed under the authority of the state salt bureau at Yujing.[26] At the same time the Song state began to sponsor settlement of this territory by Han pioneers brought in to clear the forest and cultivate the newly opened lands.[27]

FROM EXPLOITATION TO EXPROPRIATION

The shift towards a more aggressive and expansionist frontier policy had been building since Wang Anshi's inauguration as prime minister in 1069. Wang's grandiose vision of dynastic renewal was predicated on the prospect of harvesting new revenues through state control of frontier trade, colonization of frontier lands, and exploitation of the mines and forests of the frontier. He ardently championed proposals to take the offensive against the Tanguts in the northwest and seize control over the lucrative trade routes reaching westward to the fabulous mercantile capitals of central Asia. To divert the profits of trade away from the merchant cartels and into military expansion and agricultural reclamation, Wang's administration established the first Bureaux for Markets and Exchange in the northwestern frontier.[28] Armed with the emperor's full confidence, Wang pressed for a broader mandate for frontier expansion that would encompass Sichuan, Hunan, and Guangxi as well as the northwest. The case of Hunan provides striking parallels to the history of frontier expansion in Sichuan. It was in Hunan that Wang Anshi and his coterie first developed the policies, institutions, and personnel which later would be transplanted to Southern Lu and adjacent areas. In both regions, the primary objective of frontier expansion was to gain control of the virgin lands and untapped resources of the tribal territories.

Wang Anshi's pursuit of these intertwined policies of economic intervention and frontier expansion had produced heated controversy over frontier policies in Hunan just a year before the Li Man case erupted in Luzhou. At the inception of the Song dynasty, the peoples of the "streams and grottoes" occupied roughly half of the modern province of Hunan: Miao of the Peng lineages dominated the lower course of the Yuan River, while various Klao and Yao/Miao groups shared its upper reaches; the Meishandong Yao inhabited the northern portion of the Snowpeak Mountains, primarily to the east of the Zi River; other Yao, gradually pushed out of the lowlands by Han settlers, retreated into the Nanling ranges separating Hunan from the southern littoral of Guangdong and Guangxi. As in Sichuan, the Song initially relinquished native territories once claimed by the Tang and refrained from all but the most perfunctory contacts with native polities. But internecine conflict among the native chieftains provided an opportunity for conquest and expansion into the tribal pale.[29]

The first serious native uprising in the Yuan valley occurred in 1055–1057, when rival claimants for leadership of the Peng confederation involved Song officials and eventually Song troops in their struggle for power. The court's discovery that local officials had surreptitiously lent assistance to a conspiracy to overthrow the chief, Peng Shixi, smoothed the way for a reconciliation between the Song and Peng Shixi. But another crisis threatened to erupt into renewed warfare in 1070 when Peng Shixi was murdered by one of his sons, who in turn was put to death by another son, Peng Shiyan.[30]

In central Hunan the Meishandong Yao expressed no interest in an accommodating relationship with the Song. From the inception of the dynasty the Meishan brazenly plundered Han commerce between the Xiang River valley and the upper course of the Zi River. In 977 the court forbade all intercourse with the Meishan or settlement of their territories.[31] An uprising by the Meishan in the early 1060s prompted Zhang Jie, magistrate of Yiyang county and a native of nearby Dingzhou, to begin to open the Meishan territory to Han settlers. Fan Ziqi, appointed assistant fiscal intendant of Hunan in late 1070, also advocated bringing the Meishan under the direct administration of the Song bureaucracy; but his petitions at first elicited little attention.[32]

At the same time, the court of Emperor Shenzong was also beseiged with proposals to extend imperial rule over the Yuan valley. The judicial intendant of Hubei declaimed against the tyranny of the chieftains of the upper Yuan valley and asserted that the native peoples longed for the magnanimous government of the Song monarch. Most persuasive of all was a letter addressed to the court in 1071 by Zhang Qiao, an inhabitant of Chenzhou, and Li Zi, an exile residing there. Zhang and Li outlined the weaknesses of the native polities and the opportunities for the Song to establish its authority over the entire Yuan valley. The authors of the letter related that competition over territory among Klao tribes of the upper Yuan valley had erupted into a full-scale blood-feud. A number of beleagured chieftains were anxious to secure protection from the Song. Zhang and Li concluded their letter by arguing that Peng Shiyan, a weak and timid leader despite his act of vengeance against his parricidal brother, was unable to retain mastery over the far-flung and deeply divided Peng confederation. He too sought Song aid to bolster his own precarious position.[33]

Wang Anshi capitalized on this stream of reports from the Hunan frontier to set in motion a strategy for gaining the submission of the native peoples. In 1072 a new corps of officials was dispatched to the region to carry out the initiatives proposed by Zhang Qiao and Li Zi and enthusiastically endorsed by Wang Anshi. Zhang Dun, an early appointee to the Finance Planning Commission (*zhizhi sansi tiaolisi*) created by Wang in 1069 to codify his fiscal reforms, was made Imperial Inspector of Agriculture, Water Control, and Ever-Normal Granaries in Hubei Route. Other state councilors—notably the elder statesmen Wen Yanbo, who had headed the Court of Military Affairs since 1064— bitterly contested Wang's choice of Zhang Dun and his appointment to an ad-hoc office that reported directly to Wang. Wen's faction countered by entrusting responsibility for negotiations not to Zhang but to Cai Yu, the Hunan fiscal intendant and son of Cai Ting, a state councilor and opponent of Wang's expansionary policies.[34]

While Cai Yu wrote lengthy epistles cautioning the court against any hasty decisions in dealing with the Meishan Yao, Zhang Dun, at his headquarters in Chenzhou, pursued his tacit mandate to win their capitulation. In January of 1073 Zhang announced an accord with the Meishan, who agreed to subordinate their territory to the regular Song field administration and become subjects of the Song emperor. Later in 1073 Zhang reported that 4,809 native households and 260,436 *mu* of cultivated lands belonging to the Meishan had been added to the imperial realm, and consequently to the revenue base of the empire.[35] By January of 1074 the Song generals, through intimidation or conquest, had gained mastery of the territories of dozens of tribes in the upper Yuan valley. In addition, Peng Shiyan finally succumbed to the Song's entreaties and agreed to recognize Song suzerainty. Zhang Dun, his work completed, was recalled to the court to assume new responsibilities as finance commissioner.[36]

Ministers at the court, excepting hostile critics of frontier expansion, rarely spoke directly about the economic value of the newly acquired territories in Hunan, but it seems reasonable to infer that they expected to reap a fiscal bonanza by enlarging the taxable population and resources of the empire. When Zhang Qiao and Li Zi wrote to the court in 1071, they extolled the productive assets of the region: "The lands of the [native tribes] produce cinnabar, mercury, gold, hemp cloth, and yellow wax, and encompass several thousand *qing* of fertile cultivated fields."[37] In 1073, upon receiving Zhang Dun's confirmation of the acquisition of the territories of the Meishan and the Yuan valley, Wang Anshi lauded the virtue of an emperor who now reigned over an empire blessed with an unprecedented wealth of population.[38] For Confucianists imbued with the idea that human labor was the basic productive force in society, any augmentation of the population automatically increased the wealth of the nation.

Wang Anshi, driven by his unwavering conviction that exploitation of economic resources must be rationalized under state management, regarded the presumed riches of the "streams and grottoes" as fuel for the engines of economic growth. The fiscal innovations of the New Laws, such as the program of state loans to farmers to improve the productivity of their holdings and the commutation of labor service into a tax paid in coin, drastically increased the demand for cash and pressures on existing supplies. In a long critique of the New Laws written in 1074, Sima Guang fulminated against Wang's fiscal program, charging that it caused deflation and destitution: "Money becomes increasingly dear while the value of goods declines; although this is a year of dearth, the people suffer the double hardship [of meager harvests and low prices]."[39] Wang responded by adopting measures to stimulate mining production and thereby increase the supply of currency. Wang clearly hoped that aggressive exploitation of the gold, copper, silver, lead, and tin mines of Hunan (and, as we shall see, iron mines in southern Sichuan) would alleviate the chronic problem of "currency famines" (*qianhuang*) and help to finance his fiscal innovations.[40]

Equally dismaying, in the eyes of Wang Anshi's opponents, was the circumvention of regular channels of bureaucratic communication by Wang and his hand-picked officials in the field. Perhaps no aspect of the New Laws alarmed the conservative establishment more than Wang's sweeping indictment of the civil service and its methods of recruitment and operation. Drawing on the heritage of a professional corps of experts in the Song finance administration,[41] Wang envisioned a reorganization of the Song bureaucracy into autonomous task-oriented agencies empowered to extend state control over a wide range of economic activities. Paul J. Smith characterizes Wang's formula for bureaucratic appointment as one of "selecting men for specific offices on the basis of their technical qualifications rather than formal credentials, endowing them with broad and undefined functional authority, and retaining them in office long enough to accomplish their goals."[42] Wang sought to apply these principles in recruiting officials for frontier administration as well as for fiscal agencies.

Like Xiong Ben in Southern Lu, Zhang Dun received an appointment as an imperial inspector, freeing him from oversight by the route intendants and allowing him to correspond directly with the court. The office of imperial inspector was a recent innovation, begun in 1070 as a means of obtaining prompt information on harvest conditions; but Wang Anshi utilized it to carry out his policies in remote frontier areas where communication through normal bureaucratic procedures was interminably slow.[43] The debate over the respective roles of Zhang Dun and Cai

Yu reflected a contest over administrative license as much as policy. After the submission of the Meishan Yao, Wang insisted that Cai Yu's dilatory approach and calumnious criticism of Zhang disqualified him from sharing in the credit, and the emperor agreed.[44] Henceforth Wang and his successors were able to gain approval for departures from established protocol in their pursuit of imperial expansion.

The career of Xiong Ben (1026–1091) also typified the mercurial rise of ambitious but low-ranking officials to influential policymaking positions through Wang Anshi's patronage. When Emperor Shenzong inherited his father's mantle in 1068, Xiong, then foundering in a humdrum post at the Board of Punishments after more than twenty years in the civil service, strongly supported Wang's program for radical institutional reform. In 1069, Xiong was appointed to one of the newly created granary intendancies (the vanguard of Wang's fiscal reforms) and subsequently to the Secretariat Planning Commission, an agency founded by Wang to draw up plans for reorganizing the bureaucracy.[45] Xiong was serving in the finance branch of the commission at the time of his appointment as imperial inspector in Sichuan. Xiong's unequivocal successes in Southern Lu won him the complete confidence of both Wang and the emperor, who readily assented to all of Xiong's recommendations on frontier policy. The emperor even granted Xiong the privilege of choosing Li Man's successor as prefect of Luzhou, commenting that "those [in the Board of Civil Office] who would otherwise make the selection cannot compare with Xiong."[46] Until the reformers fell from power, Xiong served in a succession of crucial posts in frontier affairs and fiscal administration.[47]

The Song court's sanction of Xiong Ben's policies and actions committed it irrevocably to a policy of frontier expansion in Southern Lu. Han settlements, and especially the salt industry at Yujing and the transport route between Yujing and Jiang'an, had proven too vulnerable to depredations by hostile tribes. Only by expelling, or assimilating, the native peoples and inducing Han homesteaders to settle in the Yu valley could the Song secure the economic resources of the area. At the same time, the court anticipated that social stability could be achieved by introducing a Han agrarian regime and property relations in place of the more nebulous concepts of territory inspired by the social and economic

life of shifting cultivators. Military security was to be strengthened by
increasing the number of garrisons in Jiang'an county from two to five,
while the old security agreements with the now defunct haltered-and-
bridled territories were jettisoned in favor of new accords reached with
the leaders of the Black Tribes, clearly the ascendant political force
among the non-Han peoples. Yet the new frontier policies themselves
introduced new tensions, in the form of the enhanced power of Han
military leaders and the Black Tribes chiefs, that threatened the arrangement from the outset. Only a couple years would pass before a far
greater wave of violence and destruction racked Southern Lu.

FIVE

Political Hegemony in the Frontier Zone

Despite the rise and fall of dynasties and the migrations of the native peoples, prior to the Song the Southern Lu frontier zone had proven remarkably stable. For centuries the Yangzi River marked the boundary of effective Han sovereignty. The irruption of Song military power and political authority into native-populated areas radically reshaped the political context of Han frontier settlement. The Song began to annex native territories—to the extent that its organizational and technological capabilities made annexation feasible—as simple accretions to the existing field administration of the empire. Although the Song possessed a vastly more sophisticated system of political organization and control, its technological superiority over the native polities was not nearly so overwhelming. The productive techniques of Han settlers, like those of the native peoples, were impeded by ecological constraints which inhibited intensive agricultural exploitation. Without a revolution in the technology of production—or destruction—the Song resorted to manipulating levers of social control to impose its political hegemony. As the Song leaders soon learned to their dismay, the costs of achieving hegemony threatened to deplete the state's resources at an astonishing rate. Unlike the Spanish conquistadors in the New World, the Song could not take advantage of an existing state structure among their new subjects but had to institute bureaucratic rule over myriad autonomous societies.[1]

The shift from a policy of exploiting frontier resources to one of expropriating them brought about changes within the internal political structure of the native societies. Even before the phase of expansion that began in the 1070s, conflict among native groups had led isolated Klao villages and lineages to ally. Habits of independence, however, made cohesion difficult to maintain; and the fragile unity of these new Klao polities could not withstand the onslaught of the Song's expansionary initiatives. Once native territories were absorbed into the Song domain, Klao alliances disintegrated. Loss of political autonomy increased the dependence of the Klao on the dominant Han society and hastened the pace of assimilation.

Paradoxically, Song frontier expansion also contributed to the political ascendancy of the transfrontier chiefdoms of the Black Tribes of the Luo Clan in western Guizhou and the Bozhou Yang, a large haltered-and-bridled confederation in central Guizhou. These societies had always maintained a greater degree of political cohesion than the Klao; but the Song incursions into Southern Lu enhanced the power of the paramount chiefs, who handled diplomatic relations with the Song and mobilized resources for warfare. The interaction between the Song and these chiefdoms stimulated greater diversity within the political economy of the latter. The formation of more centralized political institutions among the Black Tribes and the Bozhou Yang favored the augmentation of their territories and populations. The powerful chiefdoms that would vex the Ming rulers originated in policies cultivated by the Song from the 1070s onward.

WARS OF CONQUEST, 1078–1082

Five years of turbulence that began in 1078 and claimed thousands of lives can be traced back to a street quarrel over a meal of fish and bamboo shoots. The argument between a Han inhabitant of Naqi named Su Sanqi and a tribesman named Miukdəki, from Laγokiek, led to blows; and Su killed Miukdəki. Miukdəki's fellow villagers, acting in accordance with their agreement with the Song, filed charges with the garrison commander at Naqi and also with the magistrate of Jiang'an; but none of the Song officials was willing to take any action on their suit. The customary agreement between the Han and the haltered-and-bridled tribes stipulated that a Han found guilty of murdering a tribesman would be condemned to death. In addition the Song officials would be obliged to redeem the crime with "blood money" to be paid to the victim's village. When it became clear that in this case the officials would do nothing, the tribesmen took justice into their own hands, raiding, looting, and burning Han settlements. The ferocity of their attacks convinced the garrison commander at Naqi to abandon the fort and seek refuge across the river.

The prefect at Luzhou, Ren Ji, the first civil official to serve in that office during the eleventh century, advocated appeasing the Layuokiek and negotiating a new truce. He was overruled by the assistant fiscal intendant, Cheng Zhicai, whose brother Cheng Zhiyuan had conducted the massacre of the Sanli leaders several years earlier. Cheng convinced the court, at that time already embroiled in several frontier wars, to mobilize a massive army of Shaanxi veterans to suppress the Layuokiek. The decision to use overwhelming force to crush a minor uprising reflected the desire to enforce, and to justify, the new frontier policies laid down by Wang Anshi and Xiong Ben a scant five years before. The judicial intendant, Mu Xun, reported that Han immigrants only recently settled in Southern Lu had begun to flee from the area because of Layuokiek reprisals. Mu also insinuated that if the Song hesitated to suppress this uprising, the Black Tribes would gain an opportunity to inflame the native peoples' hatred of the Han and challenge Song authority in the area. The military intendant, Wang Guangzu, likewise recommended dispatching Shaanxi troops to Southern Lu. Measured against the rare unanimity of opinion among the route's triad of intendants, Ren Ji's pleas for a more conciliatory approach weighed little.[2]

Ren Ji defended a negotiated resolution to the conflict on the grounds that the Layuokiek were "cooked tribesmen" with a legitimate grievance and not a "raw tribe" violating the territorial sovereignty of the Song. Ren drew a conclusion opposite to Mu Xun's: Suppression would drive "cooked tribes" like the Layuokiek into the arms of the Black Tribes, creating unified opposition to Han rule where no unity had existed before. In desperation Ren submitted a motion of censure against Cheng Zhicai, appending a long list of abuses. Cheng retaliated with an indictment blaming the uprising on Ren's incompetence. Despite support from Xiong Ben, who had initially sponsored Ren Ji for the Luzhou post and endorsed Ren's reappointments in 1076 and 1078, the court relieved Ren of his duties and imprisoned him pending an investigation. Cheng was retained in his office, which involved supervising logistical support for the expeditionary army.[3]

The acrimonious confrontation between Ren Ji and Cheng Zhicai would seem to be an unlikely dispute. Both were Sichuanese, fellow countrymen from Meishan county, which at just this time was gaining national prominence as the birthplace of many leading scholars and statesmen. Cheng's cousin and Meishan's most famous son, Su Shi, also was a close friend of Ren Ji and composed a commiserating poem which he sent to Ren in prison.[4] Their enmity might have had hidden roots in family quarrels; eminent families from the same locality do not always share identical interests. Yet the division between Ren Ji and Cheng Zhicai paralleled a divergence of opinion among the Sichuanese elite on the issue of the native problem. Ren, representative of the professional bureaucrats, espoused a policy of paternalistic magnanimity towards "the emperor's children." Cheng's insistence on swift and severe punishment of "the children of wolves," on the other hand, was heartily endorsed by the local magnates, keen to add new conquests to their domains. Cheng's policy triumphed, but the bitter clash ruined the careers of both men. Ren died in prison in the spring of 1080, before the censorate completed its investigation. In December of 1082 the court debarred Cheng from the civil service for making false accusations about Ren's conduct in office.[5]

In 1078, as the summer drew to a close, the court ordered Han Cunbao, a general with long experience on the northwestern frontier, to march to Luzhou with his army of five thousand steppe footsoldiers and one thousand cavalry. Setting out from Naqi in October, Han's army met little opposition. The Layuokiek belonged to a confederation of fifty-six Klao villages known as the Eight Mǝu Surnames (Bamuxing), distributed throughout the valley of the lower Na River. Within two months, fifty-one of the villages had capitulated, most without a struggle. Inhabitants of the remaining five fled into the forest rather than submit. The court directed Han to pursue the renegades and enlist the aid of the Black Tribes in tracking them down. The Song offered a reward of twenty bolts of silk for each adult, male head that the Black Tribes presented to Han.[6] While Han's soldiers searched for the remnants of the insurgents, Cheng Zhicai laid the foundations of a new Han order. Cheng's clerks registered the thousand-odd inhabitants of the vanquished villages under the fiscal categories of headmen, able-bodied adults, and elderly or children, and assessed their cultivated lands for taxation. Henceforth the new Song subjects were required to pay the twice-a-year land tax and the labor service commutation levy, but at lower rates than their Han neighbors. The differential tax schedule was intended to offset the two-fold obligations, to both the Song state and to the tribal chieftain, borne by "double-fealty tribesmen" (*liangshuyi*).

Cheng also requested that the Song build a garrison on the former site of Layuokiek, a strategic point that marked the upper limit of the navigable course of the Na River. Cheng recognized that a Song garrison at Layuokiek had considerable strategic value because it could choke off the advance of the Black Tribes from the south. The Black Tribes and the Eight Surnames were enemies of long standing. The Black Tribes had refused to trade with the Han at Naqi Garrison because they could reach Naqi only by passing through the river's narrow gorges, bristling with the Eight Surnames' warriors. Thus the Black Tribes stood to gain an important outlet for trade in the aftermath of a Song conquest of the Layuokiek territory. Unsurprisingly, a Black Tribes chieftain, K'iatdiei, who had succeeded his father Piuomiuang Kaśio after the latter's death in early 1078, was only too willing to collaborate with the Song in the suppression of the Eight Surnames. The Song officials remained wary of embracing K'iatdiei too tightly. Rather than allow K'iatdiei's warriors to accompany the Song army, Han Cunbao merely ordered them to secure their own territory and round up any of the Layuokiek who took refuge there.[7]

Once the Layuokiek were captured or dispersed and Han's army withdrew, K'iatdiei seized the opportunity to inflict a blow against his other enemies among the indigenous Klao. Given safe passage by his allies in the Yu River valley, K'iatdiei launched attacks on the confederations of the Seven Surnames and the Nineteen Surnames in the valley of the Nanguang River. The defeated villagers were forced to pay homage and tribute of slaves and livestock to the triumphant K'iatdiei.

While returning to his own territory, K'iatdiei took a detour that brought his army to the county seat of Jiang'an, where the tribesmen encamped outside the town. K'iatdiei sent his lieutenant Iɪtmau to demand that the magistrate fulfill the promise made by his superiors to reward the Black Tribes for their cooperation in subduing the Eight Surnames. The frightened magistrate and townfolk hurriedly erected makeshift barricades against the expected attack; but after three days, K'iatdiei quietly departed. He left behind Iɪtmau and another lieutenant, a Song army deserter known by his tribal name of Laiɪt, to present gifts to the magistrate. The latter refused to receive the tribesmen, who then left to rejoin K'iatdiei. A few miles beyond Jiang'an, at the village of Iɪilau, rival tribesmen ambushed Iɪtmau's party and Iɪtmau himself was killed. Laiɪt, or Yang Jie as the Han knew him, fled back to Jiang'an, where the magistrate promptly arrested and imprisoned him. Laiɪt tried to bribe the Song officials to gain his freedom but was led to the executioner's block nonetheless, to serve as an admonitory example of the risks of colluding with the native peoples.[8]

K'iatdiei was indifferent to the fate of Laiɪt but vowed revenge against the villagers of Iɪilau. Ren Ji's replacement as prefect of Luzhou, Qiao Xu, adopted his predecessor's conciliatory posture and made repeated entreaties asking K'iatdiei to agree to a truce. Finally K'iatdiei accepted Qiao's offer. In the spring of 1080, he brought his host of warriors to Naqi and sent forth his brother Adzi to perform the ritual oath-swearing with Qiao Xu. Upon leaving Naqi, however, K'iatdiei attacked and occupied the village of Lakamiəu, claiming that the village's inhabitants owed him tribute. The garrison commander at Naqi, a local magnate named Ren Guangxiu, immediately hastened to Jiang'an to inform the magistrate that K'iatdiei had blatantly violated the oath consummated only days before and assaulted a village within the imperial domain. Ren claimed that Lakamiəu was one of the villages vanquished by Xiong Ben and subordinated to direct Han rule in 1074. A later investigation revealed that although the village had begun to submit taxes in 1077, it was not liable for the twice-a-year tax and properly belonged to the haltered-and-bridled district of Yanzhou, which by this time had become a tributary of the Black Tribes, rather than the Song domain. Ren, a native of Jiang'an, certainly must have known the village's real status; but the court accepted his word and dispatched the battalion of imperial guards at Jiang'an, under General Wang Xuan, to retake Lakamiəu.

K'iatdiei protested that the Lakamiəu matter had nothing to do with the Song, but Ren Guangxiu goaded Wang Xuan into making a reckless assault against K'iatdiei's warriors. The tribesmen routed the Song army, killing eight hundred Song soldiers, including Wang Xuan and all his officers—with the sole exception of Ren Guangxiu, who had judiciously fled.[9] The crushing defeat of Wang's army stirred the chagrinned court to mount a massive expeditionary force to suppress K'iatdiei. The emperor dismissed all of the officials who had been involved in negotiations with K'iatdiei and resolved to end the Black Tribes menace to Southern Lu once and for all. Once again Han Cunbao was called upon and charged with "penetrating deeply into the tribal realm and eradicating the bandits." The court also broke with precedent by inviting the "double-fealty tribes" to accompany the Han army on the campaign. On November 8, 1080, Han's army of 32,309 soldiers, 1,907 horses, and over thirty thousand bearers departed from Jiang'an and struck out overland towards K'iatdiei's lair.[10]

Han's soldiers, accustomed to the treeless plateaux of the loess region, proceeded slowly through the tangled brush and canebrake of the semi-tropical forest. Blind in the jungle, Han's troops were susceptible to bushwhacking raids. Han Cunbao himself became apprehensive and indecisive. Ren Guangxiu, who met and accompanied Han during his march to Luzhou, wormed his way into Han's confidence and became his tactical advisor. Early in the campaign Ren directed Han to attack Tiɛibuongpau, a group of villages clustered on a small, fertile basin near the Singa River. Ren, perhaps motivated by a personal grudge, charged that the tribesmen there had given clandestine aid to K'iatdiei. Han naively accepted Ren's counsel and sent his main force to attack the astonished and defenseless natives. The Song soldiers slaughtered over eleven hundred people. Departing from Tiɛibuongpau, Han's army ascended into the wilderness known in more recent times as the Endless Canebrake (Wanlijing). Han soon decided that his army was too vulnerable and retreated to the safer ground of Tiɛibuonggiang, above the Sian River. From there Han was content to send small expeditions to raid individual villages. On occasion the Song razed the wrong villages and swelled K'iatdiei's ranks with vengeful refugees.

K'iatdiei had little taste for pursuing the quarrel with the Song and, through the Demon Master Ṣats'iuo Lukluo, offered to submit to a truce. Han had received frequent directives from the court, impatient with his lack of progress after two months, to plunge forward with the campaign of extermination; but he was inclined to accept K'iatdiei's offer and withdraw as quickly as possible. K'iatdiei's emissary Ṣadziĩ Angie presented a letter of surrender and performed the ritual of the blood oath before Han's tent, whereupon Han ordered his soldiers to break camp and return to Jiang'an. That same day a group of warriors from Yanzhou, revenging an unwarranted attack on their village, raided Han's supply column and seized over a thousand *dan* of rice. On the return march to Jiang'an the Song army was ambushed by another band of natives led by Təukaniei, a survivor from Tiɛibuongpau seeking revenge for Han's butchery. The junior officers pressed Han to retaliate and renew the campaign of suppression; but Han ignored their protests and proceeded with the withdrawal, arriving at Jiang'an on January 16, 1081.[11]

The vehemence of the emperor's reaction to Han's retreat stunned the court, to say nothing of Han himself. Angered and humiliated by Han's timorous conclusion of the campaign, the emperor ordered the Luzhou officials to imprison him pending the arrival of a censor to try him for cowardice. That Han would be found guilty was a foregone conclusion. On September 15 he was beheaded in the marketplace at Luzhou. Reportedly, the emperor meted out this extraordinary punishment with the intent of stiffening the backbones of the generals then engaged in a protracted and inconclusive war with the Annamite kingdom. Undoubtedly the significance of Han's execution was not lost on his successor, Lin Guang, another Shaanxi general dispatched to Luzhou to complete his unfulfilled mission.[12]

Lin Guang's resumption of the aborted campaign against K'iatdiei was preceded by overtures to gain the support of K'iatdiei's potential rivals among the native leaders. The key figures wooed by the Song were Ṣats'iuo Lukluo, the Demon Master of the Luo Clan, and Yang Guangzhen, patriarch of the Bozhou Yang. Yang's clan, based well beyond the Song frontier in the Dalou Shan, ranked among the most powerful ruling groups in the southwest; but its isolation had hindered relations with the Song. The Yang resented K'iatdiei's growing power and eagerly sought an alliance with the Song against him. In April of 1081 Yang Guangzhen presented the head of Angau, "K'iatdiei's most trusted henchman," to the Song officials as a profession of his loyalty. Yang also offered to escort Song soldiers through his territory to attack K'iatdiei from the east. The emperor in particular was elated by this opportunity to reverse the fortunes of war and readily assented to the proposed alliance. He dispatched General Peng Sun to the frontier town of Nanping, founded six years before, to meet the Song's new-found ally.[13]

Peng Sun expressed considerable skepticism about Yang's trustworthiness after the two met at Nanping, but the court ignored his misgivings and told him to proceed with plans for the offensive. The prefect at Nanping, Wei Congge, succeeded in bringing together Yang Guangzhen, Ṣats'iuo Lukluo, and the chieftains of the Klao tribes of the Tuotśiang and the Lakmau, all of whom swore allegiance to the Song and pledged to hunt down K'iatdiei and bring back his head. Peng Sun's troops never left Nanping, however, because of the difficulty of maintaining supply lines through a territory into which no Song official had ever ventured.[14]

Lin Guang from his base in Luzhou proceeded slowly and deliberately in his pursuit of K'iatdiei, taking time to clear the forest and build a series of garrisons to facilitate the passage of supply caravans. By the end of December, 1081, Lin's troops had consolidated their control over the haltered-and-bridled territories and turned southward towards K'iatdiei's strongholds in the Wumeng Shan. The winter of 1081–1082 was freakishly cold in the mountains of the Wumeng ranges. The expedition had intentionally awaited the onset of winter to escape the scourge of summer's "mist-borne pestilence and perpetual rains" only to encounter heavy snows.[15] Many soldiers lost fingers or toes from frostbite, while others succumbed to cold, disease, and hunger. Once, the Song army almost captured K'iatdiei, who under the pretext of surrendering himself tried to lead the army into an ambush. The Song soldiers overwhelmed the tribesmen but seized the wrong leader, whose corpse, mutilated by soldiers fighting over it to claim the emperor's lavish reward, turned out to be not K'iatdiei but his brother, Adzi.

Ever mindful of Han Cunbao's failure, and fate, Lin continued his relentless pursuit through "the land of death," to quote one of his aides, where the mountains "pierce the heavens like upright daggers and swords." On February 4, 1082, Lin's soldiers crossed the Mount Beyond the Crow's Reach (Yafeibudao Shan; the crow was renowned for its ability to fly to places inaccessible to other creatures) and three days later reached K'iatdiei's home village. They found only "empty thatch huts, large and small, about a hundred rooms altogether." With no hope of tracking down K'iatdiei in the mountains, Lin Guang reluctantly ordered his army to return to Luzhou, fully expecting to share in Han Cunbao's fate. However, the emperor's special envoy produced a secret directive that granted Lin permission to withdraw provided that "the bandits' lairs have been flushed out" and that supply lines could no longer be maintained. K'iatdiei was never found, though from time to time rumors of his death reached the ears of the Song officials at Luzhou. In 1087 K'iatdiei's son Akiəi announced his father's death.[16]

Victory over K'iatdiei exacted a heavy toll of lives and fiscal resources. Feeding the soldiers in the Wumeng Shan became an insurmountable problem, and many more soldiers died from starvation than from wounds inflicted in battle. The soldiers received a daily allowance of two *sheng* (1 ⅓ liters) of rice per day; but the bearers—civilians from Luzhou and neighboring prefectures fulfilling their labor duty or hired laborers from all over Sichuan—received no rations and were left to shift for themselves. Many died from exhaustion and hunger, or deserted. Sima Guang wrote that over forty thousand of the Song army and its supernumerary retinue perished during this campaign, and six or seven thousand more died when a plague swept through the army camp at Luzhou upon the soldiers' return. These figures seem improbably high; but if accurate, the number of men lost totaled half of Lin Guang's army of ninety-three thousand troops and bearers. Another source records that the figure of forty thousand represented the death toll for the whole period from 1078 to 1082.[17] The fiscal burden also weighed heavily upon the population of Sichuan. The one million *guan* expended on this expedition, equivalent to 1.5 percent of the total annual income of the Song state, was taken almost entirely from the revenues of the Sichuan fiscal administration.[18] Such were the human and social costs of acquiring, as critics put it, "a land barren of even a single ear of grain."

IMPLANTING THE NEW ORDER, 1082–1121

The war of suppression against K'iatdiei and the subsequent annexation of the territories of the "cooked tribes" of Southern Lu left the Song state with formidable administrative problems. With Xiong Ben's strategic alliance between the Song and the Black Tribes now in tatters, the court sought to restore stability by fashioning a new set of alliances. The Song assiduously cultivated the loyalty of Ṣats'iuo Lukluo and Yang Guangzhen, acknowledging their rule over fragments of K'iatdiei's confederation in return for help in tracking down K'iatdiei himself.[19] Yet at the same time the court was becoming chary of relying on ambitious and powerful tribal leaders to ensure the safety of Han subjects. The turmoil and tremendous costs, in lives and expenditures, of the preceding decade of warfare convinced the court that the state itself had to assume the burden of occupying and defending the vast area now in its possession.

Anticipating that the Southern Lu region would require a strong military presence for years to come, the court created a special military zone comprising Luzhou, Xuzhou, and the newly acquired territories. A new military office, the Pacification Intendancy for the Southern Lu Frontier (*Lunan yanbian anfushi*), superseded Luzhou's prefect. The pacification intendant served as both the civil authority in Luzhou and the military intendant of Zizhou and Kuizhou Routes. Departing from precedent, the court accorded the pacification intendant sole authority over border affairs, thus dispensing with the usual interlocking decision-making structure of route-level government. The first incumbent, Wang Guangzu, a veteran of the Xiong Ben, Han Cunbao, and Lin Guang campaigns, lived up to the expectations of critics of this bureaucratic license and was impeached in 1085 for his imperious and brutal treatment of the native peoples.[20]

In 1091 Fan Zuyu, a prominent opponent of Wang Anshi's military adventurism, petitioned to separate the Military Intendancy from the Pacification Intendancy and return it to its original station at Suizhou. Fan denounced the delegation of broad military, civil, and diplomatic powers to a single "parochial garrison commander," as he styled the current incumbent. Emphasizing that an official posted to a distant frontier was poorly situated to deal with police responsibilities in all of central and eastern Sichuan, he insinuated that the rest of the new intendant's jurisdiction was vulnerable to a recrudescence of unrest not unlike the rebellions of 993–995. The court weighed Fan's objections but ultimately rejected them. Henceforth the pacification intendant served concurrently as the military intendant of Zizhou Route.[21]

Lin Guang's soldiers had built a new infrastructure of social control: roads, bridges, signal towers, and fortresses. During the immediate postwar years, a standing army of ten thousand regular troops occupied Southern Lu; but at Lü Tao's urging, this force was abandoned in 1087 in favor of a less costly militia system.[22] The Song adopted a two-tiered system of border defense. As in the past, the state conscripted ablebodied Han males to serve in the "Sons and Brothers" militias. In changed circumstances, however, the officials failed to obtain sufficient numbers of conscripts. Whereas in the 1050s the "Sons and Brothers" manned five garrisons, by the end of 1082 there were eighteen garrisons scattered throughout Southern Lu. Since 1073 the state had encouraged Han to settle in Southern Lu by offering them lands in return for periodic military service, but officials encountered considerable difficulty in trying to peruade the new settlers to put down their hoes and take up sentry duty. Exasperated officials finally decided, in 1087, to allow the "Sons and Brothers" to take responsibility merely for defending "the area of their own homes" (*benjia difen*) rather than compel them to serve stints at the garrisons. Thus the state partially restored the autonomy of the militias that had been curtailed by the reorganization of the garrisons under the direct control of the pacification intendant.[23]

Originally the Song intended to use the lands taken from K'iatdiei's vanquished allies to attract Han immigrants who would serve as state tenants. Wang Guangzu persuaded the court instead to give the lands to compliant native groups willing to assume the land tax and militia obligations. In the winter of 1083, Wang reported that some 16,660 tribesmen had been registered and organized into militia units. Altogether thirty-one commands (*zhihui*) were formed, organized along the lines of the traditional multi-lineage networks (Table 6). Each unit of fifty warriors was assigned a distinct bailiwick to police; they placed under the authority of their own chieftains, who were given the same titles (*xunejiang* and *bajiejiang*) as the Han garrison commanders. The pacification

TABLE 6 Native "Righteous Armies" Organized in Southern Lu in 1083

Lineage Network	Commands	Epithet
Eight Surnames of the Laśitang South of the Wild Frontier	8	"Cleaves to Transformation"
Nineteen Surnames of the Tuotang (Tuotśiang)	8	"Submits to Transformation"
Nine Districts Before and Behind the Mountain under Changning Jurisdiction	15	"Embraces Transformation"

Source: XCB 350/13a.

intendant provided the native militias with horses and conducted annual training exercises, which concluded with a grand feast.[26]

Despite this detailed organizational plan, ethnic rivalries and contradictory notions of land tenure undermined the viability of the native militia system. Two of the lineage groups, the Laśitang and the Tuotśiang, had a long history of mutual enmity; and conceivably each participated in the militia system simply to prevent the other from taking any belligerent actions under the guise of defending the interests of the Song. A Board of War report issued in 1091 noted the organizational weakness of the militias:

> Although the "Righteous Armies" of Lu and Xu have an organizational framework on paper, these units have not yet been fixed in a unified structure; and it is exceedingly difficult to arrange periodic tours of duty at the garrisons or to determine who should receive rewards and feasts for meritorious service. This confusion, we fear, may culminate in provocation and unrest. Therefore we wish to revise the [1083] agreement and allow each command [zhihui] to train in its own village. Each year a single disbursement of wine, foodstuffs, and gifts such as clothing, salt, fans, umbrellas, and the like will be made.[25]

In effect the Song acknowledged that the militia system could not work as a means of mobilizing the local populace for the common defense of Han and non-Han alike. Each village, settlement, or lineage group preferred to defend its own local community rather than comply with the broader priorities established by the Song state. The tribesmen also proved to be erratic in meeting their new tax obligations. In 1087 a censor, noting that the "taxable lands often have been abandoned and lie uncultivated," recommended that the Song halt the practice of turning over lands to the native militias.[26] For shifting cultivators, "property" in the Han sense held little meaning; nor did grants of landed property exert their predicted civilizing influence.

The ascendancy of Cai Jing as the dominant figure at the court in 1103 spurred another expansionary thrust in the southwest. Cai welcomed and encouraged the expropriation of tribal territories, sending a clear signal, through a calculated series of promotions and dismissals, that border officials who added new lands to the Song realm would be munificently rewarded.[27] In 1108, after the court accepted Cai's program of "opening the frontiers and acquiring new territories" (*kaibian natu*), one chieftain after another submitted their lands. East of Luzhou, several Muk lineages, the Bozhou Yang, the Ren lineages of Upper and Lower Yizhou, and the Lak lineage in the Fuzhou area all conceded sovereignty to the Song. In 1113, under pressure from the ambitious assistant fiscal intendant of Zizhou Route, Zhao Yu, nine chieftains in the Nanguang River valley submitted their territories to the Song. The chieftains received both Han surnames and personal names such as "Forever Obedient" and "Loyal for Generations" that bespoke their new status as humble subjects of the "Radiant Theocrat" (see Table 7). Two new prefectures were established in the Nanguang valley and one in the Anle River valley, although each prefecture was subdivided into several "faces" ruled by autonomous native chieftains. The Song undertook a more substantial administrative initiative in raising Yujing's status from an industrial agency to a military prefecture, renamed "Enduring Tranquility" (Changningjun).[28]

The terms of the pacts surrendering native lands to the Song mandated that the Song officials register the lands and assign tax quotas to the various tribal groups. In addition, they opened wilderness lands in the newly acquired territories to Han settlement. The native peoples were recognized as "new subjects" (*xinmin*) and placed on an equal footing, in principle, with the "common folk of Han families" (*Hanjia baixing*). In most areas the *kaibian natu* policy produced little substantive change. The already overextended field administration of the Song state never assumed actual control of the newly opened territories, nor were Han settlers willing to venture into them without assurance of vigilant protection by the Song army. Native chieftains who flocked to

TABLE 7 The "New Subjects" in Southern Lu, 1108–1113

Han Names Bestowed on Chieftains	Epithet	Territory
Wang Zhongshun	"Loyal and Obedient"	Southern Face of Chunzhou
Huangfu Shizhong	"Loyal for Generations"	Southern Face of Xiangzhou
Li Shigong	"Deferential for Generations"	Northern Face of Xiangzhou
Shi Shiqin	"Reverential for Generations"	New Subjects of Shimen
Hui Shijin	"Prudent for Generations"	New Subjects of Nanguan
Luo Yongshun	"Forever Obedient"	Northern Face of Chunzhou
Xu Yongning	"Forever Tranquil"	New Subjects of Mahu
Zhang Yongshun	"Forever Obedient"	New Subjects of Nanguan
Wang Yonghuai	"Forever Cherishes (Virtue)"	New Subjects of Nanguan
Se Yongyang	"Forever Nurtures (Virtue)"	New Subjects of Nanguan

Source: SHY fanyi 5/36b–37b.

the courts of local magistrates to "surrender" their territories did so to buttress their personal authority among their fellow tribesmen and within the larger community of native peoples. The Song offered rich compensation in return for nominal sovereignty, lavishing gifts of gold, silver, and silks on the tribal chieftains. More importantly, through investiture as "prefects" and Song recognition of the principle of hereditary succession, the native chieftains secured their own position against internal and external challengers.

In the new prefecture of Changning, however, the claim of Song sovereignty signified more than embroidered rhetoric. The infusion of Han settlers and selective adoption of native chieftains as Song surrogates ignited the smoldering animosities and passions that the wars of 1078–1082 had failed to extinguish. The incumbent pacification intendant, a career soldier named Jia Zongliang, could muster few diplomatic skills in trying to resolve competing claims and demands. Jia also earned the resentment of the tribal peoples by imposing levies of bamboo and timber, exactions that had never been conceded in formal agreements between the Song and the chieftains. In 1114 Jia ordered the arrest of the recusant chieftain Təukabuang and others on fraudulent charges. The prisoners were beaten, tattooed, banished to other areas, and in some cases put to death for their alleged crimes, even though, as the Song later admitted, they had the right to be tried under tribal law, which stipulated that their penalty could not exceed compensation in goods or livestock.

Outrage against Jia's tyrannical actions solidified into a chorus of protest demanding his head. Disparate native groups—the six "counties" of Yanzhou, the twelve villages of the Yu valley, the 135 villages of the Lašitang lineages, the confederation of the "ten prefectures and five fortified villages," and the independent "county" of Singa—joined forces under the leadership of Puklɔu, chief of the twenty-one villages of the Takang surname. The united tribesmen assaulted seven garrisons in Southern Lu, including the prefectural seat at Changning, but succeeded in capturing only one, Meilingbao. The Song detachment sent to disperse the insurgents was routed; and over one hundred soldiers, including the commanding officer, were killed. At this juncture Zhao Yu assumed authority over the situation and hastened to Legongcheng, the principal Song fort in Southern Lu. Zhao exceeded the bounds of his authority in doing so, but as Cai Jing's protégé he escaped serious punishment.

A steady stream of imperial directives followed Zhao Yu to Legongcheng instructing him to pursue a peaceful resolution to the conflict. The garrison commander at Legongcheng had greatly complicated Zhao's task with yet another perfidious atrocity. The commander, Pan Hu, had persuaded several dozen chieftains to agree to a truce. To celebrate and consecrate the pact, Pan invited the tribesmen to put down their weapons and join him in a banquet. Midway through the feast Pan's soldiers seized and executed the intoxicated chieftains, whose heads were sent in a box to Zhao Yu. This abhorrent act was swiftly followed by imperial justice, and Pan Hu himself was beheaded in the marketplace at Legongcheng several months later.

To the delight of the court, Zhao Yu succeeded in reaffirming the pacts of friendship through painstaking negotiations, chieftain by chieftain. But the truce was short-lived. As the emperor's personal envoy phrased it, "the blood smeared on their lips [in the ritual oath of allegiance] had not yet dried before the bandits violated the borders and committed crimes," including the seizure of salt merchants' vessels. Zhao immediately requested a large-scale effort to suppress the tribesmen, but the court instead instructed him to negotiate while continuing to make defensive preparations. Zhao insistently called for sterner measures and twenty thousand Shaanxi troops. Finally, late in the summer of 1115, Zhao received the message he was looking for: a hand-drafted imperial directive notifying him that seven thousand soldiers were on their way to assist Zhao in inflicting a decisive defeat on the insurgents. The court gave Zhao full authority to take whatever measures he deemed necessary to achieve a lasting peace.[29]

Reading Zhao Yu's own narrative of the 1115 war, one is struck by the entirely different tone of this hand-drafted directive, which departed completely from the conciliatory themes sounded in the court's previous instructions. The emperor composed hand-drafted directives (*shouzhao*) when "behind the curtain," that is, in the inner sanctum of the palace where only the most intimate advisers were allowed to tread. I suspect that Cai Jing, who strongly approved of Zhao's recommendations and was instrumental in promoting Zhao to high office, used his privilege of access to the sequestered emperor to win the latter's acquiesence to Zhao's strategy. By having the emperor issue a hand-drafted directive, Cai could circumvent the apparatus of court discussion and consensus, which heretofore weighed heavily against another massive military undertaking in the southwest.

The war of 1115 bore a gruesome resemblance to earlier campaigns in Southern Lu. The Laśitang lineages, which had wavered in their support of the insurrection from the beginning, capitulated almost immediately to Zhao Yu. Elsewhere the tribesmen resisted fiercely and were put to the sword. Within a month's time Zhao's army had captured and burned sixty-five villages (*cun*) and twenty fortified villages (*tun*). Eighteen chieftains and 586 other captives were taken alive; a reported 3,132 persons had surrendered or fled; and 7,025 natives were killed and beheaded.[30]

If these figures are credible, roughly two-thirds of the population of the eighty-five villages had perished in a matter of weeks. The Song victors sent the survivors back to their villages, now smouldering in ruins, with the legend "Surrendered in Awe during the Era of Regnant Harmony" (*Zhenghe weixiang*) tattooed on their foreheads.

The war of 1115 was the last war of conquest in Southern Lu for three hundred years, bringing to a close a century of bloody strife between the Han conquerors and the indigenous tribes. Twelve years after Zhao Yu's triumphant return from Luzhou, the Jurchen sacked Kaifeng and shattered the myth of empire. During the Southern Song neither the refugee court at Hangzhou nor the warlords of Sichuan expressed any interest in initiatives to expand the southwestern frontier. The tasks of the "Mid-dynastic Restoration" (*zhongxing*), salvaging the empire and retaking the north, became the all-consuming passion of statesmen and generals.

In 1115, though, with the flush of victory still glowing brightly, Zhao Yu revived Xiong Ben's vision of a new Han order in Southern Lu. Zhao strongly advocated Han settlement of the newly conquered areas on the model of the "Bow and Arrow Covenants" (*gongjianshe*) of the Shaanxi frontier. Both Han immigrants and natives would be enrolled in local militias and employed as tenants on state lands. Zhao initially estimated that the state possessed enough land to give one hundred *mu* to each of a projected twenty-seven hundred militiamen. In the following year, Zhao's successor, Sun Yisou, reported that over twenty-four hundred men had responded to the summons for militia.[31] A memorial from 1118 gave a somewhat lower figure:

> The lands under the jurisdiction of the various forts and garrisons have been divided into categories of "cultivable" and "barren." From the presently enrolled militia we have selected 1,491 robust and battle-hardened soldiers and in addition summoned 235 immigrants, who will be provided with ploughing oxen and farming tools. They will build thatch cottages and reside there undisturbed. They will also receive loans of cash, provisions, and rice from government stores and be entrusted solely with the task of opening new lands for cultivation. . . . All will live contentedly with secure employment and will serve periodic tours of duty to defend the forts and garrisons.[32]

Despite this new plan, the perennial problems of mustering militia to serve in the garrisons continued to plague local officials. Lands disappeared from the government registers, perhaps abandoned by their tenants or sold off to others. In 1181 only 754 militiamen, occupying 100,600 *mu* of land, were listed on the registers. By 1205 the lands assigned to militiamen had dropped to 94,400 *mu*, though officials expressed doubt that even this figure bore any relation to reality.[33]

Zhao Yu also continued Xiong's work of laying the foundation of a formidable military infrastructure in Southern Lu. Soldiers and laborers built six new garrisons on the sites of former native villages. This building project raised the number of garrisons in Southern Lu to thirty, all established within the previous century. Sun Yisou brought to completion, at a cost of 230,000 *guan*, the long-delayed construction of a permanent city wall at Luzhou.[34] The court broadened the civil responsibilities of the pacification intendant to include Xu and Changning prefectures as well as Luzhou. Since the militia system enacted in 1082 and revised in 1115 worked erratically at best, a large contingent of imperial guards was stationed permanently at Luzhou to shore up local defense. Luzhou's quota of three thousand imperial guards represented one-fourth of Sichuan's total allotment.[35]

The formidable costs of maintaining this extensive military establishment elicited sharp criticism. The Song state had spent 1.96 million *guan*,[36] or twice as much as in 1080–1082, on the 1115 war at a time when profligate state spending, epitomized by the "Flower and Stone Flotillas" (*huashigang*) hauling exotic shrubbery and odd-looking stones from the southeast to Kaifeng, was whipping up widespread protest. Cai Jing's warmongering and rapacious demands for revenues precipitated the devastating Fang La rebellion in the lower Yangzi Basin in 1120, forcing Cai to resign as prime minister. In 1121 Feng Ji boldly condemned the insupportable costs of Cai Jing's ill-conceived annexations in a famous indictment delivered to the Huizong emperor:

> The border officials in Sichuan and Guangxi recommended adopting the policy of annexing territories and persuading the frontier peoples to accept the status of cooked tribes. These officials came to the court, one in the footsteps of another, seeking gold, silver, and silks from the Board of Civil Office to sate the appetites of the chieftains and to request lofty titles and munificent emoluments to corrupt the chieftains' hearts. They opened the barren wilderness for settlement and hastily carved out administrative jurisdictions. Each tribe

comprised no fewer than three or four prefectures, and twice as many counties. The tribal peoples entered upon the taxation registers remain meaningless names. They make no contribution towards filling the storehouses and treasuries; but the expenses for the maintenance and salaries of officials and clerks, for the provision of armies and garrisons, and for the upkeep and repair of the walls and buildings of new administrative seats increases day by day, month by month. . . . The government has had no alternative but to spend revenues budgeted for other purposes and revise tax rates upward.[37]

Feng Ji requested that the intendants of Sichuan and Guangxi review the entire process of expansion under the *kaibian natu* policy and make recommendations to eliminate, amalgamate, or retain the new territories. Since the route-level fiscal administrations shouldered most of the burden of added administrative and military costs, they readily rejected Cai Jing's expansionary policies. Four months after Feng wrote his memorial, eight prefecture-level units along Sichuan's southern frontier and six in Guangxi were abolished.[38]

The renunciation of the *kaibian natu* policy in 1121 brought to a close the phase of Han expropriation of tribal lands in Southern Lu. The Song abolished the three prefectures created in 1108 and 1113 and struck the "new subjects" from the tax rolls, but retained Changning prefecture and all thirty garrisons. In 1116 the office of the pacification intendant, formerly the preserve of the military hierarchy, was attached to the civil service, which was less likely to dabble in military adventurism.[39] Under intendants such as Feng Ji himself (who served at Luzhou from 1143 to 1152, by far the longest tenure of any intendant), relationships between the Song and the native tribes reverted to the pre-1073 formula of haltered-and-bridled territories exempted from direct taxation and granted full autonomy over internal affairs.[40]

Of course, most of the old haltered-and-bridled territories no longer existed. The peoples inhabiting the lands incorporated into the Song realm after the wars of 1073, 1078–1082, and 1115 still remained Song subjects. These groups moved about freely within the Song borders, cultivated lands nominally owned by the Song state, and mingled with the Han in the marketplace. Lu You, on an excursion to Xuzhou in 1178 to view stone carvings of Huang Tingjian's calligraphy, stumbled upon a knot of tribesmen gambling with dice in the halls of a famous Buddhist temple.

While playing they shouted and guffawed, making sounds like the bellowing of wild beasts. Coiled sinuously on a felt mat, they looked exceedingly complacent. With their mallet hairstyles and barbarian faces they hardly seemed kin to men. They barely took notice of the Han around them. At this time the season had advanced to the middle of the fifth month, but all of them wore felt clothes on their backs which smelled so bad that you could not approach them.[41]

The unrestricted freedom of movement between the Han and native settlements granted to the Klao "cooked tribes" encouraged contact and assimilation. Zhu Fu, who commented on the proclivity of the Klao of western Hunan to move from their own "grottoes" and resettle within Han territories, considered them eminently capable of "transformation by our king" (*wanghua*).[42]

Despite the growing influence of Han civilization in all aspects of life, visitors from the capital were most impressed by Luzhou's tawdry provincialism. Fan Chengda, passing through the region in 1177, a year before Lu You, remarked that "although Luzhou in recent times has been designated the military headquarters of the route, the town itself is still a wild, untamed place, and has not yet become a true metropolis."[43] The geographer Fan Zichang, who served as prefect of Luzhou a generation later, struck a more positive note in assessing the quality of life there, but added a predictable caveat:

> The *Annals of the Southwestern States* relates that the local character of Luzhou inclined towards simplicity and rusticity, and few classical scholars could be found here. Today, though, the population has grown and filled up the countryside. The customs and habits of the region, by comparison with the old style, have become increasingly refined. The inhabitants reckon that they can lead a prosperous life here, and thus seven out of ten persons are immigrants who have left their native places and taken up residence in Luzhou. Still, Luzhou borders on the region of Kui and Yu [the Gorges region] where the people venerate shamans and undertake profligate sacrifices to appease the spirits. The locals here still imitate such behavior.[44]

Yet for the poet Tang Geng, a native of Meishan who made his home in Hejiang after the 1115 war, changes in the landscape, unremarkable elsewhere perhaps, presaged a quiet revolution:

> *In recent times customs and habits have undergone great changes.*
> *With gonfalons and battle standards furled and packed away, tavern*
>   *pennants flutter in the breeze.*

Oxen and sheep, villages dot the landscape, evening's gloaming descends,
Hearth-fire smoke rises above storied pavilions at the sun's setting
moment.[45]

THE HAN CONQUEST OF THE BUƏK RIVER VALLEY

The aftershocks of the wars of conquest in Southern Lu caused repercussions in adjacent frontier regions, fracturing political alliances and creating new fault lines of tension and conflict. The events in Southern Lu led to a similar thrust of Han expansion into the valley of the Buǝk River (now known as the Qi River) immediately to the east. The demise of K'iatdiei's confederation and the Song alliance with the Bozhou Yang brought the latter into political prominence over the indigenous peoples in an area extending from the edges of Southern Lu to the Wu River in central Guizhou. As the frontiers of the Song and the Bozhou Yang closed in around them, many smaller groups resorted to desperate but futile attempts to protect their territories and their independence.

Unlike the uplands of Southern Lu, the valley of the Buǝk River, which snakes through the heavily forested foothills of the Dalou Shan, was familiar territory to the Han. Han settlement of the Buǝk valley dated from the Tang dynasty, when Han immigrants began to cultivate tea on the steep hills. The Han shared the valley with many small native tribes, "inhabitants of the streams and grottoes who dwelled in a thousand cavern chambers," upon whom the reins of Song authority rested lightly. In the 1040s, a Song official recommended bringing this region, known officially as Nanzhou, within the regular field administration; but the court merely assigned a detachment of soldiers to defend the Han populace.[46] This isolated outpost was of minor significance, however, and the local populace instead fell under the thrall of powerful local hegemons, both Han and non-Han.[47]

In the 1060s, three native leaders in the area known as the Three Streams established small satrapies reminiscent of the fortified garrisons of the Han magnates. The three had adopted Han surnames, a common practice of the native chieftains in this area, but were not recognized by the authorities. On the contrary, their coercive tactics and growing military power, symbolized by the fortified redoubts built to defend their realms, gave Song officials cause for alarm. Sun Gou, recently commissioned by Wang Anshi to become the fiscal intendant of Kuizhou, urged that the court take immediate steps to rectify this situation:

> The three cooked tribes lineages of Li Guangji, Wang Yan, and Liang Chengxiu of Nanchuan and Ba counties each possess guests bonded to the soil [*dike*] numbering several thousand families. Included among them are Han households who have been induced or coerced to assume this station because of the power and influence wielded by these three. Those who refused to submit were slaughtered and their lands confiscated. Usually people voluntarily pledged themselves and became guest households, a practice known as "submitting oneself to bondage" [*nashen*]. The government officers took all the taxes and levies they owed from substitute sources. Not one dared to investigate, nor did anyone try to determine what had happened to the people who disappeared or lost their lives. Instead, it was reported simply that several hundred families had been lost in border raids by the Lau. When the soldiers arrived to pursue and capture the invaders, the local populace would say that the Lau had already fled. This practice, oft repeated, became a typical occurrence.[48]

In 1071 Sun Gou dispatched his deputies to demand that the trio pay the taxes due on the properties now under their control. Interestingly enough, no mention was made of the condition of subservience to which the Han settlers were subjected. Li and the others refused to comply and soon found their forts besieged by a Song army. The Song soldiers drove the natives from their strongholds and pursued them into the jungle, where they eventually captured and executed Li Guangji. The other two surrendered shortly afterwards. The court was jubilant at the success of this maneuver but immediately sent civil officials to reassure neighboring chieftains that the Song was concerned solely with collecting taxes on the lands of Han subjects and did not intend to interfere with the native communities.[49]

Despite such disarming blandishments, Song officials took steps to secure the defense of Han settlements. The nearby garrison of Binhua, attached to Yuzhou, was raised to the status of a county seat; and Song garrisons were established at Fuhuan (Piuoxuang) and Rongyi (Jiuangiei), the former sites of Wang Yan's and Li Guangji's forts. The central government appointed a Han native of the area, Wang Caijin, as marshal and gave him authority to police both Han and non-Han areas; but Wang died shortly afterwards, and the post was left unfilled.

These actions stirred resentment among the native peoples of the Buək valley, especially the chieftains of the Muk clan. Fuhuan and Rongyi belonged, at least nominally, to the Muk's haltered-and-bridled territory of Couzhou. The chieftains Muktəuung, Muktəutsiit, and Anuənɳiii led their warriors in raids on Han settlements to regain these lands. In 1075, shortly after the conclusion of his victorious campaign in Southern Lu, Xiong Ben was ordered to pacify the Buək valley as well. Xiong accomplished this task with his usual celerity and ruthlessness, conquering the rebels' eleven villages with the expenditure of a month's time and the lives of sixty-six natives. The Song decided upon an unusual resettlement policy for the forty-eight warriors and 133 women, children, and elderly of the Muk who surrendered. The captives were relocated in the sparsely inhabited hills between the Han and Huai rivers in Jingdongxi Route, where they were given two *qing* of land (roughly twenty-eight acres) per household and rations for a period of three years.[50] Forced removal, previously a little used technique of frontier social control, subsequently became a widespread practice, especially in Hunan and Guangxi, attesting to the new aggressiveness of the Song court under Wang Anshi's helmsmanship.

Xiong Ben reported to the court that the conquered territory was ripe for settlement and recommended that the Song enlist Han farmers to clear the forest and cultivate the virgin soil as state tenants. Xiong also urged the court to establish a new, prefecture-level administrative center at the village of Tongfoba and to raise more garrisons to protect the new arrivals. The court acceded to these requests, naming Tongfoba as the military prefecture of "Southern Peace" (Nanpingjun) and increasing the number of garrisons from three to six. The court also turned over salt and tea revenues to Xiong to finance the construction projects, while a small army of bearers was mobilized to transport stores and foodstuffs to the new frontier outposts.[51]

Tongfoba was located well within the territory of the Muk clan, much farther upstream than most of the existing Han settlements. The siting of the new prefectural seat of Nanping, like that of Changning in Southern Lu, can be readily understood in terms of its proximity to valuable mineral resources. No mention of it was made in the surviving documentation on the Han conquest of this area, but Xiong Ben and other

Song officials could not have been ignorant of the potential mineral wealth of the Nanping region. At Tongfoba the Buək River traversed the richest iron ore lode in Sichuan.[52] Indeed, the Song immediately began to exploit these deposits, building a mint which by 1079 produced sixty million iron coins a year.[53] The state mint, known as Guanghuijian, was located directly across the river from Tongfoba at a place called "Return-to-the-Mean Bank" (Guizhengba), a name that clearly betokened its beginnings as a native settlement.

Sichuan at this time suffered from a chronic shortage of iron coins. The dramatic increase in the demands for money occasioned by Wang Anshi's expansionary fiscal policies caught Sichuan's fiscal planners unprepared. In 1059 the Fiscal Office of Chengdu Route had enacted a ten-year moratorium on the minting of iron coins because of the excessive abundance of paper currency (*jiaozi*) in circulation, but the scarcity of coins after 1070 caused deflation and hardship.[54] The price of grain dropped to 1300 cash per *dan* in 1077, and fell to a mere 700–800 cash by 1087 in spite of the increased output of Sichuan's mints.[55] Thus the founding of the Guanghuijian mint at Nanping undoubtedly was intended to alleviate the critical dearth of iron coins induced by monetary policy under the New Laws.

The creation of Nanping prefecture provided the mint with a fiscal base to defray the costs of production. Ordinarily the smelters assumed responsibility for supplying their own coal, but they were unable to obtain sufficient quantities locally. The government earmarked income from lands cultivated by state tenants to purchase coal from other areas (perhaps the adjacent Southern Lu region, which has rich coal deposits although no mention of coal mining is made in Song sources).[56] At the outset the Han excavated easily recovered deposits at little cost. The relative advantage of minting coins in Nanping could not be maintained indefinitely, however. In the Southern Song the output of the Guanghuijian mint declined drastically. In 1155 the mint produced only fifteen million coins, a figure that plummeted to barely more than a million coins only five years later. Finally the mint was closed in the mid-1190s.[57] Local officials blamed the decline on insufficient supplies of cheap coal or on the exhaustion of iron ore deposits. Undoubtedly, supplies of raw materials diminished in the sense that the cost of recovering them rose.

Scarcity of labor and poor transportation made exploitation of all but the most accessible ore deposits uneconomical. Perhaps more important, though, was the decision in 1145 to reopen the mint at Lizhou. Lizhou had become the center of the Sichuan fiscal administration in the Southern Song because of its position as the break-of-bulk point for supplies destined for the armies along the Jurchen frontier, which consumed the greater part of Sichuan's tax revenues. Other things being equal, it certainly made sense to manufacture coinage at the place where the state conducted most of its cash transactions rather than at a frontier outpost far from the centers of trade and finance.

The renunciation of the territories of the "new subjects" in 1121 and the dimunition of mining activity throughout the twelfth century slowed and eventually halted Han expansion into the valleys of the Buək and Anle Rivers. Before immigration ceased, Han settlers had displaced the natives from the prime lowlands. As the frontier moved southward, agricultural settlements sprang up in its wake. The garrisons at Rongyi and Fuhuan, for example, were relocated farther south but these settlements acquired new identities as periodic rural markets.[58] The reorientation of Han settlement towards the agricultural plains well within the military boundary altered the urban geography of the region. In Hejiang county the market towns of Yaobazhaishi (where the garrison was shut down in 1213) and Xianshizhen flourished as the chief population and economic centers, while the five upstream garrisons became obsolete— by the end of the Song they existed merely to protect themselves.[59] In the Buək valley the prefectural seat of Nanping dwindled in importance as the iron industry declined. The principal tax bureaux were shifted downstream to the market town of Daqishi, which during the Ming dynasty became the administrative capital.[60]

As the strategic value of the Anle and Buək valleys declined, the national government took less interest in local affairs and transferred the responsibility for border defense back to local authorities. The Song had built a large number of garrisons in this area in a largely fruitless attempt to regulate the flow of traffic across the border. Song soldiers controlled the main routes; but the native peoples used mountain paths to cross the border, either to conduct illicit trade or raid Han settlements. Local officials had little recourse except to condone militias organized by local magnates. In 1159, for example, after raids on Han settlements near Qingqi Garrison in the sparsely populated hills between the Anle and Buək Rivers, the magistrate of Nanping reported that he had "persuaded the master householder Xun Bing to supply one hundred militiamen attached to his household" (*huxia tuding*) to man the garrison. The fort had stood empty since the death of an earlier magnate.[61]

Song officials often were unhappy with the license enjoyed by the local magnates. In 1195 the prefect of Qianzhou accused garrison commanders in Nanping of receiving bribes from native chieftains, conducting clandestine relations, and even disclosing military secrets. He also charged that the local magnates had embezzled funds for purchasing horses and lands set aside for militiamen.[62] In contrast to the territories under the jurisdiction of the Southern Lu pacification intendant, in Nanping the local magnates successfully reasserted their prerogatory control over defense and, by extension, local society.

VICTORS AND VICTIMS

Song frontier expansion took the form not of a wholesale takeover of large, contiguous territories, but rather of a gradual process of accretion through the annexation of many individual tribal domains over a long period of time. Consequently, the political closure of the Southern Lu frontier at any point in time was partial and tentative. In addition the Song imperial initiatives stimulated political developments beyond the frontier over which the Song had little control. Divided by complex ethnic and social boundaries and unable to mobilize their warriors in common defense of their homelands, the "cooked tribes" were reduced to a much weakened and vulnerable condition. Unlike the Han, who saw the frontier as a zone of conflict between civilization and barbarism, the indigenous peoples had no conception of a common racial or social identity. For some tribal leaders the Han appeared as potential allies against traditional enemies. For powerful chieftains at a safe remove from the grasp of Song authority, the new political climate presented inviting opportunities to augment their own power and domains through warfare and judicious alliances. Ironically, the Song conquests, by crushing the military capability of some tribes, contributed to the political ascendancy of others even more powerful. In this sense the Muk of Nanping were victims of frontier expansion, while the Bozhou Yang reaped substantial benefits.

After the establishment of Nanping prefecture in 1076, the remnants of the Muk clan found themselves hemmed in by advancing Han settlers to the north and powerful tribal rivals to the south. Deprived of their former homeland in the Buǝk valley and its eastern tributaries, they retreated to the hillier country west of the river. Even more disastrous for the Muk, the Bozhou Yang, their traditional enemies, had succeeded in wooing the Song frontier officials and forged a "peace-keeping" alliance after the outbreak of war between the Song and the Black Tribes. In 1081 the leader of the Bozhou Yang, Yang Guangzhen, convinced the court of the feasibility of sending an army to attack K'iatdiei's strongholds from the east. The prefect of Nanping, Wei Congge, enthusiastically supported the plan and met with Yang Guangzhen and other native leaders to make preparations. Wei then led a party of soldiers to clear a road through the Muk territory to Southern Lu. The alarmed Muk reacted by setting an ambush and massacring Wei and his companions.

One Song official, Xi Ruming, later admitted that the Muk had been caught by surprise when the Song soldiers appeared in their territory and had retaliated purely to defend their shrinking homeland. This realization did not mean that the Muk would be forgiven, but that the punishment would be scaled down to fit the crime. Xi advised that the Song use surrogates among friendly tribes to round up the Muk leaders, in order to avoid "creating another K'iatdiei."[63] Ironically the chieftains of the Kiuk lineage who eventually captured the Muk leaders had collaborated with the Muk in raids on Han settlements in 1073 and 1074.[64] The Kiuk had seen that the balance of power had shifted; the Muk learned the hard way.

The Kiuk chieftains claimed to have eradicated the entire lineage of Mukgiemńiɨi, but the clan survived into the Southern Song. In 1108 the Mukp'uan and Mukgiuei lineages responded to the *kaibian natu* summons and submitted their lands to the Song, "requesting to pay taxes as Han families and subjects." The court bestowed the imperial surname of Zhao on the Muk chieftains and turned over the uncultivated lands of the Muk to Han homesteaders.[65] Yet even under the protection of Song sovereignty, the Muk enjoyed little respite from intertribal warfare. In the early thirteenth century the Yang clan killed the chieftain Mu (Muk) Yongzhong who, they claimed, had seized lands belonging to the ruling lineage of the Yang.[66] More likely, the Yang took advantage of their police powers to deal a final, fatal blow to an old rival.

Among the spoils that the Bozhou Yang, as a victor in the frontier wars, could claim was the prerogative of writing their own history.[67] The Yang traced their ancestry back to a Han general entrusted with the defense of the Bozhou area during the last Tang-Nanzhao war in 883. When the dynasty collapsed shortly afterwards, so the legend went, the general Yang Duan remained and became the ruler of the native peoples. Yang Duan's sons united the armies of several local clans, subdued the "Lau of the Nine Streams and Ten Grottoes," and drove out the Lamiuen, a purported client of the Nanzhao who became the chief nemesis of the Yang.

The claim of Han origin, though amply documented in later clan histories, remains dubious; but the supremacy of the Yang in the western part of the Dalou Shan is incontestable. The clan organization of the Yang, however, was not centralized enough to prevent its disintegration into competing lineages. In the early eleventh century, the three sons of the fifth-generation patriarch carved the patrimonial realm into three hostile camps. While the sixth patriarch, Yang Zhao, continued to rule at the traditional capital of Puakiem, his brother Yi allied with the hated Lamiuen and established the territory of Xiazhou to the west. The youngest brother, Xian, created another principality, which he styled Yangzhou.[68] Despite the centrifugal forces which eventually spun off several dozen loosely affiliated branches, the main lineage dominated the clan as a whole. In 1073 a Song official described the seventh patriarch, Yang Guiqian, as "the most powerful of the southwestern native leaders, paramount over all the rest."[69]

In that same year the Song began to cultivate Yang Guiqian and his sons, Yang Guangzhen and Yang Guangrong, as powerful and intimidating figures whose presence would curb the excesses of smaller native groups. After the war against K'iatdiei broke out, dashing the court's hopes that K'iatdiei would perform this role, Yang Guangzhen readily offered himself as a substitute. Yang Guangzhen perceived, much more clearly than the Song did at first, that he could manipulate the alliance to make the Song's interests conform to his own. When Guangzhen impressed the emperor by presenting the head of Angau, he not only eliminated one of K'iatdiei's lieutenants but also rid himself of a close ally of the Lamiuen. Similarly, Yang's plan to mount an expedition through the Muk territory seems to have been a ploy to encroach upon the lands of another rival. If so, it worked. After K'iatdiei's defeat and subsequent disappearance, Yang Guangzhen was permitted to subdue any remaining pockets of resistance and "to make himself master over any tribal households he captures."[70] Over the next decade Yang Guangzhen acted as the agent of Song order in the remote parts of the Buǝk and Anle valleys, using his new stature and authority to dominate weaker groups.[71]

Yang Guangzhen's apparent goal of creating a powerful kingdom died with his own passing in the early 1090s.[72] His young son and heir, Yang Wenguang, lacked the prestige to dominate the other lineage heads. Guangzhen's brother Guangrong attempted to install himself as chief in Wenguang's place but was rebuffed by the rest of the clan leadership. Guangrong then fled to the haltered-and-bridled district of Gaozhou, where in concert with the ruling Lak lineage he plotted to take by intrigue or force what he had failed to gain through charisma. In the meantime the young Wenguang, with the aid of his wife's relatives, the Xie lineage, consolidated his position and continued the campaigns of conquest against the Muk and others.[73] Wenguang's sudden death in 1097 precipitated another succession crisis. Although Wenguang's brother Wenhan assumed leadership of the clan, Guangrong tried to outmaneuver him diplomatically by striking an alliance with the Song. Guangrong offered to submit his territory to Nanping prefecture in return for recognition as the Marshal of Bozhou. The local officials at Nanping took the bait and also began unauthorized negotiations with other members of the Yang clan in hopes of adding still more lands to the Song realm.

The pacification intendant at Luzhou discerned Yang Guangrong's real motives and bluntly informed the court that Guangrong sought to wrest the leadership of the clan from Wenhan while sheltered by Song military protection. The intendant warned that Guangrong might even seek assistance from the Black Tribes of the Luo Clan, an alliance that would threaten Song domination in Southern Lu. The court ultimately decided to partition the realm of Bozhou by imperial fiat and recognized Wenhan and Guangrong as separate and equal chiefs, a cavalier solution that did little to resolve the bitter feud between nephew and uncle.[74]

Over the next decade the Yang clan was riven by fratricidal strife. Wenhan's premature death and the youth of his heir, Yang Weicong, plunged the clan once more into succession disputes and internecine warfare. The elders finally accepted Guangrong as regent and leader of the clan. Unsatisfied with this temporary role, Guangrong plotted to assassinate Weicong, though none of his schemes succeeded. Finally he attempted to secure his position by submitting Bozhou to the Song when the *kaibian natu* policy was enacted in 1108.[75] Guangrong died shortly afterwards—according to the family chronicles, from drinking poisoned tea intended for Weicong—and Weicong assumed personal rule over the deeply divided clan. Not until a century later did a strong leader, the fourteenth patriarch Yang Can, reunify the various feuding lineages. Can's father had achieved a rapprochement with the long-estranged descendants of Yang Xian, who had quietly preserved their independence for seven generations. Can, however, demanded a stronger union than the fraternal pledges of the preceeding generation and forcibly imposed his own direct rule over the territory of Yangzhou. Turning towards the Yang's perennial rivals, Can scored even greater triumphs, crushing the Muk and finally subjugating the Lamiuen, whose extensive territories were incorporated into the Yang realm. By the 1230s the Yang clan dominated most of the native peoples between the Anle and the Wu Rivers.[76]

The political success of the Yang dynasty stemmed from their skillful manipulation of alliances and the geographic insularity of their realm. The Yang nurtured the friendship of other powerful clans—and potential rivals—of the Dalou Shan and exchanged daughters with them: the Xie and the Ren immediately to the east and the Tian of Sizhou along the middle course of the Wu River.[77] The Xie in particular were closely tied to the Yang rulers as kin, military allies, and confidential counselors, and played crucial roles in deciding disputes over succession.[78] Accommodation with the Song, on the other hand, was possible because the two did not compete for the same lands or resources. The Yang did on occasion raid Han settlements, but these injuries were alleviated by the healing balm of commerce. The Yang sold to the Han, sometimes clandestinely, the riches of their forests: timber of cunninghamia, nanmu, and bamboo; animal drugs such as musk, rhinoceros horn, and bezoar; gold and cinnabar; and above all honey and beeswax from the chieftains' apiaries. The garrison commanders and civil officials of Nanping achieved a certain notoriety for their accommodating tolerance of illicit trade with the Yang.[79]

In this instance the Han did not progress from trading partner to conqueror. The tide of immigration in the Buək valley had crested and begun to ebb. No navigable rivers reached into the heart of the Yangs' territory; access to Puakiem was possible only by following the sinuous threads of the mountain tracks. Thick stands of pristine forest rendered the terrain impassable even for horses, a tenth-century visitor noted: "persons of noble and mean station alike must plant their staffs and walk . . .proceeding inch by inch."[80] Here, as in the Tibetan borderlands, the frontier between the Han and the natives marked the boundary between two ecological zones. The Han did not have the determination, nor yet the means, to undertake the agrarian conquest of these mountains. Not until 1601, nearly two centuries after Guizhou became a province of metropolitan China under the Ming dynasty, did the Han vanquish the Yang and subordinate them to direct imperial rule.

Although the Yangs' dominions were not threatened from without, the segmentary organization of the clan repeatedly produced internecine conflict and subdivision of the clan's territories and ruling authority. The tripartite division of the ancestral realm among Yang Zhao and his brothers in the mid-eleventh century and the further fragmentation of Yang Zhao's share among the feuding phratry after Yang Guangzhen's death underscored the political weakness of the clan. The head of the Yang, the eldest son in a line of eldest sons descended from Yang Duan, remained paramount, despite the machinations of powerful competitors, on the strength of universal acknowledgment of his patrimony. Yet the chief of each segmentary lineage ruled supreme over his own appanage, a territorial and social base that placed him, in terms of resources if not prestige, on roughly equal footing with his brethren. To cite a later example, in 1478 the aging patriarch divided his realm of "145 farming estates, 26 tea orchards, 28 apiaries, 11 pig yards, and 13 fish ponds into four equal parts, which he gave to his four sons," thereby inaugurating a bloody struggle for supremacy.[81]

The intensity of fraternal enmity often exceeded a distrust of outsiders. Warring factions among the Yang readily allied with other clans or lineages, especially affinal kin, to fight one another.[82] Although the Song never interceded militarily in the strife among the Yang chieftains, the latter sought formal recognition by the Song as a means of establishing the territorial integrity of their chiefdoms. For the Yang, not yet on the edge of Han conquest, transfrontier alliances provided valuable leverage to resist the encroachment of a far more immediate enemy, their own kinsmen.

THE FRONTIER AS A POLITICAL PROCESS

The actions of the Song state demonstrate that the primary objective of the expropriation of native lands which began in 1073 was to secure valuable mineral resources of salt and iron. After decades of trying to exploit the mines of Southern Lu without resorting to force, the Song finally turned to war and dispossession to protect existing operations or acquire new mines. Opening virgin lands to Han farmers figured as a secondary consideration, not an objective itself so much as a means of stabilizing the frontier. In the routinized, predictable, mechanical labors of the Han husbandman the Song saw the antidote to the unsettled, scavenging life of the hunters of the forest.

In the beginning the framers of Song policy believed that political accommodation through the haltered-and-bridled arrangement would suffice to guarantee access to the coveted salt wealth of Southern Lu. The continual cycle of tension and insurrection, the realization that military dominance over the native peoples achieved no more than "a stolen peace," finally persuaded the Song leadership that the halter and bridle were not enough. The frontier, they came to believe, could only be civilized by imposing Han concepts of property and tenure, chiefly through the agency of Han immigrants, that would settle all territorial disputes and promote social stability. The bureaucratic mind saw detailed surveying, mapping, registration, and record-keeping as the simple solution to the baffling notions of homeland and territory that the natives clung to with ferocious tenacity. Song officials convinced themselves that given proper tutelage the native peoples could be induced to accept the Han way of life. Wedded to the Han polity and dressed in the garb of the stolid soldier-farmer, the tribesmen would find their places in Han society as simple peasants and laborers.[83] To ensure Han domination over the "new subjects," the state encouraged Han immigrants to gain control of productive resources by acquiring the lands of the natives through mortgage. The Han would then farm the lands themselves or lease them back to the nominal owners. Conversely, the Song outlawed the practice of allowing natives to mortgage Han property, fearing that the natives might gain control over the labor power of Han settlers by employing them as tenants, a status with strong servile overtones in this part of the Sinitic world.[84]

The pulse of Han expansion into Southern Lu and the Buǝk valley swelled and contracted with the vagaries of court politics. The expropriation phase lasted for a relatively brief period, the half-century between 1071 and 1121, or put another way, from Wang Anshi's ascension to power to the fall of his self-anointed disciple Cai Jing. The motives behind the Han occupation of the frontier areas were economic, but the timing was political, triggered by Wang Anshi's bold ideological synthesis. Wang's creed, the belief that the rational creation and distribution of wealth could best be achieved by maximizing the state's control over economic resources, spurred the exploitation of "the products of the mountains and the marshes," the traditional legacy of the emperor and his executors. When this vision of political economy fell into disfavor, the state's appetite for swallowing up the native territories in Southern Lu slackened considerably.[85]

Technological innovation played only a minor role in the Han conquest of Southern Lu. The lofty pipe salt well stimulated exploration and mining from the 1040s onward; but as part of the process of frontier expansion, this technology had a much greater impact in the area between the Tuo and Min Rivers, where the non-Han peoples already had become isolated in small enclaves. Overwhelmed by the renewed influx of Han settlers, the natives of that region ceased to exist as autonomous communities. In Southern Lu the native peoples surrendered their salt wealth to Han pioneers, but the frontier remained open.

Nor was agriculture a significant economic motive for sustaining expansion in Southern Lu, though farmers certainly far outnumbered salt miners and workers. Not enough social capital had been invested in Southern Lu to yield more than subsistence returns from farming. When the mines gave out, as many of them did in the Southern Song, frontier expansion came to a halt. The farming population continued to grow; but it was concentrated north of the Yangzi, a region better endowed with soils, transport routes, and markets.

For the indigenous communities, the intrusion of Han settlers, soldiers, and officials presented both dangers and opportunities. Direct resistance to the Han inevitably ended in defeat, subjugation, and displacement. Nominal surrender of sovereignty and acceptance of the halter and bridle allayed or deflected elsewhere the pressure to yield up lands to Han settlers. Weak native polities like the Nine Surnames in the Nanguang valley and the Muk in the Buək valley ultimately chose to accept Han rule to protect their homelands from aggressive rivals. Yet this strategy for survival proved to be illusory; eventually the Han annexed and absorbed their lands anyway. Indeed, the real victims of the expropriation phase were the "cooked tribes." By 1115 virtually all of the original haltered-and-bridled territories had come under direct Song rule, either by force or intimidation. By contrast, many of the "raw tribes" beyond the frontier grew more powerful under Song patronage.[86] When the Song made alliances with distant "raw tribes" in order to control other frontier groups that could threaten its domination, it upset the fragile balance of power among the tribal polities. In effect the Song legitimated the domination of its clients, such as the Black Tribes of the Luo Clan and the Bozhou Yang, over the smaller groups by elevating their chieftains to the rank of "Marshals of the Tribal Realm" and entrusting them with the task of maintaining order in the frontier areas. Using the fiercely independent "raw tribes" to control the supposedly friendly "cooked tribes" was by no means an uncontroversial policy. Before their change of heart Wang Anshi and Xiong Ben both insisted that there was no way to ensure that the "raw tribes" would respect Song interests.[87] Although Song officials fully realized the political advantage they had ceded to their clients, their capability for disciplining those clients was compromised by their need for "peace-keepers." The Song could not bear the costs of policing the border itself, nor could raids on Han settlements and property be allowed to go unpunished.

Forced to choose surrogates, the Song preferred large, powerful confederations that could hold in check the innumerable small native groups yet would not challenge the Song itself. The Black Tribes and the Bozhou Yang met these prerequisites. Both were based in mountainous regions that the Han considered impenetrable and of negligible economic value. Both confederations, though internally divided by lineage and patronage allegiances, had produced a paramount chief who dominated the political life of the federation. The Demon Master of the Black Tribes possessed divine qualities that set him above the lesser chieftains. In the case of the Yang, rigid adherence to the principle of hereditary succession of first-born sons produced a lineage of rulers that remained unbroken for centuries despite periodic schisms. Consequently the Song could deal with a few powerful leaders rather than attempt to master the political complexities of dozens of small groups ruled by consensual norms that dispersed decision-making authority among many persons.

Thus the Klao "cooked tribes," caught between the southward-moving Han and their traditional enemies beyond the frontier, were forced to relinquish their autonomy and mobility in order to survive. The Song offered the more attractive bargain: subjugation and assimilation, but not annihilation. For the original "cooked tribes" of Southern Lu, the frontier had closed. Loss of mobility and restriction to lands marked off by the invisible but impenetrable barriers of Han property imposed severe constraints on the social organization of the native communities. Fixed settlement patterns, private property, and the tax and labor demands of the Song government must have engendered changes in their mode of livelihood. Subjugation to the rule of Song officials would inevitably weaken traditional political institutions. The Klao chieftain, divested of prestige and power, would become an irrelevant anachronism.[88] We can, however, only speculate about social change among the native peoples under Song rule. Han historians paid no attention.

The most striking aspect of the advance of the Han frontier in Southern Lu was the central role of state power in establishing Han political domination and organizing Han settlement. Wherever new areas were opened for settlement along the frontiers of Sichuan, the state provided land grants, organized militias, and guaranteed uninterrupted shipments of vital supplies such as medicine and food. Yet in most areas, for example Shizou, Qianzhou, Nanping, and Jiazhou, the Song relied on existing social institutions—in essence, the local magnates and their networks of clientage—to maintain these services. Thus the local magnates continued to flourish in many parts of the Sichuan frontier throughout the Song period.

In Southern Lu, however, the state itself closed the frontier, replacing the anarchic warfare between Han magnates and native chieftains with an imposing bureaucratic hierarchy that stripped power from both. The state took over the private armies of the former, undermined the traditional polities of the latter, and assumed direct overlordship of the region's inhabitants. The institution of the Pacification Intendancy greatly augmented central control over productive resources, arms, and local society. The state lands system, despite its many failings, created a new class of frontier settlers beholden to the state for sustenance and protection. This set of institutional procedures deprived the local magnates of their customary freedom of action and perhaps explains the relative peace that prevailed in Southern Lu during the Southern Song in contrast to frontier areas where the power of the local magnates remained unfettered. Private initiatives to expand the frontier of Han settlement that continued apace elsewhere were curbed in Southern Lu, where the state effectively supplanted the designs of the local magnates with its own priorities. The intrusion of the state in local society on such a significant scale loosened the bonds that tied the inhabitants of Southern Lu to the local magnates. At the same time the state forged a new set of chains that linked Han settlers to the pull of political forces in the capital.

Part Three
Closing the Frontier

Lush green village after village; the litchis are crimson.
Malarial mists, verging on rain, darken the approaching bend.
Pennants unfurled, gaily we race down the Three Rapids,
A shout to the helmsman; Hark! winding gorges lie ahead.

Leisurely sailing the Lu River—where is the ancient ford?[1]
Wei Gao's monument[2] *lies broken amid the desolate hills.*
A glorious name, noble deeds—what claim have I to these?
Carefree, drifting aimlessly, we invade the tribal realm.

FAN CHENGDA, "Journey to Jiang'an," *1177*

SIX

Civilizing the Frontier (I):
Settlement and Social Control

The active role of the Song state in expropriating native lands, initiating Han settlement, and neutralizing the personal military power and social control of the local magnates set the stage for a fundamental transformation of Luzhou's social landscape. The state-enforced truce between the Han and the native tribes alleviated the perpetual fears and anxieties besetting the Han inhabitants and encouraged migration into the enlarged frontier zone. From the 1070s through the beginning of the thirteenth century, domestication of the frontier proceeded apace.

The Song state initiated the settlement of Southern Lu by issuing proclamations urging immigration to the southwest, opening state lands to Han settlers, and shaping tax policies to encourage frontier development. But the decisive transformation of frontier life was carried out by the landowners, peasants, and traders who came to live in and exploit the frontier areas. Population growth, the expansion of arable, and the founding of new towns and villages shaped Luzhou in the likeness of the core areas of Han civilization. Following the decline of the local magnates' power in Luzhou, the corporate village and the family farm—social features that only recently had begun to proliferate throughout Han rural society—spread quickly in Luzhou as well. The institution of the family farm and its tendency towards periodic fission explains in part why so many homesteaders pushed into new and as yet unexploited areas. The structure of the corporate village also contributed indirectly to frontier expansion. The rigidity of the local magnates' regime—with its enveloping bonds of clientage and circumscribed territorial range, fierce competition for the control of labor, and incessant feuding and warfare—inhibited mobility, trade, and political integration. The advent of the corporate village, in which wealth and property determined one's status and prestige, created new incentives to expand cultivation and increase one's landholdings. Although Luzhou's peasants lacked the social capital available to the builders of levees, canals, dams, and polders in the intensive rice-growing areas of the lower Yangzi basin, the subsistence farming and abundant wilderness that characterized Luzhou in earlier times gave way to more intensive cultivation, agricultural surpluses, and significant market involvement. New towns, routes, and patterns of circulation brought Luzhou's agrarian hinterland into greater contact with, and dependence upon, the larger commercial world of Song China. Part III examines the social and economic changes engendered by the penetration of the state and the market into local society and their impact on social organization and livelihood in Luzhou.

THE DEMISE OF THE LOCAL MAGNATE ORDER IN LUZHOU

By supplanting the "Sons and Brothers" garrison system with militias under the state's direct control, the Song undermined the independence of Luzhou's local magnates and ushered in a new era of frontier settlement. While the old garrisons faded into oblivion, the Song built thirty garrisons in Luzhou and Changning in the century between 1015 and 1116. No new garrisons were founded during the Southern Song, but twenty-three of the thirty still existed in 1220. The institution of the Pacification Intendancy, which exercised broad powers over fiscal policy, social control, and border defense, imposed a bureaucratic regimen on the state-run garrison system. The state continued to choose Luzhou's garrison commanders from the social stratum of local magnates even after the creation of the Pacification Intendancy in 1082, but at the same time the bureaucrats succeeded in bridling the personal authority of the garrison commanders.

The history of the Wangs of Hejiang county exemplified the trend towards local defense organized on bureaucratic principles rather than personal bondage and loyalty.[1] After mustering an army of "Sons and

Brothers" to suppress a tribal uprising in the late 990s, Wang Wen was rewarded with official recognition as the "local lord" (*tuzhu*) of his fortress at Qing Shan, on a high bluff overlooking the Anle River. In the 1050s, the Song incorporated the Qing Shan garrison into the reorganized network of "Sons and Brothers" militias and twice, in 1084 and 1116, sent the garrison's militiamen to fight border wars in northwestern Sichuan.[2] After the 1115 border war in Luzhou, which in retrospect was blamed chiefly on tyrannical garrison commanders, the Song undertook another reorganization of the local militias with the intention of reducing the autonomy of the garrison commanders even further. The commander at Qing Shan, Wang Tang, had been killed during the 1116 expedition to the northwest, but the Song awarded his son Wang Chun a military appointment to serve in his father's stead. Wang Chun was not allowed to assume control over the Qing Shan garrison, however; and in the late 1120s he was transferred to Hengjiang Garrison, a strategic outpost in Xuzhou that guarded the confluence of the Jinsha and Min Rivers. Wang Chun's two sons also received military appointments, but not as garrison commanders. One was serving as the marshal for Changning prefecture at the time of his death in 1169, while the other was appointed bailiff of his native county of Hejiang. Although the Wang family still had a prominent place in local defense, they no longer commanded their own personal army but rather served at the behest of their bureaucratic superiors.

Although the thirty garrisons under the pacification intendant's jurisdiction retained a fair degree of autonomy, the garrison commanders were subject to central oversight that did not exist elsewhere. The pacification intendant had the authority to appoint and dismiss garrison commanders, and clearly preferred to employ army officers rather than local strongmen. In 1181, after a brief uprising blamed on provocations by Han garrison commanders, the regional governor (*zhizhishi*) in Chengdu assumed the power to appoint garrison commanders in Southern Lu.[3] Judicial review of the garrison commanders chilled their arrogance; more than one found himself in exile in Lingnan. Moreover, in 1090 the Song adopted a legal code to regulate relations, particularly property disputes, between the Han and the natives in Southern Lu in an attempt to eliminate coercive tactics.[4]

The rupture of the personal bonds between the garrison commanders and their "Sons and Brothers" struck at the roots of the magnates' domination of local society. Control of labor through the obligations of personal service that the local magnates imposed on their clients was the crucial determinant of tenurial relations in the Sichuan frontier. The contest for control of the labor supply supply became an intense struggle for power:

> The prefectures of Shi and Qian are located far away in an interminable wilderness of mountains and valleys. The country is vast but underpopulated. Those who possess large landholdings need laborers to cultivate them. The wealthy magnate households compete with one another for landed guests [*dike*] and strive to attract guest households [*kehu*]. The latter on occasion arrive in large groups, bringing their entire household with them.[5]

Although this text, written in 1205, referred to the most remote areas of Sichuan's frontier, it probably can serve as a fair description of Southern Lu in the early Song. Before 1073 the central government made little effort to check the personal power of the local magnates, upon whom it relied for border defense. The new policy of frontier expansion and colonization inaugurated by Wang Anshi and his disciples brought the state into direct competition with the local magnates for tenants and militiamen. State-sponsored settlement, whereby immigrants to Southern Lu were given grants of land in exchange for militia service, threatened the patron-client relationships upon which the magnates' power rested.

From 1073 onward the Song brought in large numbers of immigrants and provided them with lands wrested from the native peoples. New arrivals were installed on "government estates within the imperial realm" (*shengdi guanzhuang;* also known as *shengzhuangtian* or simply as *guantian*). Initially, local officials in Sichuan collected rents in kind from state tenants in the form of eighteen different crops and products, including barley, wheat, beans, unhulled and polished rice, millet, buckwheat, taro, mulberry, hemp, and duck eggs.[6] Later these exactions were commuted into a lump cash payment. Tenures on state lands traditionally passed from father to son. The Wang Anshi administration, in one of its first acts after coming to power, forbade the sale of state lands under hereditary tenure to other parties.[7] Over time tenants on state lands began to claim that the right of permanent tenure (*yongye, shiye*) included the right to dispose of the lands as they pleased. Eventually many state tenants sold all or part of their holdings to others, although purchase of a permanent tenure entailed paying rent as well as the twice-a-year tax to the state.[8]

In Southern Lu the state lands offered to immigrants fell under the jurisdiction of specific garrisons. The homesteaders were expected to serve regular tours of duty at the garrison to which they were attached, as a county magistrate outlined in 1076:

> The frontier region of Luzhou spreads over a vast area of fertile and productive lands. In recent years many of the inhabitants have fled from the border troubles and no longer cultivate the fields. Now, having pacified the tribesmen of the Yu River, it is possible to recruit our subjects to cultivate the lands as tenants, granting them the privilege of permanent tenure, while gradually training them in military arts and defensive preparations.[9]

This concept became the cornerstone of state-sponsored settlement in Southern Lu. With the acquisition of sizable territories after the frontier wars of 1073, 1078–1082, and 1115, the Song was able to make lands available to large numbers of homesteaders. State lands were also distributed to compliant, "cooked" tribal groups who served in the Song militias, as can be seen in the following report from 1183:

> Within and without the city wall of Xuzhou the Buǝk and Klao [Katlau] move about in the course of their myriad affairs and live intermingled with the Han. Most of the cooked households who reside on government estates within the imperial realm serve as "Sons and Brothers" in the Righteous Armies.[10]

The framers of the state lands policy intended to use land grants to lay the foundations of a stable social base on which they could erect an enduring edifice of state control. In their view, the very act of farming, the devotion and care with which the husbandman tended his fields, would instill a strong sense of duty and social order in both the immigrant Han and the new Song subjects among the native peoples. The Song state sought to civilize the frontier by recreating a typically Han peasant society out of Han immigrants long inured to the rhythms of the agricultural cycle (including the arrival of the tax collector) and tribal peoples newly incorporated into the political economy of the Song empire.

The availability of land and assistance from the state lessened the dependence of the frontier population on wealthy landowners, just as the new garrison system usurped the magnates' former function as the guarantor of their clients' security. The state did not propose to establish itself in the place of the magnates, though. Government officials seem to have accepted the state tenants' de facto control of their tenures as long as the tenants met their tax and militia obligations. In the absence of cadasters and careful record-keeping, the state gradually lost control over homestead lands. In 1150 the pacification intendant at Luzhou, Feng Ji, requested and received an exemption from the universal land survey (*jingjie*) enacted a few years earlier to equalize the tax and labor service burdens of the poor. Spurred by the fear that powerful landowners would manipulate the surveys to reduce their own taxes even further, Feng Ji objected to the tax reassessment on the grounds that it would actually increase the taxes of state tenants already overburdened with rents denominated in cash.[11] In any case, without adequate oversight and information such as the surveys might provide, local officials could not prevent the transfer of state lands from public to private control.[12] The amount of state lands registered on Luzhou's tax rolls declined from 3,700 *qing* in 1116 to 944 *qing* by 1208.[13] In other words, 75 percent of Luzhou's state lands passed out of the state's direct control by the beginning of the thirteenth century.

In addition, the central government found itself pitted against the retaliatory efforts of local magnates to regain control of land and labor, though the state was on much stronger footing in Luzhou than elsewhere along Sichuan's frontier. The magnates frequently succeeded in persuading or coercing tenants on state lands to enter their employ. The law of 1052 enjoining the magnates in Kuizhou Route from encouraging state tenants to abandon their tenures, together with the revisions promulgated in 1184 and 1205, attest to the competition between the state and the magnates for the control of labor power. The laws mandated severe penalties for "transporting" (*banyi*) a state tenant from his assigned tenure to a private one. In enacting these laws, though, the Song government reinforced the traditions of personal bondage that still thrived along the frontier. In order to retain its own tenants and to support a border militia system based on the service obligations owed by guest households to their patrons, the Song codified the legal foundations for bondage in this region. Despite the laws against "transporting" state tenants and selling state lands to wealthy landowners, the state lands system proved to be highly susceptible to aggrandizement by magnates in areas such as Nanping, Jiazhou, and Qianzhou.[14]

Before the sustained period of colonization that began in the 1070s, the incidence of bondage seems to have been exceptionally high in Luzhou, where 90 percent of the population was classified as "guest households" in 1080. This figure included immigrant homesteaders who had arrived in Luzhou within the previous seven years. Although the state granted its tenants permanent usufruct rights on large tracts of land, at first they were exempted from land taxes and presumably classified as guest households.[15] At the time of the 1080 census, however, homesteaders probably constituted only a small portion of the prefecture's population; the major influx took place after 1082. Unfortunately, we have no breakdown of Luzhou's population on the basis of the master/ guest classification after 1080, and therefore cannot directly relate the weakening of the local magnates' power after the 1070s to a decline in the number of guest households.[16] At the same time, the 1080 guest household figure is inadmissible as evidence that the local magnates of Luzhou continued to wield their accustomed influence over the rest of local society. Certainly the reports of the tyranny of local magnates are far fewer for Luzhou than for other parts of the Sichuan frontier after the 1080s. The bureaucratization of local militias and their commanders, the influx of homesteaders endowed with state lands, and the creation of a powerful institution for state control on the local level—the Intendancy for the Pacification of Southern Lu—broke the grip of Luzhou's local magnates on the lives and activities of the frontier populace.

POPULATION CHANGE IN LUZHOU

The Han installed themselves in Southern Lu by force of arms, but it was the weight of their numbers that decisively transformed the social landscape. The Han did not expel the native peoples from the conquered territories, but they did displace them from the preferred settlement sites. Forced into the uplands, their movements constricted by the steady advance of Han settlers, the native peoples found themselves reduced to isolated enclaves, cut off from their fellow tribesmen and stranded on barren islands of forest with poor soils and worsening erosion. Eventually these castaways were forced to accept the Han world and their place in it or to slip across the frontier and rejoin the unbounded and "uncooked" peoples beyond the pale of Han settlement.

Song population figures confirm that Luzhou's population grew rapidly throughout the Song period. We possess some unique sources of data for Luzhou's population history, but crucial inconsistencies in the way this data was compiled hinder an analysis of population change over the entire period. The figures at our disposal are shown in Table 8. The richest source of information is the *Jiangyang pu*, which records the census figures, based on *baojia* registration, for each of Luzhou's eighty-five communes (*du*) circa 1220. The figures for the towns of Luzhou and Jiang'an, however, were not included, since these urban populations were not incorporated into the *baojia* networks.

Another significant omission occurs in the early Song (ca. 980) universal census, which simply lists the number of master households (2,407) and non-Han households (2,415) for Luzhou but gives no figure for guest households, probably the vast majority of the total population. Therefore we cannot measure the magnitude of population growth in Luzhou prior to the next universal census in 1080. Given the leap in the registered populations of neighboring prefectures for the period 980–1080 (107 percent in Fushun, 124 percent in Yu, 223 percent in Xu, 141 percent in Chang, 103 percent in Pu, 144 percent in Jia), we can assert with some confidence that Luzhou's population at least doubled over this span of a century. A doubling of the population from 980 to 1080 implies a net average annual increase of one percent, a high rate for a premodern society but typical for Sichuan and much of South China during the eleventh century. The expansion of the salt industry, the opening of the Yu River valley to Han settlers after 1014, and the conquest of the Na River valley in 1073 all brought substantial numbers of immigrants into Southern Lu. Moreover, at least part of the native population was entered on the household registers.

The next census period, from 1080 to 1102, spanned the devastating war against the Black Tribes and the beginning of large-scale Han

TABLE 8 Number of Households in Luzhou
in the Tang and Song Dynasties

	Luzhou (including Fushun & Changning)	Luzhou (including Changning)	Luzhou
726?	14,749	–	–
742	16,594	–	–
980	?[a]	–	–
1080	46,248	35,064	–
1102	55,852	44,611	–
1220	–	–	47,507[b]

Sources: 726: *TD* 175/929.
    742: *TPHYJ* 88/2a.
    1080: *YFJYZ* 7/15a.
    1102: *SS* 89/2219, 2221.
    1220: *JYP*, cited in *YLDD* 2217/18b–23b.

Notes: [a]Although some census data are available for the year 980, they are too fragmentary to be useful for comparisons.
[b]Excluding towns of Luzhou and Jiang'an.

immigration under state sponsorship. In most of Sichuan, demographic growth had peaked by 1080 and slowed considerably therafter. In Luzhou, however, the net annual increase during this period averaged 1.24 percent, a rate surpassed only in Zizhou (1.59 percent), Chengdu (1.56 percent) and Hezhou (1.45 percent) among the fifty-three prefectures of Sichuan. For Sichuan as a whole (excluding Kuizhou Route, for which the 1102 figures have been lost) the growth rate fell to 0.35 percent. Luzhou's sustained demographic vigor in the last quarter of the eleventh century, on a par with the major productive centers of Sichuan, attests to the initial success of the state's settlement policy.

After the debacle of 1127, the central government reversed its settlement priorities. Rather than continuing southward expansion, the Song now espoused resettlement of the war-ravaged frontier that bisected China from east to west after the Jurchen occupation of the north. The government particularly encouraged Sichuanese to migrate to Hubei, which suffered a population decline of 60 percent between 1102 and 1162. In 1156, when the pacification intendant of Luzhou requested that the central government send refugees from the north to replace the aging soldiers dispatched to Luzhou forty years before, the court replied that refugees no longer were arriving from the Jurchen territories and consequently no replacements were available.[17] More likely, the court's refusal reflected the priority on resettling refugees along the Jurchen border. The year 1156 marked the peak of the state's efforts to replenish the once populous countryside of Hubei and Huainan with southerners, especially Sichuanese.[18] Few heeded the summons, though; during the twelfth century Sichuan's population grew fastest in the most densely populated areas.[19]

As we have noted before, the state lands policy ultimately betrayed the sanguine projections of its sponsors. New settlers in Southern Lu frequently abandoned or sold off their land-grant tracts within a few years. Despairing of Southern Lu's flinty soil and hostile natives, many drifted northward across the Yangzi to the more fertile valleys long settled by the Han. By 1220 the prefecture's population was overwhelmingly concentrated along the major rivers, the Yangzi and the Tuo, and in the valley of the Chishui River, which descended from the uplands of Changzhou and debouched into the Tuo at Hu Market. In the frontier areas conquered by the Han since the beginning of the eleventh century, the registered population in 1220 stood at 3,174 households, only eight percent of the prefecture's total.

The highly uneven distribution of population cogently expressed Han settlement preferences. The pronounced relief, karst formations, and mediocre soils in the western half of the prefecture (Jiang'an county) discouraged immigration. Only one-quarter of the prefecture's population lived in Jiang'an, which comprised more than one-half of its territory, while slightly more than one-half (leaving aside the inhabitants of Luzhou city) lived in the fertile purple-black soil areas north of the Yangzi River. The higher productivity of the purple-black soil region was conducive to more concentrated settlement as well. Jiang'an county encompassed more settlements, 199 in all, than the other two counties combined, but averaged a mere 60 households per settlement, compared to the average of 201 households in the 177 settlements of Luzhou and Hejiang counties (Table 9). Even if we eliminate the settlements with non-Han placenames, the remaining settlements in Jiang'an, overwhelmingly populated by Han, still averaged only 73 households each (Table 10).

TABLE 9 Settlement and Population Distribution in Luzhou in 1220

	Luzhou	Hejiang	Northern Jiang'an	Southern Jiang'an
Number of Settlements	119	58	110	89
Population (Households)	23,992	11,601	7,472	4,479
Average Population per Settlement	201.6	200.0	67.9	50.3
Percentage of Total Population	50.5%	24.4%	15.7%	9.4%
Number of Communes	34	20	17	15

Source: JYP, cited in *YLDD* 2217/18a–23b.

TABLE 10 Han and Non-Han Settlement in Jiang'an County in 1220

	Han		Non-Han	
	Northern Jiang'an	Southern Jiang'an	Northern Jiang'an	Southern Jiang'an
Communes	11	10	9	2
Number of Settlements	58	73	52	16
Population (Households)	5,187	4,322	2,285	157
Average Population per Settlement	89.4	59.2	43.9	9.8
Percentage of County's Population	43.4%	36.2%	19.1%	1.3%

Source: JYP, cited in *YLDD* 2217/18a–23b

Local variations in soil productivity and topography influenced the distribution and siting of both Han and native settlements. The higher dispersal of settlements in Jiang'an suggests that the inhabitants occupied a greater variety of settlement sites. North of the Yangzi, villages congregated on river terraces and valley bottoms or in the numerous small basins interspersed among the hills. In Jiang'an many villages, especially those of the indigenous tribes, were found on higher slopes and hilltops. Han placenames derived from site features referred to the irrigation of river terraces or small basins for agricultural exploitation (Table 11). The most common of these words, *ba*, denoted both a flat valley bottom (a coinage unique to Sichuan) and a weir erected to divert a stream flow

TABLE 11 Placewords in Luzhou in 1220

	Luzhou	Hejiang	Jiang'an	Total
Administrative Places				
County Seat	1	1	1	3
Garrisons	–	–	10	10
Total	1	1	11	13
Markets				
Market Town (*zhen*)	6	2	–	8
Market (*shi*)	27	11	7	45
Garrison Market (*zhaishi*)	–	4	–	4
Inn (*dian*)	2	–	3	5
Total	35	17	10	62
Villages				
cun	44	16	69	129
Site Features (I)				
Valley Bottom (*ba*)	6	10	18	34
Hollow (*kan*)	7	3	2	12
Hollow (*wu*)	2	2	2	6
Channel (*gai*)	1	3	–	4
Total	16	18	22	56
Site Features (II)				
Riverine	3	7	5	15
Slope	1	3	4	8
Building	2	–	1	3
Estate	–	–	3	3
Other	4	4	2	10
Total	10	14	15	39
Non-Han Names				
lai	–	–	2	2
la	1	–	24	25
lak	–	–	13	13
muəi	–	–	9	9
təu	–	1	5	6
lang	–	–	4	4
Other	4	–	16	20
Total	5	1	73	79
Prefectural Total	111	67	200	378

Source: *JYP*, cited in *YLDD* 2217/18a–23b

onto irrigated fields.[20] "Hollow" (*kan, wu*), and "channel" (*gai*) appeared somewhat less frequently.[21] The even distribution of this categtory among the three counties underscores the strong Han preference for these sites. Nevertheless, we find no mention of placewords derived from artificial irrigation works such as levees or manmade ponds, in contrast to placenames of the lower Yangzhi Basin (compare Table 11 with Table 12).

We have no direct evidence concerning the internal layout, density, or patterns of dispersal of settlements in Luzhou. The evidence at our disposal suggests that the Han inhabitants of the purple-black soil areas lived in fairly large nucleated villages of five hundred to one thousand or more residents, although the constraints of topography necessitated some degree of dispersal. The dispersal of settlements in Jiang'an, especially in the northern part of the county, indicates that where topography precluded the formation of large nucleated villages, the Han tended to congregate in small villages rather than spread across the landscape. Given the fear and hostility that pervaded the frontier and the uncomfortable proximity of the tribal villages, isolated farmsteads presumably were regarded as unacceptably dangerous. The general pattern for both Han and non-Han seems to have been nucleated village settlement, though the size of the village varied enormously depending on topography and productive resources.

In areas where the native peoples had been compressed into constricted enclaves, as in northern Jiang'an, they became largely integrated into the Han order; but along the open frontier to the south, they remained independent of direct Han rule. Of the seventy-nine villages I have identified as non-Han on the basis of placenames, sixty-one were located north of the Yangzi and only eighteen south of the river. This skewed distribution reflected not the actual distribution of non-Han peoples, who were overwhelmingly concentrated in the south, but the marked difference in political and social integration between those groups who had lost their mobility and autonomy and were surrounded by Han, and those for whom unimpeded mobility afforded a degree of freedom. The striking disparity in the size of native settlements on opposite banks of the river (shown in Table 10) also reinforces the conclusion that the circumscribed non-Han groups had begun the transition to fixed villages, while in the south mobile settlement and shifting cultivation still prevailed. In both areas the natives continued to build their villages, called

TABLE 12 Placewords in Changshu County, Suzhou

Placename Element	Number	Placename Element	Number
Administrative Places		*Domestic Architectural Site Features*	
County Seat	1	Farmstead (*zhuang*)	55
Markets		Cottage	27
Market	33	Subtotal	82
Inn	3	*Other Site Features*	
Landing (*bu*)	1	Bridge	16
Subtotal	37	Hill	10
Villages		Lane	7
cun	30	Wood	7
Manmade Aquatic Site Features		Lake	6
Channel (*jing, du, gou, cao*)	26	Point	6
Artificial Pong (*tang*)	19	Temple	5
Levee (*yan, dai*)	8	Other	110
Estuary	10	Subtotal	167
Harbor	7	*County Total*	392
Mooring	5		
Subtotal	75		

Source: Qinchuan zhi [1196], 2

la or *lak*, on level hill crests that could be easily defended.[22]

We know of more than one hundred non-Han villages that were brought under Song rule as a consequence of the border wars during the Northern Song, yet only eighteen village names appear in the 1220 gazetteer. The fate of the rest remains uncertain. Many of the larger villages at favorable sites were simply supplanted by Han settlements. Thus the Han garrison of Pacified Tribefolk (Anyizhai) replaced the native village of Sabua in 1014; later, the Song built the garrisons of Ningyuan, Anyuan, Jiangmen, Zhenqi, Meiling, Dazhou, Legong, Bowang, Banqiao, and Meidong at sites formerly occupied by fortified native villages. In other cases the proliferation of Han settlements displaced native villages more gradually. Changes in placenames gave testimony of the squeezing out of the natives. In 1121, for example, the village of Liuongmiuekok near the Changzhou border was renamed Mijiao Village, while

Laklai, on the Tuo River, became Huaide (To Cherish Virtue) Township.[23] Renaming the landscape did not mean that the native peoples had disappeared, but they certainly were becoming less visible. The low number of Southern Lu native villages incorporated into the *baojia* networks leads us to conclude that the majority of the native villages, even those located within the nominal Song borders, were not fully subject to Song institutions of social control. In this respect the Song policy of conquest failed to integrate the tribesmen into Han society.

THE ROLE OF THE LINEAGE IN FRONTIER SETTLEMENT

Migrants to the frontier areas of Sichuan did not arrive as solitary individuals. In most cases they brought immediate families with them, while forsaking the intimacy of an extended kindred and the country of their native birth to face the uncertainty of a new life. Cut off from the guiding traditions of family and native place, pioneer settlers had to develop their own strategies for survival and reproduction. In this context marriage and inheritance customs not only shaped the formation of family and lineage but also left a distinct imprint on the pattern of settlement.

An ancient tradition particularly common in Sichuan was the practice of premortem partition of inheritance, whereby the patrimony was divided among the heirs while the head of the household still lived.[24] The male heirs typically received their endowment when they married, whereupon they moved out of their father's house and established a separate and independent household.[25] The Sichuanese custom of sons living apart from their father drew censure from the official keepers of public morality in the early seventh century, and under the Tang legal code a punishment of three years' exile was decreed for those who did so.[26] In 968 the Song court, noting that the custom of "establishing a separate household and partitioning the family estate" (*bieji yicai*) was still rampant in Sichuan, issued its own proscription. A year later the court mandated the death penalty for violators of his injunction.[27]

Contemporary opinion and the hoary canons of filial piety condemned severing the bonds of joint residence and economic dependence between son and father as a gross violation of the norms of human behavior. Once the children received their portion of the family estate, it

was feared, they would no longer devote themselves to the care and support of their parents when age and infirmity rendered the latter incapable of sustaining themselves.[28] Moreover, endowment of children at
the age of marriage weakened parental control. Yet there were also incentives for the parents to make an early transmission of property. Generally speaking, endowment at marriage was made in movables rather than
land.[29] Since equal inheritance among surviving male heirs (daughters
received a dowry equivalent to one-half of a brother's share) was the rule,
the custom of premortem partition preserved the cohesion of the family's landholdings. This issue was more pertinent in Sichuan, where
concentrated landholding lasted longer than elsewhere. Premortem partition also enabled parents to select a preferred heir who would inherit
the land and support them in their declining years. Finally, the inheritance of the family's property by a single son reinforced the family's
control over tenurial and settlement rights on its property. Thus in comparison to the egalitarian division of inheritance typical of other areas,
premortem partition could actually strengthen the father's arbitrary
authority. On the other hand, in order to provide endowments for children at the time of their marriage, the head of the household would have
to convert the family's wealth into movables or money, perhaps burden-
ing the household with debt in the process.

Another custom typical of Sichuan but offensive to the dominant
patriarchal ideology was the practice of marrying a daughter to an adoptive son-in-law (*zhuixu*) who lived with his wife's family and continued
their family line. In Sichuan such uxorilocal marriage was not confined
to families without male heirs but also was found among those who did
have sons to assure the continuity of the family, as we can see in the following report from 990:

> The wealthy of the Rivers and Gorges often bring adoptive sons-in-law into
> their families and count them among their sons. When the wealthy man dies,
> [the adoptive son-in-law] shares in his estate. Thus many poor men forsake
> their own families and offer themselves as husbands, a practice that does grave
> harm to moral custom.[30]

Presumably the intent of this form of uxorilocal marriage was to consolidate the estate and prevent the loss of property through dowries. The

Song subsequently proscribed this practice on the grounds that it was ruinous to poor families, though the numerous lawsuits brought to magistrate's courts by male heirs who did not wish to share their patrimony with their sister's husband also seems to have influenced this decision. Uxorilocal marriage remained common in Sichuan nonetheless, but the ambiguous legal status of an heir adopted in this fashion led to frequent lawsuits. In 1161 the prefect of Fuzhou, seeking a clarification of the legal uncertainty surrounding adopted sons-in-law, presented the following hypothetical case for the court's consideration:

> For example, X's wife gives birth to a single daughter but has no male children. Upon the death of his wife, X remarries; and the second wife raises X's daughter. When the latter reaches the age of maturity, an adoptive son-in-law is brought into the household. Afterwards X, fearing that he will never have any sons, bequeaths his rightful wealth and property to the adopted son-in-law. After X dies, his second wife takes in X's consanguinal nephew as her adopted son [*yangzi*]. This results in X's adopted son-in-law disputing the inheritance of X's estate with the adopted son on the basis of X's bequest and testament. The civil officials who decide the case sometimes rule that the adopted son receives the entire estate, while in other instances the verdict, based on the testament bequeathing the estate to the adopted son-in-law, favors the latter.[31]

The court ruled that an adopted son-in-law and an adopted son each had equal claim to an estate and ought to receive equal shares of an inheritance; but in the following year a modified schedule was implemented, giving the adopted son-in-law only between one-third and one-half of the inheritance.[32] Apparently the court recognized the legal claim of an adopted son-in-law only as a means of maintaining a family line; but as we shall see, the practice of uxorilocal marriage continued to serve as an important strategy for upward mobility among the rich as well as the poor.

Like premortem partition, uxorilocal marriage attracted severe censure for its detriment to the older generation, the aged parents bereft of the material and emotional support of their children.[33] Yet uxorilocal marriage's value as a means of preventing the dispersal of wealth, even to agnatic relatives, was widely appreciated. Like cross-cousin marriage, uxorilocal marriage seems to have enjoyed unprecedented popularity during the Song.[34] On the most basic level, uxorilocal marriage provided a direct heir to the family's lands—a crucial necessity, since by custom, though certainly not in law, the ownership claims of a tenant farmer often prevailed over those of a landowner's agnatic relatives should he die without direct heirs.[35] In addition, wealthy families in frontier areas utilized uxorilocal marriage to preserve the integrity of the family's land-holdings and to form alliances with other families among their social peers. The first settlers in frontier areas were mere fragments of larger lineages, most probably from junior lines of kin groups that remained firmly rooted in their native place.[36] In the absence of a strong lineage body in the frontier area, uxorilocal marriage offered a strategy for devel-oping one. The case of the Mou family of Nanping succinctly portrays the actual workings of this strategy of social reproduction.

Mou Liren was descended from an old and immensely wealthy family from Ziyang. In the early 1070s, immediately after Xiong Ben's conquest of the territory that soon became Nanping prefecture, Liren visited Nan-ping and discovered that rich and fertile lands could be had for the taking. Liren then took his share of the family's estate and brought his family to live at Rongyi Market, the former stronghold of the tribal leader Li Guangji. Within a few years' time Mou Liren's property and wealth surpassed that of nearly all his new countrymen.

Another son of a wealthy Sichuan family, Zhao Yan of Suining, arrived in Nanping at the same time and took up residence at New Market, a day's journey from Rongyi. In property and wealth Zhao Yan rivaled Mou Liren. Eventually Zhao Yan proposed that since the fore-bears of the two families came from neighboring counties (actually, Ziyang and Suining were about 130 kilometers apart), now that they found themselves in a strange land they should renew this tie through the marriage of their children. Mou Liren considered Zhao's son Zhao Zhicai a fitting husband for his daughter and accepted him as an adoptive son-in-law. Liren built a separate residence for Zhao Zhicai and his daughter, though the house's walls adjoined his own as if they were a single family. When Mou Liren divided his estate among his heirs, Zhao Zhicai received a share equal to those of Liren's natural sons. The marital alliance between the Zhao and the Mou was renewed in the next genera-tion. Zhao Zhicai's two daughters married their maternal cousins Mou

Fen and Mou Fan, both of whom were successful scholars and attained the *jinshi* degree.[37]

We can see that Mou Liren took advantage of the cheap lands suddenly thrown open to Han settlement in 1075 to invest his inheritance and found a new branch of his lineage. Mou then established a collateral lineage with his own property and the Zhao surname with which his direct heirs could trade daughters, thereby strenghtening the family's control over property transmitted to succeeding generations. The few documents we possess on marriage and inheritance in frontier areas like Nanping indicate a strong concern with establishing a local descent group through marriage alliances. The Zhang family moved from Longguizhen in Puzhou to Nanchuanzhen in the frontier area of Yuzhou in the 1050s. Zhang Shang, born the year before Xiong Ben's conquest of Nanping, later moved to Shihe Market in the conquered territories. Zhang Shang's daughter married a *jinshi* of the Qu family, while his sons, who received military degrees and served as garrison commanders, married women of the Qu family.[38] Exclusive marriage exchanges of this type also functioned as a means of limiting the dispersal of the patrimony.

In at least some cases an agnatic group moved en masse to the frontier. The five Ren brothers, originally from the Chengdu area, moved to Nanping with their families in the late 1070s: "joining together cooperatively to open the land for cultivation, they founded a village which came to be known as Five Brothers' Valley (Wudiba)."[39] Unfortunately we have no information about the marriage arrangements of the Ren, but we can safely assume that in this instance agnatic descent and transmission of inheritance played a much greater role than in the other cases mentioned above.

From the foregoing we can see how the custom of endowment at marriage produced a group of sons who were squeezed out of the long-settled parts of Sichuan, where the best lands had been taken and a strong penchant for the impartibility of landholdings discouraged division of landed property among the heirs. These sons could migrate to the frontier, using their endowment as capital to acquire lands and establish their own household. The social isolation of such households, far removed from the main lineal descent group, would encourage them to seek marriage alliances with families of roughly equal station and wealth to ensure the continuity of their own line. Uxorilocal marriage could provide a male heir to continue the family line and keep the patrimonial estate within the family.

This pattern of migration, settlement, and reproduction of the family contrasted sharply with the settlement of the underpopulated central Yangzi region during the early Song period. During the tenth century the custom of establishing a "fraternity" (*yimen*), whereby a group of agnates pledged to live in common, "sharing hearth and home" (*tongju tongcuan*) and to farm the undivided patrimonial estate collectively for generation after generation, became widespread in the Yangzi valley.[40] The archetypal case of these fraternities was that of the Chen family of Dean county, Jiangzhou, in Jiangxi. In his *Family Precepts*, compiled in 890, Cheng Chong laid down the organizational plan of the household and established the rules for the joint management of the family's lands and wealth and the education of the younger generation. Stewardship of the family estate passed agnatically rather than patrilineally; in other words, the head of the fraternity was the eldest agnatic descendant of Chen Chong. The family flourished as a fraternity for eight generations. In the 1020s, having grown to an unmanageable size of more than two thousand persons, the fraternity was dissolved and the lands divided into 291 separate farmsteads. Fraternities with several hundred members and a history of six or seven generations were particularly concentrated in Huainan and the Poyang Lake basin in Jiangxi, reaching their apogee in the early Song period.[41] Although many later manuals on family management and ritual, such as Sima Guang's *Exegeses on the Canon of Ritual*, embodied the ideology of the fraternity, the actual institution was fast disappearing by the middle of the eleventh century.[42]

Satake Yasuhiko, noting the precise temporal and geographic boundaries of the fraternities, suggests that this institution was closely connected to the rapid pace of settlement in the Yangzi valley during the tenth and eleventh centuries. Settlers in this fertile region opened new lands for cultivation using the labor- and capital-intensive techniques developed in the lower Yangzi Basin, but the scarcity of labor inhibited the expansion of these forms of agricultural exploitation. Faced with this dilemma, pioneer farmers fell back on consanguinal bonds and large families as inexpensive and reliable sources of labor and resources. Consequently fraternities occupied large tracts of land, a trend that fostered the proliferation of single-lineage villages. But by the beginning of the eleventh century, when a dense population and an ample supply of labor became firmly implanted in the valleys and lacustrine basins of the central Yangzi, the enormous fraternities, cumbersome and ridden with internecine conflict, began to give way to simpler nuclear families and small farms. The single-lineage villages also faded away and were replaced by multi-lineage villages in which landownership rather than kinship determined one's social standing.[43]

In contrast to pioneer settlement in the central Yangzi region, nowhere in the Sichuan frontier did the lineage serve as the fundamental unit of settlement and village organization. The clientage networks of Sichuan's local magnates were based on fictive rather than actual kinship. At the beginning of the thirteenth century, 55 percent of the placenames in Luzhou derived from surnames; but while the placenames probably were taken from the name of the village founder, the villages themselves do not appear to have been organized along lineage lines or even primarily composed of lineage members. In nine Luzhou villages the words "greater" or "lesser" preceded a surname-derived placename, suggesting that one village was a spin-off from the other. The Great Xian Village (Daxiancun) and Lesser Xian Village (Xiaoxiancun), for example, were located within a few kilometers of each other. We can probably infer that these villages were founded by agnatically related families, but such cases were rare. Finally, the successive waves of immigration into Luzhou reduced the founding families to a small minority.[44]

Indeed, we would expect that the domination of the local magnates inhibited the development of strong lineage institutions in the Sichuan frontier. Yet even after the power of the magnates diminished, kinship strategies for survival and social reproduction involved distinctly non-patrilineal practices such as uxorilocal marriage, non-agnatic adoption, and premorten partition of the family estate. What mattered most was retention of undivided family land and its transmission to future generations, who need not be direct male descendants of a single progenitor nor even descended through male bloodlines. Considerations of property and progeny clearly took precedence over the prevailing ideology of patrilineal descent and agnatic solidarity.[45] The desire to prevent the division of landed property encouraged endowment of movables on younger children at the time of their marriage, a practice which in turn tended to isolate nuclear families and separate the interests of the married couple from those of parents and agnatic relatives. Thus, in the long-settled Chengdu Plain as in the frontier, the custom of premorten partition often led to the fission and geographic dispersal of agnatic descent groups. Upon arriving in the frontier, individual settlers, detached from their lineages, sought to establish new patrilines.[46] Uxorilocal marriage, cross-cousin marriage, and non-agnatic adoption provided the means to hold together the new patrimony and ensure its transmission to posterity.

VILLAGE AUTONOMY AND CORPORATE INSTITUTIONS

As the bonds of fictive kinship which united magnate society weakened without being replaced by strong lineage organizations, the village emerged as the basis of social identity and control in Luzhou as in the metropolitan areas of Song China. The pattern of Han settlement reflected the demise of the local magnates' garrison towns and personal armies. During the heyday of magnate society, their mountain fortresses, which stood on high, easily defended bluffs, had dominated the landscape. The villages of the local inhabitants could not extend much beyond their protective ken; the magnates had built their strongholds to defend only their personal bailiwicks, and the villages grew up in their shadows. The state garrison network, by contrast, demarcated the edge of the frontier. Facing outwards against the native tribes, the state garrisons defined the territorial limit of the imperial realm and denied entry to the non-Han peoples. Behind this defensive bulwark a vast territory was thrown open to settlement. Subsequently major changes occurred in frontier society. The autonomous village, largely independent of both state and magnate control but rapidly producing its own forms of hierarchy and power, emerged as the basic social unit in Luzhou's countryside.

Several often-quoted portrayals of rural society in Sichuan remind us, of course, that the eclipse of the local magnates' power and influence was by no means total. In the 1070s Han Qi wrote that in Sichuan "the great houses dominate the inhabitants; each family possesses as many as three to five hundred 'guest households,' all of whom depend on the great families for their livelihood, from clothing and food to lending and borrowing."[47] Su Xun's famous polemic against the evils of unequal landownership, written about the same time, rebuked "the families of the rich . . . [who] hire itinerant laborers [*fouke*] to cultivate their vast landholdings, compelling them with whip and lash to perform their tasks and treating them as base slaves."[48] Large, concentrated landholdings indeed persisted in Sichuan much later than elsewhere. Yet a closer look at these estates shows that the organization of labor and tenurial relationships was changing drastically.

In the Chengdu Plain, for example, the "permanent sustenance fields" (*changzhutian*) of the great monasteries extended over tens of thousands of *mu*. These enormous estates were so large that most of the lands remained undeveloped. In the case of the Monastery of the True Dharma (Zhengfayuan), only twenty percent of the more than ten thousand *mu* of land bequeathed by a warlord of the Later Shu dynasty was under cultivation at the time of the Song conquest. Eventually the rest of these lands, located in the northeast corner of the Chengdu Plain, were brought under cultivation—not under the monastery's direction but by squatters who claimed title (*zhuming*) to the lands. In the 1080s, frustrated by the interminable legal wrangling over these lands, the local officials rejected the monastery's demands for a land survey of more than five thousand *mu* of the monastery's property, a decision that essentially acknowledged the squatters' claims to ownership. Not until 1105 did the monks, through appeal to the prime minister, win a reversal of this ruling and recover title to the lands.[49]

Tan Kyōji and Satake Yasuhiko have argued persuasively that the relationship between the monastery and its hundreds of tenants was a contractual one without any tinge of bondage or feudal obligation. The monks took no part in the management of the lands or in organizing field work. Their sole concern was to collect the rents. The tenants themselves organized land reclamation, irrigation projects, tax collection, and social control through village-based institutions.[50] Despite their enormous landholdings, the monks of the Monastery of the True

Dharma held little power over either the lands or the population they sustained. Tan and Satake both conclude that the landed estates of the Chengdu area bore little likeness to the manorial order described by Sudō and Niida. Instead they advance the hypothesis that a rising land-owning elite, distinct from and hostile to the hereditary aristocracy, began to dominate village life in the late tenth century. Satake associated this social transformation with the displacement of the old *xiangli* struc-ture of rural social control based on artificial units of population by new forms of local administration based on natural social groupings. The *tuanbao* system, promulgated in 958 by the Northern Zhou dynasty and retained in its essentials by the Song, grouped the rural population into artificial units of one hundred master households, but customarily these units were defined as a group of three villages. Three elders (*qizhang*), selected on a rotating basis from among the wealthiest families of each village, took responsibility for policing duties and resolving internal disputes.[51] In Sichuan the elders also collected taxes.[52]

The Song adopted a formal structure of village administration in 974 that deprived the garrison commanders and *xiangli* officers of any mean-ingful role, even though the old titles and jurisdictions were retained. The government thus placed responsibility for social control in the hands of the elders and other village officers who, under the household-ranking system, were selected from the substantial property-owners among the master households. The New Laws implemented by Wang Anshi's administration further strengthened the village-level officers at the expense of higher levels of the local administration. The *dubao* sys-tem promulgated throughout the empire in 1095, which unified local militia organization and the village-officer system, was based on a new rural administrative unit, the commune (*du*).[53] Each commune was com-prised of a group of villages, ranging from two to fifteen or more, and headed by a commune chief (*baozhengzhang*) selected from among the first-rank master households and directly responsible to the county magistrate. The commune chiefs, the elders, and the families of govern-ment officials (*guanhu*) formed a new rural elite, the "influential house-holds" (*xingshihu*), a privileged status duly recognized in the household registers.[54]

The legal status of this elite of "influential households" derived from their native residence and substantial landholdings. Guest households, on the other hand, by definition were barred from any village office. They existed in the shadows of the household-ranking system—having no rank at all—and frequently were registered merely as adjuncts of their landlord.

The authority of the village officers and the pool of "influential households" from which they were chosen extended far beyond their officially sanctioned responsibilities. In the Yangzi delta the village officers directed the construction and maintenance of irrigation projects such as dikes, polders, and levees, and supervised the operation of norias, well-sweeps, and other irrigation equipment. The massive investment of labor and capital in irrigation projects in the Yangzi delta required new forms of labor organization as well, and the village or commune became the social basis of these projects. Yanagida has shown that in Yuqian county of Hangzhou the administrative structure of the *dubao* system conformed to the contours of irrigation networks. The fragmentation and dispersal of landownership in this region forced even those with the most extensive landholdings to cooperate with smallholders, tenant farmers, and hired laborers. One of the main tasks of the commune chief consisted of organizing and directing work on such projects.[55]

In part the reorganization of work on cooperative principles, using the village or groups of villages as the social basis for recruiting labor, can be traced to new forms of technology. The most prevalent type of irrigation equpiment was the *fanche,* a square-pallet chain pump powered by hand, treadle (*tache*), or water mill (*shuiche*). Batteries of these water pumps, usually operated by women and children, lined irrigation channels in the lower Yangzi Basin. At peak periods the *fanche* were in constant use for many days, with the entire village participating in the work.[56] But even rudimentary tasks were performed by the community as a whole. Su Shi lauded the cooperative spirit of the peasants of his native county of Meishan in an essay written in 1078:

> The tillers of the fields combine their ploughing to help each other. . . . In the second month farming tasks begin. In the first quarter of the fourth month the shoots of grain are still tender, but the grasses are tough and well entrenched. The weeders all go out into the fields in groups of several dozen or even a hundred. A clepsydra is set up to mark the time and drums are sounded

to summon the host of fieldworkers. Two of their number, respected and trusted by the rest, are selected to take charge of the clepsydra and drum respectively. These two men regulate the advance and retreat of the weeders and schedules of work and rest. Penalties are meted out to those who fail to respond to the summons of the drum or who are lax in their work. The two leaders measure the amount of land and the effort contributed by each person; and when the tasks are completed, a large meeting is held. Families with large landholdings and few hands must recompense the others in cash. In the third quarter of the seventh month, when the grain is in full flower and the weeds all have been uprooted, they take the money collected from fines and compensation payments and buy lambs and pigs, and spirits and wine, to offer in sacrifice to the Ancestral Husbandman. They play music, feast, and drink, lingering until sated and soused. Over the years this has become a regular practice.[57]

Su and other authors accentuated, and to some extent idealized, the communal quality of cooperative field work. By contrast, local officials in the Yangzi Basin and the Chengdu Plain frequently bemoaned the labyrinthine, competing interests that frustrated cooperation in water control projects. The authorities constantly admonished landowners and tenants to cooperate in building dikes and dredging channels according to the principles of "providing funds on the basis of the amount of property owned" (*zhaotian chuzi*) and "compensating tenants for the labor they expend" (*yangshi dianli*). In practice, the limited means of tenants and small cultivators disqualified them from any significant role in village decision-making. Although rights to use assets such as water and uncultivated lands inhered in the village as a corporate body, the wealthiest landowners exercised actual control over communal resources.[58]

Nonetheless, the settlement patterns spawned by the rapid pace of land reclamation in the lower Yangzi Basin reflected the organization of labor based on reclamation and water control projects. Agricultural exploitation of the delta's low-lying marshes accelerated with the proliferation of poldering techniques (*weitan, yutian*), which involved building levees and water channels in order first to drain the lands and later to control the flow of water for irrigation. Villages sprouted up along the watercourses that criss-crossed the polders:

Formerly each household had a field cottage located in the midst of the polder, which they eventually made their home. Wishing to facilitate the passage of boats [to their dwellings], they breached the levees and dug small channels through the polder. . . . [Village names] such as So-and-So Family Creek, So-and-So Family Mooring, are examples of this practice.[59]

During the Southern Song wealthy landowners—particularly the "influential households"—utilized such techniques to bring under cultivation large tracts of lacustrine swamps. Work teams assigned by the landowner to a given section of the polder (*yuluo buwu*) founded new villages in their particular section. Wei Jing, in his description of agricultural reclamation in Liangzhe at the close of the twelfth century, emphasized that it was the landowner who took the initiative in the establishment of these villages:

> Polder fields mostly are found in unpopulated wilderness areas. [The landowners] first must set up farmsteads [*zhuangshe*] where tenant households will be brought together to live. Then they can proceed to expand cultivation and occupy additional lands.[60]

During this period many new villages founded in the lower Yangzi Basin were the products of new techniques of production and the organization of labor, as elements in many placenames reflect: "levee" (*yan, dai*), "dike" (*tang*), "creek" (*jing*), "runnel" (*du*), "cottage" (*she*), and "farmstead" (*zhuang*). (See Table 12.) The importance of the village as both a work and residence community in turn was mirrored in the administrative structure of the *dubao* system, which recognized that rural populations existed as social entities rather than abstract units of population.

Needless to say, settlement patterns in Luzhou differed widely from those of the lower Yangzi Basin. Yet corporate institutions, especially the village, dominated Luzhou's social landscape by the beginning of the thirteenth century. The *dubao* administrative structure that existed in Luzhou in 1220, for instance, was identical to that of Suzhou.[61] Of course, corporate institutions based on water control projects were virtually absent in Luzhou, where technological innovation lagged far behind the lower Yangzi region. But in Luzhou, as in the metropolitan areas of Song China, land and wealth had supplanted the patronage and personal power of the local magnates as the foundation of local power and social control. Under the household-ranking system, wealthy landowners assumed effective control over village life. They collected taxes, assigned labor service duties, organized police and crop-watching tasks, and adjudicated property disputes and minor litigation.[62] The state-run garrisons supervised the militias, but the militiamen lived in villages outside the garrison and held de facto title to the lands they farmed. Social insurance and charitable assistance became the responsibility of corporate groups organized under public and private auspices. A community granary (*shecang*)—an institution popularized by Zhu Xi as a means of freeing the organic, rural community from its dependence on the state—had been founded by a group of local notables in Luzhou in the late twelfth century to provide famine relief. Luzhou's poorhouse, located just south of the city wall, was refurbished in the 1210s through public subscription, and its capacity doubled to two hundred persons. A charitable cemetery (*yizhong*), where the poor were buried at public expense, was built in the early 1180s and enlarged in 1205; but acute need prompted the pacification intendant to set aside additional lands for a new charitable cemetery in 1216. For the most part the pacification intendant entrusted the management of these institutions to local notables, particularly former government officials and wealthy households.[63]

In short, while the rule of local magnates persisted in many parts of the Sichuan frontier, in Luzhou wealthy landowners, at the apex of village society, superseded the local magnates while also asserting their independence from the state. The primacy of landownership, combined with new incentives to market the agrarian surplus, also triggered economic changes. Rising market demand for foodstuffs within the regional economy of the Sichuan Basin spurred the exploitation of arable lands. As migration to the edges of the Southern Lu frontier slowed, settlement of the northern half of the prefecture, which benefited from convenient access to transport routes and market towns, accelerated. Ironically, although the exploitation of the frontier's mineral resources never fulfilled the expectations of Wang Anshi and his "fiscalist" clique, the integration of Luzhou into the regional economy of Sichuan created a new economic role for the frontier: supplying the metropolitan centers of consumption with agricultural staples.

SEVEN

Civilizing the Frontier (II): Farming and Commerce

Despite Luzhou's importance as a strategic military and commercial center, the vast majority of the prefecture's inhabitants, laboring in the
shadows of the generals' fortresses and the merchants' markets, tilled the
soil. Capitalizing on the wealth of their numbers, the peasantry slowly
transformed their wilderness habitat of serried ridges and fog-girded forest into sculpted terraces of rice fields. By the end of the twelfth century
their relentless activity had created a prosperous agricultural landscape
and irrevocably altered the forms of settlement in this corner of the
Sinitic world.

At the same time, Luzhou achieved an unprecedented prominence
within the commercial world of Song Sichuan. The Jurchen conquest of
the north sundered Sichuan's primary trade artery, the overland route
linking Chengdu with the northern capitals of Chang'an and Kaifeng.
Subsequently the Yangzi River valley became, and would henceforth
remain, Sichuan's major avenue of trade and communication with the
rest of the empire. Thus began a gradual reorientation of Sichuan's regional economy, first evident in trade flows, from its traditional focus on
Chengdu towards a new center on Chongqing (Song Yuzhou).[1] In Song
times, however, this transition was just getting underway. Demographic
growth and agricultural productivity in the Yangzi valley remained well
below the levels maintained in the northern half of the basin. A general
decline in extraregional trade offset the increase in commercial traffic
along the Yangzi. The chief centers of consumption still were located

in northern and western Sichuan. Above all, the earlier transfer of tax revenues to the government's coffers at Kaifeng was replaced by a much more grievous hemorrhage of the region's wealth to the enormous, and enormously costly, armies amassed along the Jurchen frontier.

Luzhou participated in the intensification of intraregional trade to a greater extent than any other part of the upper Yangzi valley. Yet not all of Luzhou shared in this sudden prosperity. The degree of functional integration with networks of trade and social contact varied considerably even within one prefecture. Demand for new sources of grain stimulated agricultural exploitation of the alluvial valley bottoms north of the great river, while settlement of frontier areas ebbed. Consequently Luzhou became segmented into two economic zones. As a supplier of rice, the northern half was a hinterland, fully enmeshed in Sichuan's regional grain trade. The hillier, less arable south remained a periphery valued chiefly for its strategic military significance. Moreover, Luzhou's role in the regional marketing system was limited to the export of primary products such as rice, salt, and timber. The narrow corridors of trade largely circumvented the lives of the majority of the rural populace.

THE AGRARIAN LANDSCAPE

Luzhou lies at the southern rim of the Sichuan Basin, an ancient inland sea, where it meets the escarpment of the rugged, pock-marked Yungui Plateau. Both the basin and the plateau are covered by sandstone soils underlain by limestone rock. In many parts of the plateau, especially the eastern spur that forms the Yangzi Gorges region, tectonic action has folded and elevated the limestone beds, leaving a striated landscape of steep hills with an average of elevation of 1500–2000 meters above sea level. In both the plateau and the basin, even the smallest streams cut steep, narrow gorges through the soft sandstone, creating a dissected terrain with little flat land. The major tributaries of the Yangzi—the Min, Tuo, Fu, and Jialing Rivers—have several levels of flat terraces, formed during quiescent stages of river erosion, but the great river itself has gouged out a sharply inclined valley. Alluvial deposits have built up fertile plains along the banks of the tributaries, the most notable being the

Chengdu Plain; but with the exception of the Luzhou area, little alluvial sediment accumulated in the Yangzi valley. In both the Sichuan Basin and the Yungui Plateau, flat ground is scarce; and the steep gradients of the river valleys require relatively advanced techniques of soil management to render them suitable for wet-rice cultivation.

The purple-black sandstone soils of the basin are highly permeable, rich in mineral content, and drought-resistant, amenable to a wide range of crops. This type of soil is common in parts of Luzhou north of the Yangzi River. In the hills to the south, however, one finds purple-brown sandstone soils which, though fairly productive, are susceptible to erosion. The clearing of the original broadleaf evergreen forest and extremely heavy rainfalls (averaging over 1300 millimeters of precipitation annually in Luzhou) have resulted in severe elutriation. Layers of eroded soil deposited at the foot of the hills can be cultivated with grains, but the upland areas can support little more than root and tuber crops. Acidic, easily eroded yellow soils of negligible agricultural value cover most of the Yungui Plateau. Where purple soils once existed, they have degenerated into leached podzols. Only in the dolines of the limestone region, where repeated deposition of eroded soils has led to the formation of calcareous clays, can one find fertile soils conducive to wet-rice agriculture.[2]

Thus Luzhou's natural setting confronted farmers with formidable obstacles. Yet the landscape also offered a rich lode of productive resources: a magnificent array of subtropical fauna and flora, especially fruit trees, and abundant reserves of timber, fish, and minerals, especially salt. "Salt wells and fish ponds number in the hundreds; every family possesses them," claimed a fourth-century chronicler.[3] Despite—or perhaps because of—the southward retreat of tropical flora in China, Luzhou's wealth of tropical fruits gained far-flung renown.[4] The litchis of the upper Yangzi valley, and Luzhou in particular, became favorite delicacies at the Tang court in Chang'an. In the eighth century Emperor Xuanzong, in response to the extravagant whims of his consort Yang Guifei, built a series of courier stations to bring the just-ripening crimson fruit to the capital. The litchi orchards of Luzhou, stretching out along the northern bank of the Yangzi east and west of the city, vied with one another to produce the finest varieties. Connoisseurs regarded them as unrivaled in Sichuan.[5] Betel nut (*binlang*), longan, and apricots from Luzhou were well known to readers of pharmacopeia and botanical treatises, even if they had no opportunity to taste them themselves. The fruit of the emblic myrobalan (*yuganzi*), which tasted bitter at first but became sweet when chewed, was reputed to relieve sulphur poisoning.[6] Honey from the forests of the tribal regions, bought in the markets or surreptitiously gathered by foraging parties, was another popular ingredient in the local cuisine. Luzhou's inhabitants cooked an aqueous vegetable known as pearl greens (*zhenzhucai*) in honey, or preserved it in vinegar to make a pickled concoction carried by travelers on long journeys. The bitter long pepper (*ju*), famed for its medicinal properties, was also sweetened with honey, or alternatively used to make a condiment sauce or leaven.[7]

The variety of horticultural products, wide as it was, merely supplemented the basic diet of grain and root crops. The staple foods of the hills of southwestern Sichuan were spiked millet and taro, a cultigen of the Southeast Asian highlands. Spiked millet (*setaria italica*), an adaptable plant tolerant of poor soils and requiring relatively little care, flourished as the staple crop of both Han and native shifting cultivators in the broadleaf evergreen forest belt stretching from Yunnan to China's southeastern coast.[8] Continuous cropping with millet rapidly depleted soil nutrients, though, forcing cultivators repeatedly to clear new fields or rotate millet with legume or tuber crops.

While the question of whether cultivation of root crops represented an incipient stage of agriculture prior to the introduction of grains is debatable, it is clear that taro and millet had been the basic crops of southwest China since antiquity.[9] The native peoples of Southern Lu cultivated many varieties of taro and considered one known as "red peregrine-head" to be "most precious of all."[10] The Han expressed considerably less enthusiasm for taro; but in upland areas it was a vital supplement to the meager harvest of grains, as the prefect of Chengdu informed the court in 1070:

> The four routes of Sichuan differ from the inner provinces in that the people practice shifting cultivation and their food supply is often so inadequate that they plant taro to fill their empty bellies.[11]

A poetic expression of the prominence of taro as a landscape feature in Sichuan can be found in the works of the eighth-century poet Lu Lun, who summed up the new assignment of a friend sent to Sichuan as a fiscal official in the following words:

> *Exacting fees from commerce that enriches the barbarian traders,*
> *Taxing lands grown fat with taro fields.*[12]

While Lu associated the cultivation of taro with Sichuan's purportedly semi-barbaric character, Han and non-Han alike appreciated taro for its hardiness and bountiful yields.[13]

Taro and dryland grains prevailed as major food crops even in the prosperous sugar cane and mulberry commercial farming region of the Fu River valley, as Fan Chengda revealed in a poem entitled "Finally Seeing A Flat Valley at Suining, I Gaily Composed a Short Song":

> *The fields of the plain, level as looking at one's outstretched palm,*
> *The gravel roadbed scoured clean: we seemed to cross a mirror.*
> *Taro pits and knolls of millet glistened with heavy raindrops,*
> *Mulberry groves and bamboo edged the road, chilled by the raw wind.*[14]

In 1141 the government permitted the prefectures of the Fu River valley (Zi, Sui, Guo, and He) to ship millet instead of rice to the frontier armies because of the "extreme dearth of rice fields in this area."[15] Wang Ying-chen reported in 1167 that during the winter peasants everywhere in Sichuan grew barley and wheat to supplement their inadequate harvests of rice.[16] Dryland crops in the central parts of the basin were planted in permanent fields; but in frontier areas such as Qianzhou, Han farmers practiced shifting cultivation utilizing barley and spiked millet.[17]

The level of agricultural development in Luzhou during the Song period can only be glimpsed through several brief accounts, but all of these texts imply a low level of technological sophistication compared to the intensively worked fields of the lower Yangzi Basin. Yue Shi's universal gazetteer (ca. 980) stated that the farmers of Luzhou practiced shifting cultivation (*yutian*), more commonly known as "tilling [after clearing the forest] with a knife and planting [after burning the brush] with fire" (*daogeng huozhong*).[18] No more precise description of shifting cultivation as practiced in Luzhou exists, but Fan Chengda recorded his observations on the cropping system of the Yangzi Gorges in a preface to a poem:

> *Yu* fields are the lands in the Gorges region cultivated by felling and burning the natural vegetation. With the arrival of spring [the farmers] first make cuttings in the hills, clearing away all of the forest. When the time comes to plant, they await the onset of the rains, then in one night burn the fallen trees to use the ash as fertilizer. The following day the rains come; and taking advantage of the prepared soil, they sow the seeds. In this manner the sprouts grow luxuriantly and the farmers double their harvest; but without rain, nothing of the sort will occur. The mountains are mostly covered with stony, barren soils, low in fertility, which must be repeatedly treated by the fire-field technique before planting can begin. In the spring they sow wheat and beans, from which they make cakes and dumplings to tide them over the summer season. In the autumn the grains ripen. . . . Although they may pass their entire lives without tasting rice, they have never suffered from hunger.[19]

According to an excerpt from the *Tortoise Tumulus Records*, a now-lost Song gazetteer of Fuzhou, shifting cultivation was the rule in Kuizhou Route except for the two prefectures of Fuzhou and Yuzhou, where rice paddies predominated.[20]

The limited penetration of advanced irrigation techniques restricted wet-rice cultivation to the alluvial plains of the larger river valleys and small, isolated basins. Immigrants to Luzhou took advantage of the fertile alluvial soils of the Tuo and Chishui Rivers to grow rice rather than dryland crops. By the close of the fourteenth century, Luzhou had become a rice-growing area despite topographical constraints, according to a gazetteer dating from that time:

> Of the five grains this area is better suited for rice than millet or buckwheat. The cultivated fields of thin, stony soils are located along mountain streams [which flow too rapidly] to allow irrigation dams. When the seasonal winds and rains are in harmony, the harvest is abundant. If the weather is dry and hot, famine ensues. These lands are called "thunder peal fields" [*leimingtian*], meaning that if the rains come, the farmers will obtain the water they need to irrigate the fields.[21]

In the idiom of Sichuan "thunder peal fields" referred to terraced fields irrigated solely by rainfall. The farmers constructed embankments along the contours of the hill slopes to catch the run-off from the rains.[22] The native peoples of Southern Lu utilized the same techniques to build "watered terraces on hillside slopes" (*shanpo shuizeng*).[23] Terracing also prevented the easily eroded purple-brown soils from washing away, but irrigation was the immediate concern of the farmers. Even in the humid, rainy climate of the Sichuan Basin, two weeks without rainfall in summer dried out the purple-brown soils, as evidenced by the following thirteenth-century description of farming in Bachuan county of Hezhou, just to the northeast of Luzhou:

> Our county's mountainous, uneven terrain lacks the benefits of irrigation dikes and ponds. The popular custom of describing the farmlands of his area as "thunder peal fields" implies that if five days pass without rain, the crops become parched; after ten days, the plants wither and die. Thus years of plenty are rare, years of dearth all too frequent.[24]

In such places little rice could be grown.

As the author of the early Ming gazetteer of Luzhou cited above indicated, the steep gradients of the valleys and the rapid flow of the mountain streams rendered advanced irrigation technology such as the noria impractical. One solution to this problem involved collecting rainfall in storage ponds on the higher slopes which could be released onto the rice paddies at the proper times. The prefect of Fuzhou in 1158 mentioned that without this technique, which has since become one of the most characteristic features of Sichuan's landscape,[25] rice cultivation would be virtually impossible in his district.[26] A sixteenth-century gazetteer of Hezhou likewise noted that since the hilly terrain precluded the use of well-sweeps in this area, water storage ponds provided the sole means of irrigating rice fields.[27] The well-sweep (*jiegao*), noria (*gu*), and water-shuttle (*suo*) all were used to irrigate cultivated fields in the Chengdu Plain in Song times,[28] but we have no evidence of their use in Luzhou until much later. According to a text from 1631, at that time eight-tenths of Luzhou's cultivated lands were terraced fields extending high up the hillsides and irrigated by series of ponds and well-sweeps.[29]

The same obstacles that frustrated the farming population make it difficult to estimate the degree of intensity of cultivation in the frontier areas of Sichuan. When the central government undertook an exhaustive fiscal suvey of the empire in 1077, officials in Zizhou Route claimed that they were unable to calculate the acreage of cultivated land within their jurisdiction because the fields were scattered in isolated terraces among the hills.[30] Local officials commonly identified taxable lands in terms of parcels rather than a standard acreage measure. Thus the 1211 audit of the government estate of Pingrongzhuang in Qianwei county, Jiazhou, listed the lands recovered from local magnates as 494 "slopes" (*po*) of hill fields and 1,596 parcels (*gai*) of irrigated lands.[31] Officials were interested primarily in assigning an appropriate tax levy rather than determining the actual extent of lands under cultivation.

An inventory of state lands attached to the garrisons in Southern Lu compiled in 1181 provides a rough benchmark for the intensity of cultivation along the frontier. At that time the registers of state lands listed one thousand *qing* of lands distributed among five garrisons.[32] Irrigated fields made up one-fourth of the total. The one thousand *qing* had been divided among 754 militiamen, for an average holding of 1.33 *qing* (about 18.5 acres) per militiaman. Thus the immigrants to Southern Lu who received state land grants occupied nearly seven times the amount of land deemed sufficient to support a household in the wet-rice farming regions of South China. These large tracts of land, far more than a single household could cultivate at one time, suggest not only that land use in Southern Lu was extensive rather than intensive but also that the inhabitants practiced shifting cultivation in combination with rice farming.

No actual descriptions of farming in the alluvial purple-black soil areas of Luzhou have been preserved from Song times. Nonetheless we can infer from other evidence that these areas had become a prosperous wet-rice agricultural region in the twelfth century. The high density of markets in Luzhou and Hejiang counties serves as one index of the existence of a significant agrarian surplus. The numerous placenames derived from small, flat plains, either in valley bottoms (*ba, gai*) or amidst the hills (*kan, wu*), attest to the central importance of rice cultivation in the siting of villages (see Table 11). In recent times the irrigated rice fields of Sichuan's river valleys have become known as *batian*, a designation denoting both the physical features of the valley bottoms and the use of weirs to divert water from streams into the rice paddies.[33] The meaning of *ba* as a placeword in Song Sichuan is confused by the contemporary usage of the word *batian* in the lower Yangzi Basin to refer to both diked fields and water storage ponds.[34] I believe that in Luzhou *ba* merely signified a flat valley bottom until long after the Song period. Irrigation dikes were not yet widespread in Luzhou at the close of the fourteenth century; but by the end of the Ming, complex irrigation systems and the building of water storage ponds on hillside terraces had proliferated throughout the prefecture.[35] At the beginning of the seventeenth century, Luzhou and the neighboring prefectures of Xu and Yu ranked with Chengdu as the four most productive agricultural areas in Sichuan.[36]

Most importantly, the evidence on government procurement of grain shows that Luzhou emerged as a major rice-exporting center during the twelfth century, a position it continued to hold in recent times.[37] The assumption of this new role, coupled with Luzhou's favorable location for water transport to all parts of the Sichuan Basin, enhanced the city's participation in intraregional trade and stimulated the formation of a dense network of local markets. As the following sections will show, Luzhou's market system evolved primarily in response to the demands of an external market rather than to local consumption. The structure of the local marketing system mirrored these priorities.

TRADE AND MARKET STRUCTURE IN LUZHOU

During the phase of frontier expansion in the eleventh century, the southwestern periphery of Sichuan was a heavy importer of goods and people. In the twelfth century, the Song consolidated its political control, the growth of the Han population rapidly outstripped that of native groups, and the frontier economy became much more involved in regional markets. As the availability of cheap but non-renewable resources—such as salt in Southern Lu and iron in Nanping—diminished and the agrarian population multiplied, rice population became the basis of the local economy. At the same time, Luzhou's primary economic function as a supplier to metropolitan markets remained unchanged except that rice surpassed salt as the chief export commodity. The renewed importance of an agrarian economic base in conjunction with the continued commercial orientation resulted in a proliferation of markets and market towns throughout the prefecture. A close look at the structure of Luzhou's marketing system reveals a three-fold functional differentiation of marketing activity. Rather than an interlocking and integrated structure, Luzhou's marketing system appears to have been segregated into functionally distinct spheres of frontier trade, regional commerce, and local consumption marketing. An examination of the process of market development in Luzhou can illuminate the special role of commerce in frontier settlement and in the economic life of the Song period.

FRONTIER TRADE. The frontier both obstructs the expansion of a society and provides a portal through which pass the unique products of the transfrontier world. Even amid the pervasive hostility of bitterly contested frontiers, such as the Song-Jurchen border after 1127, a lively trade can persevere despite strenuous attempts to curtail clandestine contacts.[38] The Han, ever confident of the material as well as cultural superiority of their own civilization, regarded the special products of their world as tantalizing fruits to charm and seduce benighted foreign peoples. Song leaders calculated the value of frontier trade in terms of social control as well as profit, a theme underscored by the prefect of Luzhou in a memorial of 1136:

> Each year the southwestern tribes arrive in the autumn with horses, seeking to engage in "mutual trade" [*hushi*]. The marketplace is opened to "broad exchange" [*boyi*] and ample gifts of gold and silk are used as bait to gain profits from the exchange. Trade also functions as a technique for expressing [the hierarchical relationship between ourselves] and the haltered-and-bridled peoples. Thus the significance of trade is far-reaching indeed![39]

Exchange of goods with the native peoples took three forms. Ritual trade, which established the preeminence of the Song sovereign over foreign peoples, involved a reciprocal exchange whereby the Song bestowed gifts of precious metals and silks on the native chieftains, who in return acknowledged their inferior station. The chieftains also sealed this pact by selling war horses to the Song, purportedly at prices fixed by the latter.[40] In some areas an indemnity levy (*suoshui*) was the price the Song paid to win peace with powerful chieftains. The chief of the Xioyen, for example, traveled to Longpeng Garrison in Jiazhou each year to receive an allotment of silver, cloth, tea, silk, cauldrons, and cooking pots as compensation for permitting Han settlers to cultivate lands within the tribe's territory.[41] Finally, private trade permitted under the "broad exchange" policy at certain specified marketplaces involved, as the term suggests, trade in a wide variety of goods, both staples and luxury items. This trade, which essentially took the form of an exchange of the products of the plain for those of the forest, bridged the ecological seam that divided the Han from the native territories. The Han sold grain, tea, salt, and cloth to the tribesmen in return for forest products such as horses, timber, firewood, bamboo, honey, hides, musk, medicinal plants, and beeswax.[42] Occasionally precious goods from Southeast Asia, including the supposedly aphrodisiacal rhinocerous horn, drugs, and aromatics, passed over the Yungui Plateau and reached the "mutual trade" markets of southwestern Sichuan.[43]

Song officials were keenly aware that trade between Han and non-Han might produce heated controversy and frictions with catastrophic potential. They certainly were not overly apprehensive in this regard; two of the bloodiest border conflicts of the eleventh century began with trifling arguments in the marketplace. The court insisted that prefects limit trade with native peoples to a few officially designated places under the eyes of a state official. Lu You, on his excursion through Sichuan in 1178, observed the activity at the principal frontier market of Xuzhou:

> The tribesmen cannot use their own language to communicate [with Han buyers], so in these districts there are special officials for tribal affairs [*manpanguan*] who conduct the transactions on their behalf. The *manpanguan* is a state official; but the tribesmen fear and defer to him, obeying his every word. In cases of gross inequity, though, they will assemble in the prefect's court and sue to have the transaction renegotiated.[44]

Stopping illicit trade was a constant theme of reports from border officials. Below Xuzhou, where the upper course of the Yangzi, known in Song times as the Mahu River, joins the Min River, the Song stretched iron cables across the river to prevent the natives from floating timber down into Han territory.[45] Xu Yi, prefect of Luzhou in 1210, took umbrage at the audacity of tribal leaders seeking to circumvent the official frontier trade system. No sooner had Xu expressed a willingness to consider a petition from the leader of the Bozhou Yang to incorporate Bozhou into the Song realm than he discovered that the Yang had surreptitiously floated down into Luzhou great quantities of cunning-hamia timber to sell at market. Xu angrily ordered his subordinates to seize the contraband, after which he rejected the Yangs' petition and instead made preparations to build a Han garrison on the Anle River to check any future recurrence of clandestine trade.[46]

The restrictions on private trade between Han and non-Han had a dual purpose. Private trade created problems simply by encouraging social intercourse and economic ties between two groups that the Song assiduously tried to keep separate.[47] Trade and the roads that carried it breached the "thorny hedgerow" (*fanli*) that set apart two societies perceived as fundamentally antagonistic to each other. The military governor of Sichuan confided his concerns about the erosion of natural barriers by trading relations in a dispatch to the court in 1180:

> In the prefectures of Sichuan bordering on the tribal regions, signal beacons have been raised on the frontier to indicate the "forbidden hills" [*jinshan;* in other words, the neutral zone between Han and non-Han settlements declared off-limits to both]. Over the years the inhabitants of these areas have cut down the forest and opened new lands, ravaging the landscpe without cease. Your servant requests that the restrictions closing off the mountains to settlement be enforced and the people enjoined from seeking tenements [*qingdian*], felling timber, and engaging in itinerant commerce.[48]

The restrictions against cutting forests to gouge out roads or bring new lands under cultivation dated back to 1007 but always had been difficult, if not impossible, to enforce.[49] The frequent complaints of violations of these laws, and the continual advance of the signal beacons in order to keep the official frontier between the Han and non-Han villages, underscored the effectiveness of this policy.

In addition, the Song state sought to restrict trade in order to use trading privileges as bait for luring native leaders into a conciliatory posture. Seeing how eagerly the native leaders vied for trading relations, Song officials drew the conclusion that the natives depended on the goods of the Middle Kingdom for their livelihood:

> The tribal bandits depend on the Han for the goods they require to meet their bodily needs. If the annual dispensation of rewards for meritorious service at Jiazhou is halted and mutual trade at Xuzhou suspended, the tribal peoples will suffer dearth and hardship.[50]

In 1184 the military governor of Sichuan, Zhao Ruyu, resorted to suspending trade to convince the Mahu tribesmen to cease their raids on Han settlements in Jiazhou and return prisoners taken during the course of their pillage.[51] Although the tactic of suspending trade to discourage raiding was approved as early as 1074, Zhao Ruyu apparently was the first official to use it. After all, an embargo on trade with the tribesmen hurt Han merchants and frontier inhabitants as well as the intended targets. In 1211 the judicial intendant of Chengdu Route, Li Zhi, attempted to impose an embargo on the Iituo tribesmen (one of the Mahu subgroups) in order to force them to cease their raids on Han settlers at Lidian Garrison in Jiazhou. Li found even his colleagues uncooperative. The Luzhou pacification intendant promised to suspend "mutual trade" at Xuzhou, which lay outside Li Zhi's jurisdiction, but in fact took no retaliatory action against the tribesmen. "The inhabitants of Xuzhou profit from this trade with tribal peoples," Li complained to the court, "and even barter for goods taken in the raids on Lidian."[52] Despite its questionable effectiveness, the threat of suspending trade remained a key weapon in the Song diplomatic arsenal.

Frontier trade could be beneficial in alleviating shortages of staples by widening the resource base that supported communities on either side of the border. At the same time trade in staples created dependent relationships with potentially damaging consequences. Isolated Shizhou, deep within the tribal territories of the Gorges region, required a large contingent of soldiers to defend the Han populace from the tribes that surrounded them on all sides. After a native uprising in 1000, the fiscal intendant of eastern Sichuan, Ding Wei, augmented the garrison at Shizhou with new fortifications and fresh troops. In order to feed the soldiers, though, food had to be carried overland from the Yangzi valley at great cost. Ding Wei struck an agreement with the native tribes of Shizhou whereby the Han would exchange salt, a scarce good in the eastern half of the Yungui Plateau, in return for the natives' grain, an arrangement celebrated on both sides.[53] The Song officials also wished to cultivate an amicable relationship with the natives because they had no recourse but to rely on native mercenaries to defend the Gorges should the Wang Jun rebellion, then raging in central Sichuan, threaten to spill into the central Yangzi region.[54] Yet this unseemly dependence on the

Gorges tribes for food and mercenaries clearly made the Song court uneasy. In 1005 Ding's protégé and successor, Xue Yan, recruited Han households to settle in Shizhou and neighboring Qianzhou. In the first year, he could report, the new settlers reaped a harvest of ten thousand *dan* of millet.[55] As Shizhou's Han population grew, to nearly twenty thousand households by 1080, the roles of provider and dependent reversed. By the 1070s, during years of dearth the tribal peoples of Shizhou had been reduced to procuring grain from the Han, paid for in precious metals at twice the market value.[56]

The trade that most upset Song officials was illicit dealings in lands. In 1073 the Song court reversed its previous policy and approved the purchase of tribal lands by Han settlers but continued to forbid the Han from selling lands to the tribesmen.[57] Even before 1073, powerful Han families usurped lands belonging to the native peoples.[58] During the 1060s a local magnate in Jiazhou, Wang Wenkui, "occupied and cultivated the hills and slopes of the tribal region" in an area later known as the Laiyin Estate. The court, upon learning of this breach of established borders, ordered that the lands be returned; but the Han inhabitants of Laiyin secretly negotiated to pay an annual indemnity of three hundred pieces of silk in compensation for the right to settle on these lands. Later on, though, the tribesmen demanded larger indemnities, embittering and antagonizing the Han settlers.[59] In the "submitted territories" incorporated into the Song realm during Cai Jing's tenure as prime minister, private sales of land between Han and non-Han were prohibited entirely. During the Southern Song, when refugees and immigrants from northern and central China swelled the population of Sichuan, the state was unable to prevent clandestine sales in such areas, as the following court discussion, dating from 1183, indicates:

> Recently many migrants from other prefectures and officials with their retinues have taken up residence in the county of Qingfu and the post station of Laifu [both subordinated to Xuzhou]. . . . They covet and aggrandize the lands of the tribesmen, actions which have given rise to numerous lawsuits and judicial proceedings. Everyone inside the yamen and out takes bribes from the powerful magnates. The translators bend to the will of the latter and alter the sense [of the tribesmen's petitions to the Song authorities]. For any crime, even murder, the tribal people lack recourse. . . . We request that laws prohibiting

the Han from encroaching upon or purchasing the lands and fields of the tribesmen be strictly enforced and that a heavy charge be laid on local officials to respond to, and make every effort to understand the intent of, the suits of the tribal peoples.[60]

Ordinarily the officials responsible for enforcing these restrictions were the garrison commanders, who could profit immensely by encouraging Han immigration and bringing additional lands under their own control. In some cases the garrison commanders imposed their own extra-legal demands on the native peoples. In 1164 censors dispatched by the central government accused the garrison commanders at Jiazhou of demanding "exploitative exactions of honey, beeswax, and red pepper from the tribal regions, which the tribal peoples found intolerable."[61] On the other hand, some tribal chieftains in this same area wielded sufficient power to impose their own tribute terms on their Han neighbors, leading to mutual resentment and recriminations.

The goods that passed through the frontier markets of Sichuan's southern border undoubtedly constituted an important component of local commerce. Given the sharply contrasting resources on either side of the frontier, opportunities for trade yielded benefits for producers and consumers among both Han and non-Han alike. The scale of trade was too small, and the native peoples' demand for Han goods too limited, for the border trade to exert much influence on the regional economy of Sichuan as a whole.[62] Trade could have a positive effect on inter-ethnic relations by creating bonds of mutual self-interest among trading partners, yet just as frequently commerce heightened conflict when divergent notions of a "just price" and profit-seeking clashed. As we have seen, many of the border conflicts in Southern Lu during the eleventh century grew out of disputes in the marketplace. The Song state employed trade as a political tool to extract concessions on other issues of contention that threatened to upset the stability of the frontier; but once initiated, frontier trade proved difficult to control.

REGIONAL COMMERCE. Daily reminders of the central place of salt in Luzhou's economy abounded, from the sight of salt merchants' ships plying the Yu River to the precious handful poured into a peasant's bowl in the marketplace. Yet the salt wells employed only a fraction of

Luzhou's population, while the great majority of the inhabitants tilled the soil. The salt trade, like the great rivers, flowed around rather than through the peasants' quotidian world, bound for distant and barely imagined cities. Most of the salt wells were located in tribal regions, which, from the Han point of view, were fit abodes for ne'er-do-well migrant saltworkers, perhaps, but dangerous places to stake out a homestead and raise a family. The salt trade and industry, Luzhou's primary link with the regional marketing system of Sichua, stood apart from the local economy.

Although the salt industry remained the economic base of the prefecture of Changning (created at Yujing in 1111), its relative importance in the wider economy of Southern Lu declined in the twelfth century. The paucity of data precludes anything but a rough dating of this decline. For the late Song the most we can say is that salt production continued, perhaps even at a level comparable to the Northern Song, but Changning's prominence in the intraregional salt market declined precipitously. In the mid-twelfth century, Yujing's share of the state-operated sector of Sichuan's salt industry dwindled to a mere 3.6 percent, compared to 13.4 percent in the Northern Song.[63] In 1281 the newly established Yuan dynasty set a quota of 120,000 *jin* for the Yujing salt wells, a drop of 71 percent since 1152.[64] After the thirteenth century, salt became a vestigial industry in Southern Lu. Several late Ming geographical works mention salt wells in Changning, but other contemporary sources indicate that salt production there was insignificant.[65] The salt industry continued to play an important part in the local economy during the Southern Song—salt revenues paid for all of Changning prefecture's administrative costs and nearly half of Southern Lu's military expenditures—but it no longer was expanding and attracting capital and immigrants. By contrast, the wells in Luzhou north of the Yangzi, chiefly those at Nanjing, matched Yujing's output by the beginning of the thirteenth century, while production at the Fushun wells had increased 113 percent since the late tenth century.[66] Concentration of capital and labor in the salt industry shifted permanently to the Tuo River valley.[67]

As salt production leveled off and perhaps declined in the twelfth century, the proportion of Luzhou's population involved in the salt industry shrank. The waves of immigrants that surged into Luzhou in the

1070s, 1110s, and the early decades of the Southern Song were of peasant stock, in many cases from the wheat-and-rice growing valleys of the Han and Huai Rivers. During the Southern Song, if not earlier, the hinterland of Luzhou developed into a mature rice-producing region which, though beset by the transportation problems typical of the Sichuan Basin, became fully incorporated into the regional grain market of the upper Yangzi. Along Southern Lu's frontier, on the other hand, the homesteads of the Han settlers remained isolated by the rugged terrain, dispersed settlement patterns, and marginal market involvement.

Although we have no direct evidence concerning the private grain trade in Luzhou, the state's procurement policies indicate that Luzhou generated ample surpluses which circulated throughout the regional rice markets of the Yangzi, Tuo, and Jialing River valleys. In 1136, for example, the military governor of Sichuan, Xi Yi, proposed to resolve the problem of supplying the massive armies on Sichuan's northern border by purchasing rice on the private market in the Yangzi valley prefectures of Lu, Xu, Yu, and Fu.[68] Xi's recommendation was turned down because of a lack of funds, but his proposal suggests that rice was available in the markets of the Yangzi valley at relatively low prices. By the latter half of the twelfth century, the markets of Luzhou had become an important source for state-operated procurement programs. During the devastating famine of 1167–1168, large quantities of rice were purchased in Luzhou and Yuzhou to alleviate drought-stricken areas in the Jialing valley. At the same time fiscal officials in Chengdu Route, the richest part of Sichuan, purchased 50,000 *dan* of rice in the counties of Luzhou, Jiang'an, and Nanqi in Xuzhou to supplement their own insufficient rice stocks.[69] In 1182 the government made massive purchases of rice, wheat, vegetables, and millet in Luzhou to meet the needs of famine relief in the neighboring drought-afflicted prefectures of Chang, He, Pu, and Zi.[70]

The primary stimulus for a regionwide rice market originated with the state's need to supply the standing armies defending Sichuan's northern borders against the Jurchen invasions. From the inception of the Southern Song, special fiscal agencies assumed responsibility for raising substantial revenues to support these armies. In order to obtain sufficient foodstuffs, Sichuan's fiscal planners instituted a policy of "matched purchases" (*duidi*), whereby each taxpaying household was required to sell to the state an amount of grain equal to its tax quota. Although the state was supposed to match prevailing market prices in making *duidi* purchases, in practice the taxpayers received less than half of fair market value, and in some cases no compensation whatsoever. To correct such abuses and reduce its transport costs, Sichuan's General Commissariat (*Zonglingsuo*), founded in 1140, jettisoned the *duidi* system in 1148 in favor of purchasing grain from private merchants at depots set up in the Jialing River valley.[71] Nonetheless, the state continued the compulsory sales in the slightly disguised form of "harmonious purchases" (*hedi*). In the 1170s the General Commissariat annually collected 600,000 *dan* on the private market.[72]

The documents on *hedi* and *duidi* do not refer explicitly to Luzhou, but we can infer that Luzhou contributed a significant share to these procurement programs. In the first place, the Song limited compulsory sales to Chengdu and Zizhou Routes, drastically reducing the Chengdu's share from 95 percent of the total in the 1130s to a mere 20 percent in the mid-1150s.[73] Since the Jialing River valley served as the major conduit for the shipment of grain to the frontier armies, the Yangzi valley prefectures had much easier access to the General Commissariat's procurement depots than did the Chengdu Plain. On the local level, the pacification intendancy depended on compulsory sales, totaling 20,000 *dan* of rice annually, to supply Luzhou's border garrisons.[74] Luzhou's importance as a source of grain for Sichuan as a whole was stressed in a report written by the prefect of Chengdu, Yuan Yueyou, in the 1190s. Yuan stated that the government purchased rice for its own stockpiles in the prefectures of Lu and Yu in the Yangzi valley in addition to Han, Mei, and Huai'an prefectures because those areas (1) have considerable surpluses, (2) rarely suffer years of dearth, and (3) are conveniently accessible by water transport.[75] Climate, soil, and waterways supplied the material conditions which the farming populace of Luzhou transmuted into a prosperous rice-growing region.

Virtually all of this activity in producing and marketing rice surpluses was concentrated in the prefectural county of Luzhou. In the two counties along the frontier, less intensive patterns of cultivation prevailed. No Song figures on farming acreage in Luzhou have survived; but data from the first decade of the fifteenth century show that although the prefectural county contained only 65 percent of the registered population (and presumably a much smaller percentage of its rural inhabitants), the county accounted for 82 percent of the prefecture's taxable arable lands.[76] The same source also suggests that farmland in the prefectural county was much more likely to be planted in rice than in dryland grains or tuber crops, and thus was cultivated more intensively, a conclusion reinforced by our knowledge of the differing natural resources of the two areas.

Aside from salt the frontier areas did produce another valuable commodity: timber. We have already noted that the native tribes and the Han carried on a lively, though often illegal, trade in timber. Thick stands of cunninghamia (*shan*) and nanmu evergreens covered the hills of Southern Lu at elevations above six hundred meters. These two hardwood conifers, especially prized as building material for ships and large buildings, also were used in the manufacture of fine furniture. After the Jurchen conquest of North China in 1127, the demand for timber needed for military purposes soared. In 1136 a memorialist protested that all along the frontier of southern Sichuan the Han inhabitants engaged in timber cutting, shipbuilding, and weapons manufacture, with the result that the "forbidden hills" separating the Han from the native territories had been almost completely denuded.[77] Six months later Xi Yi recommended that the state itself initiate shipbuilding in the prefectures of Lu, Xu, Jia, and Qian, using timber cut on state-owned lands.[78] Predictably, Xi Yi's proposal was rejected because of the fear of destroying the defensive screen protecting Han settlements from the depredations of the indigenous tribes. Regardless of the repeated proscriptions against illegal trade in timber, logging and clandestine trade flourished, fueled by the perennial demand for ships and military supplies. In 1197 the court reiterated the injunctions against Han felling timber or bringing goods into tribal territories to trade for timber and enjoined the tribal peoples from selling timber to the Han outside of the supervised market at Xuzhou.[79]

ECONOMIC INTEGRATION OF THE AGRARIAN HINTERLAND

The commercialization of staple goods and the formation of regional and national marketing structures during the Song period engendered an unprecedented proliferation of rural markets. In the Chengdu Plain, marketing activity achieved a particularly intense level. The great medicine fairs in Chengdu and the springtime silkworm fairs held in many of the plain's towns at the beginning of the sericulture season attracted thousands of marketgoers. Periodic markets, which in Sichuan acquired the curious name of "ague markets" (*jieshi*), took place on a frequent schedule in the countryside:

> In Shu there are "ague markets" where marketgoers gather on alternate days. The custom of naming the markets after the ague resulted from the similarity between this [market periodicity] and an attack of the ague [*jienüe*], in which a day of cold chills is followed by a day of flashes of fever.[80]

This description of market periodicity suggests a cycle of two days, a fairly active schedule; but no source refers to "ague markets" with any greater geographic specificity than Shu (that is, all of Sichuan), or western Shu, which usually signified the Chengdu Plain. Without further corroborative information we must presume that such a high frequency of market periodicity was confined to a few highly commercialized districts. The topography and limited transport facilities of the Sichuan Basin as a whole militated against such frequent and easy access to itinerant peddlers and merchants.

Still, rural markets sprang up quickly in the wake of pioneer settlement. In 1077, after the government's initial encouragement of migration to Southern Lu, the new homesteaders began to set up their own markets, prompting the central government to issue the following directive:

> In localities within Xuzhou and Luzhou where tribesmen and Han households live far from the county seats and are unable to purchase foodstuffs, salt, tea, and farming tools, those who wish to set up a rural market [*caoshi*] in their own locality and summon other households to come to live and pursue their trade there must first submit a petition to the prefecture. The prefecture in turn will ask the Fiscal Office to send an official to determine whether the market has long-term potential and make an evaluation. If permission is granted, then in accordance with existing regulations the wine levy and other taxes must be collected and transmitted to the prefecture.[81]

The rural markets of the frontier existed to meet the subsistence needs of settlers far removed from the focal points of commercial activity.

Compared to the commercialized agricultural areas north of the Yangzi, rural markets were sparsely distributed in Southern Lu; yet each market served a smaller population, roughly 570 households, than did those north of the Yangzi (Table 13). These figures accord with our view of Southern Lu as an area of dispersed, subsistence-oriented settlement, isolated from higher levels of the market structure by poor transport and low consumer demand. With the exception of the salt wells at Yujing, settlement in Southern Lu failed to stimulate secondary economic activities and urban growth. The principal urban form in Southern Lu was the garrison town. Even the Yangzi River port of Jiang'an and the salt production center of Changning, both of which contained official yamens, numbered large contingents of soldiers among their inhabitants.

In contrast to Southern Lu, a dense marketing network had emerged in the commercial agricultural areas. Excluding the county seats, the prefectural county of Luzhou averaged one market for every three settlements, Hejiang county one market for every four settlements, while Jiang'an contained only one market for every 9.5 settlements. In addition, a second order of market towns (*zhen*), which functioned as intermediate bulking centers and riverine trading ports, developed along the major water routes in Luzhou and Hejiang, though none appeared in Jiang'an (Map 4). There is little doubt that these *zhen* represent market towns rather than the old garrison towns, since none of the *zhen* listed in the 1220 gazetteer had existed in 1080.[82] The market towns became significant urban aggregations. Lugangzhen, on the Chishui River descending from Changzhou, had 587 households in 1220, while Caoshi, farther upriver, attained a population of 639 households (Table 14). These market towns equalled in size the population of the county seat of Hejiang (596 households). The proliferation and magnitude of marketing centers in Luzhou and Hejiang counties clearly indicates a high level of market activity and the growth of secondary occupations to provide services for the agrarian population.

Marketing in Southern Lu evolved along very different lines from those by which it developed in the rich agricultural areas in the northern part of the prefecture. Markets preceded settlers in the frontier, their locations determined by the needs of facilitating the shipment of salt to Luzhou and other parts of Sichuan and of supplying the military out-

TABLE 13 Markets in Luzhou, ca. 1220

	Luzhou	Hejiang	Jiang'an
Market Towns	7	3	1
County Seat	1	1	1
Other towns (*zhen*)	6	2	0
Rural Markets	29	14	20
Markets (*shi*)	27	9	7
Inns (*dian*)	2	0	3
Garrison-markets (*zhaishi*)	0	5	0
Garrisons	0	0	10
Total Number of Marketplaces	36	17	21
Settlements	111	67	199
Settlements/Marketplace	3.1	3.9	9.5
Rural Markets/Market Town	4.1	4.7	20.0
Households	22,563	13,030	11,951
Households/Marketplace	627	766	569
Households/Market Town	3,223	4,343	11,951

Source: *JYP*, cited in *YLDD* 2217/18b–23b

posts along the frontier. The siting of the latter was determined by strategic concerns rather than economic ones. Consequently few of the garrisons served as centers of rural trade; indeed, the garrisons built after 1073 tended to be located far from the people they defended. The markets in Southern Lu created their own demand in the form of saltworkers or homesteading militiamen who were given lands in the vicinity of the more important garrisons (Legong, Zhenghe, Bowang, Meiling, and Banqiao), yet these markets remained poorly integrated into the larger marketing network. The frontier inhabitants devoted nearly all of their energy and resources simply to meeting their subsistence needs.

In the northern half of Luzhou, on the other hand, rural markets and a superordinate level of market towns developed as a consequence of the intensification of settlement, production, and exogenous consumer demand. The dense network of rural markets probably reflected not a high degree of local demand but the limited range of consumers. Handicapped by a lack of roads, bridges, and navigable streams, the inhabitants

Map 4 Marketing Network and Topography of the Luzhou Region

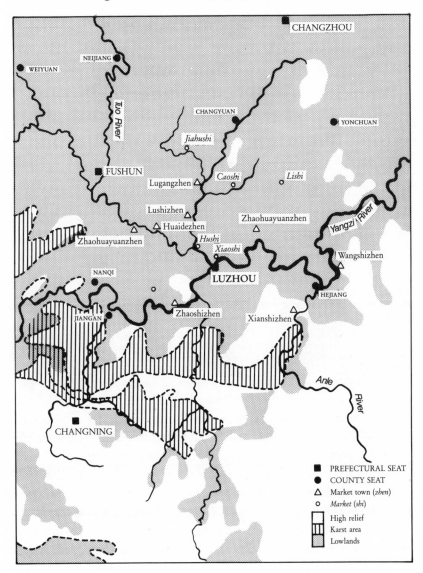

CHANGZHOU

NEIJIANG

WEIYUAN

Tuo River

CHANGYUAN

YONCHUAN

Jiahushi

FUSHUN

Lugangzhen

Caoshi

Lishi

Lushizhen

Zhaohuayuanzhen

Yangzi River

Huaidezhen

Zhaohuayuanzhen

Hushi

Xiaoshi

Wangshizhen

NANQI

LUZHOU

HEJIANG

JIANGAN

Zhaoshizhen

Xianshizhen

Anle

River

CHANGNING

■ PREFECTURAL SEAT
● COUNTY SEAT
△ Market town (*zhen*)
○ *Market (shi)*
▯ High relief
▥ Karst area
▦ Lowlands

TABLE 14 Urban Populations in Luzhou, ca. 1220[a]

	Number of Households	County
Administrative Seats:		
Luzhou	N.A.	
Jiang'an	N.A.	
Hejiang	596	
Market Towns and Markets:		
Caoshi	639	Luzhou
Lugangzhen	587	Luzhou
Xianshi	447	Luzhou
Renshi	328	Luzhou
Xiaoshi	300[b]	Luzhou
Huaidezhen and Sheming	823	Luzhou
Tuolushi and Yanjing	679	Luzhou
Xianshizhen and Yinshi	660	Hejiang
Hushi and Dawangcun	352	Luzhou

Source: *JYP,* cited in *YLDD,* 2217/18b–23b.

Notes: [a]These figures are based on the population figures for communes (*du*) comprised of one or two settlements. The distinction between urban and rural was an ambiguous one, and most likely these figures included rural families living outside the principal settlement.

[b]"Formerly the inhabitants numbered one thousand families. After the devastation of flooding [in 1214] the remnants numbered a mere one-third of the former population": *JYP,* cited in *YLDD,* 2217/22b.

of even the rich agricultural areas could not venture far to market. Metropolitan consumers' demand for rice produced in the agricultural hinterland grew steadily, though, and the range of grain merchants widened correspondingly. The market towns of Luzhou served as the collection points for grain in preparation for shipment to distant markets. The prosperity of the market towns of Luzhou, several of which had populations greater than two thousand persons, principally owed to their location along major waterways and their role in facilitating the flow of Luzhou's agricultural wealth to the metropolitan centers. The local markets remained divorced from intraregional trade, especially since staple consumer goods like rice, salt, tea, and wine all were produced in ample quantities within Luzhou's precincts.

Luzhou's position at the confluence of the Yangzi and Tuo Rivers endowed the prefectual capital with great potential as a commercial center. But like many of the port cities of the Upper Yangzi valley, notably Yuzhou (modern Chongqing) and Kuizhou, Luzhou's location on a raised river terrace surmounted by steep hills hindered its development as a local marketing center:[83]

> Mountains lie south and west of Luzhou; to the east and north the town reaches to the edge of the Great River. The hills branch off into numerous ridges of irregular height. The site is not at all suited for establishing a marketplace.[84]

Cut off from its own rural hinterland by imposing bluffs and broad rivers, Luzhou served poorly as the prefecture's central market. Another commercial center, the "Little Market Town" (Xiaoshizhen) sprang up directly across the Tuo River, connected by road to the agricultural areas north of the city. Xiaoshi became a bustling port town numbering a thousand households before it was devastated by a flood at the beginning of the thirteenth century. Subsequently Xiaoshi lost its *zhen* status, although it regained its former position as a marketing center after a protective dike was built in 1214.[85] The growth of market towns contributed to the horizontal exchange of goods and services within the prefecture but did not lead to a concentration of secondary productive activities in Luzhou, which functioned above all as a transshipment point for long-distance trade. Luzhou's physical isolation from the farming hinterland, the underutilization of the Yangzi River as a transport route, and the general orientation of trade towards the Chengdu Plain all figured in the rapid growth of market towns along the Chishui and Tuo Rivers.

From the perspective of demand, Luzhou's rural population had little propensity for market participation. The peasant devoted by far the greater part of his income to feeding his family, and the family consumed most of what it produced. If the family's income increased, its members probably enjoyed a higher standard of food consumption, more rice and perhaps wheat instead of millet, buckwheat, legumes, or taro. The bulk of the surplus went to meet the household's social dues: the landlord's rent, the moneylender's interest, the state's taxes. These three creditors not only garnered a substantial part of the peasant's income but also took the highest quality goods, such as the better grades of rice, leaving the peasant with the less esteemed red rice (*chimi*), buckwheat, or as a last resort taro, ordinarily associated with the "foraging tribesmen." Most of Sichuan's rural population cultivated rice as a cash crop, grown solely to meet obligations to creditors. During the Northern Song the state collected the land tax in Sichuan in the form of various kinds of silk cloth, forcing the peasant to sell what he produced for silk goods, often at an unfavorable rate of exchange. After 1127 the massive armies raised to defend Sichuan's northern frontier relied on substantial increases in levies on liquor and salt in addition to the program of compulsory grain sales to the state in order to meet provisioning requirements.[86] The burden of the additional taxes on consumption no doubt further diminished the peasant's propensity to consume.

The weakness of local consumer demand, the subsistence orientation of the frontier areas, and the limitation of Luzhou's participation in the regional economy of Sichuan to the export of primary products—salt, rice, and timber—betoken a general pattern of economic development during the Song. In the eleventh century the growth of cash-crop agriculture (tea, sugar, and fiber plants) and urban industries was concentrated in the Chengdu Plain, along the main transport route from Chengdu across the Qinling Mountains to Kaifeng, and to a lesser extent along the upper courses of the Fu and Jialing Rivers. The twin foci of Chengdu and Zizhou accounted for the bulk of industrial growth, mainly in artisan handicrafts and large-scale textile production.[87] In the Southern Song the transport link with Kaifeng was broken; but the major centers of consumption remained in the northern part of the Sichuan Basin, principally the cities of the Chengdu Plain and the huge army camps along the Jurchen border. The towns of the Yangzi valley did not experience a similar growth in secondary production. Instead they remained small trading points on the attenuated trade route connecting the Sichuan Basin with the lower reaches of the Yangzi River. Fan Chengda, descending the Yangzi by boat in 1177, found each town more dreary and desolate than the last. Lu You commented that Guizhou, in the midst of the Gorges, numbered only three to four hundred households and contributed a meager five thousand *dan* of rice, wheat, and millet annually in taxes, "equivalent to a single household of the lowest category in Wu [Liangzhe]."[88]

The only regionwide statistical basis for the conclusion that consumption was centered in the northern half of the basin is the table of commercial tax receipts for 1077 compiled by the court statistician Bi Zhongyan in his *Complete Report of the Secretariat* (*Zhongshu beidui*) and later copied into the *Digest of Essential Song Documents*. Statistics from a single year can induce a false sense of certitude; but Bi Zhongyan's figures represented projected revenues based on past trends, and short-term variations presumably did not unduly influence his data. Moreover these statistics accurately reflected the taxable portion of commercial activity at the height of the dynasty's economic vigor.

The Sichuan data depict a highly unbalanced distribution of commercial activity (Map 5). No city in the Yangzi valley, including Yuzhou, served as a major metropolitan center of industry, trade, or consumption. The level of commercial activity decreased as one moved down the major river routes leading away from the Chengdu Plain to the Yangzi valley. No Yangzi valley town dominated the rest. The nine principal towns, all prefectural capitals, were relatively undifferentiated links in the chain of long-distance trade. This trade route still was restricted largely to high-value goods and luxury items, above all Sichuan's famed damasks and brocades.[89] The Yangzi valley towns provided transshipment facilities for long-distance trade, while their hinterlands produced staples and regional specialties destined for metropolitan markets. Few of these goods were drawn into local consumer markets.

The evidence on marketing in Luzhou, imperfect as it is, describes a tripartite marketing structure but not a tightly nested hierarchy of marketing levels. On the most basic level, a dense network of village markets emerged to meet the needs of a peasantry dispersed throughout a frontier area with poor roads and few navigable waterways. The proliferation of these markets reflected not a high degree of market participation but rather the limited threshold of consumer demand. At the next level, strong urban demand for foodstuffs prompted wholesale merchants to increase their range in search of new sources of supply. Exogenous mercantile demand also stimulated the founding of new market towns in the rice-producing areas. In Luzhou market towns fell

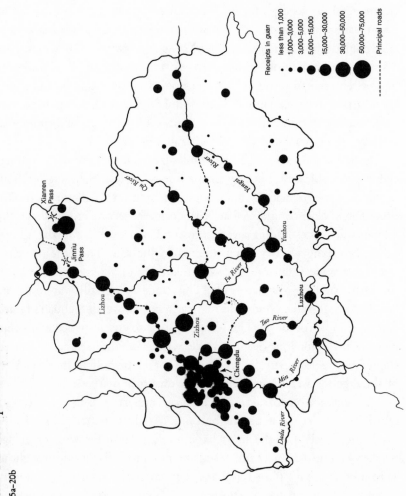

MAP 5 Commercial Tax Receipts in Sichuan, 1077

Source: SHY shihuo 16/15a–20b

into two categories. One set, commonly designated as *zhen*, enjoyed favorable access to water transport and served as collection centers for goods produced in more remote rural areas, while another set, located at the edge of the frontier, handled the trade between the Han and non-Han territories. The market towns also provided goods and services for rural areas, but these goods and services were local in nature and not products of the larger mercantile system. The third level of the marketing structure, intraregional trading cities, was with few exceptions export-oriented and facilitated the flow of mineral, forest, and agricultural products to metropolitan markets. The indigenous village markets at the bottom of this hierarchy of marketing levels had virtually no interaction with the top.

Luzhou's role in the regional economy, then, was that of a producer rather than a consumer. The marketing structure evolved from the top down, initially to expedite the delivery of salt from Yujing to Chengdu Route, and later to collect and ship rice to markets throughout Sichuan. Since salt producers were clustered together in a few places, they needed only a minimal infrastructure to convey their goods to urban markets. Rice and other agricultural products were a different matter. The procurement of rice from innumerable small producers spread widely across a hilly landscape required an elaborate commercial system. In addition to the market towns, with their inns, warehouses, and wharves, that developed along the major waterways, a network of brokers (*yaren*) and rice wholesalers (*mipuhu*) extended throughout Sichuan to handle the intraregional trade.[90] On the local level an economic elite of "influential households" and local magnates, who in their roles as landlords, moneylenders, and tax farmers gained control of local grain supplies, dominated rice markets. The commercialization of rice production resulted not from primary producers responding to market opportunities but rather from the appropriation of the agricultural surplus by the local elite who in turn sold their hoards to regional brokers and merchants. Regionwide arbitrage of foodstuffs was common in Sichuan as in other parts of South China.[91] Thus the commercial integration of Luzhou into the larger mercantile world of Sichuan led to a steady drain of the region's wealth into the centers of consumption, with little profit returning to the actual cultivators. Nor did the absorption of Luzhou into the mercantile system bring about full integration with the core areas of economic and demographic growth. At the end of the thirteenth century the exhaustion of salt and timber resources, followed by the devastation and depopulation brought about by the Mongol conquest, plunged Luzhou into the shadowy existence of a frontier backwater, from which it emerged again only in the sixteenth century.

EIGHT

A Cycle of Frontier Expansion

When Emperor Yingzong died in January, 1067, shortly after his thirty-sixth birthday, the heir apparent, known to history as Emperor Shenzong, was only twenty. Chief among the many pressing troubles facing the young emperor was the renewed menace of invasion by the Tangut Xixia kingdom. The Song had narrowly escaped total rout at the hands of Xixia twenty years before, and once again the Tanguts were advancing upon the Song's northwestern frontier. Near the end of the first year of his reign, the emperor issued a broad appeal for reform of government, opening the door to men of imagination and intellect who could rise to the challenge of "meeting the urgent priorities of governing the realm" and devising "secret strategems for repulsing the enemy."[1] Within a year's time he had found his paladin in Wang Anshi, whose bold and forceful vision of a renascent empire impressed the fledgling monarch.

Ten years before, Wang Anshi had composed a striking dissertation on the reform of government that foreshadowed the activist and interventionist administration he led from 1069 to 1077. Wang's "Ten-Thousand Word Memorial" of 1058 focused on the twin goals of shoring up frontier defenses against foreign invaders and relieving the economic misery of the vast majority of the population. Wang, like most statesmen of his time, viewed the threat of annihilation at the hands of the Tanguts or the Khitan as the greatest peril confronting the dynasty. He denounced the common run of bureaucrats for coveting positions of prestige within the civil service while sloughing off the vital responsibility for the defense of the realm onto a class of "common soldiers, frequently unreliable men of shameful repute who would not have forsaken family and friends to answer the summons for enlistment if their conduct and talents had merited them an honorable station in their home villages."[2] By belittling and underpaying officers and civil servants who served in frontier posts, Wang warned, the leading statesmen of the day had inflicted grave injury to the state by abandoning responsibility for perhaps the most sensitive task of government.

In addition to homiletic prescriptions for combining the roles of scholar and warrior in the person of the ideal statesman, Wang sketched out several substantive proposals to reinvigorate state and society. The first concerned regaining control of key economic resources, properly the estate of the emperor, usurped by a rentier class of nefarious "aggrandizers" (*jianbing zhi jia*). The rentiers had not only seized control of crucial sectors of commerce vital to the defense of the realm, such as tea, salt, grain, and international trade, but also had dispossessed the bulk of the peasantry and deprived them of their means of livelihood. Wang, in accord with many of his contemporaries, attributed the impoverishment of the peasantry to the rentiers rather than to exorbitant taxation. Wang admitted that corruption was rife throughout the Song bureaucracy and that taxation weighed heavily on the populace, but he denied that the appropriation of surplus wealth by the state was inherently evil:

> We must exploit the wealth of the realm in order to meet the fiscal costs of the realm. Since antiquity, it is not insufficiency which the rulers of every age regard as the common misfortune of the realm; rather, misfortune lies in not understanding the Way of managing wealth.[3]

Wang subscribed to the popular notion that the Song had ceded control over commerce and commodity prices to powerful merchants and the great commercial guilds. In 1069, within a month of his appointment to the Privy Council, Wang won approval for the creation of a Finance Planning Commission expressly charged with a mandate to recover "power over the ratios of exchange and the collection and distribution of revenues" (*qingzhong liansan zhi quan*).[4] Wang was deeply committed to the idea that enlightened and impartial control over money and commerce would result not only in the augmentation of the wealth of the realm but also its fair distribution to all social classes. This faith animated all of the programs, collectively known as the New Laws, enacted by his administration in subsequent years.[5]

Wang blamed the Song's military weakness on the distressing quality of its military leaders and the state's inability to control events in frontier areas. Many others shared this view, of course, but Wang chided the leading critics of the military establishment for trying to reform the generals by enveloping them in a complex web of bureaucratic red tape. Rather than bringing frontier policy under the court's control, he argued, these measures merely hampered the flexibility and effectiveness of frontier officials. Wang unveiled a radical alternative: Once having selected appropriate officials for frontier posts, the court should grant them long tenures—the more distant and crucial the post, the longer the tenure—in order to develop experience and expertise among those entrusted with such weighty responsibilities.[6] Wang's solution no doubt was an anathema to Song statesmen who, schooled in the lessons of the fragmentation of the Tang empire as a result of the proliferation of military satraps, objected to relinquishing any prerogatives of the central government to provincial officials. In any event, his memorial of 1058 made little impression on prevailing policy, and Wang himself refused repeated invitations to take up positions at the court until 1069.

Several months before Wang Anshi was elevated to the Privy Council, another young and ambitious official, Wang Shao, arrived at the capital in response to Shenzong's summons for men of talent. He presented an essay entitled "A Strategy for Vanquishing the Barbarians" in which he elaborated a three-pronged plan to regain control of the strategic areas of the Tao and Huang river valleys from the Tanguts.[7] First, he proposed, the Song must take the initiative in organizing the numerous petty nomadic tribes of the Gansu Corridor–Koko Nor region in common defense against the increasingly bellicose Tanguts. He then outlined an ambitious project of agricultural reclamation of this region to be jointly undertaken by the Song and its allies among the local tribes. Finally, Wang Shao predicted that driving the Tanguts from the Gansu Corridor would enable the Song to wrest control of the profitable international trade that passed along the routes leading westward into Inner Asia.

Both the emperor and Wang Anshi admired the ingenuity and audacity of Wang Shao's proposals. The court immediately dispatched Wang Shao to the northwestern frontier to put his strategy into operation, giving him an appointment as Intendant of Agricultural Colonies, Markets and Exchange in the Tribal Territories (*tiju fanbu yingtian shiyisi*). Through the Bureau of Markets and Exchange, set up under Wang's direction, the Song would use the profits collected from international trade to finance the acquisition and development of waste lands by Han colonists. Wang Shao confidently predicted that an investment of merely thirty thousand *guan* would bring one thousand *qing* of land under cultivation and generate an annual surplus of two hundred thousand *dan* of grain, enough to feed thirty thousand soldiers for a year. Overcoming strong opposition from officials at the court and in the northwestern frontier, Wang Shao won approval for his plans to create a powerful military and commercial center at Guweizhou in the Wei River valley.

In June, 1072, Wang Anshi notified the court that he had received a letter from Wang Shao stating that over three hundred thousand tribesmen had submitted to Song rule, and that the Song, with the cooperation of the tribal leaders, had begun to establish agricultural colonies and a profitable liquor industry. In an audience before the emperor Wang Anshi affirmed his faith in the ability of the Song to transform the tribal peoples into productive Song subjects:

> If we can gradually "tighten the reins" on this host of 300,000 by applying the laws of civil society, before long they will have been transformed into Han people. . . . The native tribes value goods but attach little importance to land. If the Han engage in trade with the natives, the Han will gain control of the lands, while the tribes will obtain the goods they desire. Each side will get what it wants; the lands will be brought under cultivation; the augmentation of wealth will proceed unhindered; and the tribes and the Han will become one.[8]

Four months later Wang Shao reported that his army had inflicted a decisive defeat over the Tanguts and had driven them from the Tao valley. Wang Anshi wrote to Wang Shao urging him to pursue a victory on the battleground of commerce to cap his military triumph:

> We must enlist men of means among both the Han and the native tribes, lend them capital from government reserves, encourage them to build marketplaces

and set up shops, and ensure that both the Han and the native tribes, public and private interests, will profit from trade. Then we can easily secure the frontier and quickly attract merchants and settlers.[9]

The Song created the new Route of Xihe to cement its administrative control over the Tao, Huang, and upper Yellow River valleys. The indigenous populations of this region were brought under Song suzerainty as "double-fealty households" (*liangshuyi*) subject to the rule of both their own chieftains and the Han administrative order. Wang Anshi believed that this form of joint sovereignty would provide the social foundations for increasing the territory, population, and wealth of the Song empire.

The process of frontier expansion in the northwest cogently exemplified the convergence of the goals and methods of frontier policy and fiscal policy under the New Laws.[10] From the outset the Bureau of Markets and Exchange was an essential instrument of frontier policy in the northwest, where the first bureau was founded at Wang Shao's urging. In court debates over Wang Shao's request, Wang Anshi insisted that duties on foreign trade garnered by the bureau would provide the revenues necessary to support the large army raised against the Tanguts. To the emperor's query whether trade and expansion of arable were an inseparable part of the policy for subduing the native tribes, Wang Anshi replied emphatically, yes.[11] Permission to proceed with the creation of the bureau was granted shortly afterwards, in November, 1070. Wang Anshi also presumed that the Bureau of Markets and Exchange would foster growth in the volume of international trade by breaking the debilitating monopoly power of the merchant guilds and providing inexpensive credit to wholesalers purchasing goods from foreign merchants.[12] Both the concept and institutional structure of state management of trade that were applied to the domestic sector following the creation of the Superintendency of Markets and Exchange at Kaifeng in June of 1072 derived from the prior experiment with state control of foreign trade in the northwest.[13]

In the domestic as well as the international sphere, the underlying rationale for state control of trade emphasized exploiting the wealth of the realm for the public good. Defending the state's involvement in the pedestrian business of fruit wholesaling at Kaifeng, Wang Anshi spelled out the crucial importance of commercial revenues: "The performance of proper government requires us to curb the aggrandizers and to take from them the surplus profits needed to revive the commonweal and succor the distressed and afflicted."[14] Under Wang's leadership, fiscal agencies aggressively broadened the state's role in stimulating investment, production, and trade, especially in the tea, salt, iron, and copper industries.[15] In addition, the government took measures to increase the money supply and increase investment in agriculture. The frantic scramble to gain new sources of scarce resources and the push to bring new lands under cultivation—in short, the whole project of frontier expansion—were essential components of this grand political design.

Wang Shao's scheme for frontier expansion provided the inspiration for military conquest, commercial exploitation, and agricultural colonization of the southern frontiers as well as the northwest. Between 1071 and 1075 the Song launched wars of conquest in southern Sichuan, western and central Hunan, and Guangxi, opening a phase of frontier expansion that lasted, except during anti-reform interregnum of 1085–1093, until the collapse of the Northern Song in the 1120s. The same principles also motivated the colonization of internal frontiers. Beginning in 1069, in a massive project to resettle the Han River highlands, an area that had never recovered from the chronic warfare of the tenth century, the Song used the state's financial resources and the labor power of refugees from Hebei and Hedong to reclaim waste lands and build a vast network of irrigation works.[16]

Many Song statesmen had long coveted the latent wealth of the southern lands, Guangxi in particular. In 1038 Su Shen had outlined a plan for the conquest of the tribal territories of Guangxi predicated on the mobilization of a massive army to humble the tribal leaders, a policy of forcible removal of recalcitrant natives to the Song interior, and vigorous state sponsorship for settlement of Guangxi by Han colonists. Su also recommended that this strategy be employed throughout the country of "streams and grottoes" in southern Sichuan and western Hunan wherever perennial conflict with native tribes posed a threat to the peace and security of the Han inhabitants.[17] Su Shen's proposals were warmly received at the court; but the outbreak of war with the Tanguts and a series of insurrections in all the areas mentioned by Su, culminating in the Nong Zhigao rebellion of 1049–1052, which devastated over fifty Han towns and cities in Guangxi, injected a tone of subdued caution into court debates on frontier policy. When Xiao Zhu resurrected Su Shen's proposals in the late 1050s, he encountered a fierce storm of criticism and eventually was removed from office.[18] The trials of the turbulent decades of the 1040s and the fiscal hardships that lingered for many years afterwards had quelled any sentiment for frontier expansion.

In spite of the reluctance to commit the state's fiscal and human resources to what seemed to be quixotic expeditions of conquest, the question of the economic value of the southern lands remained a central political preoccupation. Su Xun's essay "On Giving Due Weight to the Frontiers," written about 1056, expressed the concern, later echoed by Wang Anshi, that neglect of frontier administration had jeopardized national defense and wasted opportunities to develop important sources of revenues. Su emphasized that while the northern provinces provided the bulwark against foreign enemies, the abundant wealth of the southwest, which fed, armed, and equipped the Song armies, was equally vital to the fortunes of the dynasty. Su addressed himself primarily to the problem of eliminating official corruption, which taxed the population and deprived the central government of much-needed revenues; but he also reiterated the popular conception that the Song could greatly profit by exploiting the fabulous riches of the southlands:

> The security of the Middle Kingdom rests on [the northern provinces], which form the defensive frontier against the "two caitiffs" [the Tanguts and the Khitan]. Guangnan and Sichuan are the springs of wealth and goods, and the northern provinces depend on them for provisioning. Bringing the southern tribes under control is an urgent priority. The products of these regions are enormously valuable and varied. Their brilliant pearls, large cowries, fine brocades, and silks are all extremely exquisite and finely crafted. Carried overland or shipped by water routes, these goods emerge from the frontier with their value magnified a hundredfold.[19]

Wang Anshi and others shared this view of the southern lands as inexhaustible springs of wealth, a potent resource for the embattled dynasty.[20] But Wang Anshi drew a connection between the exploitation of wealth and the might of the nation that appalled conservative theorists: "If we select and promote men of talent who will rationalize the use of wealth and devote themselves to enriching and protecting the common people, then we need not fear the foreign invaders. . . . If fiscal resources suffice, then the state can wage war, whether justified or not."[21] Having added this Machiavellian twist to stock notions of the untapped riches of the tribal territories, Wang embarked on his quest for imperial supremacy.

In the southern campaigns, as in the northwest, we can discern the main tenets of dynastic rejuvenation adumbrated by Wang Anshi in the "Ten-Thousand Word Memorial" of 1058: taking the offensive against foreign rivals; using state control of key economic resources to exploit wealth for the greatest public benefit; and upgrading frontier administration by enhancing the prestige and power of frontier posts and by nurturing an experienced corps of officials who enjoyed long tenures and considerable personal authority. Because the inertia of normal bureaucratic institutions limited their usefulness in his imperial design, Wang created a profusion of extraordinary plenipotentiary posts and special administrative zones through which he could direct the unfolding process of frontier expansion. The careers of men like Xiong Ben, Zhang Dun, and Wang Shao were notable for their specialization in frontier administration and its attendant fiscal concerns. This pattern of career specialization also was found at lower echelons of the frontier administrative hierarchy, in such men as Wang Guangzu, who served in successive special military posts in Southern Lu for more than fifteen years.

Despite the success of Wang Anshi and his key advisers in reshaping the bureaucracy, their sanguine expectations of imperial supremacy were never fulfilled. Wang Shao, upon returning to the capital from the northwest in 1076, was showered with a hero's acclaim; but his victories already were becoming tarnished by the mounting fiscal burden of subsidizing Xihe Route, on the scale of three to four million *guan* per year.[22] The agricultural colonies of the northwest foundered and eventually were abandoned. The Song launched several attempts to reinvigorate settlement and agricultural exploitation of the region, but the drain of the state's fiscal resources to Xihe continued unabated. In 1082 the Tanguts crushed the Song armies in the battle of Yonglecheng, a devastating blow that threw the Song on the defensive once again. After Shenzong's death in 1085, calls to abandon Xihe became legion, leading to a gradual withdrawal to a more constricted defensive perimeter.

In the southwest the Song was more successful in establishing an enduring presence. During the period 1070–1085 the Song annexed large territories and extended its domain over many non-Han peoples. Although the anti-reform factions that held power from 1085 to 1093 rolled back the frontiers and relinquished some of the areas conquered since 1070, the revival of an aggressive frontier policy under Cai Jing expanded Song political control to or beyond the 1085 borders. But the vaunted treasures of the southern frontiers, the chimera of "waters pregnant with gold and jade,"[23] remained elusive. The mines of Sichuan, Hunan, and Guangxi did indeed yield up their troves of gold, silver, tin, copper, cinnabar, iron, and salt; but this transfusion of mineral wealth failed to revive the ailing dynasty.

Instead of the heralded lands of riches, the Song found itself in possession of vast wilderness areas without roads or towns, a land of forests and swidden cultivation where the plough was virtually unknown. The technological means at the disposal of the Song empire-builders were far too limited to accomplish the wholesale transformation of the frontier landscape which they had originally anticipated. Moreover, the territorial gains of the Song were by no means permanent. Depopulation and the disruption of Sichuan's regional economy following the Mongol conquest in the thirteenth century led to a contraction of Han settlement.[24] The native population of Southern Lu appears to have increased in the early Ming period even as Han settlers pushed southward in the wake of new trade routes extending into Yunnan and Guizhou. The cycle of frontier expansion and the displacement of native peoples began once again in the 1570s, resulting in a new influx of Han colonists.[25] The reprise of the familiar pattern of conflict, expansion, and frontier settlement during the last quarter of the sixteenth century raises the question of whether the Song phase of frontier expansion had any lasting effect on the social landscape of the southwest. In response I would suggest that frontier expansion and settlement in the Song did indeed alter the frontier in significant ways, resulting in the establishment of Han sovereignty, the disruption of society and polity among the indigenous peoples, and the incorporation of the frontier into the regional system of the Sichuan Basin.

First, we must acknowledge the significance of the reformers' confidence in the native peoples' capacity for adopting Han civilization as the catalyst for frontier expansion. Although the wilderness landscape of the southwestern frontier presented formidable obstacles to Han settlement, the reformers did not perceive the native peoples themselves as an impervious barrier to productive use of frontier resources. Wang Anshi concluded that, however intractable and capricious in their "wild" state, the natives could be civilized by subjecting them to the laws and discipline of civil society (*wenfa*).[26] Apologists for frontier expansion espoused the belief that once Han patterns of land tenure, taxation, labor service, and magisterial authority took root, the indigenous peoples gradually would be transformed into productive subjects. No attempt was made to enslave the conquered tribal peoples; but Han landowners often exploited the labor of natives who had become enmeshed in the web of land tenure, tenancy, and debt bondage spun by their Han overlords.

The reformers' misplaced faith in the transformative power of their civilization and its social institutions betrayed their aspirations for rapid imperial dominance. The Song initiatives to expropriate and exploit the southwestern frontier zones were only part of a larger frontier process encompassing geography, forms of livelihood, ecological change, population movements, and indigenous social changes among both local Han and native peoples. The complex interaction between these processes precluded the quick resolution that the proponents of frontier expansion anticipated. Still, over the long term their original goals—to increase the territory, population, and wealth of the empire—were achieved. The Song's efforts to colonize southwestern Sichuan set the stage for later assaults against the mountain fastnesses of Yunnan and Guizhou. Later historians shrilly denounced the warmongering of Wang Anshi and his disciples for impoverishing and weakening the empire.[27] Yet the seventeenth-century political philosopher and ardent nationalist Wang Fuzhi paused, in the middle of his jeremiad on the evils of the New Laws, to break with conventional opinion and acknowledge the reformers' contributions to the Chinese nation. Whatever their motives, Wang wrote, they had advanced the civilizing mission of the Han by extending humane governance to the benighted peoples, who in Wang's view were not barbarians but true subjects of the Subcelestial Realm. Regrettably, Wang lamented, their work was left unfinished.[28]

The native peoples of Southern Lu varied widely in their capacity for resistance to the penetration of Han settlement. Inclusive, acephalous groups inhabiting lowland areas, such as the Klao (Gelao), lacked strong political process of frontier expansion. Groups that in response to the Han as both potential allies and potential enemies achieved a certain numbers only forty thousand people. The Yi, characterized by an exclusive, centralized, and highly stratified social order, fiercely resisted assimilation and often achieved at least a stalemate against Han intrusions into their homelands. Furthermore, the inhospitality of their mountain habitat shielded the Yi from the brunt of Han expansion. Internal changes within native polities also affected the outcome of the political process of frontier expansion. Groups which in response to the Han as both potential allies and potential enemies achieved a certain degree of centralized authority under a paramount chief were able to preserve their autonomy and even expand their own domains. The disappearance of weaker groups such as the Klao, by contrast, created ecosocial voids which attracted immigrants from elsewhere. By the late Ming, Yi from southwestern Guizhou and westward-moving Miao had superseded the Klao as the major non-Han populations of Southern Lu.

Han control of the major land and water routes not only fragmented tribal societies but also forced them into isolated enclaves in upland areas where the soils and forests, subjected to overly intensive woodcutting and grazing, rapidly degenerated. The penurious and barbaric conditions ascribed to the indigenous peoples by later observers probably resulted, to some extent, from a decline in living standards subsequent to the degradation of the natural environment they inhabited. Enclavement, the segregation of indigenous groups within restricted territories, thus set in motion social and ecological changes that culminated in the fission, dispersal, and isolation of native polities.[29]

Conclusive settlement of the frontier was contingent upon its integration into the larger Sinitic world. Once the political dominance of the Han was assured, the paramount defensive and strategic considerations of the initial phase of frontier expansion gradually were supplanted by economic priorities. The implantation of Han civilization became irreversible only after the focus of settlement shifted to the exploitation of the soil and the alteration of the landscape to meet the needs of Han farmers. The original political motives for frontier expansion in southern Sichuan, nourished by the fiscalist and bullionist proclivities of the reformers, emphasized securing or acquiring valuable mineral resources. The wars of conquest in the 1070s and 1080s inaugurated a period of intensive mining; but over the course of the Southern Song, yields from the Yujing salt wells and the iron mines of Nanping steadily diminished and the stress of Han immigrants to the mining areas ran dry. Nonetheless, the patterns of circulation created during the heyday of intensive mining and forest exploitation continued to sustain settlement and trade. After 1127 Luzhou emerged as a major rice-exporting area with strong ties to the regional grain market of the Sichuan Basin. Growth in cultivated acreage and marketing activity was mostly confined to areas north of the Yangzi River, but Luzhou's waxing economic prominence was accelerated by the long-term reorientation of Sichuan's regional economy away from its original nucleus, the Chengdu Plain, and towards the Yangzi valley.

The epochal shift in Sichuan's demographic and productive center of gravity to the Yangzi valley was an integral part of the spatial transformation of post-Tang China. Frontier settlement of southern Sichuan during the Song spurred demographic growth throughout the Yangzi, Tuo, and lower Min River valleys. Initially, the port cities of the Yangzi valley served as little more than transshipment points for intraregional trading networks centered on Chengdu, but by Ming times the Yangzi had become the chief avenue of immigration into Sichuan and the primary trade route linking the basin with national markets. At the same time, the Tuo and lower Min valleys achieved unprecedented prominence as the productive heartland of the Sichuan Basin.[30]

Situated at the intersection of the primary arteries of commerce, Luzhou prospered as a hub of regional and interregional trade. Completion in 1387 of the dredging of the Na River (since known as the Yongning River) made Luzhou the terminus of the major transport route connecting the upper Yangzi valley to Yunnan.[31] Merchant route-books of the late Ming era describe Luzhou as the chief break-of-bulk point for cargo shipped between Chengdu and the Yangzi valley.[32] Indeed, the picture of commercial traffic drawn from Ming route-books and gazetteers demonstrates Luzhou's central position with the trading system of the Sichuan Basin. Luzhou's commercial efflorescence in turn stimulated intensification of cultivation and the development of specialized industries, particularly timber and forest products, along the frontier.[33] Thus the incorporation of Luzhou into the regional system of the Sichuan Basin initiated by the Song phase of frontier expansion subsequently withstood the demographic catastrophe of the Mongol conquest and solidified during the Ming period.

The crucial role of external political and economic forces in shaping regional and interregional systems of circulation and production prompts us to reconsider the spatial transformation of China in Song times and afterwards. The models of regional systems advanced by G. William Skinner and Robert Hartwell are based on an implicit assumption that indigenous demand and productive surpluses stoked the furnaces of demographic and economic expansion within a regional system. An examination of the evolution of expansion, settlement, and economic change in Luzhou, to the contrary, indicates that along Sichuan's southern frontier the structure of regional integration conformed to priorities, articulated through political and economic institutions, determined in the metropolitan centers. In the core areas surrounding the Chengdu Plain, to be sure, production was oriented towards local demand, and markets circulated goods to meet local needs. In Luzhou, however, marketing systems were tributaries to the flow of exports out of the frontier into the centers of consumption.

The conceptual approaches of Skinner and Hartwell suffer from an overemphasis on the distinction between core and periphery to the neglect of the relationship between the two. Skinner defines regional systems as physiographic macroregions "characterized by the concentration in a central area of resources of all kinds—above all, in an agrarian society, arable land, but also, of course, population and capital investments—and by the thinning out of resources toward the periphery."[34] Peripheries figure in Skinner's model largely as obstacles to transport, trade, and interregional integration. Hartwell has given greater weight to the role of peripheries in regional cycles of development by drawing attention to the stimulative impact on peripheral areas induced by increases in population and agricultural productivity within the core. Indeed, he defines the "rapid development" stage in regional cycles as one in which the periphery achieved a higher rate of population growth than the core.[35] Yet Hartwell's concept of periphery, like Skinner's fails to address the question of the relationship between periphery and core within a regional system. In particular, their models overlook the unique functions a frontier serves within a regional system, as the boundary between competing societies, as an arena for the reproduction of social institutions, and as a source of scarce goods. To redress this conceptual imbalance I propose an alternative analytical approach which stresses the historical context of frontier settlement and the process of regional integration. In my view, frontier areas can be classified into three types, which I designate as *borderland, periphery* and *hinterland.*

Pioneer Han arrived in *borderland* areas as intruders who soon began to compete with the indigenous peoples for access to and control of land, water, and other resources. The attenuated reach of the distant state, conflicts between Han and natives, and conflicts among the natives themselves all abetted the political ascendancy of local potentates on both sides of the frontier. Yet the power of native chieftains and Han local magnates alike was circumscribed by the limits of personal clientage. The technological and organizational gap between pioneer Han settlers and indigenous groups remained fairly narrow. Both societies, isolated from wider networks of social intercourse and economic exchange, devoted themselves to subsistence production. Beholden to the local magnates who provided them with protection, Han frontier inhabitants became enmeshed in a system of bondage whereby they subordinated themselves and their households to the will of the magnates. Personal bondage in turn fostered coercive tenurial relations. Local magnates gained control not only over scarce economic resources—principally labor, but land and commerce as well—but also over the reproduction of labor, by regulating the marriage arrangements of their dependents and making personal bondage a hereditary status. The magnate society formed by these overlapping ties of dependency embodied a complex system of social and economic control resistant to encroachment by external political and economic forces.

In the case of Luzhou, political motives provided the main impetus for incorporating the borderland territory into the Han realm. Sustained frontier expansion sponsored by the Song state from 1070 to 1120 established a coherent structure of political and economic integration within the Southern Lu frontier zone, but one designed to satisfy political goals. Lacking a decisive advantage in arms or numbers, the Song relied on the extension of a comprehensive apparatus of territorial control to exploit frontier resources. The political supremacy of the Song rested on the systematic elaboration of a hierarchical, tightly-structured bureaucratic administration throughout vast contiguous territories. Whereas both the native chieftains and Han local magnates mainly sought to control the labor power of particular social groups, the Song state attempted to dominate an entire territorial range, including its population, lands, resources, and routes. The authority of tribal chieftains and Han magnates extended no further than their personal influence, mediated through clientage and personal bondage. The Song state, however, defined the frontier with a ring of garrisons demarcating the boundaries of civil society and built military camps, fortified towns, and post stations to control strategic land and water routes. Lands seized from the natives were allotted to homesteaders who provided military service to the Song; commerce, too, was subjected to government regulation and supervision. Consequently the intrusion of state power vitiated the authority of magnates and chieftains in Southern Lu, though they continued to flourish in other parts of the Sichuan frontier.

The transfer of sovereignty to the Song state did not immediately entail wholesale social transformation. After the wars of conquest that concluded in 1115, Southern Lu remained a *periphery*, characterized by extensive rather than intensive agriculture, a large and largely unassimilated non-Han population, and only intermittent contact with the metropolitan core. For the most part the local elite continued to regulate social and economic exchange on the local level. The transport and communication networks connecting the periphery to the core conformed to the logistical requirements of frontier expansion. Those networks, rather than taking the form of a central place hierarchy based on the intensification of rural demand for goods and services, exhibited a dendritic structure: trade and transport moved along a few trunk routes connecting military and administrative seats.[36] The resulting structure of regional integration, while conducive to the exercise of political control, organizing troop movements, and extracting strategic resources, otherwise had little impact on the great majority of frontier inhabitants. Moreover, this structure often proved to be a fragile one, readily shattered by exogenous shocks or superannuated by shifts in political priorities.

A peripheral frontier zone within a regional system undergoing rapid growth could serve as an outlet for migration and a source of staple goods, thus acquiring new status as a *hinterland*. During the twelfth century Sichuan's sustained demographic growth and rising metropolitan demand for food, fuel, timber, and other basic commodities led to a reorientation from subsistence to commercial production in Luzhou. Following the demise of magnate society in this area, impersonal economic relationships supplanted ties of personal bondage. The penetration of centralized political control and external market forces facilitated the transfer of the agricultural surplus to the state and to a commercially oriented elite of wealthy landowners, moneylenders, and merchants. The institutionalization of the power of these groups marked the transition from pioneer frontier society to the dominant Han social order. In northern Luzhou this process was largely completed by the beginning of the thirteenth century, while the prefecture's southern rim remained a periphery.

The metropolitan core of Sichuan, centered on the Chengdu Plain, heartland of ancient Shu, was defined by a concentration of population and arable lands and a systematically organized grid of competitive market centers. The core developed around the administrative capital of Chengdu, but economic growth within the core was based on agrarian surpluses, efficient transport, and high levels of public and private consumption. A sizable agrarian surplus and higher standards of consumption stimulated specialization of production in the countryside as well as the cities. To a large degree the boundaries of the core area were congruent with the threshold of demand for urban goods within the regional system. Like the frontier, though, the core was not an inert entity. Its spatial configuration expanded and contracted in accordance with long-term cycles of growth and decline.

A crucial feature of the core was that even though it produced considerable surpluses beyond the minimum requirements of subsistence, the core remained a net importer of goods from the frontier zones. In essence, the core was characterized by a consumption deficit resulting from its high concentration of population and wealth and its correspondingly high level of demand for foodstuffs and other staples as well as luxury goods. Following Carol Smith, I would stress that the structure of regional economic integration was determined not by the mode of production or level of agricultural technology (as, for example, Yanagida's work suggests), but rather by control of the surplus and the terms of exchange.[37] Frontier settlers were largely at the mercy of officials and traders who provided protection, controlled transport, and supplied vital goods like salt, tea, medicines, and tools. The trader exercised little power over the self-sufficient frontiersman. But as the pioneer farmer became enveloped in a web of obligations, paying taxes to the state, rent to the landlord, and interest to the moneylender, his dependence on the market increased.[38] By controlling the terms of exchange, the state and traders controlled the surplus and shaped the marketing system to serve their own interests.

Frontier zones, then, functioned as borderlands, peripheries, or hinterlands. Borderlands existed as largely autochthonous societies, independent of direct political control by the state to which they nominally belonged. Peripheries and hinterlands developed significant and vitally important links to the metropolitan core. It is important to note that the spatial relationship between core and hinterland areas retained the dendritic structure of the core-periphery relationship. While hinterland areas (unlike peripheries) formed strong economic ties with the core, the primary stimulus for economic integration arose from exogenous rather than local demand. The economic integration of the Sichuan Basin in Song times was predicated on metropolitan demand for hinterland goods and the availability of cheap water transport. Consequently the structure of the regional marketing system derived from the network of long-distance trade routes connecting the hinterland to the core, which in turn conformed to the pattern of major navigable waterways. Thus the geographic articulation of the regional marketing system exhibited a dendritic form oriented towards the principal centers of consumption, Chengdu above all. Peasants in frontier villages did trade with one another at local markets, but these markets were not integrated into higher levels of the marketing system. In contrast to the periodic markets of the countryside, which developed in response to the limited range of isolated settlers, market towns and riverine port cities existed to channel goods from the hinterland into the core. These two spheres of trade remained poorly integrated. As a result the regional marketing system and the traders who operated it proved much more responsive to metropolitan demand than hinterland needs.[39]

The three types of frontier described here do not represent a unilinear sequence of regional development and integration. The function of each frontier type depended upon its place within the regional system as a whole. Incorporation into a regional system of exchange did not necessarily entail integration with the core area, nor did incremental growth in population or the size of agricultural surpluses invariably lead to absorption into the core.[40] Hinterland areas, such as Luzhou in the Southern Song, produced significant surpluses without developing a diversified local economy. Consequently settlement in Luzhou, while intensified by incorporation into commercial networks, remained partial and tentative. Short-term crises or exogenous shocks readily ruptured the links between the frontier and the core and often brought about depopulation, declining productivity, and a devolution of political control.[41] In the late thirteenth century Luzhou underwent just such a regression from hinterland to periphery. Even the restoration of a stable central government, the return to expansionist frontier policies, and the extension of long-distance trade routes across Luzhou into Guizhou and Yunnan during the early Ming did not touch off a new wave of settlement in Southern Lu. Only with accelerating population growth and rising regional demand after 1550 did Luzhou once again attract Han settlers and regain its role as an agrarian hinterland.

Notes
Bibliography
Glossary
Index

Abbreviations Used in the Notes

BS	Li Yanshou, et al., *Bei shi*
CBBM	Yang Zhongliang, *Tongjian changbian jishi benmo*
CSJC	Congshu jicheng collectanea
CYZJ	Li Xinchuan, *Jianyan yilai chaoye zaji*
FYSL	Zhu Mu, *Fangyu shenglan*
GXJBCS	Guoxue jiben congshu collectanea
HYGZ	Chang Ju, *Huayang guozhi*
JGLBS	Gu Yanwu, *Tianxia junguo libing shu*
JYP	Cao Shuyuan, *Jiangyang pu*
LCGM	*Liangchao gangmu beiyao*
QTS	*Quan Tang shi*
QTW	*Quan Tang wen*
SBBY	Sibu beiyao collectanea
SBCK	Sibu congkan collectanea
SHY	*Song huiyao jigao*
SKQSZB	Siku quanshu zhenben collectanea
SS	Ouyang Xuan et al., *Song shi*
SWJC	Fu Zengxiang, *Songdai Shuwen jicun*
TD	Du You, *Tongdian*
TPGJ	Li Fang, *Taiping guangji*
TPHYJ	Yue Shi, *Taiping huanyu ji*
WXTK	Ma Duanlin, *Wenxian tongkao*
XCB	Li Tao, *Xu zizhi tongjian changbian*
XNYL	Li Xinchuan, *Jianyan yilai xinian yaolu*
XTS	Ouyang Xiu, Song Qi, et al., *Xin Tang shu*
YDJS	Wang Xiangzhi, *Yudi jisheng*
YFJYZ	Wang Cun, *Yuanfeng jiuyu zhi*
YHJXZ	Li Jifu, *Yuanhe junxian tuzhi*
YLDD	*Yongle dadian*

YSJZ   Song Lian, "Yangshi jiazhuan," *Song xueshi wenji*
ZXSZ   *Huang Song zhongxing liangchao shengzheng*
ZYYY   *Zhongyang yanjiuyuan lishi yuyan yanjiusuo jikan*
ZZTJ   Sima Guang, *Zizhi tongjian*

Notes

PREFACE

1. Katō Shigeshi, *Shina keizaishi kōshō*.
2. For the classic expositions of their views, see Sudō Yoshiyuki, "Sōdai shōensei no hattatsu," in his *Chūgoku tochi seido shi kenkyū*, pp. 195–288; Niida Noboru, "Chūgoku no nōdō, kōyōjiɴ no hōteki mibun no keisei to henshitsu," in his *Chūgoku hōseishi kenkyū: dōrei nōdō hō, kazoku sonraku hō*, pp. 147–193. An extreme version of this view is expounded in Mark Elvin, *The Pattern of the Chinese Past*, pp. 69–83.
3. Miyazaki Ichisada, "Sōdai igo no tochi shoyū keitai," *Ajia shi kenkyū*, IV, 87–129. For a review of the debate and an overview of scholarship on Song society in general see Peter J. Golas, "Rural China in the Song," *Journal of Asian Studies* 39.2:291–325.
4. Shiba Yoshinobu, *Sōdai shōgyōshi kenkyū*. Shiba's work has been partially translated by Mark Elvin: Shiba, *Commerce and Society in Sung China*.
5. Yanagida Setsuko, "Sōdai tochi shoyūsei ni mirareru futatsu kata," *Tōyō bunka kenkyūsho kiyō* 29:95–130.
6. Satake Yasuhiko, "Sōdai Shisen Kishuro no minzoku mondai to tochi shoyū mondai," *Shirin* 50.6:801–828, 51.1:44–74; and Satake, "TōSō henkakuki ni okeru Shisen Seitofuro chiiki shakai no hembō ni tsuite," *Tōyōshi kenkyū* 35.2:275–308. See also Kawahara Yoshirō, "Shisen shiro no tochi mondai to shōgyō shihon," *HokuSōki tochi shoyū no mondai to shōgyō shihon*, pp. 257–318.
7. Tan Kyōji, "Sōsho no shōen ni tsuite — Seitofu Kōshoku koku setsudoshi Ten Kinsen no shoryō o chūshin to shite," *Shichō* 87:2–3.
8. Joseph P. McDermott, "Charting Blank Spaces and Disputed Regions: The Problem of Sung Land Tenure," *Journal of Asian Studies* 44.1:13–41. In my view McDermott strives overmuch to minimize the prevalence and significance of coercive tenurial relations in Sichuan and Hunan/Hubei, although I fully agree with his contention that the evidence for a labor-repressive agrarian regime in the central and upper Yangzi regions must not be generalized as typical of the Song

as a whole (for an example of this misuse of evidence see Elvin, pp. 71–73).

9. G. William Skinner, "Marketing and Social Structure in Rural China," *Journal of Asian Studies* 24.1:3–43, 24.2:195–228, 24.3:363–399, and his set of essays in Skinner, ed., *The City in Late Imperial China.*

10. An exception would be Shiba's studies of Huzhou and Ningbo: "Sōdai no Kōshū ni okeru shinshi no hensen ni tsuite," in *Enoki hakushi kanreki kinen tōyōshi ronsō,* pp. 225–238; "Sekkō Kōshū ni okeru teijū no enkaku" in Kimura Eiichi, ed., *Chūgoku tetsugakushi no tembō to mosaku,* pp. 603–633; and "Ningpo and Its Hinterland," in Skinner, ed., *City,* pp. 391–439.

11. D. W. Meinig, "The Continuous Shaping of America: A Prospectus for Geographers and Historians," *American Historical Review* 83.5:1195.

12. Owen Lattimore, "The Frontier in History," in his *Studies in Frontier History: Collected Papers, 1929–1958,* pp. 480–481.

INTRODUCTION

1. The full magnitude of the social and economic transformations of the Tang-Song transition was first enunciated in Miyazaki Ichisada's pioneering work, *Tōyōteki kinsei.* A cogent survey of the major advances in productivity, demographic and urban growth, transport, credit instruments, marketing, and technology is presented in Elvin, pp. 111–199. For a recent analysis of these changes from a different perspective, see Robert M. Hartwell, "Demographic, Political, and Social Transformations of China, 750–1550," *Harvard Journal of Asiatic Studies* 42.2:365–442.

2. In the past few years a sudden efflorescence of scholarship on Song Sichuan has appeared. For studies devoted particularly to the political integration of Sichuan during the first century of the Song, see Christoph Schifferli, "Recherches sur l'histoire du Sichuan vers la fin du Xe siècle: la formation d'une province chinoise"; Klaus-Peter Tietze, *Ssuch'uan vom 7. bis 10. Jahrhundert: Untersuchungen zur Frühen Geschichte einer Chinesischen Provinz;* Winston W. Lo, *Szechwan in Sung China: A Case Study in the Political Integration of the Chinese Empire.* The role of state fiscal policy in the incorporation of Sichuan into the Song polity is studied in Paul J. Smith, "Taxing Heaven's Storehouse: The Szechwan Tea Monopoly and the Tsinghai Horse Trade, 1074–1224."

3. Howard Lamar and Leonard Thompson, "Comparative Frontier History," in Lamar and Thompson, eds., *The Frontier in History: North America and Southern Africa Compared,* p. 7.

4. The concept of "civilization" that I am proposing here borrows from Meinig's concept of "cultural landscape": Meinig, "The Continuous Shaping of America," p. 1191. In addition I am indebted to two French scholars who first developed the concept of "agrarian civilization": Marc Bloch, *French Rural History: An Essay on Its Basic Characteristics,* and Pierre Gourou, *La terre et l'homme en Extrême Orient.*

5. On the relationship between tribal sociopolitical structure and the capacity to resist encroachment, see Robert Berkhofer, Jr., "The North American Frontier as Process and Context," in Lamar and Thompson, pp. 56–66.

6. The best introductions to Wang Anshi's political program are James T. C. Liu, *Reform in Sung China: Wang An-shih (1021–1086) and His New Policies,* and Qi Xia, *Wang Anshi bianfa.* Unfortunately, neither work gives much attention to Wang's foreign and frontier policies. Contrary to the prevailing view, I maintain that Wang's domestic economic policies were inextricably linked to his foreign policy, an argument propounded also in Smith, "Taxing."

1. THE CIVILIZATION OF THE FOREST

1. He Guangyuan, *Jianjie lu,* 6/40. He's account identifies the general as Wen Zong-yuan; but the historical record of the Former Shu dynasty indicates that this name is a corruption of Wang Zongruan, one of the adopted sons of the founder of the Former Shu: Ouyang Xiu et al., *Xin wudai shi,* 63/786. Wang passed through Luzhou on several occasions, but from the context He's account undoubtedly refers to the 906 campaign. See *ZZTJ* 265/8657.

2. *CBBM* 141/2b.

3. Fan Chengda, *Wuchuan lu,* xia/17.

4. See Miyazaki Ichisada, "Sōdai ni okeru satsujin saiki no shuzoku ni tsuite," *Ajia shi kenkyū,* V, 117–126; Wen Chongyi, *Chu wenhua yanjiu,* pp. 125–154; Fan Zichang, *Huangzhou junxian zhi,* cited in *YLDD* 2217/26a; *SS* 300/9966; Du Zheng, "Tiaozou bianmin wushi," *Xingshantang gao,* 6/9b–11b.

5. *SHY* xingfa 2/133a. Zhu Xi regarded the prevalence of human sacrifice in Hunan/Hubei as a survival of the customs of ancient Chu: Zhu Xi, *Chuci jizhu,* 7/135. On human sacrifice in the Song, see Miyazaki, "Satsujin saiki," pp. 100–144.

6. For studies of ancient flood myths, see Henri Maspero, "La société et la religion des chinois anciens et celles des Tais modernes," in his *Le Taoisme et les religions chinoises,* pp. 261–266; Shirakawa Shizuo, *Chūgoku no shinwa,* pp. 63–67. See also the wide range of myths related to Yu assembled by Wolfram Eberhard in *Lokalkulturen im alten China,* I, 326–328; and in *Local Cultures in South and East China,* pp. 349–362.

7. Du Fu, "Yumiao," *QTS* 229/2489.

8. On the euhemerization and secularization of the divine world in Tang poetry, see Edward H. Schafer, *The Divine Woman: Dragon Ladies and Rain Maidens in T'ang Literature.*

9. *QTS* 198/2044. Translation from Schafer, pp. 47–48.

10. *YDJS* 153/5a, 7a.

11. *HYGZ* 3/30–31; Li Fang, *Taiping guangji,* 291/2316.

12. Max Kaltenmark, "Le dompteur des flots," *Han-hiue, bulletin du Centre d'Études Sinologiques de Pekin* 3:36–42.

13. Ouyang Xiu, "Huangniu xia," *Ouyang Xiu quanji,* jushi waiji 1/4; Su Shi, "Huangniu miao," *Su Dongpo quanji,* xuji 1/14.

14. Kaltenmark, passim. Han generals renowned for their victories over the native peoples of the southwest also figured in legends concerning the Dragon Woman. One such tale relates that the Dragon Woman switched her allegiance from the Nanzhao to the Tang in 740: Huang Xiufu, *Maoting kehua,* 5/10a–b.

15. *YDJS* 153/7b.

16. *JGLBS* 19/88a; *Guizhou tongzhi* [1555], 2/53a; Claudine Lombard-Salmon, *Le Province du Gui zhou au XVIIIe siècle: un exemple d'acculturation chinoise,* p. 265; Kaltenmark, p. 74.

17. Wei Liaoweng, "Xuzhou Zhuge wuhou zhonglingmiao bei," *Heshan xiansheng daquan wenji,* 44/1b–2a.

18. Zhang Tingyu, et al., *Ming shi* 212/5620. Early Song visitors to Yunnan were duly impressed by the authority that the injunctions of the long-dead Zhuge exercised over the peoples of Yunnan. See the excerpt from Xin Yixian's *Yunnan zhidao lu* (ca. 994) quoted in Hong Mai, *Rongzhai suibi,* 4/55–56.

19. *BS* 83/3155; *TD* 187/999; *WXTK* 328/2579a. These stories were still part of the standard corpus of Han lore on the natives of Guizhou in early Qing times: Lu Ciyun, *Dongqi qianzhi,* 3a.

20. Bao Ruji, *Nanzhong jiwen,* 18.

21. For a parallel periodization of the history of Han expansion in southwestern Sichuan by a Han native of the area, see *Qianwei xianzhi* [1934], 3/5b–6a.

22. See the textual references collected in Ruey Yih-fu (Rui Yifu), "Boren kao," *ZYYY* 23.1:247–251.

23. In Han times the placeword *dao* (circuit) designated areas populated by non-Han peoples: Chen Cheng-siang (Chen Zhengxiang), *Zhongguode diming,* pp. 58–60.

24. *HYGZ* 3/38. See also Yü Ying-shih, *Trade and Expansion in Han China,* p. 111.

25. *Wenwu kaogu gongzuo sanshinian, 1949–1979,* pp. 377–378. Judith Treistman, *The Early Cultures of Szechwan and Yunnan,* pp. 60–63; Michèle Pirazzoli-t'Serstevens, *La civilisation du royaume de Dian à l'époque Han, d'après le materiel exhumé à Shizhai shan;* Magdalene Von Dewall, "The Tien Culture of South-west China," *Antiquity* 41:8–21; Kwang-chih Chang, *The Archaeology of Ancient China,* pp. 453–467.

26. Tong Enzheng, "Jinnianlai Zhongguo xinan minzu diqu Zhanguo, Qin, Han shidaide kaogu faxian jiqi yanjiu," *Kaogu xuebao* 1980.4:417–442; Tong Enzheng, "Sichuan xinan diqu dashimu zushu shitan," *Kaogu* 1978.2:104–110. The historian Sima Qian, writing in the first century B.C., emphasized the basic cultural affinity of the peoples of this area: *Shi ji,* 116/2991.

27. *HYGZ* 3/41.

28. *HYGZ* 4/45.

29. Feng Hanyi, "Yunnan Jinning Shizhaishan chutu tonggu yanjiu," *Kaogu* 1963.6:319–323.

30. *HYGZ* 4/53–54.

31. Zhang Zengqi, "Cong chutu wenwu kan Zhanguo zhi Xihan shiqi Yunnan he zhongyuan diqude miqie guanxi," *Kaogu xuebao* 1973.2:32–33.

32. On the White Tribes, see Fujisawa Yashimi, *Seinan Chūgoku minzokushi no kenkyū,* pp. 14–45, 56–83, 96–126. The ethnic identity of the White Tribes remains a controversial issue (see ibid., pp. 105, 114, 120), and my identification of the White Tribes with the Buək/Buk must remain tentative until further archaeological research is done. In light of present knowledge, however, my identification seems justified. In Tang times the White Tribes were recognized as the "original" inhabitants of the Yunnan Plateau, which certainly suggests a connection to the Buək/Buk of antiquity.

33. *LCGM* 13/2a.

34. *BS* 83/3155; *HYGZ* 9/125. See Liu Lin, "Liaoren rushu kao," *Zhongguoshi yanjiu* 1980.2:119–122.

35. See *XTS* 222C/6327.

36. On ethnic nomenclature used in Sichuan during the Six Dynasties and Tang periods, see *HYGZ* 1/2; Wei Zheng et al., *Sui shu,* 29/830.

37. Ruey Yih-fu, "Liao wei Gelao shizheng," *ZYYY* 20:348–350. See also E. G. Pulleyblank, "The Chinese and Their Neighbors in Prehistoric and Early Historic Times," in David N. Keightley, ed., *The Origins of Chinese Civilization,* pp. 431–434.

38. *XTS* 197/5632, 222C/6327.

39. Cf. Ruey Yih-fu, "Liaoren kao," *ZYYY* 28.2:741–742.

40. "Sichuan Gongxian Boren xuanguan ji yanhua diaocha ji," *Wenwu ziliao congkan* 2:187–195.

41. See *TPHYJ* 88/3b; Li Jing, *Yunnan zhilüe,* cited in Cao Xuequan, *Shuzhong guangji,* 36/3b–5a; Tang Jiahong, "Duzhangman he Tuliao," *Wenwu* 1980.11:34–38. In Jianzhou, northwest of Luzhou, the Ńiang, a Lau group, exposed the corpse in the hills and, when the flesh had rotted away, placed the dried bones in a coffin. The coffin then was burned and the ashes placed in a mountain cave: *TPHYJ* 76/11b. The earliest description of cliff burial dates from the late Tang:

> The tribes of the Five Streams [i.e., western Hunan, an area inhabited by Klao and Miao-Yao peoples] set out the corpses of their deceased parents outside the village. After three years they are interred. The mourners strike drums and chant, feasting their kin and neighbors, with much dancing and performances. This continues for a month or more. During the days they spend their time making a coffin. Halfway up a high cliff above a river they chisel out a hole to inter the deceased and suspend the coffin with ropes from the top of the cliff. The higher the coffin is, the more filial grace is bestowed on the mourners. Throughout the rest of their lives,

though, they do not sacrifice to or worship their ancestors. For the first three years of mourning they are prohibited from eating salt. [Zhang Zhuo, *Chaoye qianzai,* 9b].

Inez de Beauclair ascribed a variant of the suspended-coffin burial to the modern Gelao: "The Keh Lao of Kweichow and Their History According to Chinese Records," *Studia Serica,* 5:36.

42. "Yibinxian Shuanglong, Hengjiang liangqu yanxuemu diaochaji," *Kaogu yu wenwu* 1984.2:46–58. On the *ganlan* style of architecture in southwestern China, see An Zhimin, "'Ganlan' shi jianzhude kaogu yanjiu," *Kaogu xuebao* 1963.2:65–83.

43. "Yibinxian yanxuemu," pp. 54–57.

44. See the recent symposium report on suspended-coffin burials: Lin Xiang, "Zhongguo xuanguanzang xueshu taolunhui jiyao," *Wenwu* 1981.8:24–29. For the burial practices of the Tibetans, see *TD* 190/1022–1023 and Wang Zhong, *Xin Tang shu Tufanzhuan jianzhu,* p. 10. For the B'iu, see the detailed description in *BS* 96/3193; for the cist-tomb culture, see Feng Hanyi and Tong Enzheng, "Minjiang shangyoude shiguanzang," *Kaogu xuebao* 1973.2:41–59; on Miao-Yao mortuary practices see Wei Zheng, et al., *Sui shu* 31/897–898.

45. This discussion is based on Jean-Thierry Maertens, *Le jeu du mort: essai d'anthropologie des inscriptions du cadavre,* pp. 13–20, 47–71.

46. *TPHYJ* 88/3b; Su Shi, "Cao Dan zhi Nanpingjun chi," cited in *Qijiangxian xuzhi* [1938], 4/17b; Li Jing, *Yunnan zhilüe,* in Cao Xuequan, 36/5a.

47. "Yibinxian yanxuemu," pp. 52–53; "Sichuan Boren xuanguan," p. 188.

48. Teeth-breaking was a unique and widely noted feature of the Klao. Song texts mention the practice among the Klao of Southern Lu (*TPHYJ* 79/3a) and western Hunan, where it was a mark of the women's passage into adulthood: Zhu Fu, *Ximan congxiao,* 3a–b. The Ming author Tian Rucheng reported that the Gelao of central Guizhou were known as the "Teeth-breaking" Gelao: *Yanjiao jiwen,* 4/18b.

49. See *Sichuan chuanguanzang fajue baogao* and Kwang-chih Chang, *Archaeology,* pp. 446–447.

50. *YDJS* 167/3a.

51. Lombard-Salmon, pp. 150–151.

52. On tea-picking by the Klao in Luzhou, see Li Shangyin, "Wei Jingzhao gong qi liu Luzhou cishi Xi zongli zhuang," *QTW* 772/15b; *TPHYJ* 88/4b; Li Jing, *Yunnan zhilue,* in Cao Xuequan, 36/5a.

53. Wang Zao, "Jingzhou yingzao ji," *Fuxi ji,* 19/5b–6a; Zhu Fu, *Ximan congxiao,* 4b.

54. *TPHYJ* 88/3a.

55. Tang authors traced the distinction between the White Tribes and the Black Tribes to the predominant colors of the two groups' clothing, but the terms appear to have deeper roots in ethnic nomenclature. The term Black Tribes (Wuman) probably derived from the Yi word for "native people" (*wuzuo* in modern transcription). The prefix *wu* appears in many Yi tribal names. The term White

(M.C. *buak,* phonetically a close approximation of Buǝk) Tribes gained currency during the Later Han period, about the same time that the Black Tribes appeared in Yunnan. It seems that the strong cultural differences between the indigenous Buǝk and the intrusive Yi was expressed in the metaphorical contrast between white and black. See Ling Shunsheng, "Tangdai Yunnande Wuman yu Baiman kao," *Renleixue jikan* 1.1:74–75.

56. Fan Chuo, 1/31, 35.
57. *SS* 496/14238; *Guizhou tongzhi* [1555], 3/20a; Hu Qingjun, *Ming Qing Yizu she-huishi luncong,* pp. 9, 48. According to Yi legends written down ca. 1700, buck-wheat was the "mother" of grains, wheat and barley the "grandchildren": *Xinan Yizhi xuan,* p. 474.
58. Bao, p. 2; *Guizhou tujing xinzhi* [ca. 1488–1505], cited in Hu Qingjun, *Ming Qing Yizu,* p. 9.
59. *XTS* 222C/6315.
60. Fan Chuo, 1/31.
61. *XTS* 222C/6317–6318; *SS* 496/14231. Hu Qingjun, "Songdai Yizu xianmin diqu nuli zhidude fanrong fazhan," *Sixiang zhanxian* 1980.4:60–61.
62. See Wang Chi-wu, *The Forests of China,* pp. 129–155.
63. Matsuo Takane, "Rice Culture in China," in Association of Japanese Agricultural Scientific Societies, ed., *Rice in Asia,* pp. 157–169; Ueyama Shumpei, Sasaki Kōmei, and Nakao Sasuke, *Zoku shōyō jurin bunka,* pp. 46–62.
64. Li Hui-lin, "The Domestication of Plants in China: Ecogeographical Considera-tions," in Keightley, ed., *The Origins of Chinese Civilization,* p. 42; Wang Ning-sheng, "Yuangu shiqi Yunnande daogu caipei," *Sixiang zhanxian* 1977.1:98–102.
65. Treistman, pp. 31, 63–67.
66. Pirazzoli-t'Serstevens, pp. 17–18; Wang Ningsheng, *Yunnan kaogu,* p. 127.
67. Wang Ningsheng, *Yunnan kaogu,* pp. 126–127; Fujisawa, pp. 509–517.
68. Fan Chuo, 7/171–172.
69. Hu Qingjun, *Ming Qing Yizu,* p. 10.
70. Chang Tsuen-kung maintains that all of the early Chinese words for taro derive from transliterations of words in the indigenous languages of the southwest. Chang argues convincingly for a southwestern origin of taro in China, although his claim is based on linguistic and ethnographic rather than phytogeographic evi-dence: "Taro in Ancient China," in Laurence Thompson, ed., *Studia Asiatica: Essays in Asian Studies in Felicitation of the Seventy-fifth Anniversary of Professor Ch'en Shou-yi,* pp. 39–58.
71. Lombard-Salmon, p. 78, n. 3.
72. Wang Chi-wu, *Forests,* p. 110.
73. *JGLBS* 19/110a.
74. Li Rongcun, "Xidong suyuan," *Guoli bianyiguan guankan* 1.1:16–17.
75. Pulleyblank, p. 430.
76. "Sichuan Boren xuanguan," pp. 187–195.

77. Xu Songshi interprets the similarity of Tai toponyms to those of other peoples of the southwest as evidence that virtually all of the southwestern minorities derive from Tai stock, while ignoring strong ethnographic and linguistic evidence to the contrary: *Yuejiang liuyu renminshi,* pp. 83–89, 183–220. Unfortunately no research has been done on the origins of these toponyms.

78. *TPHYJ* 88/11a.

79. *CBBM* 141/9b.

80. Cao Xuequan, 36/10a–b. Zhu Fu described the "bird-perch plateaus" (*niaoluoping*) of the Klao of western Hunan in similar terms: *Ximan congxiao,* 4a. In 1213 the Song raised a fort on a plateau near Kiəutsiɪ to take advantage of the same defensive features: *SHY* fangyu 19/37a–38a.

81. *BS* 83/3154.

82. *XTS* 222B/6327. Hong Mai informs us that among the Klao of southwestern Hunan a warrior who has killed a man is accorded the special status of *nəi:* "Quyang mansu," *Rongzhai suibi,* sibi, 16/799. Thus it seems likely that the designation *buanəi* is an honorific form of *nəi,* a conclusion that reinforces the contention that the Klao chief's primary role was that of leading the tribe in warfare.

83. *XCB* 294/8a; *SHY* fanyi 5/24b.

84. *JYP,* cited in *YLDD* 2217/20b–22a.

85. Cited in Satake, "Sōdai Shisen Kishuro (II)," pp. 47–48.

86. Among the Klao of western Hunan, on the other hand, we find a greater degree of political centralization and status differentiation. Zhu Fu commented on the self-importance ("far more arrogant than the Yao") of the Klao chieftains in Hunan, who were known as *duigong,* and the subservience of the rest of the tribesmen, known as *duixia: Ximan congxiao,* pp. 3b, 4b.

87. *Xinan Yizhi xuan,* pp. 85–86, 95–96, 121–122.

88. Hu Qingjun, *Ming Qing Yizu,* pp. 14–22.

89. My analysis of Yi social and political structure has benefited from the theoretical insights of Jack Goody and Maurice Godelier: Goody, *Technology, Tradition, and the State in Africa;* and Godelier, "The Concept of 'Tribe': A Crisis Involving Merely a Concept or the Empirical Foundations of Anthropology Itself?," in his *Perspectives in Marxist Anthropology,* pp. 70–96.

90. *SHY* fanyi 5/21a; *XCB* 244/10a, 245/2a–b, 253/3a–b.

91. Hu Qingjun, *Ming Qing Yizu,* pp. 31–39; see also Gu Zuyu, *Dushi fangyu jiyao,* 123/4875–4876. One of the consequences of the development of more regularized political institutions was the disappearance of the shamanistic role of the chiefs, who no longer were known as "Demon Masters." In late imperial times Yi shamans, often women, came from the subject peoples: *Zhongguo shaoshu minzu,* pp. 311–312.

92. Fan Chengda, *Guihai yuheng zhi,* cited in *WXTK* 330/2588b.

93. *TPHYJ* 88/5a–8a.

94. Zeng Gongliang, *Wujing zongyao,* qianji 19/14a, 17b.

2. HAN SOCIETY IN SICHUAN'S TURBULENT FRONTIER

1. *YDJS* 180/3b.
2. Wei Zheng et al., *Sui shu*, 29/830.
3. C. Martin Wilbur, *Slavery in China During the Former Han Dynasty*, 206 B.C.–A.D. 25, p. 269; Li Yenshou et al., *Bei shi* 83/3155; *TD* 187/999; *TPHYJ* 88/3b.
4. *ZZTJ* 199/6261–6262.
5. *ZZTJ* 206/6537; Wang Pu, *Tang huiyao*, 75/1331–1332.
6. Fan Zichang, *Huangzhou junxian zhi*, cited in *YLDD* 2217/26b.
7. *XTS* 180/5332; Matsui Shūichi, "Tōdai kōhanki no Shisen–kanryo shihai to dogōsō no shutsugen o chūshin to shite," *Shigaku zasshi* 73.10:1430–1434.
8. *XTS* 197/5632.
9. Matsui, "Tōdai kōhanki no Shisen," pp. 1445–1448.
10. My account of Wei Junjing is based on Kurihara Masuo, "Tōmatsu no dogōteki zaichi shiryoku ni tsuite–Shisen no I Kunsei no baai," *Rekishigaku kenkyū* 243:1–14. The primary source on Wei Junjing is "Tang Wei Junjing bei," in Liu Xihai, *Jinshiyuan*, pp. 189–193.
11. Umehara Kaoru, "Sōdai chihō shōtoshi no ichimen–shin no hensen o chūshin to shite," *Shirin* 41.6:35–36.
12. Kurihara, pp. 6–9.
13. Wang Jian's Former Shu kingdom attempted to capitalize on this structure after Wei's death in 897. In 899, after the Former Shu swallowed up central and eastern Sichuan, Wang Jian removed the five prefectures of Sui, Chang, He, Lu, and Yu (an area roughly comparable to the territorial range of Wei Junjing's militia network) from the province of the Eastern Sichuan military governor and established a separate governorship: *ZZTJ* 261/8517.
14. One of the "personal follower" officers named in the organizational chart of Wei Junjing's militia network was a certain Zhao Shike, probably from Changzhou. Given their territorial propinquity, the shared surname and generational signifier *shi*, and the fact that twenty names on the stele are illegible, there is sufficient evidence to at least suggest that the Zhaos were related and that Zhao Shiru may have participated in Wei's regional network.
15. Sun Guangxian, *Beimeng suoyan*, 4/29. On the same journey Liu Pi encountered a certain Mou Nuan, son of a bandit leader who had won recognition as a garrison commander and eventually became a prefect. Although unschooled, Mou Nuan boldly went up to Liu and showed him some of his writings. Much to the amazement of his disciples, Liu lavishly praised and encouraged Mou. Later on, when his disciples inquired about this unseemly display of cordiality, Liu Pi replied:

> Great troubles have arisen in Ba and Shu; local magnates prevail everywhere.
> Alone among them all, this son of a military officer aspires to do good.

If I do not encourage and recommend him, he will lose heart; if I praise him, others will esteem him. In this way, perhaps, we can reduce the number of bandits in the countryside by a handful. Is this not proper? [Ibid., 4/22].

16. *ZZTJ* 225/8282.

17. *SS* 304/10064. A slightly different version was preserved in *SHY* xingfa 2/5b–6a: In the past certain inhabitants of Ba and Shu have made themselves lords over others by means of their wealth and power. Every wealthy person has a retinue of bonded dependents numbering several thousand households. The small people each year submit rent and labor service, an arrangement regarded by all as extremely satisfactory.

18. See the citations in note 17 above; the quotation is taken from the *SHY* text. The military intendant was one of the senior officials at the route level, the basic unit of the Song field administration. Each route was placed under the authority of the supervisors (*jiansi*), a triumvirate of officials which included a fiscal intendant (*juanyunshi*), a judicial intendant (*tidian xingyu*), and a military intendant (*qianxia*), who jointly deliberated over the affairs of the route. The supervisors had no legislative and little executive authority. All changes in legal statutes and disbursements of funds had to be authorized by the court. Moreover, the supervisors in all of the routes except Chengdufu had their official yamens in different cities. In Zizhou Route, for example, after 1082 the fiscal intendant (the most powerful and prestigious of the three) was stationed in Suizhou, the judicial intendant in Zizhou, and the military intendant in Luzhou.

19. *XCB* 61/2a–b. According to a law adopted in 961, garrison commanders supposedly were limited to policing the town within the walls: *SHY* zhiguan 48/92a. In 966 the court ordered the garrison commanders of Sichuan to refrain from harassing the people and demanding extortion payments on the pretext of investigating salt smuggling and illegal liquor stills: *XCB* 7/13b.

20. *SHY* bing 2/11b–12a.

21. *XNYL* 198/3349; *SHY* fangyu 19/26b–27a.

22. *SHY* bing 29/41b–42a (for 1181); *SHY* fangyu 19/34b–35b (for 1206).

23. *LCGM* 13/35a–36a; *CYZJ*, yiji 20/13b–15b; on the state's inability to control *tuding*, see Wu Yong, "Zhoubing tuding cewen," *Helin ji*, 33/17a–19a. Magnates flourished in the prefectures of Jia and Li bordering the Liang Shan. Two other examples from Southern Song sources are those of Zhang Zhaotong, the "custodian of the peace" (*bajie*) of Shuiwei Village in Lizhou, who controlled fifteen hundred "local conscripts," half of whom were his personal "guest households," and Wang Xun, garrison commander at Baiyai in Jiazhou, who was tried in 1211 for having aided the tribesmen who sacked Lidian garrison (perhaps to inflict a blow on a rival magnate?): Sun Xinghua, *Chaoye zaji yiji jiaokan ji*, 3/668; Wei Liaoweng, "Dali shaoqing zhibao moge Yang gong muzhiming," *Heshan xiansheng daquan wenji*, 81/16b.

24. *SS* 391/12030 *SHY* zhiguan 72/33b, 35b, 37a–b.

25. Zhou Bida, "Qi qie ling Qianzhou kaiju Sizhouren suomai neidi tiantu," *Zhou yiguo wenzhonggong wenji,* zouyi 11/5a–6a. See also *SHY* fanyi 5/100b, 101b.

26. According to Huang Tingjian, before the conquest of Qianjiang in the Tang the county seat had been the site of a Klao (Kalaman) village. Huang wrote that when he lived there (1095–1097), the county numbered twelve hundred Han households (only eighty-five of which owned sufficient property to be liable for labor service), while 570 natives had become Han subjects. In addition, 2,900 of the haltered-and-bridled tribesmen served in the "Righteous Militias": "Qianzhou Qianjiangxian timing ji," *Yuzhang Huang xiansheng wenji,* 17/176–177.

27. The magnates of the Gorges region long resisted the encroachment of central authority upon their military power. In the Ming dynasty the magnates of the Gorges region continued to fulfill their familiar roles as guardians of the local community. The *Kuizhou zhi* [1555], cited in *JGLBS,* 19/107a, recorded the following description of the magnates in Wanzhou around the beginning of the fifteenth century:

> In the southern part of Ba [eastern Sichuan] the rich and powerful fear the incursions of the tribesmen. They have taken it upon themselves to build forts in strategic and easily defended places for their own protection, a practice called "raising a garrison" (*lizhai*). Availing themselves of their excellent view of the terrain far and wide, and relying on the numbers and strength of their "household conscripts" (*jiading*), they submit no taxes or labor service to the government; nor do they heed the warrants or summons of the officials.

These mountain fortresses proliferated in the Gorges once again during Zhang Xianzhong's butchery of Sichuan in the seventeenth century, and continued to serve as refuges from bandit depredations in the early Qing: *Quyang zhi* [1740], 4/18a–19a; *Guangyuan xianzhi* [1757], 2/11a–b.

28. This important distinction between abode and residence is summarized in G. William Skinner, "Urban and Rural in Chinese Society," in Skinner, ed., *City,* pp. 265–266.

29. Nakagawa traces the historiography on *kehu* in Nakagawa, "Tōsō no kyakko ni kan suru shomondai," *Shakai keizai shigaku* 31.1–5:243–255. For his own views, see "Tōdai no toko, fuko, kyakko ni kan suru oboegaki," *Hitotsubashi ronsō* 50.3:339–345; and "Tōdai no kyakko ni yoru tōkiten no hoyū," *Hitotsubashi ronsō* 53.1:72–90.

30. Yanagida Setsuko, "Sōdai kyakko ni tsuite," *Shigaku zasshi* 68.4:1–38; Yanagida, "Sōdai kokka kenryoku to nōson chitsujo—kotōsei shihai to kyakko," in *Niida Noboru hakushi tsuitō ronbunshū,* I, 337–364; Umehara Kaoru, "Sōdai no kotōsei o megutte," *Tōhō gakuhō* 41:402–405.

31. The severity of the problem of aggrandizement, first expounded in detail in an edict of 752 (Wang Qinruo et al., *Cefu yuangui,* 495/24a–26a), was reiterated constantly in discussions of land tenure throughout the late Tang. Denis Twitchett

noted that the Tang court accepted the de facto proliferation of great estates, although the equal-field regulations remained the law of the land. Official consternation over the concentration of landholding abated once the Tang turned to the exploitation of non-agricultural sources for the bulk of its revenues: D. C. Twitchett, *Financial Administration Under the T'ang Dynasty*, pp. 16–23.

32. Nakagawa Manabu, "Tōdai no ryūyō ni tsuite," *Tōyōshi kenkyū* 26.2:131–149.

33. Shogabe Shizuo, "Chūgoku no chūsei oyobi Sōdai no kyakko ni tsuite," *Shakai keizai shigaku* 27.5:474–481. Critics blamed the state's fiscal policies, particularly labor service demands, for exacerbating the problem of displacement. Chen Ziang, writing in 698, estimated that over thirty thousand displaced persons in the eastern Sichuan prefectures of Peng, Qu, Guo, He, and Sui sought security by accepting the patronage of the "great lineages and local magnates," but found that their patrons imposed equally harsh taxes and forced labor: Chen Ziang, "Shang Shuchuan anwei shi," *QTW*, 211/1a–2b. The mid-eighth-century historian Liu Fang condemned the fiscal policies of Yuwen Rong and his successors for doubling the number of displaced households and driving them into the clutches of the aggrandizers: Liu Fang, "Shihuo lun," *QTW*, 372/5b–7b.

34. Ouyang Xiu, "Yuanbi," *Ouyang Xiu quanji*, jushi waiji 9/422.

35. For discussions of the fragmented Song legal texts on these issues, see Niida, "Chūgoku no nōdō, kōyōjin no hōteki mibun no keisei to henshitsu" and Takahashi Yoshirō, "Sōdai tenko no mibun mondai," *Tōyōshi kenkyū* 37.3:390–417.

36. *SHY* shihuo 69/66b–67a.

37. The question of the amount of government lands (*guantian*) in Kuizhou Route has been the subject of much controversy. Satake Yasuhiko argues that state lands amounted to 37 percent of all cultivated lands in Kuizhou Route: "Sōdai Shisen Kishuro no minzoku mondai to tochi shoyū mondai (I)," p. 807. Satake uses the 1077 land statistics from Bi Zhongyan's *Zhongshu beidui* preserved in *SHY* as the basis of his assertion, adding the *zhitian* (lands to support local officials) figure to the *guantian* figure and dividing the sum by the total of cultivated lands (*kentian*). However, Satake wrongly interprets the *guantian* figure of 223 *mu* as a textual error for 223 *qing* (22,300 *mu*). Adding up the *guantian* figures for the other routes and subtracting them from the total figure given by Bi Zhongyan does indeed yield a figure of 220-odd *mu* for Kuizhou, a figure that amounts to only 0.1 percent of the total cultivated acreage for the route, rather than the 17 percent registered by Satake's calculation. Joseph McDermott exploits this figure of 0.1 percent to refute Satake's inference that the significant percentage of government-owned lands indicated an extensive system of bondage: McDermott, p. 22. However, I would reject all of the cultivated acreage statistics for Kuizhou Route as useless, since the totals in every category are impossibly low. To take them at face value would require us to believe that in the least intensively cultivated part of China a household on average cultivated a mere 0.88 *mu*, compared to the national average of 28 *mu* per household. The Kuizhou statistics may reflect fiscal

units rather than the actual amount of land under cultivation, but in any case they do not shed much light on land tenure in this region.

38. *SHY* shihuo 69/67a.

39. For examples of native chieftains "transporting" Han settlers, see *SHY* bing 29/44b–45b; *XCB* 219/2b–3a.

40. *SHY* shihuo 69/68a–69b.

41. The proviso permitting daughters and widows of guest households to make their own marriage arrangements also served to thwart attempts to claim a bondage relationship on the basis of actual social relations rather than legal contract. Although Song documents do not address this issue, in late Ming times, when the legal grounds for bondage were more strictly defined, customary law recognized a history of providing material support (*jiyang*) and the master's right to arrange marriages (*hunpei*) as proof of de facto servile status even in cases where the alleged servant provided no labor service to the master: Oyama Masaaki, "Mindai no daitochi shoyū to dōboku," *Tōyō bunka kenkyūsho kiyō* 62:86–88. On social relations as grounds for personal bondage, see Takahashi Yoshirō: "Minmatsu Shinshoki dōboku, kokōjin mibun no saihen to tokushitsu," *Tōyōshi kenkyū* 41.3:519–527.

42. Song law permitted indentured labor service, validated by contract, up to a maximum of ten years. A master retained the right to transfer the services of an indentured servant to a third party for any portion of the period of indentureship, a practice known as *juangu*. The law, however, explicitly prohibited the practice of requiting debt through indentured labor, even if the parties involved drew up a contract. In addition, persons who mortgaged their lands bore no responsibility for cultivating the lands or performing labor service on behalf of the holder of the mortgage. Thus the 1205 regulations in Kuizhou Route were entirely consistent with existing laws (cf. Takahashi, "Tenko," pp. 390–417). But it is clear that in the frontier areas of eastern Sichuan and western Hunan/Hubei indentured service, mortgage, and debt default commonly resulted in involuntary personal bondage. The evidence also suggests that the patron could sell the labor power of his client guest households to another. For examples of concurrent sales of tenant guests and lands, either separately or together in the same deed, in the Gorges region, see Yanagida, "Tochi shoyūsei," pp. 106–109.

43. Marc Bloch, *Feudal Society*, I, 272–274.

44. The Finance Commission noted in 1020 that the burden of labor service on the convoys bringing Sichuan's tax receipts to the capital fell on the shoulders of "the little guests registered under other households" (*huxia xiaoke*): *XCB* 96/26a–b.

45. Xin Yuanlong, "Shang Jinghu zhizhishi Zhao gong lun yuliu shu," *Chongbian Guyun hongcheng Xin qingjie gong Songyuan wenji*, 2/6a. This part of Hubei shared with Sichuan the historical heritage of personal bondage described here; see von Glahn, "The Country of Streams and Grottoes" (diss.), pp. 377–382.

46. Yuan Cai, in his precepts on family management set down for the instruction of

his descendants, recommended a similar pattern of a ring of "estate cottages" (*zhuangwu*), inhabited by tenants "numbering many able-bodied men in their household," encircling the main house of an estate located in an isolated upland area. Since Yuan was a native of Liangzhe, this defensive precaution was intended to ward off bandits rather than tribal uprisings: *Yuanshi shifan*, 3/45.

47. *Qianzhou tujing*, cited in *YDJS* 176/3b.
48. *SHY* fanyi 5/103b.
49. In Sichuan these towns usually were fortified by enclosing the settlement within a wooden palisade (*zha*). Very few towns in Sichuan, including prefectural capitals, had stone or earthern walls until the late Song or even Ming periods.
50. Umehara, "Chihō shōtoshi," pp. 35–39.
51. *YFJYZ* 7 & 8.
52. Twenty of the thirty non-Han names in this sample began with *lai*, a word of uncertain meaning but unmistakably of non-Han origin. Like other non-Han placewords, *lai* took the form of a preposed object and has no discernible meaning in Chinese. According to *YDJS* 167/3a, the Klao of western Fushun were concentrated in two settlements known as Laiyizhen and Lainiuzhen. The word *zhen* undoubtedly was added by the Han and simply signified a fortified settlement. Laiyizhen appears on the 1080 list of *zhen* in Fushun, but Lainiu does not (though the list does include a Laijingzhen). In the late tenth century, eight of the thirty-three salt wells in Lingzhou, northwest of Fushun, bore names beginning with *lai*: *TPHYJ* 85/7a–b. The word *lai* also appeared frequently in tribal territories beyond the Song borders.
53. Tietze, p. 156.
54. According to *ZZTJ* 201/6362 (entry for 669), the governors-general made these appointments in the circuits of Qianzhong, Langzhong (two of the four governor-generalships in the Ba region of Sichuan) and in Lingnan.
55. According to Wen Yanbo, the ban against assigning native Sichuanese to local offices in Sichuan was rescinded in the second decade of the eleventh century: Wen Yanbo, "Qi xuanchai chuanxia zhoujun zhizhou," *Lugong wenji*, 14/9b–10a. On local administration in Sichuan during the early Song, see Tietze, pp. 146–157, and Smith, "Taxing," pp. 98–103.
56. *XCB* 280/17b, 309/11a.
57. *SHY* zhiguan 48/18a.
58. Lu You, *Ru Shu ji*, p. 56.
59. Du Zheng, "Chongqingfu daoren tiaozou bianmin wushi," *Xingshantang gao*, 6/13a–15a. Yu Gangjian, judicial intendant of Kuizhou at the same time, also expressed grave concern over the paucity of regular officials in the border areas of Sichuan. Yu's recommendation was to revive the *baojia* formula to create a local bureaucratic structure independent of the local magnates: *SHY* bing 2/48a–49b.
60. *SHY* shihuo 54/3a–b.
61. *SHY* fangyu 12/21a.

62. *CYZJ* jiaji 14/17a–b. In 1189 the Song halted commercial tax collection at ten markets and market towns in Yuzhou precisely because of abuses committed by local magnates who had purchased *maipu* privileges: *SHY* shihuo 18/18b.

3. SALT AND THE SETTLING OF THE SICHUAN FRONTIER

1. Deng Wan, "Luzhou qiaomen ji," in *SWJC* 17/7a–8a.
2. On the geology of well salt, see H. C. T'an and C. Y. Lee, "Salt Deposits and Industry of Szechuan Province," *Bulletin of the Geological Survey of China* 22:39–78; Kenneth K. Landes, "The Geology of Salt Deposits," in Dale W. Kaufmann, ed., *Sodium Chloride: The Production and Properties of Salt and Brine*, pp. 32–61.
3. *TD* 10/55 mentions five salt wells in Luzhou, while Li Jifu lists ten wells for Luzhou, all located north of the Yangzi: *YHJXZ* 33/23b. *ZZTJ* 255/8249 states that at the time of Han Xiusheng's rebellion in 883 (see chapter three) "the roads to Yun'an and Yujing were cut off and the people suffered from a dearth of salt." Zhu Mu, citing a lost work, the *Shizhou wutun ji*, recorded that by the reign of Emperor Xizong of Tang (874–889), Yujing was providing salt to the rest of Sichuan: *FYSL* 65/7a.
4. *YDJS* 166/1b, 6a.
5. *YDJS* 166/3b; *Qingyuan yanguan ji*, cited in *YDJS* 166/3b.
6. *Yuan yitong zhi*, cited in *YLDD* 2218/2b.
7. The evolution of Sichuan's salt administration is condensed in *SS* 183/4471–4476. The Song acknowledged and sanctioned a unified salt distribution and commercial region in Sichuan in 988: *SHY* shihuo 23/22b; *SS* 183/4471.
8. *SS* 183/4471; *WXTK* 15/155a. The 663 wells operating in Sichuan at the end of the tenth century produced, on average, 25,000 *jin* per well annually.
9. Su Shi, *Dongpo zhilin*, 6/8b–9a. On the technology of salt mining in Sichuan, see also *ZXSZ* 55/22b; Ma Ji, *Yanjing tushuo*, cited in *JGLBS*, 19/99b–101a; and Joseph Needham, *Science and Civilisation in China*, vol. 4, part 2, pp. 141–143.
10. *SS* 183/4471–4472; *LCGM* 2/11a. The *WXTK* 15/155a figure of 663 wells for the early Song omits the salt wells in Rongzhou, which according to *TPHYJ* 185/9b numbered 57 at that time.
11. Wen Tong, "Zouwei qi chai jingchaoguan zhi Jingyan xianshi," *Danyuan ji*, 34/256.
12. Guo Zhengzhong, "BeiSong Sichuan shiyan weiji fenxi," *Zhongguoshi yanjiu* 1981.1:88–90. For the views of eleventh- and twelfth-century observers on the causes of the Wang-Li rebellion, see Schifferli, pp. 94–98, 126–130.
13. *XCB* 249/6a–b.
14. *XCB* 252/4b; 255/8b–9b. The Bureau of Markets and Exchange never actually took over responsibility for the tea and salt monopolies in Sichuan, but instead relinquished this authority to the Tea Market Agency: see Smith, "Taxing," pp. 282–286.

15. *XCB* 274/10b–11a, 15a–16a.
16. Lü Tao, "Fengshi huizou shishizhuang," *Jingde ji,* 4/15a–16b. Lü estimated that the proscription against lofty pipe wells cost two to three thousand families in Jingyan their means of livelihood.
17. *SHY* shihuo 24/10a–11a; *XCB* 279/7b–8a.
18. *XCB* 279/7b–8a. By contrast the price of salt in the capital fluctuated between 35 and 40 cash: Shen Gua, *Mengqi bitan,* 11/78.
19. Lü Tao argued that the primary effect of the salt monopoly in Chengdu Route was to inflate the price of the salt of mediocre quality produced at Pujiang: "Fengshi huizou shishizhuang," *Jingde ji,* 4/15a–16b.
20. *XCB* 263/22a–24a, 274/15a–16a, 280/17b–21b.
21. *XCB* 281/8b, 290/6a–b; *CBBM* 76/7a–8a; *SHY* shihuo 24/16b–17a; Sima Guang, *Sushui jiwen,* 15/167–168. While Li Tao claimed that Zhou Yin's critique prompted the recission of the salt monopoly in Sichuan, Sima Guang instead emphasized the collapse of the Shaanxi salt voucher system. Given that complaints such as Zhou Yin's invariably fell on deaf ears, I am inclined to accept Sima's interpretation. Pu Zongmin, intendant for the Sichuan Tea Market Agency, also linked the suspension of the Sichuan salt monopoly to the falling value of Shaanxi salt vouchers: *XCB* 290/6a–b.
22. *XCB* 347/1b–2b.
23. *XCB* 369/13a–14b; *SHY* shihuo 24/27a.
24. *XCB* 421/11a–b.
25. *XCB* 255/9a–b.
26. *SHY* shihuo 24/6b. Unfortunately, no mention is made of how many furnaces were sold off. An estimate perhaps can be inferred from information about refining salt at Guiping in Lingzhou in the tenth century. According to Du Yu's *Yizhou ji* (cited in *JGLBS* 19/93b), two furnaces (*zao*) and twenty-eight cauldrons (*huo*) were used at Guiping to decoct 4 *dan* of salt per day. Yujing in the tenth century produced an average of 43.5 *dan* per day, suggesting that several hundred furnaces and cauldrons were in operation. Without further specific information on the size of these implements, though, it would be hazardous to make any absolute claims about the number of furnaces at the state saltworks at Yujing.
27. *WXTK* 15/155a; *CYZJ* jiaji 14/10b; *SS* 183/4472; *XNYL* 163/2674.
28. Ouyang Xiu, "Shangshu zhuke langzhong Liu jun muzhiming," *Ouyang Xiu quanji,* jushi waiji 29/202.
29. For a concise summary of Zhao Kai's sweeping restructuring of the Sichuan fiscal administration, see his funerary inscription composed by Li Tao: "Zhao daizhi Kai muzhiming," *SWJC* 54/1a–8a. See also Smith, "Taxing," pp. 452–458, 513.
30. For examples, see Hong Mai, "Ren si wei niu," *Yijian zhi,* jiazhi 17/147; *LCGM* 2/13a; *ZXSZ* 55/22a; Yuan Xingzong, "Yi xu e shu," *Jiuhua ji,* 6/8a–b. In 1086 an imperial directive forbade the imposition of any surtaxes on salt in Sichuan, but the 1132 monopoly system added a long list of new taxes: *SHY* shihuo 24/27a; *CYZJ* jiaji 14/9b; *XNYL* 58/1013.

31. *LCGM* 12/25b–26a.
32. *XNYL* 141/2273–2274. Yu was paraphrasing Guanzi's classic axiom, "Grain is the Lord of Destiny for the people."
33. Yoshida Tora, "NanSō no engyō keisei—seisanmen o chūshin to shite," *Tōyō shigaku ronshū* 5.1:133–134.
34. *ZXSZ* 55/23b.
35. Guo, pp. 79–94.
36. *SHY* shihuo 23/18a, 21a, 22b; *WXTK* 15/155b.
37. *XCB* 135/2a; *SS* 181/4417; Guo, p. 87.
38. Fan Zhen, writing in the 1080s, observed that although the lofty pipe wells could be counted in the hundreds and thousands, because of the equally great increase in mouths to feed, the price of salt remained high: *Dongzhai jishi*, 4/5b–6a.
39. Based on production figures in *WXTK* 15/155a and population figures in *TPHYJ*.
40. *SHY* shihuo 24/10b.
41. *CYZJ* jiaji 14/9a. Sichuan's population in the mid twelfth century probably ranged between thirteen and sixteen million people, estimates which would place average annual consumption of salt at 3.8 to 4.6 *jin* (population estimates based on figures cited in *CYZJ* jiaji 17/15b).
42. *TPHYJ* 85/9b; *SHY* shihuo 23/11b–12b.
43. Wen Tong, "Zouwei qimian Lingzhoujing nazhai zhuang," *Danyuan ji*, 34/255.
44. Wen Tong, "Zouwei qichai jingchaoguan zhi Jingyan xianshi," *Danyuan ji*, 34/256–257.
45. *TPHYJ* 85/6a, 8a; *WXTK* 15/155a. Gu Yanwu, citing the now-lost *Lingzhou tujing*, stated that output during the summer and autumn was 3,447 *jin* per day, rather than 1,447 as recorded in *TPHYJ* (*JGLBS* 19/99a). Since the point of the passage was to emphasize the seasonal difference (winter and spring output averaged 3,817 *jin* daily), I believe that Gu's figure represents a textual error.
46. Quoted in *YDJS* 167/6a.
47. Lu You, "Wandeng Hengqige (II)," in *Lu Fangweng quanji*, Jiannan shigao, 6/99.
48. *YDJS* 167/4a.
49. *Lingzhou tujing*, cited in *TPGJ* 399/3206–3207; *Renshou xianzhi* [1802], 1/37b–38a, citing *YHJXZ*. This passage is not found in available editions of *YHJXZ*, much of the text of which has been lost.
50. *XNYL* 165/2693; *WXTK* 90/824c.
51. *TPGJ* 424/3455. Many salt wells were called by the name "propitious" (*rui*).
52. *YDJS* 145/8b. Yet all of the authors who commented on the salt riches of Jianzhou emphasized that the rewards were distributed highly unevenly: a few became immensely wealthy, while the rest were exceedingly poor: *YDJS* 145/2b; *ZXSZ* 55/23b.
53. *FYSL* 65/8b. According to a legend dating back at least to the Jin dynasty, the Spring of Avarice was located in the mountain pass leading from Ganzhou in Jiangxi province into Lingnan. The legend explains that the reason officials posted to Lingnan became dazzled and corrupted by the fabled riches of the

tropics was that they drank at this fount on their journey southward: Fang Xuanling et al., *Jin shu*, 90/2341.

54. *YDJS* 145/8b.

55. *YDJS* 160/5a.

56. Zhang Shangying, "Song Wang Mengyi mubiao," in Liu Xihai, *Jinshiyuan*, pp.
451–452. Earlier, in the aftermath of the Wang Jun rebellion of 1000–1001, the
Sichuan Fiscal Office annulled the debts of several hundred well owners as a
gesture of conciliation: *XCB* 48/2b.

57. *YDJS* 166/2a; *ZXSZ* 63/9b. According to *SS* 409/12318, half of the government's
revenues from Yujing's salt wells was allocated to the prefecture for its annual
budgetary expenditures, while the other half was transferred to Chengdu.

4. "A Stolen Peace": Frontier Expansion under the New Laws

1. Deng Wan, "Luzhou qiaomen ji," *SWJC* 17/7a–8a.

2. *TPHYJ* 88/7a.

3. *SHY* fanyi 5/14a–16b; *SHY* bing 10/2b–3b; *XCB* 72/1b–2a, 73/3b. Shiqi Wei was
reproved later in 1009 for murdering ambassadors from the native peoples of the
Liang Shan: *XCB* 72/14a.

4. *SS* 301/9988–9989; *XCB* 63/9b.

5. The earliest reference to the Boji militia dates from 1005 when Kou Xian, then
special envoy at Shizhou, mobilized several hundred "Sons and Brothers of Boji"
(the name Boji derives from a thorny shrub planted as a protective, or defensive,
hedge) to build a palisade and defend the Han settlements from tribal incursions:
SS 301/9988. Thus the Boji militias in both Shizhou and Luzhou seem to have
been inventions of Kou Xian. He did not, however, invent ex nihilo. In 1014,
when the court dispensed rewards after the Song army prevailed over the Luzhou
insurgents, it cited a certain Zhao Jilong, who held the military post of *yajiao*
for Lu and Fushun prefectures, as the leader of the Sons and Brothers of Boji.
The same document commended a local notable of Luzhou, Bo Gu, for having
mobilized "country recruits" (*xiangding*) to accompany the regular army on its
campaign: *XCB* 82/18b. Kou Xian may, therefore, have coined the designation
"Sons and Brothers of Boji"; but it seems likely that this unit, or collection of
units, was an amalgamation of pre-existing militias organized by local magnates.

6. *XCB* 81/16a–17a, 82/5b–6a; *SHY* fanyi 5/17a–19b.

7. *XCB* 83/9b, 89/11b. The short duration of these tours of duty was prompted by
concern over the debilitating effects of malaria in the Yujing area.

8. *SHY* bing 27/21a–b.

9. On these uprisings see *SHY* fanyi 5/21b–22a; Yu Jing, "Lun Manshi (II)," *Yu
Xianggong zouyi*, xia/5b–6b.

10. Wen Yanbo, "Qichai Jia Mei Yi Li tunbing jiuying Yujingzhen geng buchai Qing-
zhou bing," *Lugong wenji*, 15/1a–2b.

11. *CYZJ* yiji 17/5b. In neighboring Yuzhou a similar system prevailed, according to *SS* 191/4744:

> The master households include, within their households, the "Sons and Brothers" guest conscripts [*zidi keding*]. In the event of a bandit scare, the latter are all placed under the authority of their masters [to defend the locality].

12. *YDJS* 163/4b.

13. In 1055 the "Sons and Brothers of Boji" began to serve tours of duty alongside the regular Song soldiers in the five garrisons then existing in Southern Lu: *CYZJ* yiji 17/6a.

14. *XCB* 166/7a. In 1061 the fiscal intendant, frustrated by the inflexible and violent solutions favored by the saltworks officials in settling disputes with the indigenous peoples, demanded joint judicial control together with the military intendant over tribal affairs in Yujing: *SHY* fanyi 5/23a.

15. *XCB* 185/1b–2a.

16. *XCB* 244/5b–6b.

17. The following month Li was ordered to explain his actions in a report to the court, which ultimately found him guilty of inciting border conflicts: *XCB* 245/4b; *SHY* zhiguan 66/14b.

18. *XCB* 245/9b–10a.

19. *XCB* 244/10a–b, 245/9b–10a, 246/2b.

20. In 992 the court issued a decree enjoining Han from crossing the Shaanxi frontier to collect firewood, trade with the native peoples, or occupy their lands. In 1026 another injunction barred the Han from mortgaging, renting, or forming partnerships with non-Han landowners to cultivate (*hezhong*) tribal lands in Shaanxi; but in the following year the emperor was persuaded to permit the practice of *hezhong*: *SHY* shihuo 27/22b–24a; *XCB* 104/2a.

21. *XCB* 245/12b–13a, 247/10a. Purchases of tribal lands along the Shaanxi border had won imperial approval in the previous year: *XCB* 238/7b.

22. *XCB* 246/1b, 2b, 17b–18b, 256/14b. The statements by the emperor and Wang Anshi implied that Li Man's fellow Sichuanese in the censorate had suppressed evidence of Li's crime. This was not, however, a case of a factional polarization between court and province. Fan Bailu, a native of Sichuan, did not hestitate to indict Li, while Li Tao, also from Sichuan, adopted a censorious tone towards Li in his chronicle of the Northern Song.

23. *XCB* 244/10a, 247/12b–13a, 253/3a–b.

24. *XCB* 248/16a–b.

25. *XCB* 248/16a–b, 249/6b–7a; *SS* 334/10730.

26. Li Tao, in *XCB* 271/18b, cited the *Veritable Records* as his source. See also *YFJYZ* 17/15b; *YDJS* 166/3a; *SS* 89/2219. A report of the previous year (eleventh month of 1074) stated that the Fiscal Office of Zizhou Route had persuaded the tribesmen of (1) the "ten haltered-and-bridled districts before and beyond the moun-

tain," (2) the "Eight Surnames," and (3) Duwu (should read Wudu, a tribe in the Nanguang River valley) to submit to Song rule: *XCB* 258/7b.

27. *XCB* 249/7a.
28. This point is forcefully argued by Inoue Takanori, "Enhen no shiekihō–tokuni Kinei-Gembō aida no Kikaro shiekishi o chūshin to shite," *Kyūshū kyōritsu daigaku kiyō* 12.2:2. On frontier policy in the northwest, see Smith, "Taxing," pp. 265–286.
29. On Han expansion in Hunan, see von Glahn, pp. 295–359.
30. *SS* 493/14179; *XCB* 215/3b–4a.
31. *XCB*, cited in *YLDD* 12307/9a; *XCB* 18/16a; *SHY* fanyi 5/73b–74a; *SS* 494/14186.
32. *XCB* 236/2b–3a; *SS* 494/14196–14197.
33. *XCB* 236/2b–3a. Li Tao attributed sole authorship of this letter to Zhang Qiao; but Wei Tai, writing a half-century earlier, states that Li Zi co-authored it: *Dongxuan bilu*, 6/41.
34. *XCB* 236/2b, 238/14a–15a.
35. *XCB* 240/6a, 242/6b–7a, 245/7a–b.
36. *XCB* 238/15b, 248/19b–20a, 252/21a, 253/1b–2a; Wei Tai, *Dongxuan bilu*, 6/41.
37. Wei Tai, *Dongxuan bilu*, 6/41.
38. *XCB* 247/16a–b.
39. *XCB* 252/16a.
40. Wang's policies succeeded in doubling the output of the Song's copper mines and tripling the minting of bronze currency by 1075, but the scourge of deflation proved intractable. On the relationship between monetary policy and mining in Hunan, see von Glahn, pp. 396–412. A further embellishment of the conquest of the Yuan valley was the construction in 1084 of a road linking the Yuan valley with Song outposts in Guangxi, celebrated as a vital link between the salterns and gold and silver mines of Guangxi and the markets of the Yangzi valley: ibid., pp. 326–327.
41. The development of a corps of career specialists in fiscal matters prior to the New Laws has been demonstrated in Robert M. Hartwell, "Financial Expertise, Examinations, and the Formulation of Economic Policy in Northern Sung China," *Journal of Asian Studies* 30.2:281–314.
42. Smith, "Taxing," p. 314. For Smith's copious research on the recruitment and deployment of bureaucratic entrepreneurs in Sichuan's Tea Market Agency under the New Laws, see pp. 310–401.
43. *SHY* zhiguan 42/62a–63a. The institution of imperial inspectors never became a permanent fixture of the reforms. The six officials appointed to this office in 1071–1073 whom I have been able to trace were all dispatched on delicate missions involving frontier or fiscal matters, but Wang Anshi later replaced the imperial inspectors with permanent special agencies. Not surprisingly, all six officials—Li Chengzhi, Zhang Dun, Deng Runfu, Xiong Ben, Shen Gua, and

Pu Zongmin—had served an apprenticeship either in Wang's Finance Planning Commission or his Secretariat Planning Commission (*bianxiu zhongshu tiaolisi*).

44. *XCB* 236/2b–4a, 238/14a–15a, 245/7a–b, 276/7b–8b.

45. *SS* 334/10730; *SHY* zhiguan 43/2a.

46. *XCB* 247/13a.

47. Particularly noteworthy were his appointment in 1075 to manage the fiscal affairs of the territories recovered from the Tanguts and his return to southern Sichuan in 1076 to deal once again with border conflicts. Also significant was his role, performed jointly with Finance Commissioner Shen Gua, to supervise the collation of regulations and decrees concerning a broad range of fiscal and military affairs. Contemporary critics protested that these tasks formerly were the province of far more senior officials (e.g., the prime minister or the commissioner of military affairs) than Xiong, then serving as a special drafting official (*zhizhigao*): *XCB* 279/10b; *SHY* zhiguan 4/43a. Xiong's early career, primarily spent in minor military posts, is recounted in his recently excavated funerary inscription: "Song Yuanyou banian Longtuge daizhi Xiong Ben muzhiming," *Wenshi* 17 (1983), p. 216.

5. *POLITICAL HEGEMONY IN THE FRONTIER ZONE*

1. For illuminating discussions of the Spanish conquest of Mexico and Peru from the perspective of comparative frontier history see Berkhofer, pp. 54, 64–65; and D. W. Meinig, "A Macrogeography of Western Imperialism: Some Morphologies of Moving Frontiers of Political Control," in Fay Gale and Graham Lawton, eds., *Settlement and Encounter: Geographical Studies Presented to Sir Grenfell Price*, pp. 216–219.

2. *SHY* fanyi 5/24b–25b; *XCB* 290/2b–3a; Qin Guan, "Luzhou shijun Rengong mubiao," *Huaihai ji*, 33/119–120.

3. *XCB* 296/2a.

4. Su Shi, "Guo Xinxi liushi xiangren Ren Shizhong shi," *Su Dongpo quanji*, qianji, 11/166. See also his eulogy to Ren Ji: ibid., 35/416.

5. Qin, "Rengong mubiao," *Huaihai ji*, 33/120; *XCB* 331/2a.

6. *SHY* fanyi 5/25b–26a; *XCB* 294/5a–b.

7. *XCB* 294/8a–b; *SHY* fanyi 5/27a.

8. Qin, "Rengong mubiao," *Huaihai ji*, 33/120; *SHY* fanyi 5/27a: *XCB* 295/12b–13a.

9. *XCB* 295/12b–13a, 303/15b–16a, 18a. Eighty surviving Song soldiers were exiled for cowardice, though Ren was not among them: *XCB* 304/16b. Belated justice was meted out in 1081, when Ren was sentenced to death for "making false claims for rewards and trafficking in human heads": *XCB* 317/3a.

10. *XCB* 303/4a–b, 304/15b–16a, 17b, 305/11b–12a, 307/2b–3a, 310/11a–b, 311/1a.

11. *XCB* 311/1a–3b.

12. *XCB* 311/1a, 4b–5a, 314/7a–8a.

13. *XCB* 311/21a–b, 22a–b, 318/12a–b.

14. *XCB* 312/15a–b, 313/2b–3a, 315/2a, 9b, 14a–b. Wei Congge was killed by enemies of the Yang only a few days later, an act that gave the Song cause to hesitate to send Peng Sun into the jungle.

15. Later geographical works record that snowfalls were common in the Wumeng Shan as far north as modern Yongning, and in the heart of the Wumeng the first snows came as early as the eighth or ninth month (that is, September/October): Xie Zhaozhe, *Dian lüe*, 2/24b; *Guizhou tongzhi* [1697], 6/35b.

16. *XCB* 320/13a–b, 321/10a–b, 323/4a–5a. Ṣatṣ'iuo Lukluo's descendants became, in the eyes of the Song at least, the heirs of K'iatdiei's role as peace-keepers in the tribal areas: *SHY* fanyi 5/41b–42a.

17. Sima Guang, *Sushui jiwen*, 14/155; Fan Zichang, *Huangzhou junxian zhi*, cited in *YLDD* 2217/26b. According to the Zizhou fiscal intendant, the expedition mobilized forty thousand troops, three thousand cavalry, fifty thousand bearers, and ten thousand pack animals: *XCB* 312/2b–3a.

18. The figure of 1,000,000 *guan* is taken from Sima Guang, *Sushui jiwen*, 14/155; cf. Fan Zichang, *Huangchao junxian zhi*, cited in *YLDD* 2217/26b. The Zizhou Fiscal Office reported two disbursements of funds to Lin Guang's army totalling 400,000 *guan* and 100,000 *dan* of rice (*XCB* 311/3a, 330/9a); but these figures probably do not represent the total sum expended for supplying Lin Guang's army, nor do they include the cost of Han Cunbao's two expeditions.

19. *XCB* 328/14b.

20. *XCB* 359/2b; *SS* 350/11078; Lü Tao, "Fengshi huizhou shishi zhuang," *Jingde ji*, 4/4b–5a.

21. *SS* 337/10791; *XCB* 465/1b–4b; *SHY* zhiguan 48/111b–112a.

22. Lü Tao, "Fengshi huizhou shishi zhuang," *Jingde ji*, 4/4b–5a; *XCB* 393/5a–6a.

23. *SHY* bing 1/10a–b.

24. *CYZJ* yiji 17/5b–7b. In the early 1080s, government outlays in Luzhou "increased ten-fold," and 30,000 *dan* of rice had to be shipped from Meizhou and Jiazhou to support the army in Southern Lu. According to Wang Guangzu's proposal, tribesmen receiving land grants from the Song were required to pay taxes in tea and wax rather than grain: *Jiangyang pu bieji*, cited in *YLDD* 7516/7b.

25. *XCB* 459/12b.

26. *XCB* 394/5b.

27. *SS* 348/11041, 472/13723–13725.

28. *SHY* fanyi 5/34a, 35b, 93a–b; *YDJS* 166/2a.

29. My account of the 1115 insurrection is based on *CBBM* 141/1a–13b, which was pieced together from Zhao Yu's narrative of the campaign, *Gongtao Yanyi lu*, and from Zhao's own "Record of Official Conduct" (*xingzhuang*). See also Zhao's biography in *SS* 348/11043–11045.

30. *CBBM* 141/12b. Reports of the death total may have been inflated in order to reap greater bounties. Nevertheless, the bounties for bringing in the severed heads of

rebels gave the soldiers and their tribal allies plenty of incentive to kill prisoners, and the actual figures were probably high.

31. *CYZJ* yiji 17/6b–7a; *SS* 191/4741.
32. *SHY* fangyu 19/21a–b.
33. *CYZJ* yiji 17/7a–b.
34. Although stone walls were built around Yujing and Jiang'an early in the eleventh century, the court had long resisted appeals to build a stone wall at Luzhou, where the spring floods repeatedly washed away the wooden palisades and earthworks foundations along the bank of the Yangzi. Substantial repairs of the timber palisades had to be made after floods in 1051, 1062, 1064, 1083, and 1106 (in addition, the inhabitants regularly pilfered timber to burn as fuel). The court finally approved the replacement of the timber-and-earth construction with a stone wall in 1108, but work was delayed until the conclusion of the 1115 war. Only the side fronting the Yangzi, slightly less than half of the total length of the wall, was built of stone: *JYP,* cited in *YLDD* 2217/13b–15b. The ramparts were covered with galleries sheltered by low, sweeping eaves of thatch to protect them from heavy rains, a building style unique to the upper Yangzi valley and Guangxi: Fan Chengda, *Wuchuan lu,* xia/17.
35. *XNYL* 173/2852–2853, citing the figures for 1156.
36. Fan Zichang, *Huangchao junxian zhi,* cited in *YLDD* 2217/26b. Since Fan Zichang had access to the military archives when he served as pacification intendant in Luzhou in 1215, we can assume that this figure is accurate.
37. Feng Ji, "Shang Huizong lun yanbian natu sanhai," in Zhao Ruyu, *Guochao zhuchen zouyi,* 143/13a–14a.
38. Li Zhi, *Huang Song shichao gangyao,* 15/13a.
39. In 1125 the court decided to move the office of the military intendant to Zizhou (which recently had been renamed Tongchuanfu), but this directive was countermanded before it was enacted: *SHY* zhiguan 48/114b. After the Jurchen conquest of the north, the Military Intendancy did become a separate position at Tongchuan; but in 1169 the pacification intendant at Luzhou again resumed both offices: *SHY* zhiguan 41/108b–109a, 113b. From this time on, Southern Lu (comprising Lu, Xu, and Changning prefectures) was a totally unique administrative region, with military and civil authority vested in a single official. This situation ran counter to the general trend of weakening the position of key military leaders in the provinces. From the 1160s onwards, the court divided military authority at the route level between the military intendant and an officer with the newly created title of General Commandant (*zongguan*): Zhao Yanwei, *Yunlu manchao,* 10/142.
40. *YDJS* 166/2a.
41. Lu You, *Laoxuean biji,* 3/19, in *Lu Fangweng quanji.*
42. Zhu Fu, *Ximan congxiao,* 3b, 4a.
43. Fan Chengda, *Wuchuan lu,* xia/17.

44. Fan Zichang, *Huangchao junxian zhi*, cited in *YLDD* 2217/26a.
45. Tang Geng, "Yunnan laoren xing," *Meishan Tang xiansheng wenji*, 7/6b.
46. "Ru Xiaobiao muzhiming," cited in *YDJS* 180/5b.
47. *XCB* 225/7b, citing Sima Guang's diary, records that in this part of Kuizhou Route the local "headmen" (*youling*—apparently referring both to Han and native leaders) arrogated all judicial and military authority to themselves and thereby attained great wealth.
48. *XCB* 219/2b–3a. *SHY* fanyi 5/85a describes the three as "native taxpaying households" (*yishuihu*).
49. *XCB* 219/2b–3a, 225/18b–19a. Sima Guang and Deng Wan both protested that Han settlers, with the tacit approval of Song officials, had illegally occupied tribal lands, provoking the natives to retaliate. Zhang Dun was sent to investigate. Zhang reported that the tribesmen had disemboweled pregnant women and cut out and eaten the hearts of Han, a grisly tale that persuaded the court to sanction Sun's military initiative: *XCB* 225/7b. Reprieved, Sun Gou was rewarded for his victory over Li and the other chieftains with a promotion to fiscal intendant of Hubei, where he assisted Zhang Dun in the conquest of the Yuan River valley: see von Glahn, pp. 317–322.
50. *XCB* 225/18b–19a.
51. *XCB* 270/9a–b.
52. A 1944 geological survey estimated that this vein contained nearly two million metric tons of high-grade hematite: Zhou Kaiqing, *Sichuan jingji zhi*, p. 78.
53. *YDJS* 180/4b.
54. *XNYL* 169/2673. The ten-year moratorium in fact was only partially implemented. The Jizhongjian mint at Xingzhou, for example, reduced production by one-half to thirty-one million coins, then raised production to eighty million in 1080 and to one hundred million in 1081: Lü Tao, "Fengshi huizou shishi zhuang," *Jingde ji*, 4/13a–14a. The mint at Yazhou was reopened in 1081, and a new mint was founded at Wanzhou in 1083: *XCB* 310/7b, 335/4a.
55. Lü Tao, "Zou qi mian kuansheng yiqianzhuang" and "Fengshi huizou shishi zhuang," *Jingde ji*, 1/1a–2b, 4/7b. The value of iron coins relative to the bronze currency in use throughout the rest of the Song empire rose steadily throughout the eleventh century, and then jumped dramatically in the 1070s. In 1027 the ratio between iron and bronze coins was about 5.5:1 (see Robert Hartwell, "The Evolution of the Early Northern Sung Monetary System, A.D. 960–1025," *Journal of the American Oriental Society* 87.3:288); but in the 1070s the ratio dropped to 2:1. In 1079 officials in Sichuan, citing the rising value of iron coins, asked that the official conversion rate be set at 1.5:1 (*XCB* 301/6a–b).
56. *XNYL* 187/3138.
57. *YDJS* 180/4b.
58. *YDJS* 180/5a.
59. In 1213 the Luzhou pacification intendant attempted to rationalize the garrison

system by eliminating redundant posts and shifting units to the largely unde-fended country between the Anle and Buək Rivers: *SHY* fangyu 19/37a–38a.

60. *YDJS* 180/5a; *Qijiang xianzhi* [1826], 9/1b.
61. *SHY* fangyu 18/23b–24a.
62. *SHY* bing 29/46b; see also Du Zheng, "Chongqingfu daoren tiaozou bianmin wushi," *Xingshantang gao,* 6/12a–b.
63. *XCB* 315/2a, 328/8a–9a, 336/2a–b.
64. *XCB* 268/3b.
65. *SHY* fanyi 5/35a–b, 93b; *YDJS* 180/4b.
66. *YSJZ,* p. 253. This text uses Mu (M. C. Miuk) throughout in place of Muk, but there is no doubt that it refers to the same group.
67. The most important sources on the Yang are *YSJZ,* compiled in the 1370s by the noted writer and editor of the Yuan dynastic history, Song Lian, under commis-sion from the Yang, and the funerary inscription of the sixteenth patriarch Yang Wen, recently excavated from Yang Wen's tomb: "Zunyi Gaoping 'Bozhou tusi' Yan Wen deng sizuo muzang fajue ji," *Wenwu* 1974.1:62–70.
68. *YSJZ,* p. 252.
69. *XCB* 245/1a.
70. Ṣats'iuo Lukluo also received the same sanction: *XCB* 328/14b.
71. For example, in 1089 Song officials suspected that the chieftain Laduosiii had resorted to banditry because of depredations inflicted on his tribe by Yang Guangzhen, but the Song relied on Yang to suppress Laduosiii anyway: *XCB* 419/5a.
72. The exact date of Guangzhen's death is uncertain. He was alive in 1091 (see *XCB* 468/15b), but an account from 1097 mentions in passing that Guangzhen had been assassinated: *XCB* 488/5b.
73. *YSJZ,* p. 253.
74. *XCB* 488/5b; *SHY* fanyi 5/33a–b. The latter source claims that Wenhan was Guangrong's brother, which he certainly was not; but Li Tao notes that their rela-tionship was unclear. Since Wenhan shared the same generational signifier as Wenguang, the two probably were brothers (making Guangrong Wenhan's uncle), or perhaps cousins: Wenhan is not listed among the five sons of Guangzhen in *YSJZ,* p. 253.
75. *YSJZ,* p. 252. According to *SHY* fangyu 7/10a, the Bozhou territories were sub-mitted by Wenguang's brother Yang Wengui. The Yang are not mentioned in either Cai Jing's memorial of 1108 on the territories submitted by the south-western peoples (*SHY* fanyi 5/93a–b) or Zhao Yu's catalogue of the "new sub-jects" written in 1115 (*SHY* fanyi 5/38a–b). *FYSL* 61/7b records that the lands of Zhenzhou, a haltered-and-bridled territory east of Bozhou, were submitted by the rulers of the upper and lower lineages of the Lak, Luo Shihua and Luo Wen-gui. The latter name possibly is a corruption of Yang Wengui. A much later source, the *Sichuan zongzhi* [1619], 13/18a, states that Yang Guangrong submitted

the territory which became the "new subject" prefecture of Zizhou along the eastern bank of the Anle River. The relevant text on Zizhou in Song records has been lost (see *SHY* fanyi 5/35b); but this statement is substantiated by a Southern Song document stating that the territory of Yang Guangrong lay alongside Hejiang county, whose border was the Anle River (*SHY* fangyu 19/37a). It is entirely likely that Wengui and Guangrong submitted their territories to the Song separately, since, in the eyes of the Song at least, the Yang realm had been divided in two by imperial edict in 1097.

76. *YSJZ*, pp. 252–253. Yang Can asked that Bozhou be incorporated into the Song as a standard prefecture, but was rebuffed when the Luzhou pacification intendant discovered that Can illegally traded in timber with the Han: Wei Liaoweng, "Xu gong Yi shendaobei," *Heshan xiansheng daquan wenji*, 68/9b. Yang Wen's funerary inscription (1265) proclaimed that the Yang realm extended as far east as Yuan, Jing, and Rong, the westernmost Song prefectures in Hunan and Guangxi, but this claim seems far-fetched: "Zunyi Yang Wen muzang," p. 69.

77. Legend recorded that Yang Duan married a woman of the Xie clan; Wenguang's wife was also a Xie (*YSJZ*, pp. 252–253). Yang Quan was allied to the Ren by marriage (*SHY* fanyi 5/96a–b), while Yang Wen's wife was a Tian (see his funerary inscription, cited in note 67 above).

78. *YSJZ*, passim.

79. *SHY* zhiguan 73/8b; *SHY* bing 29/46b; Du Zheng, "Chongqingfu daoren tiaozou bianmin wushi," *Xingshantang gao*, 6/16b–17a; Wei Liaoweng, "Xu gong Yi shendaobei," *Heshan xiansheng daquan wenji*, 68/9b.

80. *TPGJ* 483/3984.

81. He Qiaoxin, *Kanchu Bozhou shiqing shu*, cited in "Zunyi Yang Wen muzang," p. 68.

82. Affinal kin loomed large in the internal politics of the clan leadership. Yang Wenguang's mother's family, the Xie, were instrumental in preventing Yang Guangrong from usurping Wenguang's place at the head of the clan (*YSJZ*, p. 253). In 1161, upon the death of Yang Quan, son of Wenguang's brother Wenxi, Quan's wife, a woman of the Ren lineage, took it upon herself to request that the Song recognize her son's claim to her husband's title and domains (*SHY* fanyi 5/96a–b). The woman Ren's role in this matter suggests that despite the strongly patrilineal bias of the Yang segmentary clan, matrilineal claim to succession also had an important, if more subtle, place in the structure of clan organization. The involvement of affinal relatives no doubt sharpened the competition for territories and resources.

83. Wang Anshi and his followers broke sharply with conventional wisdom on the capacity of non-Han peoples to become sinicized. Wang himself argued that the natives, by adopting Han social and economic institutions, indeed would become "sinicized" (*hanhua*). Others spoke more guardedly of a "royal transformation"

(*wanghua*), which implied deference to the sovereign authority of the Song monarch without necessarily entailing cultural assimilation (e.g., *SHY fanyi* 5/34b; Zhu Fu, *Ximan congxiao*, 3b–4a). Conservative critics of Wang Anshi's reformist zeal maintained the traditional view that the non-Han peoples of the southwest were utterly incapable of sinicization, and efforts to assimilate them would prove futile. See, for example, the court discussion of 1093 recounted in *XCB* 482/7a–8a.

84. The Song also actively encouraged homesteading by Han settlers in the frontier territories of Hunan seized from native polities from 1070 onwards. Two principal objectives lay behind this homesteading policy: (1) to establish a dependable revenue base to defray the costs of maintaining political control; and (2) to improve the "customs and habits" of the native peoples by enmeshing them in Han institutions designed to stabilize their social and economic life; von Glahn, pp. 332–342.

85. The resurgence of the anti-reform factions following the death of Emperor Shenzong in 1085 unleashed a concerted effort to roll back the tide of Song expansion along the southern frontiers. The Song did begin to abandon frontier outposts in Hunan and Guangxi, but continued to sponsor frontier settlement in Sichuan. The death of the regent empress dowager in 1093 brought an end to the political ascendancy of the conservative factions, and the Song once again returned to a policy of aggressive frontier expansion until Cai Jing's disgrace in 1120: von Glahn, pp. 328–331.

86. Similarly, Charles Backus has shown that the rise of the Nanzhao kingdom in Yunnan during the eighth century was abetted by alliance with the Tang against the Tang's more immediate adversaries, the White Tribes of eastern Yunnan and the Tibetans pressing on Sichuan's western border: Backus, *The Nan-chao Kingdom and T'ang China's Southwestern Frontier*, pp. 55–68.

87. Compare their statements in *XCB* 245/2a–b and their reversal of opinion in *XCB* 247/12b–13a, separated by an interval of only five months.

88. Astonishingly, the great native insurrection of 1514–1517 in Southern Lu, which united an extremely diverse group of peoples, was a millenarian movement led by Maitreyan Buddhist cultists: *Sichuan zongzhi* [1619], 23/38b–42a. The implantation of a foreign creed as a social ideology suggests the extent to which traditional norms of political legitimation had eroded.

PART THREE: EPIGRAPH

1. According to a spurious legend, Zhuge Liang crossed the Yangzi at Luzhou on his march to conquer the peoples of Yunnan.

2. In 810 a stele was raised at the confluence of the Mahu and Min Rivers, near Xuzhou, to commemorate Wei Gao's victory over the Tibetans.

6. CIVILIZING THE FRONTIER (I): SETTLEMENT AND SOCIAL CONTROL

1. Li Shi, "Wang Chengxin muzhiming," *Fangzhou ji*, 15/10a–12a.
2. Ibid.; *CYZJ* yiji 17/7a.
3. Throughout the Southern Song the court received a steady stream of complaints about the conduct and qualifications of bureaucratic appointees to garrison posts in Luzhou and Jiazhou. Most of these complaints focused on the need for experienced hands in the often tense dealings with tribal leaders. Bureaucratic appointees served for a maximum of only three years in one place and then were transferred elsewhere, while the local magnates had developed a life-long familiarity with "the disposition and moods of the tribal peoples." In addition, the bureaucratic appointees supplemented their meager stipends with venal exactions imposed on the local populace: *XNYL* 198/3348–3349; *SHY* fangyu 19/26b–27a; *SHY* bing 29/41b–42a. In 1206 the pacification intendant at Luzhou, seeking to reform the garrison system and enhance his own authority as well, proposed that the court (1) return the power to make appointments to garrison posts in Luzhou to the pacification intendant; (2) increase the pay of the garrison commanders; and (3) amend the civil service statutes to allow the pacification intendant to reappoint garrison commanders to the same post while giving them promotions in protocol rank. The court acceded to these requests: *SHY* fangyu 19/34b–35b.
4. *XCB* 331/15b; *SHY* fanyi 5/33a; note that the date of the *XCB* text (1081) is incorrect. Zhang Keming, then the pacification intendant at Luzhou, advised the court to ratify a treaty with the native chieftains stipulating punishments for crimes committed against each other's subjects. Zhang had negotiated an identical treaty with the natives of Qianzhou fifteen years before, in 1075. Murder, injury, and theft were to be redeemed only by fines denominated in cash, with allowances for commutation to livestock, implements, and weapons of equal value: *XCB* 263/22a.
5. *SHY* shihuo 69/68a–b.
6. *CYZJ* jiaji 16/1b; *SHY* shihuo 70/126b.
7. *WXTK* 7/80a.
8. *CYZJ* jiaji 16/1b. From virtually the beginning of the dynasty, the Song granted tenants on state lands the right of permanent tenure. The lands farmed by state tenants were considered to be permanently in the possession of the tenant household (*ruhu weiye*) and could be bequeathed to heirs. Such tenures were referred to as "ancestral tenures" (*zuye*), yet the holders of these tenures could transfer the lands to others provided that the new tenants accept the attendant obligations owed to the state. The person who acquired the tenure compensated the original tenant for his labor in improving the land with a payment called *zipei:* Kusano Yasushi, "Sōdai kanden no soshu kangyō," *Tōyōshi kenkyū* 28.1:1–27. In practice, the privilege of transferring tenure was difficult to distinguish from the right of alienability, and in many areas state lands were bought and sold as if they were

private property. This was especially true in frontier areas such as Sichuan: Wei Liaoweng, "Song gu jietian ling zhi Xinzhou Wang gong muzhiming," *Heshan xiansheng daquan wenji*, 76/11a–12b.

9. *CYZJ* yiji 17/6a.

10. *SHY* fanyi 5/101a.

11. *SHY* shihuo 70/126b; *XNYL* 161/2606; on the question of the equitableness of the land surveys in Sichuan, see *XNYL* 174/2876–2879. The three prefectures of Southern Lu (Lu, Xu, and Changning) and the four prefectures of Hainan Island were the only parts of the empire exempted from the land survey.

12. In the 1020s the central government, faced with a high rate of tax evasion and state tenants' claims to the right of alienability, embarked on a policy of selling off state-owned properties. In 1021 the Song authorized the sale of lands in Sichuan that had been forfeited to the state because of lack of an heir (*hujuetian*), on the grounds that tenants contracted to farm these lands could not afford the twin burdens of rent and land taxes: *SHY* shihuo 63/168a. The policy of selling off state lands accelerated during Wang Anshi's administration, although the reformers demanded thorough land assessments and prompt payment of taxes. Despite regulations designed to distribute these lands to the poor and landless, ownership usually fell into the hands of large landowners: Ge Jinfang, "Guanyu BeiSong guantian sitianhua zhengcede ruogan wenti," *Lishi yanjiu* 1982.3:17–32.

13. *CYZJ* yiji 17/7a–b.

14. For examples, see *SHY* bing 29/46b (Nanping, 1195) and *SHY* fangyu 18/28b–29b (Jiazhou, 1211). In the latter case, the state wound up purchasing back, at a cost of 27,000 *guan*, state lands expropriated over many years by powerful magnates and hiring four hundred state tenants to cultivate the lands and serve as local militia conscripts: *LCGM* 13/17b–18a.

15. Theoretically their status was equivalent to the "landowning but tax-exempt households" (*youtian wushui hu*) brought into the upland areas of the upper Han River valley at government initiative in the late 1060s. In accordance with a policy established by the Song in 966, lands brought under cultivation by homesteaders would be taxed at the rate for uncultivated lands, but the homesteaders were still responsible for consumption and capitation taxes: Yanagida Setsuko, "Kyakko," pp. 12–20.

16. Over the course of the eleventh century the percentage of guest households for the entire empire declined from 62 percent to 48 percent. During the New Laws period, with its unprecedented emphasis on frontier colonization and reclamation of interior lands, this trend was reversed. The number of guest households, which had fallen to 44 percent by 1072, rose to 51 percent in 1083 before resuming its downward trend: ibid., p. 4.

17. *XNYL* 173/2853.

18. In May, 1156, two months before the pacification intendant's request for more soldiers, the court issued a proclamation urging Sichuanese to migrate to Hubei.

In November, regulations for homesteading on state lands in Huainan were issued. Each family would be given one *qing* of land and one year's expenses for ploughing oxen and seed. The family would also receive a ten-year exemption from land taxes and a twenty-year exemption from the labor service levy: *XNYL* 172/2833, 175/2889–2890.

19. Between 1080 and 1223 the population of the western routes of Chengdu and Zizhou rose from 1.25 million to 1.98 million households, an increase of 58.5 percent, while in the eastern routes of Lizhou and Kuizhou the population grew from 549,000 to 608,000 households, an increase of only 10.7 percent: *WXTK* 11/115c, 117a.

20. Gu Yewang, *Yupian*, shang/13a: "The people of Shu refer to a flat river valley as *ba*." The early-nineteenth-century author Zhang Shu, commenting on this passage, noted that in his day Sichuanese used the word *ba* to refer to dikes built for flood prevention: *Shu dian*, 7/13a.

21. The word *wu*, a local variant of the graph *wu* (2), referred to an embankment, especially one encircling a village, and generally came to mean a village (see Gu Yewang, *Yupian*, shang/13b). The Ming geographer Xu Xiake used this word in the technical sense of polje or doline, the large, flat-bottomed, closed hollows typical of karst regions containing fertile deposits of eroded soil (see Lombard-Salmon, p. 78). Whether the words for "hollow" that appear in Luzhou's placenames explicitly referred to these land forms is not clear, but certainly a geological possibility.

22. In the Yi language *la* is the word for *zhai*, which among the natives of the southwest signified a fortified hilltop village: Satake, "Sōdai Shisen Kishuro (II)," p. 55.

23. *JYP*, cited in *YLDD* 2217/19a, 20a.

24. This discussion of inheritance customs draws inspiration from Jack Goody, "Inheritance, Property, and Women: Some Comparative Considerations," in Jack Goody, Joan Thirsk, and E. P. Thompson, eds., *Family and Inheritance: Rural Society in Western Europe, 1200–1800*, pp. 10–36.

25. According to Niida Noboru, premortem partition occurred at the time of marriage. See the texts cited in Niida, *Tōsō hōritsu monjo no kenkyū*, pp. 579–580.

26. Wei Zheng et al., *Sui shu* 29/830. Niida notes that the legal proscriptions against premortem partition were first enacted under the Tang and strictly maintained throughout the Song, but relaxed thereafter: "Chūgoku no kafushō genryoku no kōsō," in his *Chūgoku hōseishi kenkyū: dōrei nōdō hō, kazoku sonraku hō*, pp. 354–355.

27. *XCB* 9/4a–b, 10/13b.

28. The text of the 968 edict (as recorded by Wang Cheng, *Dongdu shilüe* 2/4a) read: "Filial piety and parental love take precedence among human ethics, while reverence and courtesy are esteemed among familial relationships. One finds care and support even among dogs and horses; how much greater, then, is the injury caused to moral custom by having fathers and sons living apart from each other!"

A 1009 proclamation forbade "encouraging a person's sons or brothers to seek to divide the family's property without first consulting the venerable and elder members of the family in question" (*XCB* 71/1b). In 1019 the injunction against premortem partition was reissued (*XCB* 94/9b). During the Tang period the repeated injunctions against this practice were directed at preventing large families from breaking up into smaller units in order to avoid the heavy tax and service levy burden placed on wealthy households with large numbers of taxable individuals (see Twitchett, p. 244, n. 84). The *Tang Code* in fact permitted parents to divide their property among their sons but prohibited the sons from establishing separate households, and an ordinance of 696 required that sons living apart from their father be counted as members of the latter's household (Niida, *Hōritsu monjo*, p. 579). The same concern emerges in discussions of the issue during the Song (ibid., pp. 581–582), although tax avoidance was less of a problem since the Song assessed taxes on the household rather than the individual. But Su Shi, for one, explicitly associated premortem partition with wealthy people, and merchants in particular, seeking to avoid taxes: "Merchants, traders, and commoners often hoard fine goods. They establish separate households [for their sons] and divide up the patrimony in order to fend off the demands of the tax collectors" ("Meizhou yuanjinglou ji," *Su Dongpo quanji*, qianji 32/390). Another reason for opposing premorten partition was the fear that the children would receive unequal endowments. This reason is mentioned in the 1027 edict proscribing premortem partition in Lingnan (*XCB* 108/1b) and continued to be raised by Southern Song authors (Niida, *Hōritsu monjo*, pp. 580, 592–598). Some Southern Song commentators conceded that brothers should live apart provided that the inheritance be divided equally among them: "Brothers should live apart, and it is best to make a determination about the disposition of property early on. If brothers love one another, then even though they live apart and have divided the estate among themselves, no harm will be done to fraternal love and duty" (Yuan Cai, *Yuanshi shifan*, 1/10). This perspective was seconded by Gu Yanwu:

Today in Jiangnan the custom of premortem partition is increasingly popular. When a son takes a wife, he usually requests a portion of the family's estate as an endowment. Venerable and wise gentlemen say: "Having two women living together readily leads to suspicion and argument. The proper course, from both propriety and inclination, is to have separate hearths." Are these not indeed wise and sagely gentlemen! [*Ri zhi lu*, 5/74.]

After the Song period the legal proscriptions began to give way to widespread social practice. The authors of the Yuan legal code *Tongzhi tiaoge* [1322], while declaiming against unequal division of property and the circumstances that resulted in children living in luxury while their parents were forced to seek shelter in poorhouses, nonetheless sanctioned premortem partition of property if the older generations approved: *Da Yuan tongzhi tiaoge*, 3/2a–4a.

29. Zhao Ding, in his guide to family management compiled in 1144, urged that the

endowments be given in movables and that lands and buildings not be divided among the heirs: *Jiaxun bilu*, p. 4, article 28.

30. *XCB* 31/7b–8a.

31. *SHY* shihuo 61/65b.

32. *SHY* shihuo 61/66b.

33. During the tenth century the various claimants to the mantle of the Tang frequently adopted their generals as fictive sons, a practice which to later historians exemplified the moral decadence of the age. Consider Ouyang Xiu's opening statement in the collective biography of the "Foster Sons" (*yier*) in *Xin wudai shi*, 36/835:

    Alas! The Way of the sages has declined; the fundamental human relationships have decayed; the hierarchical principles of kinship have been inverted. Arms and weapons are raised against one's flesh and blood, while members of different families join together as father and son.

    One of the best known examples of this practice was that of Wang Jian, founder of the Former Shu dynasty, who adopted fourteen of his generals as sons. This form of fictive kinship probably was even more common in North China than in Sichuan. The Song founder, for example, adopted nine of his generals as fictive sons: Tanigawa Michio, "Hokuchōmatsu–Godai no gikyōdai ketsugō ni tsuite," *Tōyōshi kenkyū* 39.2:286–305.

34. On cross-cousin marriage, see Ch'ü T'ung-tsu, *Law and Society in Traditional China*, pp. 95–96. Hong Mai noted that although the legal code permitted marriage between maternal cousins, local officials frequently annulled such marriages: "Guju wei hun," *Rongzhai suibi*, 8/318.

35. Examples of the transformation, quasi-legal to be sure, of usufruct rights into ownership abound, especially for Sichuan. One of the first acts of the Song dynasty was to declare, in 962, that the actual cultivator could claim title to lands mortgaged for more than thirty years (*SHY* shihuo 61/56a). The beseiged Southern Tang dynasty in 973 granted tenant farmers ownership rights in a desperate attempt to rally popular support in the face of invading Song armies. In 1014 the Song court was told that tenants in South China still claimed ownership rights on the basis of the Southern Tang decree and promptly issued an edict barring any legal claim on lands rented since the Song conquest, but implicitly sanctioned claims dating prior to 973 (*SHY* shihuo 61/57a). In 1027 the prefect of Guozhou noted that when lands and dwellings in that prefecture were mortgaged, neither neighbors nor kinfolk were consulted, in contravention to the accepted notion that gave kinfolk and adjoining property owners the right of first refusal (*SHY* shihuo 61/58b). In 1018 the prefects of Zizhou and Suizhou jointly submitted a memorial reporting that disputes over properties mortgaged for long periods of time were particularly common in Sichuan:

    Invariably further investigation reveals that [the actual cultivator] acquired the lands by mortgage while the property owner was still alive. After the latter died and left no heirs, the mortgagee failed to report the mortgage contract to the authorities and instead considered the property his own. Only when neighbors began to make legal claims to the land does the mortgagee acknowledge the real status of the property and offer to purchase the land at market value. [*SHY* shihuo 63/166a–b.]

In this context we should note the near success of the tenants of the Monastery of the True Dharma in laying effective claim to ownership of the lands they rented (see p. 167). It is also worth noting that the chance of a head of household dying without heirs was fairly high. Demographic modeling has shown that for premodern societies a conjugal unit had a 20 percent chance of leaving no surviving heirs, and also a 20 percent chance of leaving only brotherless daughters: G. A. Harrison and J. R. Goody, "The Probability of Family Distributions," *Comparative Studies in Society and History* 15.1:16–18.

36. See Burton Pasternak's remarks on this question in "The Role of the Frontier in Chinese Lineage Development," *Journal of Asian Studies* 28.3:551–561.

37. "Zhao Mou shi muzhiming," *Qijiang xianzhi* [1826], 9/13a–14a. Technically this was a case of uxorilocal residence rather than uxorilocal marriage, since Zhao Zhicai retained his own surname.

38. Feng Shixing, "Zhang Jifu muming" *Jinyun wenji*, 4/3a–5b.

39. *YDJS* 180/3b.

40. Satake Yasuhiko, "TōSō henkakuki ni okeru Kōnan tōzairo no tochi shoyū to tochi seisaku—yimon no seichō o te ga karini," *Tōyōshi kenkyū* 31.4:503–516. These fraternities were similar to the *frérèche* that proliferated in France, especially in the Midi, from the mid fourteenth to the mid sixteenth centuries. Under the custom of *frérèche*, brothers agreed through formal contract to share the patrimony in common, to farm the undivided domain cooperatively, and to live together after the father's death. See Marc Bloch, *French Rural History*, pp. 164–167, and Emmanuel Le Roy Ladurie, *The Peasants of Languedoc*, pp. 33–36.

41. Satake, "Kōnan tōzairo," pp. 503–516; Niida, *Hōritsu monjo*, pp. 544–575.

42. Makino Tatsumi, *Kinsei Chūgoku sōzoku kenkyū*, pp. 11–12.

43. Satake, "Kōnan tōzairo," pp. 516–525.

44. The frequency of the Zhao surname among Luzhou's placenames merits comment. Not only does the Zhao surname appear in fourteen placenames (more than any other), virtually all in long-settled areas along the Tuo and Yangzi Rivers, but the surname is unusually prominent in the placenames of market towns. Of the seven Zhao placenames in Luzhou county, three designated market towns (*zhen*) and three designated markets (*shi*). Four were named for specific individuals: Zhao Shuncheng shi, Zhao Wangwu xiaoshi, Zhao Huayuan zhen, and Zhao Huayuan zhen (2). In these instances the towns apparently were named after a prominent resident, perhaps the founder. None of the *zhen* names appeared in the administrative gazetteer of 1080, which suggests that the *zhen* designation was not a vestige of a local magnate's stronghold but rather indicated market towns.

Still, it is difficult to dismiss the idea that the Zhao were powerful landowners who dominated many of the most flourishing parts of the prefecture. Since the Zhao left no traces in the historical records save for their village names, this question defies any satisfactory answer.

45. Recent research has emphasized these goals in Song marriage strategies and has demonstrated the importance of affinal ties in realizing them. See Robert P. Hymes, *Statesmen and Gentlemen: The Elite of Fu-chou, Chiang-hsi, in Northern and Southern Sung China;* Linda Walton, "Kinship, Marriage, and Status in Song China: A Study of the Lou Lineage of Ningbo, c. 1050–1250," *Journal of Asian History* 18.1:35–77; Patricia Ebrey, "Conceptions of the Family in the Sung Dynasty," *Journal of Asian Studies* 43.2:219–245.

46. Ebrey (ibid., pp. 232–240) defines the patriline as a descent line focused not on a single progenitor but on each individual adult male. The "patriline orientation" she describes represented a pragmatic modification of the ritual rules of the classical kinship model designed to ensure the integrity of the line and the property that provided it with a material foundation.

47. Han Qi, "Zhongxian Han Weiwang jiazhuan," 9/8a, in *Zhongxian Han Weiwang Anyang ji,* appendix.

48. Su Xun, "Tianzhi," *Jiayou ji,* 5/10a.

49. Yang Tianhui, "Zhengfayuan changzhutian ji," *SWJC* 26/7b–9b.

50. Tan Kyōji, "Sōsho no shōen ni tsuite," pp. 18–20; Satake, "Seitofuro chiiki shakai," pp. 297–303.

51. Satake Yasuhiko, "Sōdai kyōson seido no keisei katei," *Tōyōshi kenkyū* 25.3:244–274; Yanagida Setsuko, "Kyōsonsei no tenkai," *Sekai rekishi,* IX, 309–343. Ishida Yūsaku argues that the collapse of the *xiangli* system from the mid-Tang onwards resulted in the de facto devolution of local authority to wealthy landowners. In his view official sanction of this state of affairs was granted by successive dynastic houses beginning with the Later Tang in 931: "Tō–Godai ni okeru sonraku shihai to henyō," Sōdaishi kenkyūkai, eds., *Sōdai no shakai to bunka,* pp. 13–19.

52. Sudō Yoshiyuki, "Sōdai kyōsonsei no hensen katei," in his *TōSō shakai keizaishi kenkyū,* p. 570.

53. For a brief history of the genesis of the *dubao* system out of the *baojia* militia system of the reform period, see Brian E. McKnight, *Village and Bureaucracy in Southern Sung China,* pp. 31–37.

54. Yanagida, "Kyōsonsei no tenkai," p. 321. See also Yanagida, "Sōdai keiseiko no kōsei," *Tōyōshi kenkyū* 27.3:272–291.

55. Yanagida, "Kyōsonsei no tenkai," p. 331. See also Yoshinami Takashi, "Tōkeien suiri kikō no kentō–Sō igo no kokka kenryoku to sonraku," *Okayama daigaku hōbungakubu gakujutsu kiyō* 15:80–110.

56. Yanagida, "Kyōsonsei no tenkai," p. 335. On the history of the *fanche,* see Needham, *Science and Civilisation in China,* vol. 4, part 2, p. 339.

57. Su Shi, "Meizhou yuanjinglou ji," *Su Dongpo quanji,* qianji 32/390. A similar

description of cooperative field work in Sichuan was written by Gao Side, a native of Pujiang county, Qiongzhou, in the mid thirteenth century: "Ningguofu quannong wen," *Chitang cungao,* 5/34a. Francesca Bray suggests that cooperative field work originated with the practice of "paired tillage," or two-ox plough teams typical of Chinese farming since early times: *Agriculture,* vol. 6, part 2, of Joseph Needham, gen. ed., *Science and Civilisation in China,* p. 166.

58. Takahashi Yoshirō, "Sōdai Sessei deruta chitai ni okeru suiri kankō," *Hokkaidō daigaku bungakubu kiyō* 28.1:1–40; Satake, "Seitofuro chiiki shakai," pp. 283–285.

59. Jia Tan, "Lun houshi fei ditian gaotian zhi fa," in Fan Chengda, *Wujun zhi,* 19/167.

60. Wei Jing, "Lun weitian zhazi," *Houle ji,* 13/27b.

61. Sudō Yoshiyuki, "NanSō no tohōsei to kanko no tochi shoyū," in his *TōSō shakai keizaishi kenkyū,* p. 631.

62. *JYP,* cited in *YLDD* 2217/18a–b.

63. Wei Liaoweng, "Luzhou shecang yangjiyuan yizhong ji," *Heshan xiansheng daquan wenji,* 45/9a–11a.

7. CIVILIZING THE FRONTIER (II): FARMING AND COMMERCE

1. Paul J. Smith, "Commerce, Agriculture, and Core Formation in the Upper Yangtze, 2 A.D. to 1948," passim.

2. On the soils of this region, see Zhongguo kexueyuan Nanjing turang yanjiusuo, *Zhongguo turang,* pp. 652–654, and Charles Y. Hu, *The Agricultural and Forestry Land-Use of the Szechuan Basin,* pp. 43–54.

3. *HYGZ* 3/39.

4. The gradual disappearance of tropical species such as oranges, litchis, and betel, which had flourished throughout the Yangzi valley in antiquity, resulted from a long-term cooling trend that culminated in the Southern Song: Liu Zhiyuan, "Kaogu cailiao suojian Handaide Sichuan nongye," *Wenwu* 1979.12:61; Zhu Kezhen, "Zhongguo jin wuqiannian lai qihou bianqiande chubu yanjiu," *Kaogu xuebao* 1972.1:36–37.

5. Cai Xiang, *Lizhi pu,* 1a–b; *YDJS* 153/5a. Cai Xiang, a native of Fujian, remarked that the litchis of Sichuan ripened quickly, were thin-fleshed, and spoiled rapidly. Their sweetly acidic flavor, in his opinion, was comparable only to the lowest category of fruit from eastern Fujian. It is true that cosmopolitan gourmets of the Song preferred Fujian litchis, which, after all, were more easily obtained in the Song capitals. But the Ming author He Yudu rated the litchis of Luzhou and Xuzhou as Sichuan's finest: *Yibu tanzi,* shang/7a–b.

6. *TPHYJ* 88/4a; Song Qi, *Yibu fangwu lüeji,* 4a, 8b. On the identification of these fruits, see Li Hui-lin, *Nan-fang ts'ao-mu chuang: A Fourth Century Flora of Southeast Asia,* pp. 46, 111–115, 130.

7. Song Qi, *Yibu fangwu lüeji,* 6b–7a; *YDJS* 166/3a; Kou Zongshi, *Tujing yanyi ben-cao,* 15/2b–3b.

8. Edward H. Schafer, "T'ang," in K. C. Chang, ed., *Food in Chinese Culture,* p. 88.

9. Wayne Fogg has presented the hypothesis (at present a highly tenuous one) that *setaria* was first domesticated by neolithic Hoabinhian horticulturalists of the Southeast Asian highlands: Fogg, "Swidden Cultivation of Foxtail Millet by Taiwan Aborigines: A Cultural Analogue of the Domestication of *Setaria italica* in China," in Keightley, ed., *The Origins of Civilization in China,* p. 111; see also Bray, *Agriculture,* pp. 435–436. Regardless of its original provenance, foxtail millet certainly was the major cereal crop of shifting cultivators, Han or not, in southern China in Song times.

10. Song Qi, *Yibu fangwu lüeji,* 2b.

11. *XCB* 214/26a. Jia Sixie's sixth-century treatise on agriculture, citing the now-lost *Guangzhi* of Guo Yigong, stated that: "Since taro flourishes widely in Sichuan, the people rely on it for sustenance": *Qimin yaoshu xuanduben,* p. 135.

12. Lu Lun, "Song Yantie Pei panguan ru Shu," *QTS* 276/3125. In Tang Sichuan, garden vegetables—principally taro, eggplant, and ginger—were taxed at a much higher rate than grains until 830, when the tax on gardens was reduced to the level of other cultivated fields: Cui Rong, "Qing leting zashui zou," *QTW* 744/9a.

13. Though low in protein, because of its high and reliable yields taro made up in quantity for what it lacked in nutritional value: Bray, *Agriculture,* p. 530.

14. Fan Chengda, "Suiningfu shijian pingchuan xicheng duange," *Fan Shihu ji,* 16/229. The technique of pit cultivation (*outian*), a kind of intensive gardening used for taro and legumes, is described in Jia Sixie, *Qimin yaoshu xuanduben,* pp. 132–135; see also Bray, *Agriculture,* pp. 127–129, 527. "Taro pits" (*yuou*) appear frequently in poetic descriptions of Sichuan, as in Zuo Si's "Ode on the Capital of Shu" and works by Han Yu, Lu You, and Fan Chengda.

15. *XNYL* 141/2273.

16. Wang Yingchen, "Yuzha zaiwen Shuzhong hanqian," *Wending ji,* 4/39.

17. Yang Fang, "Yu Shaoqing taishou lun shizheng shu," *Ziqi ji,* 2/19b.

18. *TPHYJ* 88/3b.

19. Fan Chengda, "Lao yu geng," *Fan Shihu ji,* 16/127.

20. Cited in *YDJS* 174/2b.

21. *Luzhou tujing zhi,* cited in *YLDD* 2218/2a.

22. Another description of Sichuan's "thunder peal fields" was recorded by Ye Tingkui in his *Hailu suishi,* 17/11a:

> In Guo and He prefectures there are no flat fields. The farmers build embankments along the ridges and defiles of the hillsides to catch the run-off from the rains, planting the flooded fields with both glutinous and non-glutinous rice. These fields are called *zengtian.* In local parlance they are known as "thunder peal fields," indicating that the farmers must await the

thunder [signalling the onset of the rains] before they will have water for their crops. These fields are also found in Xuzhou.

23. *XCB* 294/8a–b.

24. Du Zheng, "Bachuan shecang ji," *SWJC* 76/5b.

25. One geographer estimated that before 1949 as much as 50 percent of the terraced fields of the Sichuan Basin was used as water-storage fields (*dongshuitian*) during the winter season: Charles Hu, pp. 41–43.

26. *SHY* shihuo 7/54a.

27. *Hezhou zhi* [1579], 1/27a–28a.

28. Sudō Yoshiyuki, "NanSō inasaku no chiikisei," in his *Sōdai keizaishi kenkyū*, p. 107. Wang Yingchen characterized the agricultural regions of Sichuan according to land and water use in a memorial of 1167:

> In Chengdu Route irrigated fields [*shuitian*] predominate, while hill fields [*shantian*] are few. Moreover, irrigation works of canals and dikes are employed in this area. In Zizhou Route hill fields predominate and no benefit is derived from irrigation. . . . Kuizhou Route encompasses the most desolate wastes and has a reputation as a land of "knife-tilling and fire-planting" [i.e., shifting cultivation]. Even in years of good harvests some of the inhabitants have no recourse but to feed on grasses, roots, and nuts. This area cannot be compared even with Zizhou Route. ["Yuzha wen Shuzhong hanqian huayi huizou," *Wending ji*, 4/33].

The noria, a treadmill-powered rotary scoop, raised water to fields well above the water level. The lightweight bamboo construction of Chinese norias made it possible to build them as large as 25 meters in diameter. Norias, however, were not practicable in the fast-flowing currents typical of much of Sichuan without further refinements in design to improve their sturdiness. The well-sweep, a counter-balanced bailing bucket used to raise water from wells, was the most common type of irrigation equipment in Sichuan; but without an elaborate system of water channels and pumps, the well-sweep was impractical for irrigating hillside fields. For a survey of irrigation engineering in China, see Needham, *Science and Civilisation in China*, vol. 4, part 2, pp. 330–362.

29. Xue Yi, "Longmatan shenying beiji," *Luzhou zhilizhou zhi* [1820], 4/34b.

30. *WXTK* 4/60b.

31. *SHY* fangyu 18/28b–29b.

32. *CYZJ* yiji 17/7a–b.

33. *Luxian zhi* [1938], 3/20b–21a; Charles Hu, p. 54.

34. In the Yangzi Basin dikes (*ba*) originally were built to form enclosed areas that were filled with water either to irrigate low-lying rice fields or simply as a means of flood prevention. In the second half of the twelfth century many of these "diked fields" (*batian*) were expropriated by powerful landowners and planted in rice. Although "polder fields" (*weitian*), as these lands came to be known,

expanded the area under cultivation, the original functions of irrigation and flood control were disrupted, leading to numerous protests, such as the following one by Wei Jing:

> In Liangzhe one finds a fairly uniform pattern of topography. The lakes are situated above the cultivated fields, which in turn lie on higher ground than the Yangzi River and the ocean. When the rivers are low, water is drawn off from the lakes to irrigate the fields. When the rivers are high, water is released from the fields and flows into the Yangzi and eventually to the ocean. Only by obtaining the benefit of both storing and releasing water can we overcome the hazards of flood and drought and turn the lands into fertile and productive fields. From the end of the Shaoxing period [1130–1162] the army has encroached upon and occupied the ponds at the edges of the lakes. The soldiers' labor has been harnessed to alter the terrain by building dikes and irrigation ditches to form fields called *batian*. Privately owned lands suffered harm at this time, yet the injury had not yet reached extreme proportions. Lands for storing water still constituted the majority. During the Longxing and Qiandao periods [1163–1174], the powerful lineages and great families followed unceasingly one upon another in extending their holdings and forcibly occupying more lands. Not a year passed without [more lands being taken]. The benefits of the ponds and lakes diminished day by day and have nearly disappeared, while the polder fields [*weitian*] have spread and filled up the entire area. ["Lun weitian zhazi," *Houle ji,* 13/28a; see also *SHY* shihuo 61/111b; *SS* 173/4183–4184].

35. *Luzhou tujing zhi,* cited in *YLDD* 2218/2a; *Luzhou zhilizhou zhi* [1820], 4/34b.
36. Smith, "Commerce," p. 35.
37. In 1939, 75 percent of the lands in Lu county were under cultivation, a percentage unsurpassed in Sichuan outside of the Chengdu Plain. About 40 percent of the cultivated lands of Luzhou were planted in rice, which was by far the major export of the county: Charles Hu, pp. 54, 75, 125. At the time, Luzhou ranked fifth in Sichuan in total volume of trade behind Chongqing, Wanxian, Chengdu, and Neijiang: Zhou Kaiqing, pp. 74–77.
38. On smuggling outside of the official Song-Jurchen markets, see Katō Shigeshi, "Sō to Kinkoku to no bōeki ni tsuite," *Shina keizaishi kōshō,* II, 247–283.
39. *SHY* bing 22/24a.
40. Purchase of horses from the non-Han peoples in Southern Lu went back at least to 1014, when the court approved such transactions: *XCB* 82/5b–6a. For a short period in 1075–1076 the Song bartered for war horses in the border prefectures of Wei, Ya, Jia, Lu, Wen, and Long because of an interruption of the trade with the Tanguts and Tibetans: *XCB* 259/7a–b. The horse trade with the steppe peoples virtually ended after 1127, forcing the Song to rely principally on horses from Tibet and the Yungui Plateau, although these were considered decidedly inferior

to steppe horses. In 1136 the prefect of Luzhou reported that the native peoples brought horses to the "mutual trade" markets every year, but few deals were made because the prices offered by the Han were considered too low: *SHY* bing 22/24a. In 1172 Li Tao, then the prefect of Luzhou, complained that new regulations issued by the Tea and Horse Intendancy stipulating that larger horses be purchased at the prevailing price for small horses had adversely affected the trade: Wang Deyi, *Li Tao fuzi nianpu*, p. 58. At the beginning of the thirteenth century the Song purchased 395 horses a year at Changning from two branches of the Black Tribes: *YDJS* 166/3a. The Song bought 300 horses a year from the tribesmen at Nanping in the mid twelfth century; but the real center of the horse trade was Lizhou, where the Song purchased 4,000 horses in 1106: *SHY* zhiguan 43/106b; *SS* 198/4977. See also Paul Smith, "Taxing," pp. 606–608.

41. *SHY* fanyi 5/103a–104a.

42. A text from 1133 informs us that the tribesmen brought horses to Luzhou each winter. Ninety-three "tribal officials" were feasted and given gifts by the Song and more than two thousand tribesmen took part in market activities. Among the goods the tribesmen brought to trade, floated down on rafts from their own territories, were white mushrooms, tea, hemp, wine, rice, hides of leopard and deer, felt, and orchids. The market lasted for three days and cost the Song a great deal: some 40,000 *liang* in silver and cloth, plus over 6,000 *jin* of salt. The silver and cloth paid out to the tribesmen in exchange for horses was disbursed from revenues collected all over Sichuan: *XNYL* 64/1095–1096.

43. *XCB* 277/4a.

44. Lu You, *Laoxuean biji*, 3/19, in *Lu Fangweng quanji*.

45. *SHY* bing 29/41b–42a; Fan Chengda, *Wuchuan lu*, xia/17. A similar tactic was used at the Zao River in Yongkang, at the northwestern corner of the Chengdu Plain: *SHY* fangyu 12/7b–9b. Eventually the Song decided simply to tax the trade rather than try to prevent it, as the following passage in *LCGM* 13/1b shows:

> In the period 976–984 trade in horses [from the Mahu tribes] began. Afterwards the tribesmen brought timber boards to sell. The most enterprising Han settlers in the border areas engaged in barter, traveling deep into the tribal region to offer grain in exchange for timber. Although the state applied strict prohibitions against this practice, it could not bring a halt to the trade. The largest of the boards were six or seven *chi* in width and more than one *chi* thick. It is said that those used in shipbuilding and construction of multi-story buildings reached a length of more than three *zhang*. The tribesmen transported the timber themselves to Jiangkou in Xuzhou and traded with the Han there. The prefect Gao Hui was the first to create a customs duty bureau, called a *choushouchang*, at Xuzhou to collect taxes on the trade. It still exists there today [i.e., ca. 1210; the date of Gao Hui's tenure is uncertain].

46. Wei Liaoweng, "Xu gong Yi shendaobei," *Heshan xiansheng daquan wenji*, 69/9b.

47. The extent of official concern over the diffusion of strategic knowledge was cogently expressed in a directive of 1090 that enjoined "anyone who has been educated at school or sat for the 'advanced scholar' examination, as well as masters of prognostication and divination, clerks formerly employed in local administration, and artisans skilled in the manufacture of weapons from entering the streams and grottoes or having intercourse with 'enlightened' tribesmen [that is, those who have submitted to Song suzerainty]": *SHY* xingfa 2/38a.

48. *SHY* bing 29/41a-b.

49. *SHY* fanyi 5/14a.

50. *SHY* fanyi 5/69a–70a. For another expression of this point of view, but one tempered by the realization that given the vicissitudes of market conditions the Han could become inordinately dependent on income earned from trade with the tribal peoples, see Wu Yong, "Hushi," *Helin ji*, 37/20b–21b.

51. *SHY* bing 29/42b–43a.

52. *SHY* fanyi 5/69a–70a. Li Zhi and the Luzhou pacification intendant, Xu Yi, engaged in a bitter battle over the resolution of this uprising. Xu had captured three bandit chieftains and intended to use them as hostages to bring a halt to the depredations of the Iituo. Li demanded that the imprisoned chieftains be turned over to him, but Xu refused. Thereafter the military governor, no doubt at Li's prompting, harassed Xu with nuisances such as an audit on uncollected taxes in Luzhou and an order to use the income from some of Luzhou's state lands to support schools in another prefecture. In disgust Xu asked for, and received, another assignment: Wei Liaoweng, "Xu gong Yi shendaobei," *Heshan xiansheng daquan wenji*, 69/9b; *LCGM* 13/7a–8a.

53. *SS* 283/9566; *SHY* fanyi 5/75a-b. Ding reported that salt was "the only thing that the tribesmen want": *XCB* 52/11a-b.

54. *XCB* 47/21a.

55. *XCB* 61/11a.

56. *XCB* 247/23a. Technically, selling grain to the natives was forbidden; but the local officials found themselves powerless to prevent these sales. The court subsequently granted permission for the natives to "borrow" grain from local officials. The natives were required to put up a security deposit of gold or silver equivalent in value to the borrowed grain, which had to be redeemed within a year's time or else forfeited.

57. This policy was upheld in an order from the fiscal intendant to the prefect of Changning in the early 1190s: *YDJS* 166/3b.

58. Zhang Fangping, "Zou Zhang Yi zhi Jiazhou," *Lequan ji*, 30/18a-b; *SS* 301/10001.

59. *LCGM* 13/2b–3a.

60. *SHY* fanyi 5/101a-b.

61. *SHY* fangyu 19/26b–27a. As noted in chapter three, Ma You, the garrison commander of Longpeng in Jiazhou, was found guilty in 1212 of having withheld

twelve years' worth of the indemnity levy owed to the Xioyen, worth 2,400 bolts of pongee silk, 4,700 *jin* of tea and salt, 100 *liang* of silver, plus livestock and wine: *LCGM* 14/7a–8b.

62. The tea trade was a notable exception. See Smith, "Taxing," passim.

63. From 780,000 *jin* out of a total 5.8 million in the late tenth century to 419,000 out of 11 million in 1152: *WXTK* 15/155a; *CYZJ* jiaji 14/10a–b.

64. For the 1152 figure, see ibid. and *XNYL* 163/2674. For the 1281 figure, see Bolanxi et al., *Yuan yitong zhi*, 5/527.

65. The existence of salt wells in Changning is mentioned in Hu Wenhuan, *Huayi fengtu zhi* [1614], 3/29b, and *Yiwo kunyu* [1627], 11/13b, but neither *Sichuan zongzhi* [1619] nor *Changning xianzhi* [1687] refer to salt production in Changning. A nineteenth-century gazetteer related a folk legend linking the dwindling of Changning's salt production to the exhaustion of native scholastic talent: "In Meishan, upon giving birth to the three Sus [Su Xun, Su Shi, and Su Che], the shrubs and trees all withered; in Yujing, after producing the two *bangyan* [candidates who achieved second place in the *jinshi* exam; this probably occurred in the mid Ming period], the salt wells subsequently declined in salinity." (*Xuzhou fuzhi* [1895], 43/65b).

66. See the sources in note 64 above and *YDJS* 153/5a.

67. At the turn of the twentieth century, the Tuo River valley produced 89 percent of Sichuan's salt, over 220,000 metric tons a year: Alexander Hosie, *Szechwan: Its Products, Industries, and Resources*, pp. 181–182.

68. *XNYL* 106/1733–1734.

69. Wang Yingchen, "Yuzha zaiwen Shuzhong hanqian," *Wending ji*, 4/39; Ye Shi, "Gu Zhaoqingjun chengxuanshi zhi dazong zhengshi zeng kaifuyi tongsansi chongguo Zhao gong xingzhuang," *Shuixin wenji*, in *Ye Shi ji*, 26/514.

70. *SS* 35/678; *SHY* shihuo 68/79b.

71. Morizumi Toshinao, "NanSō Shisen no taiteki ni tsuite," *Shien* 10:105–141.

72. Wei Liaoweng, "Chaofeng daifu fuqing Sichuan zongling caifu xizeng tongfeng Li gong muzhiming," *Heshan xiansheng daquan wenji*, 78/1b.

73. Morizumi, p. 123.

74. Wei Liaoweng, "Luzhou chanjuntian ji," *Heshan xiansheng daquan wenji*, 48/10b–11a.

75. Yuan Yueyou, "Budi Shulu shiwuzhou chuangdi qizhou guanghuicang mi shu," *Dongtang ji*, 9/9b.

76. *Luzhou tujing zhi*, cited in *YLDD* 2218/1a–2a.

77. *XNYL* 100/1646.

78. *XNYL* 106/1733.

79. The pacification intendant, who requested this decree, noted that most of the timber was used in shipbuilding and weapon-making: *SHY* xingfa 2/128a–b. Li Tao had issued an injunction against woodcutting for shipbuilding purposes in Southern Lu in 1172: Wang Deyi, p. 58. A similar ban was issued at Shizhou in

1201: *SHY* xingfa 2/131b. Many of the ships used by the government itself, such as convoy ships transporting supplies to the armies on the Jurchen frontier, were built in the southwestern part of Sichuan, specifically in the prefectures of Lu, Xu, Jia, and Mei; but it is unclear whether these ships were built in private or state-operated shipyards: *SHY* shihuo 50/23a–b.

80. Wu Chuhou, *Qingxiang zaji*, 3/3a. For other texts on ague markets see Shiba Yoshinobu, *Sōdai shōgyōshi kenkyū*, pp. 349–350.

81. *XCB* 281/13a–b.

82. As previously noted, Huaidezhen, the major market town on the Tuo River between Luzhou and Fushun, grew out of a native settlement. Some of the old garrison towns were reborn as market towns, as in the case of Chishuizhen, which became Hu Market: *JYP*, cited in *YLDD* 2218/5b.

83. Fan Chengda observed that Yuzhou and Kuizhou stood on large, stony outcrops without adequate supplies of drinking water: *Wuchuan lu*, xia/18, 20. Lu You recorded in his diary that Kuizhou city had been moved from the Tang dynasty site of Baidicheng, on a bluff overlooking the river, to an alluvial river terrace farther downstream that was more level and broad, but still surrounded by high hills: *Ru Shu ji*, 6/56.

84. *JYP*, cited in *YLDD* 2217/17a.

85. *JYP*, cited in *YLDD* 2217/22a.

86. By 1160 taxes on production, trade, and consumption of salt, tea, and liquor amounted to 59.9 percent of the revenues of the Sichuan General Commissariat: *CYZJ* jiaji 17/11a–13a.

87. Kawahara Yoshirō, "Shisen shiro no tochi mondai to shōgyō no shihon," in his *HokuSōki tochi shoyū no mondai to shōgyō shihon*, pp. 257–318.

88. Fan Chengda, *Wuchuan lu*, xia/20; Lu You, *Ru Shu ji*, 6/56. Another observer described Wanzhou as "exceedingly desolate and wild, with virtually no markets or shops": Hong Mai, "Shu Liang erhu," *Yijian zhi*, zhiding 5/1005.

89. Little information on trade through the Gorges exists. Because of the great cost of transporting grain from Sichuan to the capital, the *shanggong* tax receipts were collected in cloth rather than rice. Silk and hemp cloth were shipped in great quantities through the Yangzi Gorges to Jiangling and Shashi and thence to Kaifeng: *CBBM* 13/1a; *XCB* 13/18a. Six hundred sixty thousand bolts of cloth collected as tax revenues were shipped along this route in 1020, although even more may have been shipped overland: *XCB* 96/26a–b. In 1077 the total tax receipts in cloth collected in Sichuan amounted to more than 3.5 million bolts: Shiba, *Sōdai shōgyōshi kenkyū*, pp. 274–276.

90. Wang Yingchen, "Zaizou Shu hanqian," *Wending ji*, 4/34.

91. Ibid., 4/34, 38–39.

8. A CYCLE OF FRONTIER EXPANSION

1. *SHY* zhiguan 60/3a–4a.
2. Wang Anshi, "Shang Renzong huangdi yanshi shu," *Wang Linchuan ji,* 39/221.
3. Ibid., 39/222–223.
4. "Qi zhizhi sansi tiaoli," ibid., 70/445.
5. Wang believed that the proliferation of aggrandizers resulted from the degeneration of social custom and the unrestrained pursuit of self-interest which had prevailed in the world since the passing of the age of the sage kings ("Jianbing," in ibid., 4/22; "Fengsu," in ibid., 69/440–441; cf. Liu, *Reform in Sung China,* pp. 40–42). Although correcting this evil was ultimately a question of inculcating proper customs, Wang offered immediate institutional remedies. For example, in 1070, responding to a query by the emperor concerning whether state control of prices was appropriate, Wang replied: "The office of the Treasurer of the Money Supply (*Quanfu*) enabled the kings of antiquity to hold in check the aggrandizers and ensure that equitable provision would be made for the poor and weak. This institution provides the means whereby we can mobilize the wealth of the realm, and cause its bounty to issue from a single source" (*XCB* shibu 4/5a–b). The task was by no means an easy one. A few months later Wang Anshi conceded that given the aggrandizers' powerful grip on landholding, laws designed to curb the concentration of landownership were doomed to failure (*XCB* 213/14b–15a). Nonetheless, he remained firmly convinced that the state could break the aggrandizers' control over commerce and prices. His proposals for farm loans (*XCB* shibu 5/19a–20a) and the establishment of the Bureau for Markets and Exchange (*XCB* 240/2b–5a) were drafted with the specific aim of wresting economic power from the aggrandizers.
6. "Shang Renzong huangdi yanshi shu," ibid., 39/224.
7. On Wang Shao's career, see the classic study by Enoki Kazuo, "Ō Sō no Kika keiryaku ni tsuite," *Mōko gakuhō* 1:87–168.
8. *XCB* 233/10a–b.
9. "Yu Wang Zichun shu," *Wang Linchuan ji,* 73/465.
10. While many scholars have denied a close link between Wang Anshi's expansionary initiatives and his domestic economic policies, I would stress their interdependence. On this point see the recent study of Inoue Takanori, "Enhen no shiekihō–tokuni Kinei-Genbō aida no Kikaro shiekishi o chūshin to shite," *Kyūshū kyōritsu daigaku kiyō* 12.2:1–18.
11. *XCB* 214/11b.
12. *SHY* shihuo 37/14a–15b.
13. On the evolution of the Xihe Route Bureau of Markets and Exchange and its integration first into the Sichuan Tea Market Agency and later into the Kaifeng superintendency, see Smith, "Taxing," pp. 278–286; Inoue, "Enhen no shiekihō,"

pp. 11–12; Kumamoto Takashi, "KitaSō Shinsōki no kokka zaisei to shiekihō," *Bunka* 45.3–4:145–152.

14. *XCB* 240/2a.

15. On state initiatives in the tea and salt industries, see Smith, "Taxing," pp. 433–520; on mining, see von Glahn, pp. 396–412.

16. Yanagida, "Kyakko," pp. 13–18; Kawahara Yoshirō, "Sōsho ni okeru jisakunō ikusei katei ni miru Jōshū suiriten no kaihatsu ni tsuite," *Shigaku kenkyū* 51:26–39.

17. *SS* 294/9809–9813; *XCB* 122/11b–13b.

18. *XCB* 190/15b–16a, 193/1b–2a; Wei Tai, *Dongxuan bilu*, 8/57. Wang Shao's opponents, in accusing Wang of squandering funds on untrustworthy tribal chieftains, likened him to Xiao Zhu: *XCB* 230/8a.

19. Su Xun, "Zhongyuan," *Jiayou ji*, 4/8a–b.

20. The strategic value of the wealth of the south was underscored in a proposal made by Wang's Finance Planning Commission in 1069 urging the court to unify control of the mineral resources and foreign trade of South China under the authority of a single official. The emperor warmly endorsed this proposal in a private communication to the official appointed to this new office. Doubtlessly alluding to the predicament of the Song in his own day, the emperor noted that Wu-Yue and Southern Han, two of the South China kingdoms of the Five Dynasties period, derived sufficient revenues from mining and foreign trade to repel invasions from the north: *XCB* shibu 5/23a–b.

21. *XCB* 221/10a–b.

22. Enoki, "Ō Sō no Kika keiryaku ni tsuite," pp. 145–146.

23. To quote the Tang poet, Liu Yuxi, "Lianzhou cishi tingbi ji," *QTW* 606/9b.

24. On the demographic consequences of the Mongol invasions, see Paul Smith, "Commerce," p. 1; Hartwell, "Demographic," pp. 373–376.

25. On relations with the native tribes in Southern Lu during the Ming, see *Sichuan zongzhi* [1619] 23/32b–59b. The recrudesence of aggressive, expansionist policies after 1570 coincided with a new cycle of economic growth in Sichuan: Hartwell, "Demographic," pp. 375–376.

26. In this respect Wang rejected the body of thought, extending back at least to Sima Qian, which posited that different lands produced different societies appropriate to their own ecological milieu.

27. Within a few years of his death Wang Anshi was widely vilified by contemporary historians for squandering lives and resources on futile campaigns of foreign expansion. Particularly notable for the vehemence of their attacks on Wang's policies were Fan Zuyu (1041–1098) and Chen Guan (1057–1122): Fan Zuyu, "Lun xiezheng zhazi," *Fan Taishi ji*, 26/1b–2a; Chen's writings are liberally cited in *CBBM* (e.g., *CBBM* 87/2b–3b). In the Southern Song, historians blamed the Jurchen conquest of North China on Wang, claiming that Wang's debilitating

foreign wars sapped the Song's military preparedness. This view was forcefully expressed by Wang Mingqing in his *Yuzhao xinzhi*, published in 1198. Wang Mingqing's opinion subsequently was quoted by Li Tao in his definitive assessment of the reform era: Wang Mingqing, *Yuzhao xinzhi*, 1/1a; *XCB* 353/4a.

28. Wang Fuzhi, *Song Lun*, 6/131–133.

29. James Lee points out that the introduction of New World food crops sparked intensive exploitation of the southwestern hills by Han immigrants after 1700 and eventually broke down the vertical segregation of Han and non-Han settlements. But by that time few non-Han groups could be described as polities in any meaningful sense. James Lee, "The Legacy of Immigration in Southwestern China, 1250–1850," *Annales de demographie historique* 1982:297–298.

30. On the spatial transformation of Sichuan from the Tang to the Qing, see Paul Smith, "Commerce," passim, especially pp. 4–5, 23, 46–54.

31. *Guizhou tongzhi* [1697], 6/34b; Tao Chengqing, *Shangcheng yilan*, shang/9a, 10; see also Lombard-Salmon, p. 94.

32. Huang Bian, *Yitong lucheng tuji*, 7/1b, 4b.

33. Smith, "Commerce," p. 54; Hu Wenhuan, *Huayi fengtu zhi*, 3/22a, 29a, 39b. On the onerous burden of timber exactions along the Southern Lu frontier in the late Ming, see Huang Bian, *Yitong lucheng tuji*, 2/8b–9a; Chen Zilong et al., eds., *Huang Ming jingshi wenbian*, 423/1a–5a, 427/1a–3a.

34. Skinner, "The Structure of Chinese History," *Journal of Asian Studies* 44.2:280. See also Skinner, "Cities and the Hierarchies of Local Systems," in Skinner, ed., *City*, pp. 281–288.

35. Hartwell, "Demographic," pp. 373–374.

36. The basic features of dendritic market systems are analyzed in E. A. J. Johnson, *The Organization of Space in Developing Countries*, pp. 83–92. Carol A. Smith presents a meticulous critique of central place theory and discusses a number of alternative marketing models, including dendritic systems, in her essay "Regional Economic Systems: Linking Geographic Models and Socioeconomic Problems," in Smith, ed., *Regional Analysis*, I, 3–63. Edward Fox, in developing his models of "linear" and "areal" societies to describe the dichotomy between the commercial trading network and the agrarian base of ancien-regime France, also stresses the dendritic structure of the commercial system. Fox perhaps goes too far, however, in emphasizing the discontinuity between the commercial world and the agrarian hinterland. See his *History in Geographic Perspective*, especially pp. 33–53.

37. Carol Smith, "Exchange Systems and the Spatial Distribution of Elites," in Smith, ed., *Regional Analysis*, II, 312. The significance of the disposition of the surplus as a determining element in the type of agrarian regime also has been noted by Michel Cartier, "L'exploitation agricole chinoise de l'antiquité au XIVe siècle: évolution d'une modèle," *Annales: Economies, Sociétés, Civilisations* 33.2:373–375, 381–383.

38. On this point see William H. McNeill, *The Great Frontier: Freedom and Hierarchy in Modern Times,* p. 27.
39. The class structure of consumption in the Song still awaits detailed study. For a preliminary foray into this issue see Shiba, *Sōdai shōgyōshi kenkyū,* pp. 467–482 (summarized in Shiba, *Commerce,* pp. 202–206).
40. Carol Smith, "Exchange Systems," in Smith, ed., *Regional Analysis,* II, 314.
41. This point has also been made by Skinner, "The Structure of Chinese History," pp. 286–287.

Abbreviations Used in the Bibliography

CSJC   Congshu jicheng 叢書集成 collectanea. Shanghai: Shangwu, 1935–1937.

GXJBCS   Guoxue jiben congshu 國學基本叢書 collectanea. Shanghai, 1936.

SBBY   Sibu beiyao 四部備要 collectanea. Shanghai: Zhonghua shuju, 1936.

SBCK   Sibu congkan 四部叢刊 collectanea. Shanghai: Shangwu, 1936.

SKQSZB   Siku quanshu zhenben 四庫全書珍本 collectanea. Taipei, 1969– .

Bibliography

An Zhimin 安志敏 . "'Ganlan' shi jianzhude kaogu yanjiu" 干兰式 建筑的考古研究, *Kaogu xuebao* 1963.2:65–83.

Backus, Charles. *The Nan-chao Kingdom and T'ang China's Southwestern Frontier*. Cambridge: Cambridge University Press, 1981.

Bao Ruji 包汝楫 . *Nanzhong jiwen* 南中紀聞 . CSJC ed.

Berkhofer, Robert, Jr. "The North American Frontier as Process and Context," in Howard Lamar and Leonard Thompson, eds., *The Frontier in History: North America and Southern Africa Compared*. New Haven: Yale University Press, 1981.

Bloch, Marc. *Feudal Society*. 2 volumes. Chicago: University of Chicago Press, 1961.

———. *French Rural History: An Essay on its Basic Characteristics*. Berkeley and Los Angeles: University of California Press, 1966.

Bolanxi 李蘭肹 et al. *Yuan yitong zhi* 元一統志 . Edited by Zhao Wanli 趙萬里 . Shanghai: Zhonghua shuju, 1966.

Bray, Francesca. *Agriculture*. Vol. 6, part 2, Joseph Needham, gen. ed., *Science and Civilisation in China*. Cambridge: Cambridge University Press, 1984.

Cai Xiang 蔡襄 . *Lizhi pu* 荔枝譜. CSJC ed.

Cao Shuyuan 曹叔遠 . *Jiangyang pu* 江陽譜 , in *Yongle dadian* 2217–2218.

Cao Xuequan 曹學佺 . *Shuzhong guangji* 蜀中廣記 . SKQSZB ed.

Cartier, Michel. "L'exploitation agricole chinoise de l'antiquité au XIVe siècle: évolution d'une modèle," *Annales: Economies, Sociétés, Civilisations* 33:365–388 (1978).

Chang Ju 常璩 . *Huayang guozhi* 華陽國志. CSJC ed.

Chang, Kwang-chih. *The Archaeology of Ancient China*. 3rd edition. New Haven: Yale University Press, 1977.

Chang Tsuen-kung. "Taro in Ancient China," in Laurence Thompson, ed., *Studia Asiatica: Essays in Asian Studies in Felicitation of the Seventy-Fifth Anniversary of Professor Ch'en Shou-yi*. San Francisco: Chinese Materials Center, 1975.

Changning xianzhi 長寧縣志 . 1687.

Chen Cheng-siang (Chen Zhengxiang) 陳正祥 . *Zhongguode diming* 中國的地名 . Hong Kong: Shangwu yinshuguan, 1978.

Chen Zilong 陳子龍 et al., eds. *Huang Ming jingshi wenbian* 皇明經世文編 . Reprint of Ming ed. Taipei: Guofeng chubanshe, 1964.

Ch'ü T'ung-tsu. *Law and Society in Traditional China*. Paris: Mouton, 1961.

Da Yuan tongzhi tiaoge 大元通制條格 . Reprint of Ming ed. Beijing: National Peiping Library, 1930.

de Beauclair, Inez. "The Keh Lao of Kweichow and Their History According to Chinese Records," *Studia Serica* 5:1–44 (1946).

Du You 杜佑 . *Tongdian* 通典 . Shitong 十通 ed.

Du Zheng 度正 . *Xingshantang gao* 性善堂稿 . SKQSZB ed.

Eberhard, Wolfram. *Lokalkulturen im alten China*. 2 volumes. Leiden: E. J. Brill, 1942.

——. *Local Cultures of South and East China*. Leiden: E. J. Brill, 1967.

Ebrey, Patricia. "Conceptions of the Family in the Sung Dynasty," *Journal of Asian Studies* 43:219–245 (1984).

Elvin, Mark. *The Pattern of the Chinese Past*. Stanford: Stanford University Press, 1973.

Enoki Kazuo 榎一雄 . "Ō Sō no Kika keiryaku ni tsuite" 王韶の熙河經略に就いて , *Mōko gakuhō* 1:87–168 (1940).

Fan Chengda 范成大 . *Fan Shihu ji* 范石湖集 . Hong Kong: Zhonghua shuju. 1974.

——. *Guihai yuheng zhi* 桂海虞衡志 , in Ma Duanlin, *Wenxian tongkao*, 328–330.

——. *Wuchuan lu* 吳船錄 . CSJC ed.

——. *Wujun zhi* 吳郡志 . CSJC ed.

Fan Chuo 樊綽 . *Manshu jiaozhu* 蠻書校注 . Edited by Xiang Da 向達 . Beijing: Zhonghua shuju, 1962.

Fan Zhen 范鎮 . *Dongzhai jishi* 東齋記事 . Shoushange congshu 守山閣叢書 ed.

Fan Zhiming 范致明 . *Yueyang fengtu ji* 岳陽風土記 . Gujin yishi 古今逸史 ed.

Fang Xuanling 房玄齡 , et al. *Jin shu* 晉書 . Beijing ed.

Feng Hanyi 馮漢驥 . "Yunnan Jinning Shizhaishan chutu tonggu yanjiu" 云南晉宁石寨山出土銅鼓研究 , *Kaogu* 考古 1963:319–329.

Feng Hanyi and Tong Enzheng 童恩正 . "Minjiang shangyoude shiguanzang" 岷江上游的石棺葬 , *Kaogu xuebao* 1973.2:41–59.

Feng Shixing 馮時行 . *Jinyun wenji* 晉雲文集 . SKQSZB ed.

Fogg, Wayne H. "Swidden Cultivation of Foxtail Millet by Taiwan Aborigines: A

Cultural Analogue of the Domestication of *Setaria italica* in China," in David M. Keightley, ed., *The Origins of Chinese Civilization.* Berkeley & Los Angeles: University of California Press, 1983.

Fox, Edward Whiting. *History in Geographic Perspective: The Other France.* New York: Norton, 1971.

Fu Zengxiang 傅增湘. *Songdai Shuwen jicun* 宋代蜀文輯存. Facsimile of 1943 ed. Hong Kong: Longwen shudian, 1971.

Fujisawa Yashimi 藤澤義美. *Seinan Chūgoku minzokushi no kenkyū* 西南中國民族史の研究. Tokyo: Daian, 1969.

Gao Side 高斯得. *Chitang cungao* 恥堂存稿. SKQSZB ed.

Ge Jinfang 葛金芳. "Guanyu BeiSong guantian sitianhua zhengcede ruogan wenti" 关于北宋官田私田化政策的若干问题, *Lishi yanjiu* 1982.3:17-32.

Godelier, Maurice. "The Concept of 'Tribe': A Crisis Involving Merely a Concept or the Empirical Foundations of Anthropology Itself?" in his *Perspectives in Marxist Anthropology,* pp. 70–96. Cambridge: Cambridge University Press, 1973.

Golas, Peter J. "Rural China in the Song." *Journal of Asian Studies* 39:291-325 (1980).

Goody, Jack. "Inheritance, Property, and Women: Some Comparative Considerations," in Jack Goody, Joan Thirsk, and E. P. Thompson, eds., *Family and Inheritance: Rural Society in Western Europe, 1200-1800.* Cambridge: Cambridge University Press, 1976.

——. *Technology, Tradition, and the State in Africa.* Cambridge: Cambridge University Press, 1971.

Gourou, Pierre. *La terre et l'homme en Extrême Orient.* Paris: Armand Colin, 1940.

Gu Yanwu 顧炎武. *Ri zhi lu* 日知錄. GXJBCS ed.

——. *Tianxia junguo libing shu* 天下郡國利病書. SBCK ed.

Gu Yewang 顧野王. *Yupian* 玉篇. SBBY ed.

Gu Zuyu 顧祖禹. *Dushi fangyu jiyao* 讀史方輿紀要. Beijing: Zhonghua shuju, 1955.

Guangyuan xianzhi 廣元縣志. 1757.

Guizhou tongzhi 貴州通志. 1555.

Guizhou tongzhi 貴州通志. 1697.

Guo Zhengzhong 郭正忠. "BeiSong Sichuan shiyan weiji kaoxi" 北宋四川食盐危机考析, *Zhongguoshi yanjiu* 1981.1:79-94.

Han Qi 韓琦. *Zhongxian Han Weiwang Anyang ji* 忠獻韓魏王安陽集. Ming Wanli period ed.

Harrison, G. A., and J. R. Goody, "The Probability of Family Distributions," *Comparative Studies in Society and History* 15:16–18 (1973).

Hartwell, Robert M. "The Evolution of the Early Northern Sung Monetary System, A.D. 960–1025," *Journal of the American Oriental Society* 87:280–289 (1967).

——. "Financial Expertise, Examinations, and the Formulation of Economic Policy in Northern Sung China," *Journal of Asian Studies* 30:281–314 (1971).

——. "Demographic, Political, and Social Transformations of China, 750–1550," *Harvard Journal of Asiatic Studies* 42:365–442 (1982).

He Guangyuan 何光遠. *Jianjie lu* 鑒誡錄. CSJC ed.

He Yudu 何宇度. *Yibu tanzi* 益部談資. Hubei xianzhe yishu 湖北先哲遺書 ed.

Hezhou zhi 合州志. 1579.

Hong Mai 洪邁. *Rongzhai suibi* 容齋隨筆. Shanghai: Shanghai guji chubanshe, 1978.

——. *Yijian zhi* 夷堅志. Taipei: Mingwen shuju, 1982.

Hosie, Alexander. *Szechwan: Its Products, Industries, and Resources*. Shanghai: n.p., 1922.

Hu, Charles Y. *The Agricultural and Forestry Land-Use of Szechwan Basin*. Chicago: University of Chicago Press, 1946.

Hu Qingjun 胡庆钧. "Songdai Yizu xianmin diqu nuli zhidude fanrong fazhan" 宋代彝族先民地区奴隶制度的繁荣发展, *Sixiang zhanxian* 1980.4:58–67.

——. *Ming Qing Yizu shehuishi luncong* 明清彝族社会史论丛. Shanghai: Shanghai renmin chubanshe, 1981.

Hu Wenhuan 胡文煥. *Huayi fengtu zhi* 華夷風土志. 1614.

Huang Bian 黃汴. *Yitong lucheng tuji* 一統路程圖記. 1570.

Huang Song zhongxing liangchao shengzheng 皇宋中興兩朝聖政. Wanwei beicang 宛委別藏 ed.

Huang Tingjian 黃庭堅. *Yuzhang Huang xiansheng wenji* 豫章黃先生文集. GXJBCS ed.

Huang Xiufu 黃休復. *Maoting kehua* 茅亭客話. Linlang bishi congshu 琳瑯祕室叢書 ed.

Hymes, Robert P. *Statesmen and Gentlemen: The Elite of Fu-chou, Chiang-hsi, in Northern and Southern Sung*. Cambridge: Cambridge University Press, 1986.

Inoue Takanori 井上孝範. "Enhen no shiekihō—tokuni Kinei-Gembō aida no Kikaro shiekishi o chūshin to shite" 沿辺の市易法－特に熙甯元豊間の熙河路市易司を中心として, *Kyūshū kyōritsu daigaku kiyō* 12.2:1–18 (1978).

Ishida Yūsaku 石田勇作. "Tō–Godai ni okeru sonraku shihai to henyō" 唐五代における村落支配と変容, in Sōdaishi kenkyukai, eds., *Sōdai no shakai to bunka* 宋代の社会と文化. Tokyo: Kumiko shoin, 1983.

Jia Sixie 賈思勰. *Qimin yaoshu xianduben* 齊民要術選讀本. Edited by Shi Shenghan 石聲漢. Beijing: Nongye chubanshe, 1961.

Johnson, E. A. J. *The Organization of Space in Developing Countries.* Cambridge: Harvard University Press, 1970.

Kaltenmark, Max. "Le dompteur des flots," *Han-hiue, bulletin du Centre d'Études Sinologiques de Pekin* 3:1–112 (1948).

Katō Shigeshi 加藤繁. *Shina keizaishi kōshō* 支那經濟史考證. 2 volumes. Tokyo: Toyo bunko, 1952–1953.

Kawahara Yoshirō 河原由郎. "Sōsho ni okeru jisakunō ikusei katei ni miru Jōshū suiriten no kaihatsu ni tsuite" 宋初に於ける自作農育成過程にみる襄州水利田の開發について, *Shigaku kenkyū* 51:26–39 (1953).

———. *HokuSōki tochi shoyū no mondai to shōgyō shihon* 北宋期土地所有の問題と商業資本. Fukuoka: Nishi Nihon gakujutsu shuppan-sha, 1964.

Kou Zongshi 寇宗奭. *Tujing yanyi bencao* 圖經衍義本草. Daocang 道藏, no. 536.

Kumamoto Takashi 熊本崇. "KitaSō Shinsōki no kokka zaisei to shiekihō" 北宋神宗期の国家財政と市易法, *Bunka* 45.3–4:145–162 (1981/82).

Kurihara Masuo 栗原益男. "Tōmatsu no dogōteki zaichi shiryoku ni tsuite—Shisen no I Kunsei no baai" 唐末の土豪的在地勢力について—四川の韋君靖の場合, *Rekishigaku kenkyū* 243:1–14 (1960).

Kusano Yasushi 草野靖. "Sōdai kanden no soshu kangyō" 宋代官田の租種管業, *Tōyōshi kenkyū* 28:1–27 (1969).

Lamar, Howard, and Leonard Thompson, eds. *The Frontier in History: North America and Southern Africa Compared.* New Haven: Yale University Press, 1981.

Landes, Kenneth K. "The Geology of Salt Deposits," in Dale W. Kaufmann, ed., *Sodium Chloride: The Production and Properties of Salt and Brine.* American Chemical Society Monograph Series. New York: Reinhold Publishing Corp., 1960.

Lattimore, Owen. "The Frontier in History," in his *Studies in Frontier History, Collected Papers, 1929–1958.* London: Oxford University Press, 1962.

Le Roy Ladurie, Emmanuel. *The Peasants of Languedoc.* Urbana, Illinois: University of Illinois Press, 1974.

Lee, James. "The Legacy of Immigration in Southwestern China, 1250–1850," *Annales de demographie historique,* 1982:279–304.

Li Fang 李昉. *Taiping guangji* 太平廣記. Beijing: Renmin wenxue chubanshe, 1959.

Li, Hui-lin. *Nan-fang ts'ao-mu chuang: A Fourth Century Flora of Southeast Asia.* Hong Kong: The Chinese University Press, 1979.

———. "The Domestication of Plants in China: Ecogeographical Considerations," in David M. Keightley, ed., *The Origins of Chinese Civilization*. Berkeley and Los Angeles: University of California Pres, 1983.

Li Jifu 李吉甫 . *Yuanhe junxian tuzhi* 元和郡縣圖志 . Jifu congshu 畿輔叢書 ed.

Li Rongcun 李榮村 . "Xidong suyuan" 溪峒溯源 , *Guoli bianyiguan guankan* 1.1:7–23 (1971).

Li Shi 李石 . *Fangzhou ji* 方舟集 . SKQSZB ed.

Li Tao 李燾 . *Xu zizhi tongjian changbian* 續資治通鑑長編 . Taipei: Shijie shuju, 1961.

Li Xinchuan 李心傳 . *Jianyan yilai chaoye zaji* 建炎以來朝野雜記 . Shiyuan congshu 適園叢書 ed.

——. *Jianyan yilai xinian yaolu* 建炎以來繫年要錄 . CSJC ed.

Li Yanshou 李延壽 et al. *Bei shi* 北史 . Beijing ed.

Li Zhi 李塸 . *Huang Song shichao gangyao* 皇宋十朝綱要 . Facsimile of Liujingkan congshu 六經勘叢書 ed. Taipei: Wenhai chubanshe, 1980.

Liangchao gangmu beiyao 兩朝綱目備要 . SKQSZB ed.

Lin Xiang 林向 . "Zhongguo xuanguanzang xueshu taolunhui jiyao" 中国悬棺葬学术讨论会纪要 , *Wenwu* 1981.8:24–29.

Ling Shunsheng 凌純聲 . "Tangdai Yunnande Wuman yu Baiman kao" 唐代雲南的烏蠻與白蠻考 , *Renleixue jikan* 1.1:57–86 (1938).

Liu, James T. C. *Reform in Sung China: Wang An-shih (1021–1086) and his New Policies*. Cambridge: Harvard University Press, 1959.

Liu Lin 刘林 . "Liaoren rushu kao" 僚人入蜀考 , *Zhongguoshi yanjiu* 1980.2:119–134.

Liu Xihai 劉喜海 . *Jinshiyuan* 金石苑 . Shike shiliao congshu 石刻史料叢書 ed.

Liu Zhiyuan 刘志远 . "Kaogu cailiao suojian Handaide Sichuan nongye" 考古材料所见汉代的四川农业 , *Wenwu* 1979.12:61–67.

Lo, Winston W. *Szechwan in Sung China: A Case Study in the Political Integration of the Chinese Empire*. Taipei: University of Chinese Culture Press, 1982.

Lombard-Salmon, Claudine. *La province du Gui zhou au XVIIIe siècle: un exemple d'acculturation chinoise*. Paris: École Française d'Extrême-Orient, 1972.

Lu Ciyun 陸次雲 . *Dongqi qianzhi* 峒溪纖志 . Xiaofanghu zhai yudi congchao 小方壺齋輿地叢鈔 ed.

Lü Tao 呂陶 . *Jingde ji* 淨德集 . SKQSZB ed.

Lu You 陸游 . *Laoxuean biji* 老學庵筆記 , in *Lu Fangweng quanji*. Taipei: Shijie shuju, 1980.

——. *Lu Fangweng quanji* 陸放翁全集 . Taipei: Shijie shuju, 1980.

——. *Ru Shu ji* 入蜀記 . CSJC ed.

Luxian zhi 瀘縣志 . 1938.

Luzhou zhilizhou zhi 瀘州直隸州志 . 1820.

Ma Duanlin,馬端臨 . *Wenxian tongkao* 文獻通考 . Shitong 十通 ed.

Maertens, Jean-Thierry. *Le jeu du mort: essai d'anthropologie des inscriptions du cadavre.* Paris: Aubier Montaigne, 1979.

Makino Tatsumi 牧野選 . *Kinsei Chūgoku sōzoku kenkyū* 近世中國宗族研究 . Tokyo: Nikko shoin, 1949.

Maspero, Henri. "La société et la religion des chinois anciens et celles des Tais modernes," in his *Le Taoisme et les religions chinoises.* Paris: Gallimard, 1971.

Matsui Shūichi 松井秀一 . "Tōdai kōhanki no Shisen–kanryo shihai to dogōsō no shutsugen o chūshin to shite" 唐代後半期の四川－官僚支配と土豪層の出現を中心として , *Shigaku zasshi* 73:1418–1461 (1964).

Matsuo Takane. "Rice Culture in China," in Association of Japanese Agricultural Scientific Societies, ed., *Rice in Asia.* Tokyo: University of Tokyo Press, 1975.

McDermott, Joseph P. "Charting Blank Spaces and Disputed Regions: The Problem of Sung Land Tenure," *Journal of Asian Studies* 44:13–41 (1984).

McKnight, Brian E. *Village and Bureaucracy in Southern Sung China.* Chicago: University of Chicago Press, 1971.

McNeill, William H. *The Great Frontier: Freedom and Hierarchy in Modern Times.* Princeton: Princeton University Press, 1983.

Meinig, D. W. "A Macrogeography of Western Imperialism: Some Morphologies of Moving Frontiers of Political Control," in Fay Gale and Graham Lawton, eds., *Settlement and Encounter: Geographical Studies Presented to Sir Grenfell Price.* Melbourne: Oxford University Press, 1969.

——. "The Continuous Shaping of America: A Prospectus for Geographers and Historians," *American Historical Review* 83:1186–1205 (1978).

Miyazaki Ichisada 宮崎市定 . "Sōdai igo no tochi shoyū keitai" 宋代以後の土地所有形體 . *Ajia shi kenkyū* アジア史研究 . Vol. 4, pp. 87–129. Kyoto: Toyoshi kenkyukai, 1964.

——. "Sōdai ni okeru satsujin saiki no shuzoku ni tsuite" 宋代における殺人祭鬼の習俗について " *Ajia shi kenkyū.* Vol. 5, pp. 100–144.

Morizumi Toshinao 森住利直 . "NanSō Shisen no taiteki ni tsuite" 南宋四川の對糴に就いて , *Shien* 10:105–141 (1935).

Nakagawa Manabu 中川學 . "Tōdai no toko, fuko, kyakko ni kan suru oboe-gaki" 唐代の土戸,浮戸,客戸に関ゔる覺書 , *Hitotsubashi ronsō* 50:339–345 (1962).

——. "Tōdai no kyakko ni yoru tōkiten no hoyū" 唐代の客戸による逃棄田の保有 . *Hitotsubashi ronsō* 53:72–90 (1965).

——. "TōSō no kyakko ni kan suru shomondai" 唐宋の客戸に関する諸問題 , *Shakai keizai shigaku* 31:243–255 (1966).

——. "Tōdai no ryūyō ni tsuite" 唐代の流庸について , *Tōyōshi kenkyū* 26:131–149 (1967).

Needham, Joseph. *Science and Civilisation in China.* Vol.. 4, part 2. Cambridge: Cambridge University Press, 1965.

Niida Noboru 仁井田陞. *Tōsō hōritsu monjo no kenkyū* 唐宋法律文書の研究. Tokyo: Toho bunka gakuin Tokyo kenkyusho, 1937.

———. *Chūgoku hōseishi kenkyū: dōrei nōdō hō, kazoku sonraku hō* 中國法制史研究, 奴隸農奴法. 家族村落法. Tokyo: Tokyo daigaku shuppankai, 1962.

Ouyang Xiu 歐陽修. *Ouyang Xiu quanji* 歐陽修全集. Taipei: Shijie shuju, 1971.

Ouyang Xiu et al. *Xin wudai shi* 新五代史. Beijing ed.

Ouyang Xiu, Song Qi 宋祁, et al. *Xin Tang shu* 新唐書. Beijing ed.

Ouyang Xuan 歐陽玄 et al. *Song shi* 宋史. Beijing ed.

Oyama Masaaki 小山正明. "Mindai no daitochi shoyū to dōboku" 明代の大土地所有と奴僕, *Tōyō bunka kenkyūsho kiyō* 62:77–131 (1974).

Pasternak, Burton. "The Role of the Frontier in Chinese Lineage Development," *Journal of Asian Studies* 28:551–561 (1969).

Pirazzoli-t'Serstevens, Michèle. *La civilisation du royaume de Dian à l'époque Han, d'après le matériel exhumé à Shizhai shan.* Publications de l'École Française d'Extrême-Orient. Paris, 1974.

Pulleyblank, E. G. "The Chinese and Their Neighbors in Prehistoric and Early Historic Times," in David M. Keightley, ed., *The Origins of Chinese Civilization.* Berkeley and Los Angeles: University of California Press, 1983.

Qi Xia 漆俠. *Wang Anshi bianfa* 王安石變法. Shanghai: Shanghai renmin chubanshe, 1959.

Qianwei xianzhi 犍為縣志. 1934.

Qijiang xianzhi 綦江縣志. 1826.

Qijiangxian xuzhi 綦江縣續志. 1938.

Qin Guan 秦觀. *Huaihai ji* 淮海集. SBCK ed.

Qinchuan zhi 琴川志. 1192.

Quan Tang shi 全唐詩. Beijing: Zhonghua shuju, 1960.

Quan Tang wen 全唐文. Reprint of 1814 ed. Beijing: Zhonghua shuju, 1983.

Quyang zhi 渠陽志. 1740.

Renshou xianzhi 仁壽縣志. 1802.

Ruey Yih-fu (Rui Yifu) 芮逸夫. "Liao wei Gelao shizheng" 僚(獠)為仡佬(犵狫)試證, *Zhongyang yanjiuyuan lishi yuyan yanjiusuo jikan* 20: 343–356 (1948).

———. "Boren kao" 僰人考, *Zhongyang yanjiuyuan lishi yuyan yanjiusuo jikan* 23:245–278 (1951).

———. "Liaoren kao" 僚人考, *Zhongyang yanjiuyuan lishi yuyan yanjiusuo jikan* 28:727-770 (1956).

Satake Yasuhiko 佐竹靖彦. "Sōdai kyōson seido no keisei katei" 宋代郷村制度之形成過程, *Tōyōshi kenkyū* 25:244-274 (1966).

———. "Sōdai Shisen Kishuro no minzoku mondai to tochi shoyū mondai" 宋代四川夔州路の民族問題と土地所有問題, *Shirin* 史林 50:801-828 (1967); 51:44-74 (1968).

———. "TōSō henkakuki ni okeru Kōnan tōzairo no tochi shoyū to tochi seisaku-yimon no seichō o te ga karini" 唐宋變革期における江南東西路の土地所有と土地政策 - 義門の成長を手がかりに, *Tōyōshi kenkyū* 31:503-536 (1973).

———. "TōSō henkakuki ni okeru Shisen Seitofuro chiiki shakai no hembō ni tsuite" 唐宋變革期における四川成都府路地域社会の變貌について, *Tōyōshi kenkyū* 35:275-308 (1976).

Schafer, Edward H. *The Divine Woman: Dragon Ladies and Rain Maidens in T'ang Literature.* Berkeley and Los Angeles: University of California Press, 1971.

———. "T'ang," in Kwang-chih Chang, ed., *Food in Chinese Culture.* New Haven: Yale University Press, 1976.

Schifferli, Christoph. "Recherches sur l'histoire du Sichuan vers la fin du Xe siècle: la formation d'une province chinoise." Thèse de troisième cycle, Université de Paris VII, 1980.

Shen Gua 沈括. *Mengqi bitan* 夢溪筆談. CSJC ed.

Shiba Yoshinobu 斯波義信. *Sōdai shōgyōshi kenkyū* 宋代商業史研究. Tokyo: Kazama shobo, 1968.

———. *Commerce and Society in Sung China,* tr. Mark Elvin. Michigan Abstracts of Chinese and Japanese Works on Chinese History. Ann Arbor: Center for Chinese Studies, University of Michigan, 1970.

———. "Sōdai no Kōshū ni okeru shinshi no hensen ni tsuite" 宋代の湖州における鎮市の変遷について, *Enoki hakushi kanreki kinen tōyōshi ronsō* 榎博士還暦紀念東洋史論叢, pp. 225-238. Tokyo: Yamagawa shuppansha, 1975.

———. "Sekkō Kōshū ni okeru teijū no enkaku" 浙江湖州における定住の沿革, in Kimura Eiichi 木村英一 ed., *Chūgoku tetsugaku shi no tembō to mosaku* 中国哲学史の展望と模索. Tokyo: Sobunsha, 1976.

———. "Ningpo and Its Hinterland," in G. William Skinner, ed., *The City in Late Imperial China.* Stanford: Stanford University Press, 1977.

Shirakawa Shizuo 白川靜. *Chūgoku no shinwa* 中国の神話. Tokyo: Chuko bunko, 1980.

Sichuan chuanguanzang fajue baogao 四川船棺葬發掘報告. Beijing: Wenwu chubanshe, 1960.

"Sichuan Gongxian Boren xuanguan ji yanhua diaocha ji" 四川珙县僰人懸棺及岩画调查记, *Wenwu ziliao congkan* 2:187–195 (1978).

Sichuan zongzhi 四川總志. 1619.

Sima Guang 司馬光. *Sushui jiwen* 涑水紀聞. CSJC ed.

——. *Zizhi tongjian* 資治通鑑. Beijing: Zhonghua shuju, 1956.

Sima Qian 司馬遷. *Shi ji* 史記. Beijing ed.

Skinner, G. William. "Marketing and Social Structure in Rural China." *Journal of Asian Studies* 24.1:3–43 (1964); 24.2:195–228 (1965); 24.3:363–399 (1965).

——, ed. *The City in Late Imperial China*. Stanford: Stanford University Press, 1977.

——. "The Structure of Chinese History," *Journal of Asian Studies* 44:271–292 (1985).

Smith, Carol A., ed. *Regional Analysis*. 2 vols. New York: Academic Press, 1976.

Smith, Paul J. "Taxing Heaven's Storehouse: The Szechwan Tea Monopoly and the Tsinghai Horse Trade, 1074–1204." Ph.D. dissertation, University of Pennsylvania, 1983.

——. "Commerce, Agriculture, and Core Formation in the Upper Yangtze, 2 A.D. to 1948." Paper prepared for the Conference on Spatial and Temporal Trends and Cycles in Chinese Economic History, 980–1980. Bellagio, Italy; August 17–23, 1984.

Sogabe Shizuo 曾我部靜雄. "Chūgoku no chūsei oyobi Sōdai no kyakko ni tsuite" 中国の中世及び宋代の客戸について, *Shakai keizai shigaku* 27:474–481 (1962).

Song huiyao jigao 宋會要輯稿. Facsimile of 1809 manuscript. Taipei: Xinwenfeng chuban gongsi, 1976.

Song Lian 宋濂. *Song xueshi wenji* 宋學士文集. SBCK ed.

Song Qi 宋祁. *Yibu fangwu lüeji* 益部方物略記. Hubei xianzhe yishu 湖北先哲遺書 ed.

Su Shi 蘇軾. *Dongpo zhilin* 東坡志林. Baihai 稗海 ed.

——. *Su Dongpo quanji* 蘇東坡全集. Taipei: Shijie shuju, 1982.

Su Xun 蘇洵. *Jiayou ji* 嘉祐集. SBBY ed.

Sudō Yoshiyuki 周藤吉之. *Chūgoku tochi seido shi kenkyū* 中國土地制度史研究. Tokyo: Tokyo daigaku shuppankai, 1954.

——. *Sōdai keizaishi kenkyū* 宋代經濟史研究. Tokyo: Tokyo daigaku shuppankai, 1962.

——. *TōSō shakai keizaishi kenkyū* 唐宋社會經濟史研究. Tokyo: Tokyo daigaku shuppankai, 1965.

Sun Guangxian 孫光憲. *Beimeng suoyan* 北夢瑣言. CSJC ed.

Sun Xinghua 孫星華. *Chaoye zaji yiji jiaokan ji* 朝野雜記乙集校勘記. CSJC ed.

Takahashi Yoshirō 高橋芳郎 . "Sōdai tenko no mibun mondai" 宋代佃戸 の身份問題 , *Tōyōshi kenkyū* 37:390–417 (1978).

——. "Sōdai Sessei deruta chitai ni okeru suiri kankō" 宋代浙西デルタ 地帯におけ る水利慣行 , *Hokkaidō daigaku bungakubu kiyō* 28:1–40 (1981).

——. "Minmatsu Shinshoki dōboku, kokōjin mibun no saihen to tokushitsu" 明末清初期奴僕, 雇工人身份の再編と特質, *Tōyō- shi kenkyū* 41:516–541 (1982).

Tʼan, H. C., and C. Y. Lee. "Salt Deposits and Industry of Szechuan Province," *Bulletin of the Geological Survey of China* 22:39–78 (1933).

Tan Kyōji 丹喬二 . "Sōsho no shōen ni tsuite–Seitofu Kōshoku koku setsudoshi Ten Kinsen no shoryō o chūshin to shite" 宋初の莊園につ いて – 成都府後蜀國節度使田欽全の所領を中心 として, *Shichō* 87:1–25 (1964).

Tang Geng 唐庚 . *Meishan Tang xiansheng wenji* 眉山唐先生文集 . SBCK ed.

Tang Jiahong 唐嘉弘 . "Duzhangman he Tuliao" 都掌蠻和土僚 , *Wenwu* 1980.11:34–38.

Tanigawa Michio 谷川道雄 . "Hokuchōmatsu–Godai no gikyōdai ketsugō ni tsuite" 北朝末五代の義兄弟結合について , *Tōyōshi kenkyū* 39:286–305 (1980).

Tao Chengqing 陶承慶 . *Shangcheng yilan* 商程一覽 . Ming Wanli period ed.

Tian Rucheng 田汝成 . *Yanjiao jiwen* 炎徼紀聞 . 1808 ed.

Tietze, Klaus-Peter. *Ssuchʼuan vom 7. bis 10. Jahrhundert: Untersuchungen zur Frühen Geschichte einer Chinesischen Provinz.* Münchener Ostasiatische Studien. Wiesbaden: Franz Steiner, 1980.

Tong Enzheng 童恩正 . "Sichuan xinan diqu dashimu zushu shitan" 四川 西南地區大石墓族屬試探 , *Kaogu* 1978.2:104–110.

——. "Jinnianlai Zhongguo xinan minzu diqu Zhanguo, Qin, Han shidaide kaogu faxian jiqi yanjiu" 近年来中国西南民族地区战国秦汉 时代的考古发现及其研究 , *Kaogu xuebao* 1980:417–442.

Treistman, Judith. *The Early Cultures of Szechwan and Yunnan.* Cornell University East Asia papers. Ithaca, NY: Cornell University China-Japan Program, 1974.

Twitchett, Denis. *Financial Administration under the Tang Dynasty.* 2nd edition. Cambridge: Cambridge University Press, 1963.

Ueyama Shumpei 上山春平 ; Sasaki Kōmei 佐々木高明 ; and Nakao Sasuke 中尾佐助 . *Zoku shōyō jurin bunka* 続照葉樹林文化. Tokyo: Chuko shinsho, 1976.

Umehara Kaoru 梅原郁 . "Sōdai chihō shōtoshi no ichimen–shin no hensen o chūshin to shite" 宋代地方小都市の一面 ─鎮の変遷を中心として , *Shirin* 41.6:35–51 (1958).

———. "Sōdai no kotōsei o megutte" 宋代の戸等制をめぐって , *Tōhō gakuhō* 41:375–414 (1970).

Von Dewall, Magdalene. "The Tien Culture of South-west China," *Antiquity* 41:8–21 (1967).

von Glahn, Richard. "The Country of Streams and Grottoes: Geography, Settlement, and the Civilizing of China's Southwestern Frontier, 1000–1250." Ph.D. dissertation, Yale University, 1983.

Walton, Linda. "Kinship, Marriage, and Status in Song China: A Study of the Lou Lineage of Ningbo, c. 1050–1250," *Journal of Asian History* 18:35–77 (1984).

Wang Anshi 王安石 . *Wang Linchuan ji* 王臨川集 . Hong Kong: Guangzhi shuju, n.d.

Wang Cheng 王偁 . *Dongdu shilüe* 東都事略 . Facsimile of Qing ed., edited by Cheng Tinglu 程庭鷺 . Taipei: Wenhai chubanshe, 1967.

Wang, Chi-wu. *The Forests of China.* Maria Moors Cabot Foundation publication. Cambridge: Harvard University Press, 1961.

Wang Cun 王存 . *Yuanfeng jiuyu zhi* 元豐九域志 . Wuyingdian juzhen banshu 武英殿聚珍版書 ed.

Wang Deyi 王德毅 . *Li Tao fuzi nianpu* 李燾父子年譜 . Taipei: Zhongguo xueshu zhuzuo jiangzhu weiyuanhui chubanshe, 1963.

Wang Fuzhi 王夫之 . *Song lun* 宋論 . Beijing: Zhonghua shuju, 1964.

Wang Mingqing 王明清 . *Yuzhao xinzhi* 玉照新志 . Song Yuan ren shuobu congshu 宋元人説部叢書 ed.

Wang Ningsheng 汪宁生 . "Yuangu shiqi Yunnande daogu caipei" 远古时期云南的稻谷栽培 , *Sixiang zhanxian* 1977.1:98–102.

———. *Yunnan kaogu* 云南考古 . Kunming: Yunnan renmin chubanshe, 1980.

Wang Pu 王溥 . *Tang huiyao* 唐會要 . GXJBCS ed.

Wang Qinruo 王欽若 et al. *Cefu yuangui* 冊府元龜 . Hong Kong: Zhonghua shuju, 1960.

Wang Xiangzhi 王象之 . *Yudi jisheng* 輿地紀勝. Facsimile of Yueyatang Wushi 粵雅堂伍氏 ed. Taipei: Wenhai chubanshe, n.d.

Wang Yingchen 汪應辰 . *Wending ji* 文定集 . CSJC ed.

Wang Zao 王藻 . *Fuxi ji* 浮溪集 . SKQSZB ed.

Wang Zhong 王仲 . *Xin Tang shu Tufanzhuan jianzhu* 新唐書吐番傳箋注. Beijing: Kexue chubanshe, 1958.

Wei Jing 衛涇 . *Houle ji* 後樂集 . SKQSZB ed.

Wei Liaoweng 魏了翁 . *Heshan xiansheng daquan wenji* 鶴山先生大全文集 . SBCK ed.

Wei Tai 魏泰 . *Dongxuan bilu* 東軒筆錄 . CSJC ed.

Wei Zheng 魏徵 et al. *Sui shu* 隋書 . Beijing ed.

Wen Chongyi 文崇一 . *Chu wenhua yanjiu* 楚文化研究 . Taipei: Zhongyang yanjiuyuan minzuxue yanjiusuo, 1967.

Wen Tong 文同 . *Danyuan ji* 丹淵集 . SBCK ed.

Wen Yanbo 文彥博 . *Lugong wenji* 潞公文集 . SKQSZB ed.

Wenwu kaogu gongzuo sanshinian, 1949–1979 文物考古工作三十年
Beijing: Wenwu chubanshe, 1979.

Wilbur, C. Martin. *Slavery in China During the Former Han Dynasty, 206 B.C.–A.D.
25*. Field Museum of Natural History, Anthropological series. Chicago, 1943.

Wu Chuhou 吳處厚 . *Qingxiang zaji* 青箱雜記. Hanfenlou 涵芬樓
ed.

Wu Yong 吳泳. *Helin ji* 鶴林集. SKQSZB ed.

Xie Zhaozhe 謝肇淛 . *Dian lüe* 滇略. Ming ed.

Xin Yuanlong 辛元龍 . *Chongbian Guyun hongcheng Xin qingjie gong Songyuan
wenji* 重編古筠洪城辛清節公松桓文集. Ming woodblock ed.

Xinan Yizhi xuan 西南彝志选 . Guiyang: Guizhou renmin chubanshe, 1982.

Xu Songshi 徐松石 . *Yuejiang liuyu renmin shi* 粵江流域人民史 .
Shanghai: Zhonghua shuju, 1939.

Xuzhou fuzhi 敘州府志 . 1895.

Yanagida Setsuko 柳田節子. "Sōdai kyakko ni tsuite" 宋代客户に
ついて, *Shigaku zasshi* 68.4:1–38 (1958).

——. "Sōdai tochi shoyūsei ni mirareru futatsu kata" 宋代土地所有制
にみられる二つ型 , *Tōyō bunka kenkyūsho kiyō* 29:95–130 (1963).

——. "Sōdai kokka kenryoku to nōson chitsujo–kotōsei shihai to kyakko" 宋
代国家權力と農村秩序－戸等制支配と客户 , *Niida
Noboru hakushi tsuitō ronbunshū* 仁井田陞博士追悼論文集
vol. 1, pp. 337–364. Tokyo: Tsuyokikusa shobo, 1967.

——. "Sōdai keiseiko no kōsei" 宋代形勢戸の構成 , *Tōyōshi kenkyū*
27:272–291 (1968).

——. "Kyōsonsei no tenkai" 鄉村制の展開 , in *Sekai rekishi* 世界歷史
. Vol. 9, pp. 309–343. Tokyo: Iwanami shoten, 1970.

Yang Fang 陽枋. *Ziqi ji* 字溪集 . SKQSZB ed.

Yang Zhongliang 楊仲良 . *Tongjian changbian jishi benmo* 通鑑長編
紀事本末. Facsimile of Guangya shuju 廣雅書局 ed. Taipei: Wenhai
chubanshe, 1967.

Ye Shi 葉適 . *Shuixin wenji* 水心文集 , in *Ye Shi ji* 葉適集 . Beijing:
Zhonghua shuju, 1961.

Ye Tingkui 葉廷珪 . *Hailu suishi* 海錄碎事 . Facsimile of 1598 ed.

"Yibinxian Shuanglong, Hengjiang liangqu yanxuemu diaochaji" 宜賓縣
双龙横江西区岩穴墓调查记 , *Kaogu yu wenwu* 1984.2:46–58.

Yiwo kunyu 一握坤輿. 1627.

Yongle dadian 永樂大典. Beijing: Zhonghua shuju, 1960.

Yoshida Tora 吉田寅. "NanSō no engyō keiei—seisanmen o chūshin to shite" 南宋の鹽業経営 －生産面を中心として, *Tōyō shigaku ronshū* 5:71–138 (1960).

Yoshinami Takashi 好並隆司. "Tōkeien suiri kikō no kentō—Sō igo no kokka kenryoku to sonraku" 通済堰水利機構の檢討－宋以降の國家權力と村落, *Okayama daigaku hōbungakubu gakujutsu kiyō* 15:80–110 (1962).

Yu Jing 余靖. *Yu Xianggong zouyi* 余襄公奏議. Edited by Huang Zibo 黃慈博. N.p.: n.p., 1930.

Yü, Ying-shih. *Trade and Expansion in Han China.* Berkeley and Los Angeles: University of California Press, 1967.

Yuan Xingzong 員興宗. *Jiuhua ji* 九華集. SKQSZB ed.

Yuan Yueyou 袁説友. *Dongtang ji* 東唐集. SKQSZB ed.

Yue Shi 樂史. *Taiping huanyu ji* 太平寰宇記. Facsimile of 1805 ed. Taipei: Wenhai chubanshe, n.d.

Zeng Gongliang 曾公亮. *Wujing zongyao* 武經總要. SKQSZB ed.

Zhang Fangping 張方平. *Lequan ji* 樂全集. SKQSZB ed.

Zhang Shu 張澍. *Shu dian* 蜀典. 1876 ed.

Zhang Tingyu 張廷玉 et al. *Ming shi* 明史. Beijing ed.

Zhang Zengqi 張增祺. "Cong chutu wenwu kan Zhanguo zhi Xihan shiqi Yunnan he zhongyuan diqude miqie guanxi" 從出土文物看战国至西汉时期云南和中原地区的密切关系, *Kaogu xuebao* 考古学报 1973.2:31–37.

Zhang Zhuo 張鷟. *Chaoye qianzai* 朝野僉載. Jifu congshu 畿輔叢書 ed.

Zhao Ding 趙鼎. *Jiaxun bilu* 家訓筆錄. CSJC ed.

Zhao Ruyu 趙汝愚. *Guochao zhuchen zouyi* 國朝諸臣奏議. Facsimile of Ming ed. Taipei: Wenhai chubanshe, 1970.

Zhao Yanwei 趙彥衛. *Yunlu manchao* 雲麓漫鈔. CSJC ed.

Zhongguo kexueyuan Nanjing turang yanjiusuo 中国科学院南京土壤研究所. *Zhongguo turang* 中國土壤. Beijing: Kexue chubanshe, 1978.

Zhongguo shaoshu minzu 中国少數民族. Beijing: Renmin chubanshe, 1981.

Zhou Bida 周必大. *Zhou yiguo wenzhonggong wenji* 周益國文忠公文集. 1808 ed.

Zhou Fagao 周法高 et al. *Hanzi gujin yinhui* 漢字古今音彙. Hong Kong: The Chinese University Press, 1974.

Zhou Kaiqing 周開慶. *Sichuan jingji zhi* 四川經濟志. Taipei: Taiwan shangwu yinshuguan, 1972.

Zhu Fu 朱輔 . *Ximan congxiao* 溪蠻叢笑 . Gujin shuobu congshu 古今說部叢書 ed.

Zhu Kezhen 竺可楨 . "Zhongguo jin wuqiannian lai qihou bianqiande chubu yanjiu" 中國近五千年来气候变迁的初步研究 , *Kaogu xuebao* 1972.1:15–38.

Zhu Mu 祝穆 . *Fangyu shenglan* 方輿勝覽 . Facsimile of Kongshi Yuexuelou 孔氏嶽雪樓 ed.

Zhu Xi 朱熹 . *Chuci jizhu* 楚辭集注 . Shanghai: Shanghai guji chubanshe, 1979.

"Zunyi Gaoping 'Bozhou tusi' Yang Wen deng sizuo muzang fajue ji" 遵义高坪播州土司杨文等四座墓葬发掘记 , *Wenwu* 1974.1:62–70.

Glossary

The glossary contains characters for the names of persons who appear in the text but not in the bibliography, for place names not found on maps in the book, and for romanized Chinese and non-Han, native words. A few readily identifiable names (e.g., Wang Anshi) have been omitted.

Anju 安居
Anning River 安寧河
Anyi 安夷
Anyuan 安遠

Ba 巴
ba 壩, 埧
Baidicheng 白帝城
Baiyai 白崖
bajie 把截
Bamuxing 八母姓
banyi zhi jia 般移之家
Banqiao 板橋
baojia 保甲
baozhengzhang 保正長
batian 壩田
bazi 霸子
benjia difen 本家地分

Bi Zhongyan 畢仲衍
bianxiu zhongshu tiaolisi
　　編修中書條例司
bieji yicai 別籍異財
binlang 檳榔
Bo Gu 白固
Bo Jinfeng 白進豐
Bodao 孿道
Boerzi 白兒子
Boji zidi 白芨子弟
boyi 博易
bu 步
buqu 部曲
buyi 布衣

Cai Jing 蔡京
Cai Ting 蔡挺
Cai Yu 蔡煜

cao 漕

caoshi 草市

Caoshi 曹市

chafangshi 察訪使

chang 場

changchan 常產

changzhutian 常住田

Chen Chong 陳崇

Chen Guan 陳瓘

Chen Jingxuan 陳敬瑄

Chen Shunyu 陳舜俞

Chen Ziang 陳子昂

Cheng Zhicai 程之才

Cheng Zhiyuan 程之元

Chenzhou 辰州

chimi 赤米

Chiyai 赤崖

chong 衝

choushouchang 抽收場

Chu 楚

Couzhou 湊州

Cuan 爨

cun 村

daguizhu 大鬼主

dai 埭

dan 石

daogeng huozhong 刀耕火種

Dawangcun 大王村

Daxiancun 大先村

Deng Runfu 鄧潤甫

Deng Wan 鄧綰

Dian 滇

dianke 佃客

dianmai 典買

dike 地客

ding 丁

Ding Wei 丁謂

dingkou 丁口

Dingzhou 鼎州

dong 洞, 峒, 嵩

dongshuitian 冬水田

du 都

du 瀆

Duan Jie 段介

dubao 都保

duda guizhu 都大鬼主

duidi 對糴

duigong 隊公

duixia 隊下

Fan Bailu 范百錄

Fan Sun 范孫

Fan Ziqi 范子奇

fanche 翻車

Fang La 方臘

Fang Shan 方山

fanli 蕃籬

Feng Ji 馮檝

fouke 浮客

foulangke 浮浪客

Fuhuan 扶歡

gai 溉

gai 咳
ganlan 干欄
Gao Hui 高輝
Gelao 仡佬
gongjianshe 弓箭社
Gongjingzhen 公井鎮
Gongxian 珙縣
gou 溝
gu 穀
guan 貫
Guan Qisun 關耆孫
Guanghuijian 廣惠監
guanhu 官戶
guantian 官田
Guanzi 管子
gui 櫃
gui 槓
Guiren 歸仁
guitian 櫃田
Guizhengba 歸正壩
guizhu 鬼主
gujia 骨價

Han Cunbao 韓存寶
Han Jiang 韓絳
Han Xiusheng 韓秀昇
hanhua 漢化
Hanjia baixing 漢家百姓
hedi 合糴
Hezhang 赫章
hu 斛
Hu Market 胡市

Hu Yuanzhi 胡元質
Huaidezhen 懷德鎮
Huang River 湟水
huanju 環居
Huangtukan 黃土坎
huashigang 花石綱
hujuetian 戶絕田
hunpei 婚配
huo 鑊
hushi 互市
huxia kehu 戶下客戶
huxia tuding 戶下土丁

Jia Zongliang 賈宗諒
jiading 家丁
jian 監
jianbing zhi jia 兼并之家
Jiangkou 江口
Jiangyang 江陽
jianmin 賤民
jiansi 監司
jiao 蛟
jiaozi 交子
jiaren 家人
jiawu 甲午
jiaye wenhou 家業溫厚
jiegao 桔橰
jienüe 痎瘧
jieshi 痎市
jiguan 籍貫
jimizhou 羈縻州
Jin 晉

jing 涇
jinghu 井戶
jingjie 經界
jinshan 禁山
jinshi 進士
Jinyun 進雲
jiguan 籍貫
jiyang 給養
Jizhongjian 濟忠監
ju 蒟
juangu 轉雇
juanyunshi 轉運使
juntian 均田
junxian 郡縣

kaibian natu 開邊納土
kaiyu dianzhong 開畬佃種
kan 坎
kehu 客戶
kentian 墾田
kōshin 後進
Kou Xian 寇瑊
kuqiao 苦蕎

Lainiu 賴牛
Laiyi 賴易
Laiyin 賴因
Langzhong 閬中
Legongcheng 樂共城
leimingtian 雷鳴田
Li Bing 李冰
Li Chengzhi 李承之

Li Gou 李覯
Li Guangji 李光吉
Li Man 李曼
Li Qi 李杞
Li Shun 李順
Li Zhi 李直
Li Zi 李資
Liang Chengxiu 梁承秀
liangshuyi 兩屬戶
Liaogui 撩鬼
Lin Guang 林廣
Lin Su 林栗
Lingnan 嶺南
Liu Fang 劉芳
Liu Pi 劉辟
Liu Zuo 劉佐
liuyong 流庸
lizhai 立寨
Longguizhen 龍歸鎮
longnü 龍女
lu 路
Lu Hongxuan 盧弘宣
Lunan yanbian anfushi
　盧南沿邊安撫使
Luo Shihua 駱世華
Luo Wengui 駱文貴
Luochagui 羅刹鬼
Luogui (= Luoshi guizhu)
　羅氏鬼主

Ma You 馬樞
Ma Yuan 馬援

Mahu 馬湖
maipu 買撲
Man 蠻
manpanguan 蠻判官
Meidong 梅洞
Meilingbao 梅嶺堡
Meishan 眉山
Meishandong Yao 梅山洞猺
Meng 孟
Miao 苗
Mijiao 靡角
Minjia 民家
mipuhu 米舖户
Mou Fan 牟蕃
Mou Fen 牟蕡
Mou Liren 牟里仁
Mou Nuan 牟餪
mu 畝
Mu Xun 穆珣
Mu Yongzhong 穆永忠

Nanchuan 南川
nanmu 楠木
nashen 納身
natu 納土
neichen 内臣
neishu 内屬
Nong Zhigao 儂智高
nuli 奴隸

outian 區田

Pan Hu 潘虎
pangfu 旁婦
panghu 旁户
pangshu 旁屬
pangxia kehu 旁下客户
panwa 盤窪
Peng Shixi 彭仕義
Peng Shiyan 彭師晏
Peng Sun 彭孫
Pingrongzhuang 平戎莊
po 坡
Poyang Lake 鄱陽湖
Pu Zongmin 蒲宗閔

Qian Neng 阡能
qianhuang 錢荒
Qianjiang 黔江
Qianwei 犍為
qianxia 鈐轄
qianyin 錢引
Qianzhong 黔中
Qiao Xu 喬敍
qing 頃
qingdian 請佃
Qingfu 慶符
Qingqi 清溪
Qing Shan 青山
qingzhong liansan zhi quan 輕重斂散之權
qizhang 耆長
Qu 瞿
Qujing 曲靖

Ren 任
Ren Guangxiu 任光秀
Ren Ji 任伋
Renshi 任市
Rongyi 榮懿
ruhu weiye 入户為業
rui 瑞

Sanjiangzhen 三江鎮
Sanli 三里
senshin 先進
shan 杉
shanggong 上供
shanpo shuizeng 山坡水曾
Shashi 沙市
she 舍
shecang 社倉
Sheming 蛇鳴
shengdi guanzhuang 省地官莊

Shengjienan 生界南
Shengnan 生南
shengyi 生夷
shengzhuangtian 省莊田
Shihe Market 實合市
Shiqi Wei 侍其旭
shiyisi 市易司
shizhou wutun 十州五囤
shōensei 莊園制
shouzhao 手詔
Shu 蜀
Shu Han 蜀漢

shuiche 水車
shuitian 水田
Shuiwei 水尾
shuyi 熟夷
siming 司命
Su Che 蘇轍
Su Sanqi 蘇三七
Su Shen 蘇紳
suishen 隨身
Sun Gou 孫構
Sun Yisou 孫義叟
suo 梭
suoshui 索稅

tache 踏車
taishou 太守
Tan Ruyi 譚汝翼
tang 塘
tanquan 貪泉
Tao River 洮河
Tian 田
Tian Rubi 田汝弼
Tian Zuzhou 田祖周
tidian xingyu 提點刑獄
tiju 提舉
tiju fanbu yingtian shiyishi
提舉藩部營田市易司
Tongchuanfu 潼川府
Tongfoba 銅佛壩
tongju tongcuan 同居同爨
touan 偷安
toumai 投買

tuanbao 團保
tuding 土丁
tuhao 土豪
tuhu 土戶
Tulaman 秃剌蠻
Tulaoman 土橑蠻
tun 囤
Tuolu 陀魯
tuzhu 土主

Wanlijing 萬里箐
Wang Caijin 王才進
Wang Chun 王椿
Wang Guangzu 王光祖
Wang Huaixin 王懷信
Wang Jian 王建
Wang Jun 王均
Wang Luan 王鸞
Wang Mengzheng 王蒙正
Wang Shao 王韶
Wang Tang 王堂
Wang Wen 王文
Wang Wenkui 王文樑
Wang Xiaobo 王小波
Wang Xuan 王宣
Wang Xun 王壎
Wang Yan 王兖
Wang Zongruan 王宗阮
Wang Zongwang 王宗望
wanghua 王化
wei 尉
Wei Congge 魏從革

Wei Gao 韋皋
Wei Junjing 韋君靖
weitian 圍田
Wen Zongyuan 文宗院
wenfa 文法
wu (1) 垭
wu (2) 塢
Wudiba 五弟壩
Wudu 武都
Wuman 烏蠻
Wuyi Shan 武夷山
wuzuo 烏撮

Xi Ruming 席汝明
Xi Yi 席益
xian 縣
xiang 鄉
xiangbing 鄉兵
xiangding 鄉丁
xiangli 鄉里
xianju 見居
Xianshi 先市
Xiao Zhu 蕭注
xiaomin 小民
Xiaoqikou 小溪口
Xiaoshizhen 小市鎮
Xiaoxiancun 小先村
xidong 溪洞
Xie 謝
Xihe 熙河
Xin Yixian 辛怡顯
xinfu kehu 新附客戶

xingju 星居

xingshihu 形勢戶

xingzhuang 行狀

xinmin 新民

Xinpu 新浦

Xiong Ben 熊本

xiongbian zidi 雄邊子弟

Xu Xiake 徐霞客

Xue Yan 薛顏

Xun Bing 荀炳

xunejiang 巡遏將

xunjian 巡檢

Yafeibudao Shan 鴉飛不到山

yajiao 牙校

yan 堰

Yang Can 楊粲

Yang Duan 楊端

Yang Guangrong 楊光榮

Yang Guangzhen 楊光鎮

Yang Guifei 楊貴妃

Yang Guiqian 楊貴遷

Yang Jie 楊節

Yang Quan 楊銓

Yang Shili 楊師立

Yang Wen 楊文

Yang Weicong 楊惟聰

Yang Wenguang 楊文廣

Yang Wengui 楊文貴

Yang Wenhan 楊文瀚

Yang Wenxi 楊文錫

Yang Xian 楊先

Yang Zhao 楊昭

yangshi dianli 養食佃力

yangzi 養子

Yanjing 鹽井

Yao 猺

yaren 牙人

Yelang 夜郎

Yi 彝

yi qi shen 役其身

yier 義兒

yijun 義軍

yimen 義門

yinci 淫祠

Yingling 應靈

Yinshi 尹市

yishu 役屬

yishuihu 夷稅戶

Yiyang 益陽

yizhong 義塚

Yongkang 永康

Yonglecheng 永樂城

Yongning 永寧

yongye 永業

youling 酋領

youtian wushui hu 有田無稅戶

yu 芋

Yu 禹

Yu Ruli 喻如礪

Yuan River 沅江

yuganzi 餘甘子

yuluo buwu 隅落部伍

Yunnan zhidao lu
雲南至道錄

Yun'an 雲安

yunü 玉女

yuou 芋區

Yuqian 于潛

yutian 圩田

yutian 畲田

Yuwen Rong 宇文融

Zang Hu 臧滸

zao 灶

zengtian 曙田

zexi 則溪

zha 柵

zhai 寨

zhaijiang 寨將

zhaijiang zidi 寨將子弟

Zhang Dun 章惇

Zhang Jie 張頡

Zhang Qiao 張翹

Zhang Shang 張商

Zhang Xianzhong 張憲忠

Zhang Yan 張繽

Zhang Zhaotong 張昭通

Zhang Zijin 張子瑾

Zhao Huayuan zhen (1)
趙化原鎮

Zhao Huayuan zhen (2)
趙化元鎮

Zhao Jilong 趙繼隆

Zhao Kai 趙開

Zhao Ruyu 趙如愚

Zhao Shike 趙師恪

Zhao Shiru 趙師汝

Zhao Shunchen shi 趙舜臣市

Zhao Wangwu xiaoshi
趙王五小市

Zhao Yan 趙言

Zhao Yu 趙遹

Zhao Zhicai 趙之才

zhaotian chuzi 照田出資

zhen 鎮

zheneshi 鎮遏使

Zhengfayuan 正法院

Zhenghe 政和

Zhenghe weixiang 政和畏降

zhenjiang 鎮將

Zhenzhou 珍州

zhenzhucai 真珠菜

zhihui 指揮

zhihuishi 指揮使

zhitian 職田

zhizhigao 制置誥

zhizhi sansi tiaolisi
制置三司條例司

zhizhishi 制置使

zhongling 忠靈

Zhongshu beidui 中書備對

zhongxing 中興

zhou 州

Zhou Yin 周尹

Zhuang 獐

zhuang 莊

zhuangding 壯丁

zhuangke 莊客

zhuangshe 莊舍

zhuangwu 莊屋

zhuangyuan 莊園

zhudian zhi fen 主佃之分

Zhuge Liang 諸葛亮

zhuhu 主户

zhuhu mingxia 主户名下

zhuhu zhuangding 主户壯丁

zhuixu 贅壻

zhuming 主名

zhupu 主簿

zhupu zhi fen 主僕之分

zhuotongjing 卓筒井

Zi River 資水

zidi 子弟

zidi keding 子弟客丁

Ziliujing 自流井

zimo 兹莫

zipei 資陪

zongguan 總管

Zonglingsuo 總領所

zuye 祖業

Non-Han Words

Adzi 阿子

Akiəi 阿機

Angak 阿訛

Antsi 晏子

Anuənɲiii 安穩二

bua 婆

Buak 白

buanəi 婆能

Buaɲiəum 婆然

Buk 濮

Bukia 僕夜

Buək 襮

Iɪtmau 一毛

Iɪilau 夷牢

Iɪituo 夷都

ka 牁

Kaiem 牁陰

Kalaman 歌羅蠻

Katlau 葛獠

Kiəulau 屈獠

Kiəutsiɪ 九支

Kiuk 菊

La 羅

Laduosiɪi 羅杜肆

lai 賴

lai 來

Laiɪt 羅一

lak 落

Lak 駱

Lakamiəu 羅箇牟

Lakamuo 羅箇募

Laklai 落來

Lakmau 落莫

Lamiuen 羅闐

lang 浪

Lásitang 羅姶黨

Lau 獠

Laɣuokiek 羅胡苟

Liangliɪm 雨林

liuɪn 輪

Liuɪnpiuo 輪夫

Liuongmiuekok 龍靡角

Miukdəki 目特異

Miuətdɛng 勿鄧

Muk 木

Mukgiuei 木櫃

Mukgiemńiɪi 木琴二

Mukgiemdai 木琴大

Mukiaeu 木鷂

Mukp'uan 木攀

muəi 梅

Muəitsək 梅則

Məu 母

Ńiang 獽

nəi 能

Piuomiuang Kaśio 甫望箇恕

P'iungbua 豐琶

pua 播

Puakiem 白錦

Pukləu 卜漏

Sabua 婆婆

Şadziɪi Angie 沙自阿義

Şats'iuo Lukluo 沙取祿路

si 思

Sian 思晏

Singa 思裁

ta 多

Takang 多岡

tiɛi 底

Tiɛibuonggiang 底蓬強

Tiɛibuongpau 底蓬褒

Tsio 苴

tuo 都

Tuotang 都黨

Tuotśiang 都掌

Təkkai 得蓋

təu 斗, 鈄

Təuiin 斗引

Təukabuang 斗箇旁

Təukai 斗蓋

Təukaniei 斗箇嬭

Təulakmuəi 斗落梅

Təulangtś'iuɪn 斗浪春

Təumiuang 斗望

Təuśiaet 斗設

Təuɣuan 斗還

Xioɣan 虛恨

Index

Note: Names of native tribes or confederations are designated by (NT)

Harvard East Asian Monographs

21. Kwang-Ching Liu, ed., *American Missionaries in China: Papers from Harvard Seminars*

22. George Moseley, *A Sino-Soviet Cultural Frontier: The Ili Kazakh Autonomous Chou*

23. Carl F. Nathan, *Plague Prevention and Politics in Manchuria, 1910–1931*

24. Adrian Arthur Bennett, *John Fryer: The Introduction of Western Science and Technology into Nineteenth-Century China*

25. Donald J. Friedman, *The Road from Isolation: The Campaign of the American Committee for Non-Participation in Japanese Aggression, 1938–1941*

26. Edward Le Fevour, *Western Enterprise in Late Ch'ing China: A Selective Survey of Jardine, Matheson and Company's Operations, 1842–1895*

27. Charles Neuhauser, *Third World Politics: China and the Afro-Asian People's Solidarity Organization, 1957–1967*

28. Kungtu C. Sun, assisted by Ralph W. Huenemann, *The Economic Development of Manchuria in the First Half of the Twentieth Century*

29. Shahid Javed Burki, *A Study of Chinese Communes, 1965*

30. John Carter Vincent, *The Extraterritorial System in China: Final Phase*

31. Madeleine Chi, *China Diplomacy, 1914–1918*

32. Clifton Jackson Phillips, *Protestant America and the Pagan World: The First Half Century of the American Board of Commissioners for Foreign Missions, 1810–1860*

33. James Pusey, *Wu Han: Attacking the Present through the Past*

34. Ying-wan Cheng, *Postal Communication in China and Its Modernization, 1860–1896*

35. Tuvia Blumenthal, *Saving in Postwar Japan*

36. Peter Frost, *The Bakumatsu Currency Crisis*

37. Stephen C. Lockwood, *Augustine Heard and Company, 1858–1862*

38. Robert R. Campbell, *James Duncan Campbell: A Memoir by His Son*

39. Jerome Alan Cohen, ed., *The Dynamics of China's Foreign Relations*

40. V. V. Vishnyakova-Akimova, *Two Years in Revolutionary China, 1925–1927*, tr. Steven I. Levine

41. Meron Medzini, *French Policy in Japan during the Closing Years of the Tokugawa Regime*

42. *The Cultural Revolution in the Provinces*

43. Sidney A. Forsythe, *An American Missionary Community in China, 1895–1905*

44. Benjamin I. Schwartz, ed., *Reflections on the May Fourth Movement: A Symposium*

45. Ching Young Choe, *The Rule of the Taewŏn'gun, 1864–1873: Restoration in Yi Korea*

STUDIES IN THE MODERNIZATION OF THE REPUBLIC OF KOREA: 1945–1975

90. Noel F. McGinn, Donald R. Snodgrass, Yung Bong Kim, Shin-Bok Kim, and Quee-Young Kim, *Education and Development in Korea*

91. Leroy P. Jones and Il SaKong, *Government, Business and Entrepreneurship in Economic Development: The Korean Case*

92. Edward S. Mason, Dwight H. Perkins, Kwang Suk Kim, David C. Cole, Mahn Je Kim, et al., *The Economic and Social Modernization of the Republic of Korea*

93. Robert Repetto, Tai Hwan Kwon, Son-Ung Kim, Dae Young Kim, John E. Sloboda, and Peter J. Donaldson, *Economic Development, Population Policy, and Demographic Transition in the Republic of Korea*

106. David C. Cole and Yung Chul Park, *Financial Development in Korea, 1945-1978*

107. Roy Bahl, Chuk Kyo Kim, and Chong Kee Park, *Public Finances during the Korean Modernization Process*

94. Parks M. Coble, *The Shanghai Capitalists and the Nationalist Government, 1927-1937*

95. Noriko Kamachi, *Reform in China: Huang Tsun-hsien and the Japanese Model*

96. Richard Wich, *Sino-Soviet Crisis Politics: A Study of Political Change and Communication*

97. Lillian M. Li, *China's Silk Trade: Traditional Industry in the Modern World, 1842-1937*

98. R. David Arkush, *Fei Xiaotong and Sociology in Revolutionary China*

99. Kenneth Alan Grossberg, *Japan's Renaissance: The Politics of the Muromachi Bakufu*

100. James Reeve Pusey, *China and Charles Darwin*

101. Hoyt Cleveland Tillman, *Utilitarian Confucianism: Ch'en Liang's Challenge to Chu Hsi*

102. Thomas A. Stanley, *Ōsugi Sakae, Anarchist in Taishō Japan: The Creativity of the Ego*

103. Jonathan K. Ocko, *Bureaucratic Reform in Provincial China: Ting Jih-ch'ang in Restoration Kiangsu, 1867-1870*

104. James Reed, *The Missionary Mind and American East Asia Policy, 1911-1915*

105. Neil L. Waters, *Japan's Local Pragmatists: The Transition from Bakumatsu to Meiji in the Kawasaki Region*

108. William D. Wray, *Mitsubishi and the N.Y.K., 1870-1914: Business Strategy in the Japanese Shipping Industry*

109. Ralph William Huenemann, *The Dragon and the Iron Horse: The Economics of Railroads in China, 1876-1937*